GOD'S FISHERMEN, SATAN'S HUNTERS

GOD'S FISHERMEN, SATAN'S HUNTERS

The Unspoken Biblical Prophecy that Is Terrorizing the World

by
CHADWICK HARVEY

GOD'S FISHERMEN, SATAN'S HUNTERS

Copyright © 2017 by Chadwick Harvey

All rights reserved. No part of this book may be reproduced in any form or by any means—whether electronic, digital, mechanical, or otherwise—without permission in writing from the publisher, except by a reviewer, who may quote brief passages in a review.

World Ahead Press is a division of WND Books. The views and opinions expressed in this book are those of the author and do not necessarily reflect the official policy or position or WND Books.

Unless otherwise indicated, Scripture quotations are taken from the New King James Version®. Copyright © 1982 by Thomas Nelson. Used by permission. All rights reserved.

Scripture quotations marked ESV are taken from The Holy Bible, English Standard Version. ESV® Permanent Text Edition® (2016). Copyright © 2001 by Crossway Bibles, a publishing ministry of Good News Publishers.

Scripture quotations marked KJV are taken from the Holy Bible, King James Version (public domain).

Scripture quotations marked NIV are taken from Holy Bible, New International Version®, NIV® Copyright ©1973, 1978, 1984, 2011 by Biblica, Inc.® Used by permission. All rights reserved worldwide.

All italics in scriptures and quotations in this book are the author's own emphasis.

Paperback ISBN: 978-1-944212-46-9
eBook ISBN: 978-1-944212-47-6

Printed in the United States of America

DEDICATION

Dedicated to the *pure royal lineage* of Messiah, who are the descendants of Abraham, Isaac, Jacob, and David. May the Lord God of Israel, the Almighty, always bless and protect His heritage, His land, and His remnant, until His glorious second coming and millennial reign. Amen, amen, and amen.

> Numbers 6:24-26, "The LORD bless you and keep you; The LORD make His face shine upon you, and be gracious to you; The LORD lift up His countenance upon you, and give you peace."

CONTENTS

Dedication — 5
Acknowledgements — 9
Introduction — 11

1. God's Everlasting Covenants — 15
2. The Prophecy of the Fishermen and the Hunters — 37
3. God's Original Fishermen — 47
4. Satan's Original Hunters — 57
5. The Mystery of Aliyah — 99
6. God's End-of-the-Age Fishermen — 117
7. Satan's End-of-the-Age Hunters and the Aliyah of 2014–2015 From Europe — 126
8. The Aliyah From the United States — 168
9. Satan's Final Hunter — 204
10. The Time of Jacob's Trouble — 237

Conclusion — 280
Epilogue — 283
My Prayer — 289
Endnotes — 292

ACKNOWLEDGEMENTS

The highest and supreme praise, honor, glory, and thanks go to the Almighty, who is the ultimate Fisherman of all mankind, and the God of Abraham, Isaac, Jacob, and David. This book was written by His righteous, sovereign, and holy inspiration, and I am forever grateful for His omniscient, omnipotent, and omnipresent ways.

I would like to give a special thanks to my wonderful family, whose unconditional love, steadfast support, and daily prayers have been paramount during the writing of this book. I thank the Lord God for each and every one of you, and may His Majesty continue to protect and bless you forever. I love all of you very much. To my mother, thank you for your wisdom with this manuscript, your loving touch is always a blessing from God that fills my heart.

A special thank you to Ryan Hata, Franchesca Chai Aquino, Julie Favazza, Candice Douglas, Grace Lewis, and Elaine Rumley, your inspiration, prayers, and support has been supreme. May the Almighty continue to bless and shine His gracious light upon you. I would like to give thanks to all my friends who have provided prayers and support during the creation of this manuscript. I cannot overstate my love and gratitude for your inspiration and feedback. May the Lord God always guide you in wisdom, knowledge, and understanding. I love you all.

Last, but not least, I would like to thank Geoff Stone, Federico Lines, Renee Chavez, and all of the WND/WAP family. This manuscript would not be completed without the professional guidance and expert leadership you provide. I really appreciate the inspiration and support.

INTRODUCTION

As we journey toward Messiah's second coming and millennial reign, the end-of-the-age prophecies in the Holy Bible will become more apparent and clear, as each is fulfilled according to God's prophetic timeline. Today, when we carefully study the writings of the biblical prophets and observe the current events of the Middle East, there is little question as to whether or not we are witnessing the fulfillment of these awesome, yet breathtaking prophecies. In fact, once the nation of Israel was "born again" in 1948 (Isa. 66:8), and the children of Israel recaptured Jerusalem as their capital in 1967, God's prophet declared the 1967 generation as the terminal or last generation before Messiah's second coming and millennial reign (Ps. 102:16–18; Isa. 66:8–21). Therefore, day by day, month by month, and year by year, our generation continues to witness the fulfillment of the end-of-the-age prophecies written more than twenty-five hundred years ago!

While we eagerly await Messiah's glorious millennial kingdom on earth (Rev. 20), most *watchful* believers have at least a basic understanding of the end-of-the-age prophecies and what each encompasses. Throughout the generations, there is absolute certainty that most of these prophecies have been taught and passed down to the younger generation, in the hope of giving them great wisdom, knowledge, and understanding about these prophetic times and events.

However, what if I told you there is an unspoken, neglected, but very profound prophecy in the Holy Bible that is not being proclaimed and exhorted by most Bible scholars and prophecy teachers, but is currently terrorizing the world in an enormous and dangerous way? What if this prophecy could explain the increasing "birth pangs" of war among the nations and the unrelenting perpetual terrorist attacks across the globe?

At the end of the age, the Holy Bible clearly warns the world will become increasingly volatile and perilous as we enter the *beginning of sorrows* (see Matt. 24; Mark 13). Throughout the Word of God, the common theme and specific sign for this dire period of time is when nations rise against nations and kingdoms against kingdoms, which includes widespread terrorism across the globe. Since our generation is living in these exciting but treacherous times, we are certainly witnessing these catastrophic events before our very eyes. Therefore, the question is, are you a "wise virgin" who is watching, as Messiah commanded, or are you one of the foolish ones (see Matt. 25:1–13)?

In the past few decades, our generation has witnessed an increasingly alarming rate of war, which has manifested and dispersed throughout the nations. In all four corners of the world, nations are rising against nations, and kingdoms against kingdoms, just as Messiah prophesied. Terrorism has also ignited and exploded from one end of the earth to the other, including the Middle East, Africa, Asia, Europe, and even upon the shores of America. In recent years, we have seen these evil acts escalate and intensify at horrendous levels not witnessed or recorded in centuries. These barbaric and inhumane extremist groups terrorize, behead, drown, burn, mutilate, rape, crucify, and kill anyone who opposes their radical fundamentalist ideology. These wicked groups also justify the insanity of sacrificing themselves, or their children, as suicide bombers for their murderous satanic cult.

Assuredly, war and terrorism have reached a climatic and terrifying pinnacle across the globe. Today, more than ever, both seem like common, routine occurrences, because every week we are in disbelief and shock over the somber headlines on television or social media about another war or terrorist attack in the world. Within itself, this is a sign we are living at the end of the age. As the days come and go like sand through an hourglass, we find ourselves praying and mourning for another country, city, family, or individual, while seeking answers to these sickening acts of war and terrorism. As these horrific and impactful atrocities continue to escalate in velocity like dark clouds that accumulate massive, destructive thunderstorms, political, social, and religious leaders from around the world are grasping for answers to these cataclysmic, end-of-the-age events.

Is there a biblical prophecy that explains the cloud of war and terrorism that is covering the earth? Does this prophecy confirm that the widespread rage of war and terrorism will continue to occur in the world before Messiah's second coming and millennial reign? Does it correlate to God's everlasting promises in the Promised Land of Israel and the mystery of Aliyah of the children of Israel?

Before the foundation of the world, God Almighty had a sovereign, divine plan of salvation for both Jews and Gentiles (non-Jews) through Yeshua (Jesus) the Messiah (Gen. 48, Rom. 11; Gal. 3:26–29; Eph. 2:11–13). God's chief cornerstone of His quintessential plan (Messiah) is supremely concreted in His everlasting covenants, which will ultimately culminate in the Promised Land of Israel at His second coming and millennial reign. For this reason, the Holy Bible is Israel-centric, and it will continue to be forevermore. Astonishing as it may be, Israel, including the eternal capital of Jerusalem, is literally the center of the universe, both geographically and metaphysically, which affirms its strategic and permanent importance. Make no mistake: the Creator of the universe, the Almighty, left no stone unturned concerning the location of His sovereign, divine plan and its impact on the world. Benjamin Disraeli famously declared "the view of Jerusalem is the history of the world; it is more, it is the history of earth and of heaven."

All believers should understand that Israel, and its people, are the apple of God's eye (Zech. 2:8). In fact, Israel is the single greatest physical confirmation on earth that proves the God of Israel lives *forever*, and His promised covenants are *everlasting*. On the contrary, Satan, God's adversary, completely understands all biblical prophecies, including the everlasting covenants. He is totally aware of his fatal and eternal consequences of perpetual torment and endless damnation in the lake of fire and brimstone, which await him when these eternal promises reach their ultimate fulfillment (Rev. 20). Therefore, Satan, the father of lies, who was a murderer from the beginning (John 8:44), will *directly* attempt to forbid the everlasting covenants from being fulfilled, just as he always has.

Without any doubt, God's everlasting covenants have waged a generational war of biblical proportions between God's fishermen and Satan's hunters. Throughout history, Satan has used his power of influence on the ancient empires of the Egyptians, the Philistines, the Assyrians, the Babylonians, the Romans, the Ottomans, and more recent, Nazi Germany, to attempt to obliterate God's heritage and land, Israel, and His chosen people, the children of Israel (Jews), off the face of the earth. The primary reason for his actions is because of God's eternal promises to His people. However, it is imperative to understand that *all* of those empires have fallen, but the Promised Land of Israel, and the children of Israel, still exists! This is absolutely incredible, and as Winston Churchill declared, "no thoughtful man can doubt the fact that [the Jews] are beyond all question the most formidable and most remarkable race which has appeared in the world."[1] Most certainly, only through the sovereign, divine-right hand of God Almighty could this have been achieved, in order to sanctify *His* great and holy name and to fulfill *His* everlasting promises to the Patriarchs and their descendants (Ezek. 36:22–23).

What about Israel today? Why is the Promised Land the chief spiritual and geopolitical focus of world leaders? Why is this ancient piece of land, the size of New Jersey, saturated as a constant fixture on every television network across the world? Why is Jerusalem, as the prophet proclaimed, "a cup of drunkenness" to all nations (Zech. 12:2)? Has God sent out His fishermen to "fish" the children of Israel back to His land and heritage, the Promised Land? Has the Almighty allowed Satan to use his limited power to influence and ignite his end-of-the-age hunters? Have there been celestial signs in the heavens that connect to the release of God's fishermen and Satan's hunters? When will this unspoken, yet profound prophecy be *ultimately* fulfilled?

In *God's Fishermen, Satan's Hunters*, we will discover the urgent and imperative answers to these profound questions, and learn how the everlasting covenants, the prophecy of the fishermen and the hunters, and the mystery of Aliyah perfectly correlate with one another. We will also acquire great insight into who God's fishermen and Satan's hunters are, including the final hunter, and we will understand how and when all of these prophecies will be *completely* fulfilled. Finally, we will explore the role of God's fishermen at the end of the age, which includes you and me, and we will gain great wisdom and knowledge about the Great Commission in these exciting, yet perilous times. After completing our journey, we will have supreme understanding of all of these critical topics, including the undeniable fact that we are witnessing the fulfillment of the prophecy of the fishermen and the hunters. We will perceive how this prophecy has changed, is changing, and will continue to change the world we live in forever!

CHAPTER 1

GOD'S EVERLASTING COVENANTS

To completely understand the prophecy of the fishermen and the hunters, it is a prerequisite to first understand the premier reason it is prophesied, which is God's everlasting covenants. In the absence of the Almighty's eternal promises, there would be no reason for this incredible, yet sobering prophecy to be proclaimed, because it absolutely correlates with them. As we proceed, it is essential to understand that God's everlasting covenants are the concrete foundation of His salvation plan for Jews and Gentiles, and all believers should have wisdom and knowledge of them.

Before the foundation of the world, the Almighty had a sovereign, divine, and righteous plan of salvation for both Jews and Gentiles. God specifically chose one man, Abraham, whose seed would produce a great nation, known as Israel, to commence His awesome and faithful plan of salvation. In fact, Abraham's original name was Abram, which prophetically means "Great Father," or "father of a multitude" (Strong's #85[1]). God promised Abraham that he would not only be an abundant blessing to the children of Israel, but to *all* nations and families of the earth, including Gentiles.

> Genesis 12:2–3: "*I will make you a great nation; I will bless you and make your name great*; and you shall be a blessing. I will bless those who bless you, and I will curse him who curses you; *and in you all the families of the earth shall be blessed.*"

THE ABRAHAMIC COVENANT

In God's righteous sovereignty, He chose Abraham to commence His divine and perfect plan of salvation for Jews and Gentiles. Subsequently, the Almighty established an everlasting promise to Abraham called the Abrahamic covenant

(Gen. 13, 15, 17). The Abrahamic covenant is a unilateral, unconditional, and irrevocable covenant authenticated by God to Abraham and his descendants. The validity and the fulfillment of the covenant did *not* depend on Abraham or his descendants to do anything in order to receive the promise. This everlasting covenant *only* depends on God's sovereign righteousness.

> Genesis 17:1–7: "When Abram was ninety-nine years old, the Lord appeared to Abram and said to him, "I am Almighty God; walk before Me and be blameless. And I will make My covenant between Me and you, and will multiply you exceedingly. Then Abram fell on his face, and God talked with him, saying: *'As for Me, behold, My covenant is with you, and you shall be a father of many nations.* No longer shall your name be called Abram, but your name shall be Abraham; for I have made you a father of many nations. I will make you exceedingly fruitful; and I will make nations of you, and kings shall come from you. *And I will establish My covenant between Me and you and your descendants after you in their generations, for an everlasting covenant, to be God to you and your descendants after you. Also I give to you and your descendants after you the land in which you are a stranger, all the land of Canaan, as an everlasting possession*; and I will be their God.'"

In the Abrahamic covenant, the Lord unilaterally established an everlasting covenant with Abraham to be the God of Abraham and his descendants. He proclaimed, "I will . . . I will," and He declared it to be everlasting, which validates it as a unilateral, unconditional, and irrevocable promise. Make no mistake: God Almighty cannot lie or break His eternal covenants (Num. 23:19; Titus 1:2).

Now let us explore the difference between the Abrahamic and Mosaic covenants, because some believers conclude the *old covenant* includes the Abrahamic covenant, which is incorrect and theologically dangerous. In the Mosaic covenant, which is the *old covenant*, established after the exodus from Egypt at Mount Sinai (Heb. 8:7–13), God proclaimed, *"If you will . . ."* (Exodus 19), which substantiates it as a *bilateral, conditional, and revocable covenant*, because it is contingent upon the people's obedience of God's commandments.

> Galatians 3:17–18: "And this I say, that the law [Mosaic covenant], which was four hundred and thirty years later, *cannot annul the covenant [Abrahamic] that was confirmed before by God in Christ*, that

it should make the promise of no effect. *For if the inheritance is of the law, it is no longer of promise; but God gave it to Abraham by promise."*

THE PROMISED LAND OF THE ABRAHAMIC COVENANT

As we continue to discover the Abrahamic covenant in Genesis 17, we see that the Lord God also promised Abraham and his descendants a specific piece of land as their inheritance, which was called the land of Canaan, known today as Israel, the Promised Land. In Genesis, God confirmed several times to Abraham the specific boundaries of the land in the Abrahamic covenant, which validates its supreme prophetic value in His plan of salvation for Jews and Gentiles.

> Genesis 17:8: "Also I give to you and your descendants after you the land in which you are a stranger, *all the land of Canaan, as an everlasting possession; and I will be their God.*" (Also see Gen. 12:7; 13:14–17; 15:7)

> Genesis 15:18–21: "*On the same day the* Lord *made a covenant with Abram*, saying: 'To your descendants I have given this land, from the river of Egypt to the great river, the River Euphrates—the Kenites, the Kenezzites, the Kadmonites, the Hittites, the Perizzites, the Rephaim, the Amorites, the Canaanites, the Girgashites, and the Jebusites.'" (See Ex. 23:31; Num. 34; Deut. 11:24; Ezek. 47)

God's promised land can be summarized by the following boundaries: The land from the Mediterranean Sea (Great Sea) in the west, unto the Euphrates River in the northeast, to the river of Egypt in the southwest. Unfortunately, the descendants of Abraham have never occupied *all* of the land promised by God in the Abrahamic covenant, which includes the conquests of Joshua and King David. However, as we will discover, there will be a specific time when the descendants of Abraham will receive *all* of their inheritance of the promise, the Abrahamic covenant.

Promised Land

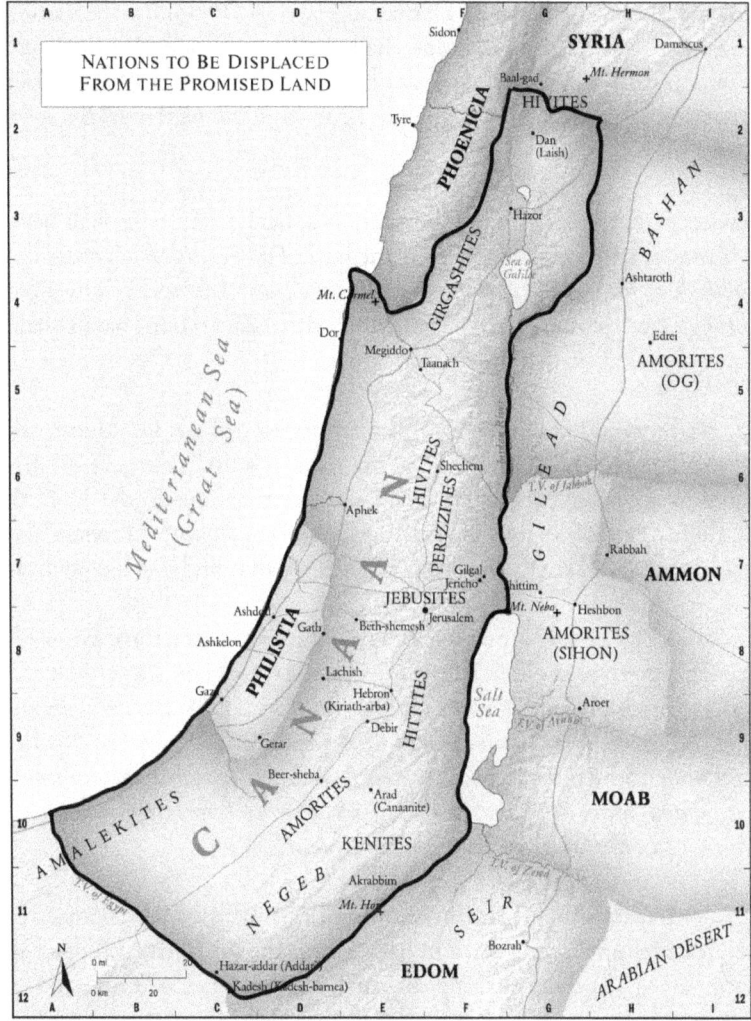

Land of Canaan

THE PROMISED SEED

In the Abrahamic covenant, God also promised Abraham a *seed*, who would continue the *pure royal lineage* to the Seed of the covenant, which is Yeshua. This remarkable revelation is found in Genesis 15, as the Lord God appeared to Abraham in a vision and proclaimed to him, "I am your shield, your exceedingly great reward" (v. 1). Subsequently, Abraham petitioned the Almighty and asked, "What will you give me, seeing I go childless, and the heir of my house is Eliezer of Damascus" (vv. 2–3)? Boldly, the Lord God prophesied to Abraham, "This one shall *not* be your heir, *but one who will come from your own body shall be your heir*" (v. 4). In Genesis 17, the Almighty substantiates who this heir is that would continue the *pure royal lineage* from Abraham unto the Seed, Yeshua.

> Genesis 17:19, 21: "Then God said: 'No, Sarah your wife shall bear you a son, and you shall call his name Isaac; *I will establish My covenant with him for an everlasting covenant, and with his descendants after him* . . . My covenant I will establish with Isaac, whom Sarah shall bear to you at this set time next year.'"

As we proceed in Genesis 15, Abraham petitioned the Lord God, asking, "how will I know that I will inherit my great reward" (Gen. 15:8)? In one of the most amazing, prophetic, and symbolic revelations in the Holy Bible, the Almighty extraordinary validates that His covenant with Abraham and his descendants is a unilateral, unconditional, irrevocable, and everlasting promise.

> Genesis 15:9–11, 17: "So God said to him, 'Bring Me a three-year-old heifer, a three-year-old female goat, a three-year-old ram, a turtledove, and a young pigeon.' *Then he brought all these to Him and cut them in two, down the middle, and placed each piece opposite the other;* but he did not cut the birds in two . . . *And it came to pass, when the sun went down and it was dark, that behold, there appeared a smoking oven and a burning torch that passed between those pieces.*"

In God's preeminent confirmation, He commanded Abraham to bring the requested animals, cut them in half, except for the birds, and place them opposite of each other, creating an "aisle of marriage." As the sun went down and it became dark, Abraham fell in a deep sleep (Gen.15:12), and he saw a smoking oven and a burning torch (God) pass *between* the animal pieces. Through God's extraordinary vision to Abraham, He substantiated the Abrahamic covenant as an "aisle of marriage," which is a sworn oath. Just as marriage today creates a permanent, concrete bond between a man and a woman, the Almighty vowed the same sentiment and sworn oath to Abraham. Keep in mind, God was the *only* one that passed between the marriage aisle. This confirms the Abrahamic covenant is a unilateral, unconditional, irrevocable, and everlasting promise from God to Abraham and His descendants, forevermore.

In E. W. Bullinger's book *Number in Scripture*, he numerically displays the profound significance of the "covenant between the parts," or the Brit bein HaBetarim. Please note, the number three symbolizes *divine perfection* and the number five signifies *grace*. Mr. Bullinger records, "The *divine seal* is seen in the choice of *three* animals, each of *three* years old (the heifer, the she-goat, and the ram). These, together with the two birds (the dove and the pigeon), made *five* in all, *marking it all as a perfect act of free-grace on the part of a sovereign God*." He continued, "therefore the number *five* (grace) shall be stamped upon this covenant by causing it to be made with *five* sacrifices—a heifer, a goat, a ram, a dove, and a pigeon."[2] Additionally, and quite remarkably, when the Lord God changed Abram's name to Abraham (Gen. 17:5), He inserted the *fifth* letter of the Hebrew *aleph bet* (alphabet) in the middle of it, which is the letter "Hey." It symbolically represents the number five (AbraHam). The "Hey" is also found in the Almighty's name (YHVH), and it validates that He stamped His grace upon the Abrahamic covenant, because this divine moment occurred during the confirmation of it (Gen. 17).[3] Of course, the Almighty is the ultimate and perfect mathematician, and He changed Abraham's name accordingly. He also commanded Abraham to summon the exact number of animals and cut them in a specific way, to numerically proclaim the number of His divine (three) grace (five) upon the Abrahamic covenant!

New York Times best-selling author Joel Richardson wrote in his book *When a Jew Rules the World* of the vital impact and supreme significance of the Abrahamic covenant. He vividly described it as "God's covenant unto death." In regard to "God's covenant unto death," Richardson also quoted Dr. Walter C. Kaiser Jr., who served as the academic dean and professor of Old Testament at Trinity Evangelical Divinity School, then as president of Gordon-Conwell Theological Seminary: "May I, God, die like these animals if I do not keep what I promised here."[4] To further substantiate, in his book, *The Holy One of Israel and His Chosen People*, Reverend Sam Clarke, M.Div., who was the first director of the Christian Office in the International Relations Department of Yad Vashem—the Holocaust Museum and Memorial in Jerusalem, also graphically describes the quintessential essence of the Abrahamic covenant, declaring it as "the walk of death."[5] Unequivocally, God Almighty, the Eternal Great I Am, who is omniscient, omnipresent, and omnipotent, cannot die, and He will keep His eternal promises forevermore, which includes the Abrahamic covenant, just as these three teachers validate.

Hebrews 6:13–18: "For when God made a promise to Abraham, because He could swear by no one greater, *He swore by Himself, saying, 'Surely blessing ... I ... will bless you, and multiplying I will multiply you.'* And so, after he [Abraham] had patiently endured, he obtained the promise. For men indeed swear by the greater, and an oath for confirmation *is* for them an end of all dispute. *Thus God, determining to show more abundantly to the heirs of promise the immutability of His counsel, confirmed it by an oath, that by two immutable things, in which it is impossible for God to lie*, we might have strong consolation, who have fled for refuge to lay hold of the hope set before us." (See Titus 1:2)

To further corroborate God's everlasting promise to Abraham, let us review how Abraham's faith was ratified. In Genesis 22, the Lord God tested Abraham by commanding him to offer his son, Isaac, as a burnt offering to Him (vv. 1–2). After Abraham saddled his donkey, summoned Isaac and two other young men, and split the wood for the burnt offering, they journeyed to the specific place the Lord commanded him (v. 3). On the *third day*, once Abraham and Isaac reached Mount Moriah, which is the same location where Messiah was crucified, Abraham placed the wood on the altar, bound Isaac upon it, and stretched out his hand to grasp the knife to slay him (vv. 4–10). Immediately, the Angel of the Lord shouted from heaven, "Abraham, Abraham," and He commanded him not to slay Isaac, because Abraham had proved that he loved and feared God more than any other, since he was going to sacrifice his son for Him (vv. 11–12).

Genesis 22:15–18: "*Then the Angel of the* LORD *called to Abraham a second time out of heaven, and said: 'By Myself I have sworn, says the* LORD, because you have done this thing, and have not withheld your son [Isaac], *your only son*—blessing I will bless you, and multiplying I will multiply your descendants as the stars of the heaven and as the sand which is on the seashore; and your descendants shall possess the gate of their enemies. *In your seed all the nations of the earth shall be blessed, because you have obeyed My voice.*'" (See Gen.15:5)

The Angel of the Lord proclaimed to Abraham, "*By Myself I have sworn, says the* LORD." The Angel of the Lord is Yeshua, as He is Lord, and He declares He is the God of Abraham. In two beautiful poetic metaphors, Yeshua declares to Abraham that He will bless him by multiplying his descendants "as the stars of heaven and as the sand on the seashore." In Abraham's days, electricity did not exist; therefore, once the bright shining sun descended and the cool desert night arrived, thousands upon thousands of stars would have illuminated the heavens, certifying the infinite measure of Yeshua's promise. If you have ever been to a remote countryside void of city lights, or ventured out to sea on a boat far from the mainland, you can relate to how many stars are visible in the sky. It seems there are thousands of visible stars! Likewise, if you visit a beach, the exponential number of grains of sand on the seashore is too mindboggling to count! Accordingly, these two metaphors symbolize the vast number of descendants from Abraham's seed. Yeshua concluded this phenomenal prophecy by proclaiming, "In your seed all the nations of the earth shall be blessed," which refers to Himself, the *promised Seed* of the Abrahamic covenant.

> Galatians 3:16–18: *"Now to Abraham and his Seed were the promises made.* He does not say, 'And to seeds,' as of many, but as of one, *'And to your Seed,' who is Christ.* And this I say, that the law [Mosaic covenant], which was four hundred and thirty years later, *cannot annul the covenant [Abrahamic] that was confirmed before by God in Christ,* that it should make the promise of no effect. *For if the inheritance is of the law, it is no longer of promise; but God gave it to Abraham by promise."*

In summary, there are six major details of the Abrahamic covenant:

1. It is a unilateral, unconditional, irrevocable, and everlasting promise by God.
2. It is stamped with the Almighty's divine grace.
3. It is an eternal covenant specifically promised to the descendants of Abraham, through Isaac, and then Jacob, and unto their descendants (See Gen. 26:24; 28:13–15).
4. It is an everlasting promise of a specific and literal piece of land (Canaan/Israel).
5. It promises a *Seed*, who will bless all nations at God's appointed time.
6. It is the foundation covenant to the Davidic and new covenants.

Psalm 105:6–12: "O seed of Abraham His servant, You children of Jacob, His chosen ones! He is the Lord our God; His judgments are in all the earth. *He remembers His covenant forever [Abrahamic], the word which He commanded, for a thousand generations, the covenant which He made with Abraham, and His oath to Isaac, and confirmed it to Jacob for a statute, to Israel as an everlasting covenant, Saying, 'To you I will give the land of Canaan [Israel] as the allotment of your inheritance.'"*

THE DAVIDIC COVENANT

The Davidic covenant is also a unilateral, unconditional, irrevocable, and everlasting promise from God to King David, who is a descendant of Abraham, Isaac, and Jacob, which is the *pure royal lineage* (Matt.1:1–17; Luke 3:23–38). Equivalent to the Abrahamic covenant, the Davidic covenant is not contingent upon David or his descendants either; both covenants *only* depend on God's righteous sovereignty. The prophet Nathan proclaimed this eternal promise to David, who was "a man after [God's] own heart" (1 Sam.13:14).

> 2 Samuel 7:10–14, 16: *"Moreover I will appoint a place for My people Israel [Promised Land], and will plant them, that they may dwell in a place of their own and move no more*; nor shall the sons of wickedness oppress them anymore, as previously, since the time that I commanded judges to be over My people Israel, and have caused you to rest from all your enemies. *Also the* LORD *tells you [David] that He will make you a house.* "When your [David's] days are fulfilled and you rest with your fathers, *I will set up your seed after you, who will come from your body, and I will establish his kingdom. He shall build a house for My name, and I will establish the throne of his kingdom forever. I will be his Father, and he shall be My son . . . And your house and your kingdom shall be established forever before you. Your throne shall be established forever."*

The Davidic covenant builds on and extends God's promises in the Abrahamic covenant. Remember: God promised Abraham that he and his descendants would inherit the Promised Land and *the Seed* would come from his pure royal lineage (descendants). Similarly, God promised David a *Seed* from the fruit of his body, who would become *Messiah* and *King* over Abraham and David's descendants in the Promised Land (vv. 10–13). The promised Seed, Messiah, and King of Israel, who is Yeshua, will build a house for God's holy name, which will occur during His millennial reign, as He rules over the descendants of Abraham and David from David's everlasting throne in Jerusalem (v.v. 13,16). At this prophetic and appointed time, the Abrahamic and Davidic covenants will be *completely* fulfilled. The Almighty will establish the throne of Messiah's kingdom forever, which establishes David's house, kingdom, and throne forever, as well (vv. 13, 16; see Dan. 7:13–14, 26).

> Psalm 132:11: "*The LORD has sworn in truth to David*; He will not turn from it: '*I will set upon your throne the fruit of your body.*'"

> Revelation 22:16: "I, Jesus, have sent My angel to testify to you these things in the churches. *I am the Root and the Offspring of David, the Bright and Morning Star.*"

To summarize, the Abrahamic covenant promised a *Seed* and a specific piece of land to the descendants of Abraham. The Davidic covenant promised the Abrahamic covenant's *Seed* would become *Messiah and King* over Abraham and David's descendants on David's everlasting throne in Jerusalem (*Promised Land*). Yeshua is the Messiah and King of Israel (John 1:49). King David also testifies Yeshua is the Seed, Messiah, and King of these sovereign, divine, and eternal covenants!

> Psalm 110:1–2, 4–6: "The LORD [God] said to my Lord [Yeshua], 'Sit at My right hand, till I make Your enemies Your footstool. *The LORD shall send the rod of Your strength out of Zion [Jerusalem]. Rule in the midst of Your enemies!* . . . The LORD has sworn and will not relent, '*You are a priest forever according to the order of Melchizedek.*' The Lord [Yeshua] *is at Your [God's] right hand*; He shall execute kings in the day of His wrath. He shall judge among the nations, He shall fill the places with dead bodies, He shall execute the heads of many countries.*" (See Acts 2:29-36, Heb. 5,7, Dan. 2:44; Rev. 19:11–16)

YESHUA, THE SON OF GOD, THE SON OF ABRAHAM AND DAVID

How can Yeshua be the Son of God, the Son of Abraham, and the Son of David? To understand this mystery, we will examine and authenticate His genealogy. The Holy Bible provides a detailed chronological ancestry lineage of Yeshua in the books of Matthew and Luke (Matt. 1:1-17; Luke 3:23–38). Look at this verse:

Matthew 1:1: "The book of the genealogy of Jesus Christ, *the Son of David, the Son of Abraham.*"

According to Matthew, Abraham and David are His ancestors of the everlasting covenants, which proves His earthly lineage is from the *pure royal lineage* (Abrahamic and Davidic covenants). At the end of the genealogy, Matthew also corroborates Yeshua's *pure royal lineage* with further details.

Matthew 1:16: "And Jacob begot *Joseph the husband of Mary*, of whom was born Jesus who is called Christ."

As we can see, Matthew lists Joseph as the *husband* of Mary, not the *father* of Yeshua, which certainly identifies His birth as a supernatural, divine event by the Almighty. This is also the reason Matthew explains that Mary was a virgin when she became pregnant with Him. How could this be?

Matthew 1:18–20: "*Now the birth of Jesus Christ was as follows*: After His mother Mary was betrothed to Joseph, *before they came together, she was found with child of the Holy Spirit*. Then Joseph her husband, being a just man, and not wanting to make her a public example, was minded to put her away secretly. But while he thought about these things, behold, an angel of the Lord appeared to him in a dream, saying, 'Joseph, son of David, do not be afraid to take to you Mary your wife, *for that which is conceived in her is of the Holy Spirit.*'" (See Isa. 7:14.)

The apostle Matthew testifies Yeshua is the Son of God, because Mary was "with Child of the Holy Spirit." Therefore, in Matthew's genealogy and testimony, he affirms Yeshua is the Son of God, and also that He is a descendant (son) of the *pure royal lineage* of Abraham and David. Please note, in the Holy Bible, ancestors were called "fathers," and descendants were called "sons." In Daniel 5, we find a great example of this "father and son" terminology. Once Belshazzar, king of Babylon, defiled the Lord God's vessels at a great feast, he witnessed the finger of God write an inscription on a wall (vv. 1–5). Once Belshazzar's countenance changed from haughty to horrified, and his wise men failed to interpret the writing on the wall (vv. 6–9), the queen spoke to him about how the prophet Daniel had interpreted dreams for his "father," Nebuchadnezzar (vv. 10–12, 18). However, Nebuchadnezzar was not Belshazzar's father, Nabonidus was,[6] which substantiates that the Holy Bible sometimes uses the term "father" when referring to an ancestor.

In the book of Luke, the writer not only explains the genealogy of Yeshua, but he also states the angel Gabriel appeared to Mary and confirmed His ultimate fulfillment of the Abrahamic and Davidic covenants.

> Luke 1:30–33: "Then the angel said to her, 'Do not be afraid, Mary, for you have found favor with God. And behold, you will conceive in your womb and bring forth a Son, *and shall call His name Jesus. He will be great, and will be called the Son of the Highest; and the Lord God will give Him the throne of His father David [Davidic covenant]. And He will reign over the house of Jacob (Israel) forever, and of His kingdom there will be no end.*'" (Abrahamic and Davidic covenants)

The angel Gabriel authenticates Yeshua is the Son of God (Son of the Highest), and the Almighty will give Him the throne of "*His father*" David, and He will reign over the house of Israel forever and ever (Abrahamic and Davidic covenants). Again, the terminology "father" ratifies Yeshua's *pure royal lineage* (Seed) from Abraham, Isaac, Jacob, and David.

In conjunction, Matthew's and Luke's accounts of Yeshua's genealogy testifies He is the Son of God, His "earthly father" was Joseph, and proves He is the pure royal heir of His ancestors: Abraham, Isaac, Jacob, and David (Abrahamic and Davidic covenants) (See Matt. 1:1–17, Luke 3:23–38).

Furthermore, Matthew's and Luke's accounts confirm both Joseph and Mary were direct descendants of David, who was a descendant of Abraham, Isaac, and Jacob, which preserves the purity of the *pure royal lineage* of Messiah. An additional purpose of Matthew's genealogy is to prove that Yeshua is the Messiah of Abraham's descendants, as the Scriptures traces it back to Abraham (Abrahamic covenant). Another reason of Luke's genealogy is to substantiate that Yeshua is the Messiah *for all of mankind, Jew and Gentile,* as it traces back to Adam.

> Psalm 89:3-4, 34–37: "I have made a covenant with My chosen, I have sworn to My servant David: 'Your seed I will establish forever, and build up your throne to all generations. My covenant I will not break, nor alter the word that has gone out of My lips. *Once I have sworn by My holiness; I will not lie to David: His seed shall endure forever, and his throne as the sun before Me; it shall be established forever like the moon, even like the faithful witness in the sky.*"

Jeremiah 33:19-22, "And the word of the LORD came to Jeremiah, saying, "Thus says the LORD: *'If you can break My covenant with the day and My covenant with the night, so that there will not be day and night in their season, then My covenant may also be broken with David My servant, so that he shall not have a son to reign on his throne, and with the Levites, the priests, My ministers.* As the host of heaven cannot be numbered, nor the sand of the sea measured, so will I multiply the descendants of David My servant and the Levites who minister to Me.'"

THE NEW COVENANT

The final covenant of God's plan of salvation for Jews and Gentiles is the new covenant. Equivalent to the Abrahamic and Davidic covenants, the new covenant is a unilateral, unconditional, irrevocable, and everlasting covenant that God promised to the descendants of Abraham, Isaac, Jacob, and David (Patriarchs). The new covenant builds upon and establishes the Abrahamic and Davidic covenants, because it encompasses *all* of the eternal promises within them.

Contrary to what some believers realize, the new covenant was *first* written and prophesied by the prophets, Isaiah, Jeremiah, and Ezekiel. Isaiah provided the first proclamation of the new covenant. He set the stage by prophesying of an Intercessor and Messiah who would manifest from the Almighty's own righteous arm to bring not only salvation and righteousness to the descendants of the Patriarchs, but also a day of vengeance upon His enemies.

Isaiah 59:15–19: "Then the LORD saw it, and it displeased Him that there was no justice. *He saw that there was no man, and wondered that there was no intercessor; therefore, His own arm brought salvation for Him; and His own righteousness, it sustained Him.* For He put on righteousness as a breastplate, and a helmet of salvation on His head; *He put on the garments of vengeance for clothing*, and was clad with zeal as a cloak. *According to their deeds, accordingly He will repay, fury to His adversaries, recompense to His enemies*; The coastlands He will fully repay. So shall they fear the name of the LORD from the west, and His glory from the rising of the sun; when the enemy comes in like a flood, the Spirit of the LORD will lift up a standard against him."

In God's infinite and supreme wisdom, He understood mankind would require an Intercessor, a Redeemer, a Messiah, who was manifested from His own righteous and divine arm (John 1). Isaiah's apocalyptic description of an Intercessor and Messiah is referring to Yeshua, God's right Arm and Hand (Ps. 110:1; Isa. 53:1; Mark 16:19, Luke 20:42–43). Isaiah went on to vividly describe the Day of the Lord, which is Messiah's second coming, when He will pour out His vengeance upon His enemies (see Isa. 34; 61:2; 63, Jer. 51:6–8; 2 Thess. 1:7–10; Rev. 19:11–16). The prophet declared that Messiah's day of vengeance and chastisement upon the nations will provoke them to "fear the name and glory of the Lord," which corroborates a "redemptive cleansing" of them. As Isaiah continued, he substantiated that the new covenant incorporates the Abrahamic and Davidic covenants.

> Isaiah 59:20–21: "'*The Redeemer will come to Zion [Jerusalem], and to those who turn from transgression in Jacob [Israel, the Promised Land],' says the* LORD. 'As for Me,' says the LORD, '*this is My [new] covenant with them [descendants]:* My Spirit who is upon you, and My words which I have put in your mouth, shall not depart from your mouth, nor from the mouth of your descendants, nor from the mouth of your descendants' descendants,' says the LORD, "*from this time and forevermore.*"

Although Isaiah did not specifically label this prophecy as the "new covenant," it certainly is a new covenant, because it perfectly correlates the Intercessor, Seed, Messiah, and King of Israel, Yeshua, to the Promised Land and the descendants of Abraham, Isaac, Jacob, and David, *forevermore.* In other words, it builds upon and establishes the Abrahamic and Davidic covenants. Isaiah proclaimed, "The *Redeemer* [Seed] will come to Zion [Promised Land] and to those who turn from transgression in Israel." He continued, "This is My covenant with them," which, again, means the descendants of Abraham, Isaac, Jacob, and David (Patriarchs). Isaiah concluded his announcement of the new covenant by describing how the Patriarchs' descendants will receive their salvation through Yeshua: "*The* LORD'S *spirit will come upon them, and His words which He will put in their mouth, shall never depart from their mouth, nor from their descendant's mouth, nor from the mouth of their descendants' descendants, from that time forth and forevermore.*"

Now, let us discover the prophecy of the new covenant of *redemption* from God through Messiah (right arm), proclaimed by the prophet Jeremiah. Before we proceed, it is worthy to note that Jeremiah 31 is a continuation from Jeremiah 30, which prophesies of the time of Jacob's trouble (last seven years of the age), indicating when the appointed time of the new covenant will be ultimately fulfilled.

> Jeremiah 31:1, 31–32: *"At the same time,"* says the Lord, *I will be the God of all the families of Israel, and they shall be My people."* Behold, the days are coming, says the LORD, when I will make *a new covenant with the house of Israel and with the house of Judah*, not according to the covenant that I made with their fathers in the day that I took them by the hand to lead them out of the land of Egypt [Mosaic covenant], My covenant which they broke, though I was a husband to them, says the LORD."

Jeremiah commenced his prophecy of the new covenant by proclaiming, "At the same time," which refers to the last verse in Jeremiah 30, "in the latter days you will consider it." The "latter days" is an eschatological term for the end of the age. In the latter days, or at the end of the age, which will culminate with Messiah's second coming and millennial reign, "the LORD [Messiah] will be the God of *all* the families of Israel, and they shall be His people." This affirms that the *ultimate* fulfillment of the new covenant will occur at the end of the age. Jeremiah continues to declare the Lord God will make a new covenant with the house of Israel and the house of Judah at that time, who are the descendants of Abraham, Isaac, Jacob, and David, and they will dwell in the Promised Land. This again validates that the new covenant establishes and builds upon the Abrahamic covenant, which promised a Seed, the Promised Land, and the inheritance of the land, and also the Davidic covenant, which promised the Seed would become Messiah and King over the descendants of the Patriarchs in the Promised Land. Of course, the new covenant does not replace or terminate the Abrahamic and Davidic covenants, but instead, it establishes and fulfills *all* of the promises in both of them. It would not be like the Mosaic covenant, which the children of Israel broke because of *their* unfaithfulness, although God Himself was faithful to it. Like Isaiah, the prophet Jeremiah clearly explained how the descendants of the Patriarchs would receive the new covenant.

> Jeremiah 31:33–34: *"But this is the covenant* that I will make with the house of Israel *after those days [latter days]* says the LORD: *I will put My law in their minds, and write it on their hearts; and I will be their God, and they shall be My people.* No more shall every man teach

his neighbor, and every man his brother, saying, 'Know the Lord,' for they all shall know Me, from the least of them to the greatest of them, says the Lord. *For I will forgive their iniquity, and their sin I will remember no more."*

In the new covenant, the Lord God will put His law [Torah] in their minds and write it on their hearts. At that divine, prophetic, and appointed time, He will be their God and they shall be His people, because He will forgive their iniquity, and their sins He will remember no more (Isa. 1:18). As of today, this promised covenant is yet to be fulfilled, because the children of Israel as a whole have not accepted their Jewish Messiah, Yeshua. Although there is a blossoming revival of a Jewish remnant occurring each and every year, the vast majority of the Patriarchs' descendants have not yet come to faith in Yeshua. Nevertheless, at the end of the age, this unilateral, unconditional, irrevocable, and everlasting covenant will be fulfilled, just as the biblical prophets have written.

> Jeremiah 32:37–42: "Behold, I will gather them out of all countries where I have driven them in My anger, in My fury, and in great wrath; *I will bring them back to this place, and I will cause them to dwell safely. They shall be My people, and I will be their God; then I will give them one heart and one way, that they may fear Me forever, for the good of them and their children after them. And I will make an everlasting covenant with them, that I will not turn away from doing them good;* but I will put My fear in their hearts so that they will not depart from Me. Yes, I will rejoice over them to do them good, and I will assuredly plant them in this land, with all My heart and with all My soul. For thus says the Lord: *'Just as I have brought all this great calamity on this people, so I will bring on them all the good that I have promised them.'"*

In Ezekiel's account of the new covenant, he also prophesied of the specific time when the Lord God would place a new heart and a new spirit within the children of Israel, which substantiates Isaiah's and Jeremiah's proclamation of it (Isa. 59:21; 60; Jer. 31:33–34). Additionally, the prophet also correlates the Promised Land of the Abrahamic covenant with the promise of the new covenant, which is the appointed time when the Patriarch's descendants, as a nation, will receive a new heart and a new spirit for Yeshua, their Jewish Messiah and King.

Ezekiel 36:22-29, "Therefore say to the house of Israel, 'Thus says the Lord G<small>OD</small>: *"I do not do this for your sake, O house of Israel, but for My holy name's sake, which you have profaned among the nations wherever you went. And I will sanctify My great name, which has been profaned among the nations, which you have profaned in their midst; and the nations shall know that I am the L<small>ORD</small>,"* says the Lord G<small>OD</small>, *"when I am hallowed in you before their eyes. For I will take you from among the nations, gather you out of all countries, and bring you into your own land. Then I will sprinkle clean water on you, and you shall be clean; I will cleanse you from all your filthiness and from all your idols. I will give you a new heart and put a new spirit within you; I will take the heart of stone out of your flesh and give you a heart of flesh. I will put My Spirit within you and cause you to walk in My statutes, and you will keep My judgments and do them. Then you shall dwell in the land that I gave to your fathers; you shall be My people, and I will be your God.* I will deliver you from all your uncleannesses.""

Just as the prophet declared, the Lord God will fulfill the new covenant with the descendants of the Patriarchs for *His sake and His holy name*, therefore sanctifying His holy name among the nations. Why? The resounding answer is because of His everlasting promises to Abraham, Isaac, Jacob, and David! Remember: the Almighty made a unilateral, unconditional, irrevocable, and everlasting promise to them. He will absolutely fulfill His covenants by giving their descendants a heart of flesh and manifesting His Spirit within them. Subsequently, they will walk in His statutes and keep His judgments, and they will inherit the promises of the everlasting covenants. At that incredible moment in time, they will be Messiah's people, and He shall be their God!

As we proceed, there are three profound misinterpretations about the new covenant. First, some believe the new covenant replaces *all* of the covenants, including the everlasting covenants God *promised* to Abraham, Isaac, Jacob, and David, and their descendants. Second, it is widely believed the new covenant is only prophesied by Messiah in the New Testament (Matt. 26), but surely, it was first announced by Isaiah, then prophesied by Jeremiah, and authenticated by Ezekiel in the Hebrew Scriptures (Old Testament). Of course, Messiah *is* the blood of the new covenant by His ultimate sacrifice at His crucifixion and resurrection (Matt.26:26-28), but as we have validated, its *ultimate* fulfillment will be when the descendants of the Patriarchs accept Yeshua as their Messiah at the end of the age. Last, some believe the new covenant is made with the Gentiles, however, the Lord God clearly proclaims the new covenant is an eternal promise to the house of Israel and the house of Judah (Jews). Gentiles are "grafted into" the everlasting promises of the Abrahamic, Davidic, and new covenants, which fulfills God's plan of salvation! In Romans, the apostle Paul provides great wisdom, knowledge, and understanding of this great mystery.

> Romans 11:17, 19-27: "And if some of the branches [Jews] were broken off, and you [Gentiles], being a wild olive tree, *were grafted in among them, and with them became a partaker of the root and fatness of the olive tree* . . . [y]ou will say then, *"Branches were broken off that I might be grafted in."* Well *said*. Because of unbelief they [Jews] were broken off, *and you stand by faith.* Do not be haughty, but fear. For if God did not spare the natural branches [Jews], He may not spare you either. Therefore, consider the goodness and severity of God: on those who fell, severity; but toward you, goodness, if you continue in *His* goodness. Otherwise you also will be cut off. *And they [Jews] also, if they do not continue in unbelief, will be grafted in, for God is able to graft them in again [new covenant]. For if you [Gentiles] were cut out of the olive tree which is wild by nature, and were grafted contrary to nature into a cultivated olive tree, how much more will these [Jews], who are natural branches, be grafted into their own olive tree?* For I do not desire, brethren, that you should be ignorant of this mystery, lest you should be wise in your own opinion, *that blindness in part has happened to Israel until the fullness of the Gentiles has come in. And so all Israel will be saved* [new covenant] *as it is written: "The Deliverer will come out of Zion, and He will turn away ungodliness from Jacob [new covenant]; For this is My covenant with them, when I take away their sins."* (See Isa. 59:20–21.)

Just as Paul authenticated, the new covenant is established with the descendants of the Patriarchs, the Jewish people, as He quoted Isaiah 59:20–21, which declares the new covenant. Paul continued to proclaim that "partial blindness" has happened to Israel until the fullness of the Gentiles come in, and afterward, "all Israel will be saved," because of the everlasting covenants. Again, Gentiles are "grafted into" the olive tree and are heirs according to the eternal promises.

> Galatians 3:26–29: *"For you are all sons of God through faith in Christ Jesus.* For as many of you as were baptized into Christ have put on

Christ. *There is neither Jew nor Gentile, there is neither slave nor free, there is neither male nor female; for you are all one in Christ Jesus. And if you are Christ's, then you are Abraham's seed, and heirs according to the promise."*

The apostle Paul testifies that if you are saved in Messiah (Christ), then you are Abraham's seed, "an heir according to the promise," which is the Abrahamic covenant. He specifically wrote this Scripture for Jews and Gentiles to understand God's plan of salvation through the everlasting covenants, which incorporates both of them. Once Jews and Gentiles are saved in Yeshua, both are included into the commonwealth of the *Israel of God*.

Ephesians 2:11–13: "Therefore remember that you, once Gentiles in the flesh—who are called Uncircumcision by what is called the Circumcision made in the flesh by hands—*that at that time you were without Christ, being aliens from the commonwealth of Israel and strangers from the covenants of promise, having no hope and without God in the world. But now in Christ Jesus you who once were far off have been brought near by the blood of Christ."*

In Jeremiah 31, as he concludes his prophecy of the new covenant, he proclaims an extraordinary and beautiful poetic confirmation from the Almighty, which corroborates the *permanence* of His everlasting promises to the descendants of the Patriarchs.

Jeremiah 31:35–37: "Thus says the LORD, who gives the sun for a light by day, the ordinances of the moon and the stars for a light by night, who disturbs the sea, and its waves roar (The LORD of hosts is His name): *'If those ordinances depart from before Me, says the LORD, then the seed of Israel shall also cease from being a nation before Me forever.'* Thus says the LORD: *'If heaven above can be measured, and the foundations of the earth searched out beneath, I will also cast off all the seed of Israel for all that they have done, says the LORD.'"* (See Jer. 33:19–26.)

Sequentially, after the Lord God prophesied His everlasting promise of the new covenant with the house of Israel and the house of Judah (Jer. 31:31–34), He substantiates it is eternal and everlasting. As we know, God Almighty controls the whole universe, including the celestial ordinances of the sun, moon, stars, and the sea, which will only be abolished when Messiah, "puts all things under His feet, including death, and gives the Kingdom to the Father, that God may be all in all" in the New Jerusalem (Ps. 8:6, 1 Cor. 15:24–28, Rev. 21–22). Furthermore, the heavens cannot be measured or the foundation of the earth cannot be searched out beneath, except by His Majesty, God Almighty, validating His everlasting promises, forevermore. In fact, by the Word of the Lord and the breath of His mouth, He created the universe!

> Psalm 33:6: "By the word of the LORD the heavens were made, and all the host of them by the breath of His mouth." (Also see Gen. 1:1–3; Ps. 135:5–7; 147:4–5; 148:1–14; Prov. 3:19–20; Isa. 40:12–15, 26; Jer. 10:12–13; 51:15–16.)

In Jeremiah 33, the prophet reiterated that the new covenant is everlasting through another incredible poetic metaphor, once more affirming the *permanence* of God's everlasting covenants with Abraham, Isaac, Jacob, David, and their descendants.

> Jeremiah 33:25–26: "Thus says the LORD: *'If My covenant is not with day and night, and if I have not appointed the ordinances of heaven and earth,* then I will cast away the descendants of Jacob and David My servant, so that I will not take any of his descendants to be rulers over the descendants of Abraham, Isaac, and Jacob. For I will cause their captives to return, and will have mercy on them.'" (See Gen. 1.)

Now, let us confirm Yeshua is the King of Israel and the fulfillment of the new covenant, who will *completely* fulfill the everlasting promises of the Almighty (Abrahamic, Davidic, and new covenants). In the Gospels, the inauguration of the new covenant is recorded when the body and blood of Yeshua the Messiah was offered as the ultimate redemptive sacrifice for the sins of His people of the everlasting covenants, which ultimately, includes Jews and Gentiles (Rom. 11, Gal. 3:26-29, Eph. 2:11-13).

> Matthew 26:26–28: "And as they were eating, Jesus took bread, blessed and broke it, and gave it to the disciples and said, *'Take, eat; this is My body.'* Then He took the cup, and gave thanks, and gave it to them, saying, *'Drink from it, all of you. For this is My blood of the new covenant, which is shed for many for the remission of sins.'"*

In conclusion, the Abrahamic, Davidic, and new covenants are *all* unilateral, unconditional, irrevocable, and everlasting covenants promised by God Almighty. All of these eternal promises *only* depend on God's sovereign righteousness. The everlasting covenants were *all* promised to Abraham, Isaac, Jacob, and David, and their descendants, and Gentiles are "grafted" into the covenants. Yeshua of Nazareth is the chosen *Seed, Messiah, and King* of the Abrahamic, Davidic, and new covenants, and He will *completely* fulfill all three of the everlasting promises at His second coming and millennial reign!

Luke 1:31–33: "And behold, you will conceive in your womb and bring forth a Son, and shall call His name JESUS. He will be great, and will be called the Son of the Highest; *and the Lord God will give Him the throne of His father David [Davidic covenant]. And He will reign over the house of Jacob [Israel] forever [Abrahamic covenant], and of His kingdom there will be no end [new covenant].*"

CHAPTER 2

THE PROPHECY OF THE FISHERMEN AND THE HUNTERS

One of the most unspoken, often neglected, yet imperative prophecies of our generation is Jeremiah's prophecy of the fishermen and the hunters. This encouraging but sobering prophecy directly and cohesively correlates to God's everlasting covenants, thus the primary reason the prophet Jeremiah proclaimed it. As we begin to explore this prophecy, it is worthy to note that God has appointed a specific time in which He will *completely* fulfill His everlasting covenants and prompt Abraham, Isaac, Jacob, and David's descendants to return to the Promised Land from *all* other nations where they have been scattered due to their sin against Him. Amazingly, the prophecy of the fishermen and the hunters bestows great wisdom and knowledge of God's appointed time for this event and also exactly how it will be fulfilled. As we journey forward, we will understand how God's everlasting covenants and the prophecy of the fishermen and the hunters are two of the major cornerstones that culminate into the time of Jacob's trouble (last seven years of the age), Messiah's second coming, and His millennial reign.

We will begin by reviewing God's call to Jeremiah to become a prophet. Afterwards, we will examine in summary the history of the children of Israel and the tragic and atrocious circumstances that led to Jeremiah's prophetic calling, which will provide us with great insight into the prophecy of the fishermen and the hunters. Upon conclusion, we will prove that the prophecy of the fishermen and the hunters is an end-of-the-age prophecy. (Please note, from this point forward, I will use "the children of Israel" or the "Jewish people" as reference to the descendants of Abraham, Isaac, Jacob, and David.)

God divinely sanctified and ordained Jeremiah to be a prophet not only to Israel, but to *all* nations and kingdoms. Jeremiah's ministry began in approximately 627 BC, and he ministered under the southern kingdom of Judah's last five kings: Josiah, Jehoahaz, Jehoiakim, Jehoiachin, and Zedekiah (586 BC).

> Jeremiah 1:4–5, 9–10: "Then the word of the LORD came to me, saying: 'Before I formed you in the womb I knew you; *Before you were born I sanctified you; I ordained you a prophet to the nations.'* . . . Then the LORD put forth His hand and touched my mouth, and the LORD said to me: '*Behold, I have put My words in your mouth. See, I have this day set you over the nations and over the kingdoms, to root out and to pull down, to destroy and to throw down, to build and to plant.*"

Before Jeremiah's ministry (627 BC), the northern kingdom of Israel had been destroyed by the Assyrian Empire (722 BC) due to their continuous disobedience to God (2 Kings 17:7–23). Although the southern kingdom of Judah vividly understood and witnessed the massive destruction of their treacherous sister, the northern kingdom of Israel, the people chose to remain "stiff-necked" and continued to rebel against God's laws and commandments (Ezek. 23, 2 Chr. 36). Slow to anger, in God's ultimate love, grace, patience, mercy, and forgiveness, He instructed Jeremiah to call the southern kingdom of Judah to repentance (Jer. 3:6–13). Rebelliously, the children of Israel persisted in their flagrant disobedience toward God, and they mocked Jeremiah's warning as they perpetuated deeper into their idolatrous lives and wicked ways. Once God's patience ended, judgment was set and His punishment was forthcoming.

> Jeremiah 1:14–16: "Then the LORD said to me: 'Out of the north calamity shall break forth on all the inhabitants of the land. For behold, I am calling all the families of the kingdoms of the north,' says the LORD; "They shall come and each one set his throne at the entrance of the gates of Jerusalem, against all its walls all around, and against all the cities of Judah. *I will utter My judgments against them concerning all their wickedness, because they have forsaken Me, burned incense to other gods, and worshiped the works of their own hands.*'"

> Jeremiah 25:8–9: "Therefore thus says the LORD of hosts: 'Because you have not heard My words, behold, I will send and take all the

families of the north,' says the LORD, '*and Nebuchadnezzar the king of Babylon, My servant, and will bring them against this land, against its inhabitants, and against these nations all around, and will utterly destroy them, and make them an astonishment, a hissing, and perpetual desolations.*'"

Babylonian Empire

Jeremiah prophesied that the king of Babylon, Nebuchadnezzar, along with his empire, would violently march from the north into Jerusalem and destroy it. He also proclaimed the Babylonian Empire would take captives from the southern kingdom of Judah and its surrounding cities to Babylon. As previously discussed, God sent Nebuchadnezzar to destroy the southern kingdom of Judah, including Jerusalem, because the people did not heed the words from His prophet Jeremiah and others, who relentlessly and painstakingly called upon their brethren to repent and turn their hearts and ways back to Him. As the Holy Bible and world history record, Jeremiah's prophecy was fulfilled in 586 BC.

Jeremiah 25:11–12: "And this whole land shall be a desolation and an astonishment, and these nations shall serve the king of Babylon seventy years. '*Then it will come to pass, when seventy years are completed, that I will punish the king of Babylon and that nation*, the land of the Chaldeans, for their iniquity,' says the LORD; 'and I will make it a perpetual desolation.'"

Jeremiah prophesied the children of Israel's captivity in Babylon would last for *seventy years*, and once fulfilled, God would judge the Babylonian Empire by allowing the Babylonians to be conquered by the Medo-Persian Empire (539 BC). The prophet Daniel records this unique prophetic event.

> Daniel 5:25–28, 30–31: "And this is the inscription that was written: MENE, MENE, TEKEL, UPHARSIN. This is the interpretation of each word. MENE: God has numbered your kingdom, and finished it; TEKEL: You have been weighed in the balances, and found wanting; PERES: *Your kingdom has been divided, and given to the Medes and Persians.* That very night Belshazzar, king of the Chaldeans [Babylon], was slain. And Darius the Mede received the kingdom, being about sixty-two years old."

Now that we have discovered God's divine, prophetic calling of Jeremiah as a prophet, the destruction of the kingdom of Israel and Judah, the seventy-year exile and captivity of the children of Israel in Babylon, and the fall of the Babylonian Empire, let us explore the prophecy of the fishermen and the hunters. In Jeremiah 16, he prophesies that the Lord will restore and redeem the children of Israel to the Promised Land of Israel *from the land of the north and from all the lands where He has driven them.*

> Jeremiah 16:14–15: "'Therefore behold, the days are coming,' says the LORD, 'that it shall no more be said, "The LORD lives who brought up the children of Israel from the land of Egypt," but, "*The Lord lives who brought up the children of Israel from the land of the north and from all the lands where He had driven them."* For I will bring them back into their land which I gave to their fathers [everlasting covenants].*'"

Is this prophecy speaking about the restoration of the children of Israel to the Promised Land *after* the seventy-year Babylonian (land of the north) captivity? At first glance, it would indicate this prophecy was fulfilled after the seventy years of Babylonian captivity, because God restored the children of Israel to the Promised Land. However, as Jeremiah continues his prophecy, he vividly describes the dramatic and specific details of exactly *how* the children of Israel will return to the Promised Land.

> Jeremiah 16:16: "'Behold, I will send for many fishermen,' says the LORD, '*and they shall fish them*; and afterward I will send for many

hunters, *and they shall hunt them from every mountain and every hill, and out of the holes of the rocks."*

Jeremiah declares the Lord God will send the fishermen to *fish* the children of Israel back to the Promised Land, *and afterward,* He will send the hunters to *hunt* them from the land of the north and from *all* of the lands where He has driven them. Ultimately, this prophecy certifies the restoration of the children of Israel into the land that God promised to Abraham, Isaac, Jacob, David, and their descendants through the everlasting covenants, which is the Promised Land of Israel (Gen. 13, 15, 17; 2 Sam. 7, Jer. 31:31–37).

Therefore, *after* the Babylonian captivity, did the fishermen *fish* and the hunters *hunt* the children of Israel back to the Promised Land, which would have resulted in the fulfillment of Jeremiah's prophecy? To discover the profound answer to this imperative question, let us continue our journey by understanding the prophet Daniel's role in the Babylonian and Medo-Persian empires. This will provide us with great wisdom, knowledge, and understanding as to who ultimately fulfills Jeremiah's prophecy. Will it be the Medo-Persian Empire, which ruled after the Babylonian Empire, or the *end-of-the-age* fishermen and hunters?

Daniel, a descendant of Jacob (Israel), was *second in command* for most of Nebuchadnezzar's reign of Babylon (Dan. 2:46–48), which lasted for more than forty years after the destruction of Jerusalem and the captivity of Judah (586 BC). Daniel would also have been *third in command* under Belshazzar's reign of Babylon if the Babylonian Empire had not been conquered by the Medo-Persian Empire in 539 BC (Dan. 5:29–31). Furthermore, once the Medo-Persian Empire became the dominant world power, Darius the Mede set Daniel as *a governor* over a province in the Medo-Persian kingdom.

> Daniel 6:1–3: "It pleased Darius to set over the kingdom one hundred and twenty satraps, to be over the whole kingdom; and over these, three governors, *of whom Daniel was one,* that the satraps might give account to them, so that the king would suffer no loss. *Then this Daniel distinguished himself above the governors and satraps, because an excellent spirit was in him. And the king gave thought to setting him over the whole realm."*

Additionally, to validate Daniel's prestigious honor, respect, and position in the Medo-Persian Empire, when the other jealous governors had conspired against him and he was unfairly cast into the lion's den, Darius the Mede made a decree after the Lord God had rescued Daniel.

> Daniel 6:25–28: "Then King Darius wrote:
> To all peoples, nations, and languages that dwell in all the earth: Peace be multiplied to you. *I make a decree that in every dominion of my kingdom men must tremble and fear before the God of Daniel. For He is the living God, and steadfast forever; His kingdom is the one which shall not be destroyed, and His dominion shall endure to the end.* He delivers and rescues, and He works signs and wonders in heaven and on earth, who has delivered Daniel from the power of the lions. *So this Daniel prospered in the reign of Darius and in the reign of Cyrus the Persian.*"

Clearly, Jeremiah's prophecy of the *hunters* did *not* occur after the Babylonian captivity and into the reign of the Medo-Persian Empire under Darius the Mede. Daniel and his brethren, the children of Israel, were not *hunted* and forced back to the Promised Land, because if it were so, he would not have been elevated to these prominent positions. Furthermore, if Jeremiah's prophecy were to be fulfilled when the Medo-Persian Empire conquered the Babylonian Empire, Darius the Mede certainly would not have honored and praised the God of Israel. Instead, he would have blasphemed and denied Him and ordered his soldiers to *hunt* the children of Israel in lieu of promoting one of their distinguished prophets.

How about Cyrus, king of Persia? Did he fulfill the prophecy of the *hunters* in Jeremiah's prophecy? Ezra, who was a Jewish priest and great leader, enlightens us with Cyrus's proclamation of God's command for him to allow the children of Israel to rebuild the Jewish temple in Jerusalem.

> Ezra 1:1–3, 7–8: "Now in the first year of Cyrus king of Persia, . . . *the* LORD *stirred up the spirit of Cyrus king of Persia, so that he made a proclamation throughout all his kingdom,* and also put it in writing, saying,
>
> Thus says Cyrus king of Persia:
> *All the kingdoms of the earth the* LORD *God of heaven has given me. And He has commanded me to build Him a house at Jerusalem which is in Judah. Who is among you of all His people? May his God be with him, and let him go up to Jerusalem which is in Judah, and build the house of the* LORD *God of Israel (He is God), which is in Jerusalem. . .*

King Cyrus also brought out the articles of the house of the LORD, *which Nebuchadnezzar had taken from Jerusalem and put in the temple of his gods*; and Cyrus king of Persia brought them out by the hand of Mithredath the treasurer, and counted them out to Sheshbazzar the prince of Judah."

After reviewing Ezra's account concerning Cyrus's proclamation of God's command to rebuild the Jewish temple in Jerusalem, which included the restoration of the children of Israel to the Promised Land, it is clear the Medo-Persians were not sent to *hunt* God's people from every mountain, hill, and rock (Jer. 16:16). Both Daniel and Ezra confirm that the return of the children of Israel to the Promised Land was not because they were hunted. In fact, it was exactly the opposite, because Cyrus did everything possible to assist the children of Israel in their prophetic restoration to the Promised Land after the seventy-year captivity (Jer. 25:11–12), which included returning the Lord's articles and vessels to them (Ezra 1:7–11). Assuredly, the Medes (Darius) and Persians (Cyrus) were not Jeremiah's prophesied *hunters*; therefore, the Medo-Persian Empire, which followed the Babylonian Empire, did not fulfill his prophecy. However, could Cyrus and Darius have been God's fishermen?

God's fishermen have a solid, deep, and intimate relationship with Him, who trust and obey Him, and take pleasure in walking in His commandments and His ways (Deut. 6:5, Matt. 22:37-38). In those ancient days, it was rare for Gentiles to have these righteous qualities, because they were called uncircumcised, unrighteous, and unholy, thus salvation was very limited to them (Rom. 11, Eph. 2:11-13). Accordingly, does Darius and Cyrus (Gentiles) meet God's requirements of His fishermen in Jeremiah's prophecy?

Although Darius the Mede and Cyrus the Persian allowed the children of Israel to return to the Promised Land, they were *not* followers (fishermen) of the Lord God of Israel. In spite of the fact that Cyrus was not a believer (fisherman), God still "anointed" him as an instrument for His divine purpose and will, which was to restore the children of Israel to the Promised Land to rebuild the Jewish temple.

Isaiah 45:1–5: "*Thus says the* LORD *to His anointed, to Cyrus*, whose right hand I have held—to subdue nations before him and loose the armor of kings, to open before him the double doors, so that the gates will not be shut: '*I will go before you and make the crooked places straight*; I will break in pieces the gates of bronze and cut the bars of iron. I will give you the treasures of darkness and hidden riches of secret places, *that you may know that I, the* LORD, *who call you by your name, am the God of Israel. For Jacob My servant's sake, and Israel My elect [everlasting covenants], I have even called you by your name; I have named you, though you have not known Me [not a fisherman]* . . . I am the LORD, and there is no other; There is no God besides Me. I will gird you, *though you have not known Me [not a fisherman]."*

Isaiah validates the fact that although God anointed Cyrus for His divine, sovereign purpose and will, Cyrus *did not know* the Lord God of Israel; thus he did not fulfill the vital requirement of a fisherman. God used Cyrus as an instrument to end the seventy-year captivity in Babylon prophesied by Jeremiah (Jer. 25:11), execute His judgment on the Babylonian Empire (Jer. 25:12; Dan. 5), and allow the children of Israel to return to Jerusalem and rebuild the temple (Ezra 1). Throughout the Holy Bible, God used unholy pharaohs, kings, and others to accomplish His sovereign, divine purposes, however, it did not qualify them as His fishermen.

Therefore, if Jeremiah's prophecy of the fishermen and the hunters was not fulfilled when God brought the children of Israel out of the north (Babylon) at the end of the Babylonian Empire and at the beginning of the Medo-Persian Empire, when will this prophecy be *ultimately* fulfilled? First, let us review the context of Jeremiah's prophecy of the fishermen and the hunters.

> Jeremiah 16:14–16: "'Therefore behold, the days are coming,' says the LORD, 'that it shall no more be said, "The LORD lives who brought up the children of Israel from the land of Egypt," but, *"The* LORD *lives who brought up the children of Israel from the land of the north and from all the lands where He had driven them." For I will bring them back into their land which I gave to their fathers.* Behold, I will send for many fishermen,' says the LORD, 'and they shall fish them; *and afterward I will send for many hunters, and they shall hunt them from every mountain and every hill, and out of the holes of the rocks.'"*

Jeremiah prophesies there will be a *specific* period of time when the Lord God of Israel will summon *all* of the children of Israel to the Promised Land, by way of the fishermen and the hunters. Needless to say, for this prophecy to commence in its fulfillment, *Israel has to be a nation, otherwise, there is no reason for the children of Israel to return to the land.* The prophet's powerful, yet sobering details of exactly how the children of Israel will return to the Promised Land authenticates that it will occur at an extraordinary and differentiating period of time. Jeremiah declares the Lord God will "send for many fishermen" to *fish* the children of Israel back to the Promised Land, and *afterwards*, He will send for many hunters, who will "*hunt* them from every mountain and every hill, and out of the holes of the rocks." As we proceed, please note the order in which God releases His fishermen and Satan's hunters. Make no mistake: when Satan's hunters are released, it will be like no other period in history, because it will be chaotic, destructive, and cataclysmic, since the Jewish people will be *hunted* from "every mountain, . . . hill, and . . . rock." So, when will this somber prophecy occur?

As we have discovered, Jeremiah's prophecy was not fulfilled by the Medo-Persian Empire, when God restored the children of Israel to the Promised Land. Since that prophetic time of restoration, in AD 70 the children of Israel were exiled from the Promised Land for the second time by the Roman Empire. Nevertheless, after the worst persecution (Holocaust) in Jewish history during World War II by Adolf Hitler (1939–1945), in 1948 Israel was "born again" as a nation (Isa. 66:8), and a remnant of the children of Israel began returning to the Promised Land for the second time. Yet, although Hitler certainly was a demonic hunter, who authorized the killing of an estimated six million Jews during that horrific time, it did *not* culminate with *all* of the Jewish people returning to the Promised Land in 1948 or thereafter. Remember: Jeremiah's prophecy specifically proclaims the hunters will hunt the Jewish people "from *every* mountain and *every* hill, and out of the holes of the rocks." Hitler's evil Nazi regime did not fulfill this prophecy, because it primarily hunted the children of Israel who lived in Europe, not other parts of the world, including the abundant Jewish population in America during that dark and tragic time. In fact, during World War II (1939–1945), America's Jewish population was approximately 4.2 million people, which accounted for nearly one-third of the total Jewry in the world. [1] As of 2015, the Jewish population in America was approximately seven million people, which accounts for nearly 40 percent of the total Jewry in the world. [2] These statistics substantiate the children of Israel were not hunted "from every mountain and every hill, and out of the holes of the rocks," as Jeremiah prophesies will occur at God's appointed time. Furthermore, just as Jeremiah prophesied, God will first send His fishermen, and *afterward*, He will allow Satan to send his hunters. Clearly, God's fishermen were not sent before Hitler's diabolic reign of terror, because Israel had not become a nation again at that point, which is a prerequisite for Jeremiah's prophecy to be fulfilled.

Therefore, since Israel's rebirth as a nation again in 1948, are we currently witnessing the fulfillment of Jeremiah's prophecy of the fishermen and the hunters, which, once *completely* fulfilled, will actualize the everlasting covenants? Does the mystery of Aliyah correlate with Jeremiah's prophecy and the everlasting covenants? Has the Lord God used His celestial bodies in the heavens as markers for the release of His fishermen and Satan's hunters? Who are God's fishermen and Satan's hunters? We will explore these questions in the chapters ahead.

CHAPTER 3

GOD'S ORIGINAL FISHERMEN

Now that we understand the supreme importance of God's everlasting covenants and Jeremiah's prophecy of the fishermen and the hunters, which proclaims God's strategies concerning their fulfillment, let us discover the identity of God's *original fishermen* in order to acquire great insight into God's *end-of-the-age* fishermen. The prophet Isaiah writes, "God declares the end from the beginning, and from ancient times not yet fulfilled" (Isa. 46:9–10). This definitively attests the need to understand the beginning (Torah, Prophets, Psalms) to have knowledge of the end, which includes God's *original and end-of-the-age* fishermen.

Just as God preordained His everlasting covenants with Abraham, Isaac, Jacob, and David, He also predestined them as His *original fishermen*, since the eternal promises were sworn through them. In other words, when God promised His everlasting covenants to the Patriarchs, He also divinely anointed these godly men as His *original fishermen*, who would bring forth the *ultimate* fishermen of Jews and Gentiles, Yeshua, the promised Seed, Messiah, and King of Israel. In the Torah, Moses proclaimed, "For you [Israel] *are* a holy people to the LORD your God; the LORD your God has chosen you to be a people for Himself, a special treasure above all the peoples on the face of the earth." Why did the Lord God choose Israel for His divine purposes and will?

> Isaiah 49:3, 6–7: "*You are My servant, O Israel, in whom I will be glorified* . . . It is too small a thing that You should be My Servant to raise up the tribes of Jacob, and to restore the preserved ones of Israel; *I will also give You as a light to the Gentiles, that You should be My salvation to the ends of the earth* . . . *The Holy One of Israel . . . has chosen You.*" (See Isa. 42:5–6, 60:3)

Isaiah is ultimately prophesying about Yeshua, the Messiah, who is God's Servant, light, and salvation to both Jews and Gentiles, and a descendant of the Patriarch's *pure royal lineage* (original fishermen). In Hebrew, the word for salvation is *Yeshua* (Strong's #3442), and, in English, Yeshua is translated as Jesus, who is God's salvation for *all* of mankind! Nevertheless, Abraham, Isaac, Jacob, David, and their descendants, the Jewish people were also commanded to be a light (fishermen) to the Gentiles.

Acts 13:47: "For so the Lord has commanded us [children of Israel]: *'I have set you as a light to the Gentiles*, that you should be for salvation to the ends of the earth.'"

In God's perfect salvation plan for all of mankind, He divinely predestined Abraham, Isaac, Jacob, David (original fishermen), and their descendants to be the light of the world and spread the name of the Lord God of Israel to *all* Jews and Gentiles. Although Messiah is the *ultimate fisherman*, in the book of Acts, Paul proclaims the children of Israel are to be the God of Israel's fishermen unto the ends of the earth (Acts 13:47).

Before Messiah's preordained crucifixion and resurrection (Ps. 118:22–29, Luke 23–24, 1 Peter 1:19–20, Rev. 13:8), salvation for Gentiles was infrequent, to say the least. The apostle Paul confirms this mystery in his epistle to the Ephesians, as he proclaims Gentiles were once "aliens from the commonwealth of Israel and strangers from the [everlasting] covenants of promise, having no hope and without God in the world" (Eph. 2:11–12). Fortunately, Paul continues, "but now in Christ Jesus you who once were far off have been brought near by the blood of Christ," referring to Messiah's ultimate sacrifice for *all* of mankind (v. 13; see Isa. 56:1–8, Rom. 9:14–24).

To be clear, Paul is not indicating that before Messiah's first coming, salvation was forbidden to Gentiles who accepted and obeyed the Lord God of Israel. It simply indicates that Gentiles as a whole were evil and unrighteous, and only a meager number of them obtained salvation before Messiah's first coming. The beautiful story of Ruth substantiates this mystery, as Ruth, a Gentile, came to salvation in the Lord God of Israel. She faithfully and boldly proclaimed to her Jewish mother-in-law, Naomi, "Entreat me not to leave you, or to turn back from following after you; for wherever you go, I will go; and wherever you lodge, I will lodge; *Your people shall be my people, and your God, my God*" (Ruth 1:16).

Ruth's unwavering and courageous faith in the Lord God of Israel validates that Gentiles *could* obtain salvation before Messiah's first coming. Just as Abraham's faith in God was counted to him as righteousness (Gen. 15:6), we can be confident Ruth's faith in Him was counted to her as righteousness, as well. In fact, through Ruth's marriage to Boaz, a Jew, she became the great-grandmother of King David, who is the direct *pure royal lineage* of Messiah (Matt. 1:1-17, Luke 3:23-38)! Ruth provides a great example of loyalty to the God of Abraham, Isaac, Jacob, and David, the God of Israel, who is Yeshua (Matt. 22:29-32; Acts 3:13). Although it was scarce, if a Gentile like Ruth believed in the Lord God of Israel, turned from his or her evil ways, and lived in righteousness before Him, that person's faith was counted as righteousness and he or she was saved.

> Ezekiel 18:21-23: "'But if a wicked man turns from all his sins which he has committed, keeps all My statutes, and does what is lawful and right, he shall surely live; he shall not die. None of the transgressions which he has committed shall be remembered against him; because of the righteousness which he has done, he shall live. Do I have any pleasure at all that the wicked should die?' says the LORD God, 'and not that he should turn from his ways and live?'"

YESHUA, GOD'S ULTIMATE FISHERMAN OF JEWS AND GENTILES

As we continue the lineage of God's *original fishermen* (Abraham, Isaac, Jacob, David), let us now discover God's *ultimate fisherman*, Yeshua, who is the fulfillment of Isaiah's prophecy (Isa. 49). Most certainly, Yeshua is God's Servant, the Light of the World, the Holy One to Israel, and the glorious and preeminent fisherman of both Jews and Gentiles. One of Messiah's most fascinating prophecies of pure love for the whole world is the Great Commission.

> Matthew 28:18-20: "And Jesus came and spoke to them, saying, '*All authority has been given to Me in heaven and on earth. Go therefore, and make disciples [fishermen] of all the nations, baptizing them in the name of the Father and of the Son and of the Holy Spirit, teaching them to observe all things that I have commanded you*; and lo, I am with you always, even to the end of the age.' Amen."

Messiah instructed His Jewish disciples, who were His fishermen (Matt. 4:19–20), to make disciples (fishermen) of *all* nations, baptize them, and teach them to observe *all* things that He had commanded them. What were these "things" that Messiah had commanded His fishermen? In the days of Messiah, the Gospels and the other God-inspired books of the New Testament were not yet written. Therefore, as the apostles (God's fishermen) verbally taught the nations the good news of the gospel, they would have certainly included and passionately emphasized to the highest degree God's everlasting promises of the Abrahamic, Davidic, and new covenants. Let us explore four major reasons God's fishermen taught these covenants to the people.

- Messiah *commanded* the apostles to teach and observe *all* things that He had commanded them, which included the everlasting covenants in the Hebrew Scriptures (Torah, Psalms, Prophets).
- The everlasting covenants are the concrete foundation of salvation for both Jews and Gentiles through the promised Seed, Messiah, and King of Israel, Yeshua.
- The eternal promises are one of the primary ways to authenticate Yeshua is the Jewish Messiah.
- Messiah will *completely* fulfill *all* of the everlasting covenants at His second coming and millennial reign.

During Yeshua's earthly ministry, He clarified and validated the reason He came at His first coming, why He will return for His second coming, and prophesied a stern warning regarding the Torah and the Prophets.

Matthew 5:17–19: *"Do not think that I came to destroy the Law [Torah] or the Prophets. I did not come to destroy but to fulfill. For assuredly, I say to you, till heaven and earth pass away, one jot or one tittle will by no means pass from the [Torah] till all is fulfilled. Whoever therefore breaks one of the least of these commandments, and teaches men so, shall be called least in the kingdom of heaven; but whoever does and teaches them, he shall be called great in the kingdom of heaven."*

This is one of the most cautionary proclamations by Messiah, not only to the disciples, but to all of His fishermen, Jew and Gentile (you and me). Messiah declares He will fulfill every "jot and tittle" of the Torah and the Prophets. Some of the prophecies in the Torah and the Prophets were fulfilled at His first coming, and the remaining prophecies will be fulfilled at His second coming and during His millennial reign, including the everlasting covenants. Messiah also declares to *all* believers (fishermen) a somber forewarning about the Torah and Prophets, proclaiming, "*Whoever breaks these commandments and teaches men to do so, will be called least in the kingdom of heaven.*" Messiah's stern warning is extremely significant and essential for us to adhere to, because God's everlasting covenants are prophesied through His *original fishermen* in the Torah and Prophets.

During Messiah's earthly ministry, He certified God's sovereign plan of salvation for both Jews and Gentiles, and He explained the divine, righteous order of it. Messiah specifically commanded His disciples (fishermen) to *first* go to their own people, the Jews, with the Great Commission.

> Matthew 10:5–6: "These twelve Jesus sent out and commanded them, saying: '*Do not go into the way of the Gentiles, and do not enter a city of the Samaritans. But go rather to the lost sheep of the house of Israel.*'"

Why did Messiah command His disciples to first go to the Jewish people with the gospel before going to the Gentiles? Note: *all* of the everlasting covenants were promised to the children of Israel, including the new covenant (Jer. 31); therefore, the gospel should first be spread to them. Although the children of Israel, as a nation, rejected Messiah at His first coming, a remnant of them understood the appointed time and accepted Him as their Messiah (disciples and followers). Accordingly, Messiah was obeying and fulfilling His Father's order of His sovereign plan of salvation exactly the way it was preordained to Him (John 14). This is the predominant reason Messiah proclaimed, "*I was not sent except to the lost sheep of the house of Israel*" and that "*salvation is of the Jews*" (Matt. 15:24; John 4:22).

What can we conclude from Messiah's statements? Keep in mind: Yeshua is a Jew, a descendant of Abraham, Isaac, Jacob, and David, and He came to fulfill the Torah and the Prophets (Matt. 5:17–20). When Messiah declares, "salvation is of the Jews," this encompasses God's plan of salvation through His everlasting covenants promised to the children of Israel—Jews—that will be *completely* fulfilled at His second coming and in His millennial reign. Remember: Gentiles are grafted into these eternal covenants. In these prophetic Scriptures, Messiah is magnifying the profound importance of the Abrahamic, Davidic, and new covenants, which includes His supreme role as the Jewish Seed, Messiah, and King. Thus, for believing Jews and Gentiles, who embody the commonwealth of the Israel of God, the need to understand and proclaim these awesome, eternal promises cannot be overstated (see Rom. 11, Gal. 3:26–29; Eph. 2:11–13).

Another key reason Messiah declared, "salvation is of the Jews," is because the children of Israel—specifically His apostles and followers—would be the first fishermen (missionaries) to spread the gospel among the nations to the Gentiles. Messiah Himself did not give the gospel directly to the Gentiles. He only taught the gospel directly to the children of Israel, which validates and fulfills God's plan of salvation through His infinite Word and everlasting covenants, first to the Jew, and then to the Gentile.

> Romans 1:16 (NIV): "For I am not ashamed of the Gospel, because it is the power of God that brings salvation to everyone who believes: *first to the Jew, then to the Gentile."* (See Isa. 42:5–6, 49:3,6–7, 60:3, Acts 13:44–48.)

Furthermore, just before Messiah ascended into heaven (Acts 1:9), He prophetically and specifically commanded His fishermen concerning the exact order in which the gospel was to be proclaimed:

> Acts 1:8–9: "'But you shall receive power when the Holy Spirit has come upon you; *and you shall be witnesses to Me in [1] Jerusalem, and in [2] all Judea and [3] Samaria, and [4] to the end of the earth.'* Now when He had spoken these things, while they watched, He was taken up, and a cloud received Him out of their sight."

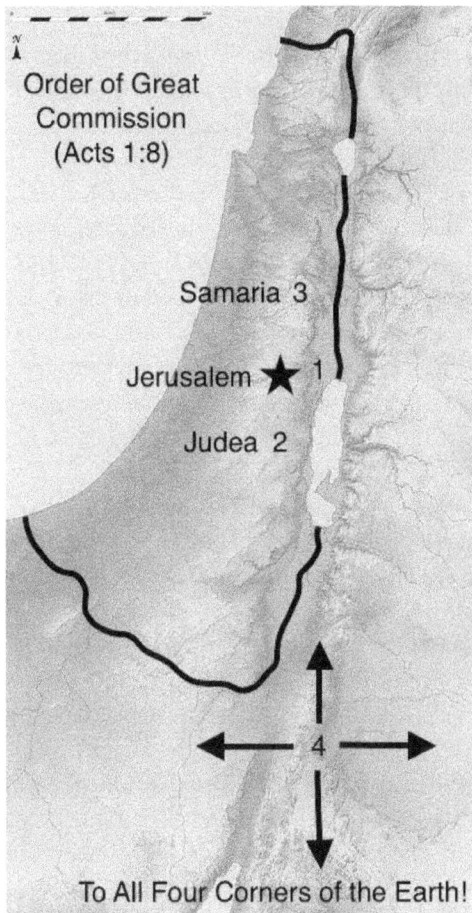

Great Commission Map

Messiah commanded His fishermen to *first* go to Jerusalem, where the Holy Spirit would be poured out (Acts 2); then to Judea and Samaria, and finally, to the ends of the earth, which upholds God's perfect plan and divine order of salvation. Once Messiah ascended into heaven and sat at the right hand of the Father (Ps. 110:1; Mark 16:19), the blessed Holy Spirit was poured out among the children of Israel in Jerusalem, just as He prophesied.

Luke 24:46–49: "Then He said to them, 'Thus it is written, and thus it was necessary for the Christ to suffer and to rise from the dead the third day, and that repentance and remission of sins should be preached in His name to all nations, *beginning at Jerusalem*. And you are witnesses of these things. Behold, I send the Promise [Holy Spirit] of My Father upon you; *but tarry in the city of Jerusalem until you are endued with power from on high.*" (See John 14:15–17.)

Acts 2:1–4, 41: "When the Day of Pentecost had fully come, they were all with one accord in one place. *And suddenly there came a sound from heaven, as of a rushing mighty wind, and it filled the whole house where they were sitting.* Then there appeared to them divided tongues, as of fire, and one sat upon each of them. *And they were all filled with the Holy Spirit and began to speak with other tongues, as the Spirit gave them utterance . . . And that day about three thousand souls were added to them.*"

The book of Acts was recorded and written by a Gentile physician named Luke, whom most people believe is the only Gentile author in the Holy Bible. Luke, who also wrote the book bearing his name, explains the Holy Spirit was first poured out unto the Jews *in Jerusalem* at Pentecost, which was originally known as the Feast of Shavuot (Lev. 23). The pouring out of the blessed Holy Spirit upon the Jews fulfilled Messiah's command to His disciples, because they were instructed to *first* go to the lost sheep of Israel in Jerusalem, then to Judea and Samaria, and last to all nations of the world (Acts 1:8). After Messiah's fishermen carried out the Great Commission to the children of Israel in Jerusalem (Acts 5:28), Judea, and Samaria (Acts 8:1–5; 9:31), they began spreading the good news of salvation to the Gentiles (Isa. 42:1, 5–6)!

John 10:16, "And other sheep [Gentiles] I have which are not of this fold; them also I must bring, and they will hear My voice and there will be one flock and one shepherd."

In the Holy Bible, the Roman centurion Cornelius, his family, and close friends were the *first* Gentiles to receive God's salvation (Yeshua) and the blessed Holy Spirit (Acts 10:24, 44–46). In retrospect, before the Holy Spirit came upon Cornelius, his family, and close friends, he and the apostle Peter had received prophetic visions from God (Acts 10:3–6, 9–16), which, once the revelations became fulfilled, would begin the "grafting in" of the Gentiles into the Israel of God (Rom. 11; Eph. 2:11–13). The Almighty spoke to Cornelius in a vision and commanded the Roman centurion to summon Peter to Caesarea, where Cornelius lived (Acts 10:24). Unlike Cornelius's vision,

Peter's vision encompassed all kinds of animals and birds of the air, and the Lord commanded him, "Rise, Peter; kill and eat" (Acts 10:12–13). However, Peter replied, "Not so Lord," because of the dietary laws commanded in the Torah (Lev. 11, Deut. 14). The Lord God gave Peter a vision he could relate to in the Torah because in Peter's day, Gentiles were considered "unclean," as most where uncircumcised and unsaved. Nevertheless, the Lord commanded Peter three times, *"What God has cleansed you must not call common [unclean]"* (Acts 10:15–16), referring to the uncircumcised Gentiles (Eph. 2:11–13). God's vision to Peter was a revelation about his role in the beginning of salvation and "grafting in" of the Gentiles through Yeshua the Messiah! (See Isa. 42, 49, Rom. 11, Eph. 2:11–13, Gal. 3:26–29)

> Matthew 16:17–18: "Jesus answered and said to him, 'Blessed are you, Simon Bar-Jonah, for flesh and blood has not revealed this to you, but My Father who is in heaven. *And I also say to you that you are Peter, and on this rock I will build My church, and the gates of Hades shall not prevail against it.*'"

When Peter arrived in Caesarea, Cornelius, his family, and close friends were waiting for him. Once Peter asked Cornelius why he had summoned him, the Roman centurion spoke of his vision from God (Acts 10:30–32), and he stated they were ready to hear Peter's commanded words from the Almighty (v. 33). Peter responded to Cornelius by declaring the Lord's words from the vision, saying, "But God has shown me that I should not call any man common or unclean" (v. 28). At that wonderful moment in time, one of the most divine and spectacular events occurred in the Holy Bible, the good news of God's salvation (Yeshua) was proclaimed to the Gentiles! Hallelujah!

> Acts 10:34–45: "Then Peter opened his mouth and said: '*In truth I perceive that God shows no partiality. But in every nation whoever fears Him and works righteousness is accepted by Him. The word which God sent to the children of Israel, preaching peace through Jesus Christ— He is Lord of all that word you know, which was proclaimed throughout all Judea, and began from Galilee after the baptism which John preached: how God anointed Jesus of Nazareth with the Holy Spirit and with power, who went about doing good and healing all who were oppressed by the devil, for God was with Him. And we are witnesses of all things which He did both in the land of the Jews and in Jerusalem, whom they killed by hanging on a tree. Him God raised up on the third

day, and showed Him openly, not to all the people, but to witnesses chosen before by God, even to us who ate and drank with Him after He arose from the dead. And He commanded us to preach to the people, and to testify that it is He who was ordained by God to be Judge of the living and the dead. To Him all the prophets witness that, through His name, whoever believes in Him will receive remission of sins.' *While Peter was still speaking these words, the Holy Spirit fell upon all those who heard the word. And those of the circumcision who believed were astonished, as many as came with Peter, because the gift of the Holy Spirit had been poured out on the Gentiles also.*"

In conclusion, God's *original fishermen* began with Abraham, Isaac, Jacob, and David, and then their descendants, through the promised everlasting covenants. Ultimately, the nation of Israel, through the *pure royal lineage*, would bring forth the *ultimate fisherman*, Yeshua, the Seed of the Abrahamic covenant, and the Messiah and King of the Davidic covenant, who will *completely* fulfill all of the everlasting covenants (new covenant) at His second coming and in the millennial reign. For Jew and Gentile, this is paramount, as both are "grafted into" the commonwealth of the Israel of God.

As Messiah fulfilled His incredible, prophetic calling of His first coming, He commanded the apostles to journey in God's exact sovereign order in which the gospel and the blessed Holy Spirit was to be proclaimed, "to the Jew first, and then to the Gentile." After the blessed Holy Spirit was poured out upon the Jews in Jerusalem at the Feast of Shavuot (Pentecost, Acts 2), the fishermen followed Messiah's plan of salvation and journeyed to Judea and Samaria, and then to the ends of the earth, as the Holy Spirit was poured out on the Gentiles. Remarkably, from that point forward, both Jew and Gentile believers became God's fishermen, including messianic rabbis, Gentile pastors, priests, missionaries, prophets, scholars, teachers, and everyday believers who spread the good news of Messiah and fulfill the Great Commission! Hallelujah!

CHAPTER 4

SATAN'S ORIGINAL HUNTERS

First and foremost, God Almighty is in complete power and control over all of the universe, dominions, powers, principalities, rulers, and kingdoms, which includes Satan and his hunters (1 Chr. 29:11). There is not any deed conceived by Satan, his angels, or his hunters that is not understood in advance by God, and is either allowed or rejected, according to His divine, sovereign will and eternal plan. From the beginning, just as God preordained His *original fishermen*, He also predetermined who He would allow Satan's *original hunters* to be in order to fulfill His everlasting Word, the Holy Bible. As discussed in chapter 2, a great example of how God uses Satan's hunters would be His use of king Nebuchadnezzar of Babylon. Although he was a pagan king who did not believe in the Lord God of Israel, the Almighty still used "His servant" for His ultimate plan (Jer. 25:9).

In this chapter, we will discover who Satan's *original hunters* were, and how they *directly attempted* to forbid God's everlasting covenants from coming to fruition through His *original fishermen*: Abraham, Isaac, Jacob, David, and the ultimate fisherman, Yeshua. By understanding who Satan's *original hunters* were, we will acquire great wisdom and knowledge concerning who Satan's *end-of-the-age hunters* are, including the final hunter, the Antichrist, whom we will discuss in a later chapter. For now, let us recall how God declares His prophetic events at the end of the age.

> Isaiah 46:9–10: "*Remember the former things of old*, for I am God, and there is no other; I am God, and there is none like Me, *declaring the end from the beginning, and from ancient times things that are not yet done.*"

Since God declares the end from the beginning, and from ancient times things that are not yet done, it would be wise to comprehend who Satan's hunters were in the beginning. Let us begin by confirming that Lucifer, better known today as Satan, is without a doubt the father of all the evil hunters.

John 8:44: "*He was a murderer [hunter] from the beginning*, and does not stand in the truth, because there is no truth in him."

Isaiah 14:12: "How you are fallen from heaven, O Lucifer, son of the morning! *How you are cut down to the ground, you who weakened the nations!*"

Ezekiel 28:16: "By the abundance of your trading *you became filled with violence within [hunter]*, and you sinned."

Since the beginning, Satan has connived and manipulated his evil plan upon his *original hunters* in order to *directly* attempt to forbid God from establishing His everlasting covenants with His *original fishermen*. Nevertheless, the Lord God of Israel laughs at Satan's evil rage of foolishness upon His holy, sovereign, and divine plan of salvation through His eternal promises (Ps. 2:3), because it always culminates with the Almighty's deliverance of His people. As previously discussed, Satan understands that once God's everlasting covenants are *completely* fulfilled, which will occur at Messiah's second coming and millennial reign, he will be tormented alive in the lake of fire and brimstone forever and ever (Rev. 20). Before we explore Satan's *original hunters*, we must examine Noah's prophetic curse on the land of Canaan. Noah's curse will convey great insight concerning Satan's *original hunters*, as well as his *end-of-the-age* hunters, and ultimately, his final hunter, the Antichrist.

NOAH'S CURSE ON THE LAND OF CANAAN

After God established the Noahic covenant (Gen. 9), Noah and his descendants, Shem, Ham, and Japheth, began populating the earth (vv.1,19). As time passed, Noah became a farmer, and he planted a vineyard and produced wine (v. 20). One day Noah drank of the wine and was drunk, and he became uncovered while lying naked in his tent (v. 21). What occurred next has echoed prophetic blessings and curses throughout the generations unto today, and they will continue to perpetuate until the completion of Messiah's second coming.

Genesis 9:22–23: "*And Ham, the father of Canaan*, saw the nakedness of his father, and told his two brothers outside. But Shem and Japheth took a garment, laid it on both their shoulders, and went backward and covered the nakedness of their father. Their faces were turned away, and they did not see their father's nakedness. So Noah awoke from his wine, and knew what his *younger son* had done to him. Then [Noah] said: '*Cursed be Canaan; a servant of servants he shall be to his brethren.*' And he said: '*Blessed be the* LORD, *the God of Shem, and may Canaan be his servant.* May God enlarge Japheth, and may he dwell in the tents of Shem; *and may Canaan be his servant.*'"

In Genesis 9, before the prophetic vineyard event transpired, it introduces us to Noah and his sons, Shem, Ham, and Japheth, and it continues to state that Ham was the father of Canaan. The text concludes by declaring "these were *the sons of Noah*, and from these the whole earth was populated" (v.v. 18-19). What is a mystery about Noah's sons is that when Ham commits his sin, instead of simply referring to Ham, the text states "Ham, the father of Canaan." Also, once Noah woke up from his drunkenness and realized what "*his son*" did to him, he cursed *Canaan instead of Ham*. What can we conclude from this?

In the Midrash (late first millennium C.E.), which is a genre of rabbinic writings that contain interpretations and commentaries on the Torah, it records renowned rabbi Eliezer's commentary on this mystery: "Noah found a vine . . . the vine still had grapes upon it . . . he planted a vineyard from this vine . . . and on that very day fruit grew . . . he drank wine from it [the vine] and he revealed himself in his tent. **Canaan came in, saw his father's nakedness**, then he went out to tell his brothers . . . **Ham came in, saw his father's nakedness** and neglecting the commandment to honor one's father, reported it to his two brothers as though he were in the market and laughing at his father. His brothers rebuked him, they took a cover, and walking backwards covered their father's nakedness . . . Noah arose from his stupor, discovered what **his youngest son** had done to him, and cursed him, as it says, "Cursed is Canaan."

According to the commentary of rabbi Eliezer, he substantiates Canaan was the *first* "son" to see Noah's nakedness. Although I believe that Noah had only three sons and Canaan was the son of Ham (Gen. 10:1,6), one thing is certain: Canaan was the *first* to see the nakedness of Noah, then Ham, because Noah cursed Canaan in the prophecy. Philo of Alexandria, a first-century Jewish philosopher wrote that Ham and Canaan were equally guilty of the sins against Noah, "for the two of them acted foolishly and wrongly and committed other sins." [1] After Canaan and Ham's exceedingly disrespectful sin, Noah prophesied a curse on the land of Canaan that would perpetuate throughout history, even unto Messiah's second coming and millennial reign.

> Genesis 9:25-27, "Then [Noah] said: '*Cursed be Canaan; a servant of servants he shall be to his brethren.*' And he said: '*Blessed be the LORD, the God of Shem, and may Canaan be his servant.* May God enlarge Japheth, and may he dwell in the tents of Shem; *and may Canaan be his servant.*'"

Land of Canaan

Promised Land

Noah prophesied that Canaan and his descendants will serve Shem and his descendants (Abraham, Isaac, Jacob, David), who are the *pure royal lineage* unto Messiah (Luke 3:23–38). Amazingly, on the account of Noah's curse, God promised the land of Canaan to Abraham, Isaac, Jacob, David, and their descendants, which are the children of Israel (Jews), through the everlasting covenants. In other words, the land of Canaan became the Promised Land, or the land that God promised in the everlasting covenants to fulfill Noah's prophetic curse upon Canaan and his descendants. Noah also declared, "Blessed be the God of Shem, and may Canaan be his servant." This ancient prophecy explains that Canaan and his descendants will serve the God of Shem (HaShem), who is the God of Abraham, Isaac, Jacob, and David, the God of Israel (Luke 3:23–38). It also proclaims and proves the land of Canaan (Promised Land) will be used for God's eternal promises and sovereign will.

Ham and his descendants were also cursed for his sin, as well, specifically, the *regions* where Ham's sons settled: Cush (Sudan), Mizraim (the Egyptians and Philistines), Put (Libya), and Canaan.

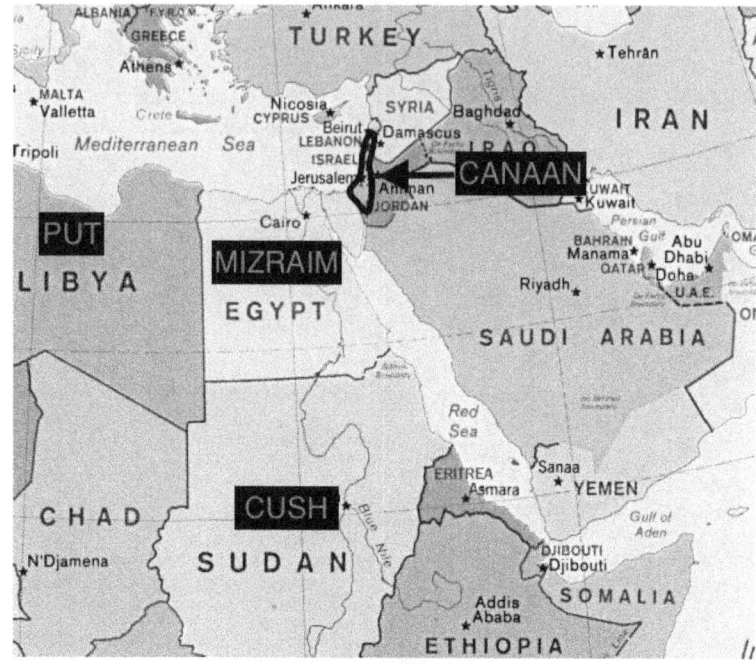

Ham's Descendants

NIMROD (SATAN'S HUNTER OF ABRAHAM – ABRAHAMIC COVENANT)

Satan's *original hunter*, who *directly* attempted to forbid the Abrahamic covenant from being promised to Abraham, was Nimrod. He was a son of Cush, grandson of Ham, and great-grandson of Noah (Gen. 10). Nimrod represents rebellion, because he was "a *mighty hunter* before the LORD" (Gen.10:9). He became the king of Babel (Babylon) and the pagan leader of the blasphemous Tower of Babel (v. 10). The Hebrew meaning of the word *Babel* means "confusion" (Strong's #894), and ultimately, God confused the language of the people at Babel and scattered them across the earth (Gen. 11:7–9).

One of the reasons Nimrod rebelled against God was because of the Great Flood (Gen. 6–8), which destroyed the earth and drowned all of mankind, except for Noah and his family (Gen. 7:23; 1 Peter 3:20). The renowned Jewish historian Flavius Josephus wrote, "Nimrod also said he would be revenged on God, if he should have a mind to drown the world again; for that he would build a tower (Babel) too high for the waters to be able to reach! And that he would avenge himself on God for destroying their forefathers!" [2]

Nimrod's ancient kingdom included Babel, Erech, Accad, and Calneh, in the land of Shinar (Gen. 10:9). As time passed, he extended his pagan kingdom to ancient Assyria and built Nineveh, Rehoboth Ir, Calah, and Resen (vv. 10–12).

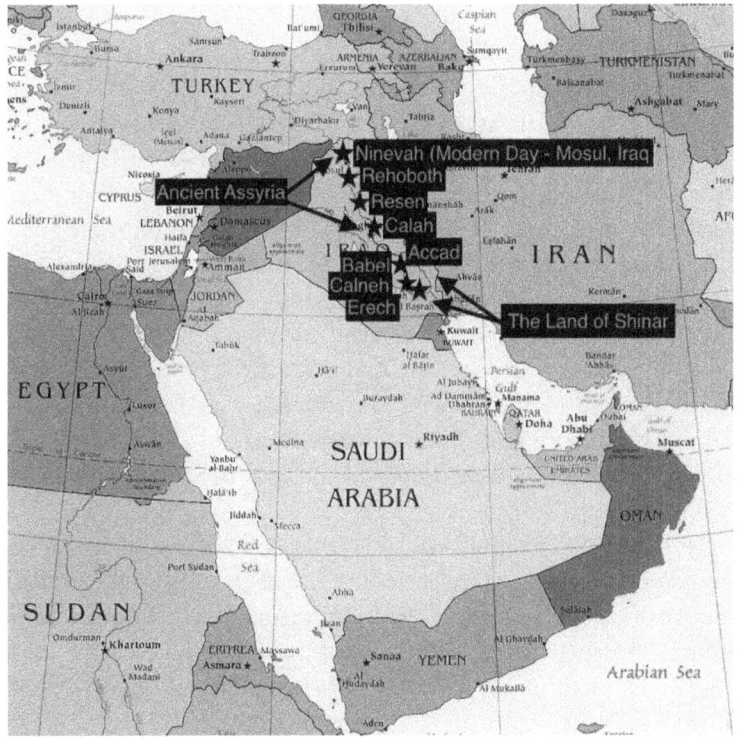

Nimrod

Nimrod's kingdom and the *region* it encompassed bestows great knowledge to us concerning Satan's *end-of-the-age hunters*. Keep in mind, God "declares the end from the beginning, and from ancient times things that are not yet done" (Isa. 46:9–10).

Now, let us explore Nimrod in the Talmud to provide us additional information about the "mighty hunter before the Lord." The Talmud is a collection of biblical history, commentaries, proverbs, and oral rabbinical teachings of the Torah, which is handed down from generation to generation by the children of Israel. To be clear, I am not suggesting or referencing the Talmud as a replacement or substitute for the Holy Bible in any way, shape, or form, because the Torah was inspired by the Lord God, and the Talmud was composed by men. I am using the Talmud only as a historical reference, because it presents additional ancient records about the history of Nimrod and others, including Abraham.

NIMROD'S COAT OF SKINS

After Adam and Eve sinned against the Lord God by eating the forbidden fruit in the garden of Eden, He made them "tunics of skin" to cover themselves (Gen. 3:21). Once Adam passed away, the coveted coat of skins was handed down to his grandson Enoch (Cain's son), and afterwards, it passed on to Enoch's son, Methuselah[3] (Gen. 4:16–18). Subsequently, Methuselah gave the coat of skins to Noah, his grandson, who brought it onto the ark. Once Noah and his family exited the ark (Gen. 8), Ham, Noah's son, stole the coat of skins, and gave it to his son Cush, who endowed it to his son, Nimrod.[4] At age twenty years, Nimrod began to wear Adam's coveted coat of skins from the Lord, and it provided him "strength and might as a *hunter and warrior*," and he subdued all of his enemies.[5] This correlates with the biblical account, as Nimrod was "the mighty hunter before the Lord" (Gen. 10:9), and he became king over the ancient regions of the land of Shinar, including Babel (Babylon) and Assyria.

After the Lord God confused the language of the rebellious people at the Tower of Babel, scattered them across the face of the earth, and divided them into nations (Gen. 11), Nimrod was still the king in power over the land of Shinar. His favorite chief officer was Terah, who begat Abraham, and was a descendant of Shem, Noah's son, *which is the pure royal lineage to Messiah* (Gen. 11:10–27).

On the exciting night of Abraham's birth, as Terah and his friends were joyously celebrating, Nimrod's wise men lifted up their eyes towards the heavens and astonishingly watched as one large, bright star consumed four smaller stars from the four corners of the earth.[6] The wise men automatically understood this glorious prophetic sign in the heavens was from God (Ps. 19:1), because it directly coincided with Abraham's birth. The Talmud records the wise men, as saying, "Verily, this is an omen connected with the newly-born child of Therach [Terah]. When he grows up he will be fruitful and increase greatly in power and excellence, and his descendants will destroy this [Nimrod's] kingdom and possess its lands." [7]

This revelation prophetically symbolized that through Abraham's descendants, God will gather His people from "all four corners of the earth" and destroy the *regions* of Nimrod's kingdom (Babel, Assyria). Greatly alarmed, the wise men immediately reported this critical heavenly warning omen to Nimrod, and they convinced him the troubling sign meant the destruction of his kingdom. [8] After reluctantly receiving the wise men's warnings, Nimrod requested their advice, and they responded, "And now, if it be pleasing to the king, we would advise him to pay the value of the child unto his father and destroy him in his infancy, lest in days to come, through him and his descendants, we and our children be utterly destroyed."[9] Accordingly, once Nimrod heard and definitively approved of the wise men's council concerning Abraham, he summoned his servant Terah, Abraham's father, and declared, "Now, therefore, give up the child, that we may slay him before misfortune falls upon us, and in payment we will fill thy coffers with silver and gold!"[10]

Once Terah heard Nimrod's horrific perplexing words, he asked the king for three days to consider the offer and speak to his wife, Amtheta. [11] After the allotted time had elapsed, Nimrod sent a stern message to Terah, demanding that he send the child, or Terah and his entire family would be destroyed.[12] Circumstantially, yet painstakingly, Terah provided the king one of his servant's children of the same age instead of relinquishing Abraham. Immediately, Nimrod, Satan's hunter, killed the child himself in hope of denying the heavenly sign and securing the protection of his kingdom for the future. [13] Although we do not understand God's ways by allowing children to die in our world, and in this case, Terah's servant's child, we most certainly are commanded to trust His ultimate wisdom concerning *all* events (Isa. 55:8–9).

This extraordinary event was Satan's *first* attempt to *directly* destroy Abraham, who was God's chosen heir to continue the *pure royal lineage* (Luke 3:23–38), which, if successful, would have forbidden God's everlasting promises of the Abrahamic covenant from ever existing. This is to say, from the very beginning of Abraham's life, Satan *directly* attempted to destroy God's eternal plan of salvation through His everlasting covenants by influencing Nimrod's decision to kill Abraham as an infant, which would have negated the Abrahamic covenant from being established.

Satan's second attempt to *directly* destroy Abraham occurred approximately fifty years later. After Terah relinquished his servant's child to Nimrod instead of Abraham, he wisely concealed Abraham and his mother, Amtheta, in a cave for ten years. Afterwards, Abraham lived with Noah and Shem (Noah's son) for thirty-nine years in order to learn the ways of the Lord. The Talmud records, "*From his earliest childhood Abram [Abraham] was a lover of the Lord. God had granted him a wise heart ready to comprehend and understand the majesty of the Eternal, and able to despise the vanity of idolatry.*" [14]

SIDE NOTE: NOAH AND ABRAHAM

Most believers do not realize Noah's life overlapped Abraham's life by fifty-eight years. Therefore, the Talmud validates that Abraham learned the Lord's statutes, laws, and ordinances from Noah and Shem. What other person would be better qualified to teach the Lord's ways than Noah, the leader of eight people he saved from the Great Flood? To confirm this mystery, we will calculate what is recorded in the Holy Bible about Noah's time line, Shem's son Arphaxad's birth, and the genealogy from that point to Abraham. Noah lived 950 years (Gen. 9:29). At the time of the Great Flood, Noah was 600 years old (Gen. 7:11); therefore, 350 years remained of his life. Shem's son Arphaxad, was born two years after the flood (Gen. 11:10), aging Noah to 602 years of age. From Arphaxad's birth to Abraham's birth totaled 290 years, aging Noah to 892 years old, which proves a fifty-eight-year overlap into Abraham's life. From Genesis 11:12–26, we can calculate the 290 years between Arphaxad's birth and Abraham's birth:

- Arphaxad lived thirty-five years (35), and begot Salah.
- Salah lived thirty years (30), and begot Eber.
- Eber lived thirty-four years (34), and begot Peleg.
- Peleg lived thirty years (30), and begot Reu.
- Reu lived thirty-two years (32), and begot Serug.
- Serug lived thirty years (30), and begot Nahor.
- Nahor lived twenty-nine years (29), and begot Terah.
- Terah lived seventy years (70), and begot Abram (later changed to Abraham by God), Nahor, and Haran.

From the detailed lineage in Genesis, Noah was Abraham's great-great-great-great-great-great-great-great-grandfather, and according to the Talmud, he taught him the ways of the Lord for thirty-nine years!

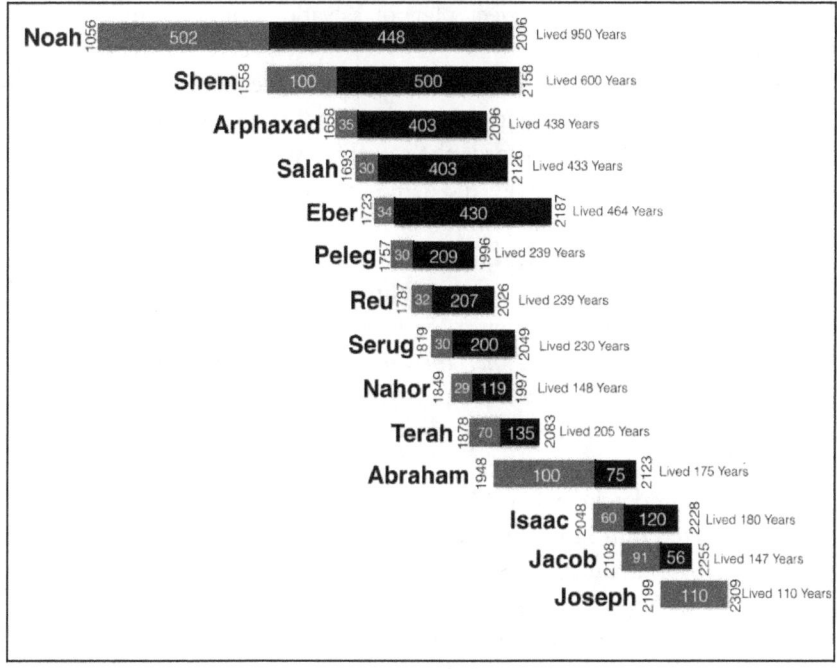

Graph Credits to Zeke Zeier

By this time, fifty years had passed, and Nimrod and his officers had forgotten about Abraham's prophetic birth. Accordingly, when Abraham was fifty, he excitingly returned to his father's home. However, once Abraham piercingly noticed all of Terah's pagan idols, he became full of wrath and destroyed all of the idols except one. [15] Once Terah heard the breaking, destructive sounds from Abraham's demolition of the idols, he angrily confronted his son.[16] Nevertheless, Abraham remained bold and strong in his godly convictions, pleaded with his father, and used an iron bar to obliterate the last idol in front of him. [17] Foolishly, Terah informed Nimrod of Abraham's actions, and Abraham was abruptly summoned before the king. [18] When Abraham condemningly challenged Nimrod about the false idols, in the king's burning anger, he commanded the officers to promptly seize Abraham and confine him for ten days.[19] During Abraham's confinement, Nimrod and his counselors sentenced Abraham to be burned to death. [20]

Just as God divinely protected Hananiah, Mishael, and Azariah from the fiery furnace in the book of Daniel (1:6–7; 3), the Almighty lovingly protected His chosen man, Abraham, to establish His sovereign, righteous, and perfect plan of salvation for Jews and Gentiles (Abrahamic covenant)!

Abraham was cast into a fiercely hot, raging furnace, but he walked upright through the burning flames without one hair on his head being singed by the fiery furnace. The Talmud records the servants' words to Nimrod; "Behold, Abraham walks unhurt through the flames, the ropes with which we bound him are consumed, yet he is uninjured." [21] In a simple twist of fate, just as we discovered with Cyrus, Darius, and Nebuchadnezzar (see chapter 2), in his absolute wonder and amazement, Nimrod also acknowledged the God of Israel. He declared to Abraham, "*Servant of the God of Heaven, come forth from the fire and stand before me. Then the king looked on Abram with awe, and made him valuable presents, and parted him in peace.*" [22] Subsequently, Abraham humbly and graciously bestowed thanks and praise to the Lord God Almighty!

Once Nimrod acknowledged the God of Abraham, showered him with gifts, and parted him in peace, Satan influenced Nimrod to *directly* attempt to forbid the Abrahamic covenant for a third time by defying the Lord God yet once again. Approximately two years after God's deliverance of Abraham from the fiery furnace, Nimrod had a dream. [23] The dream foretold Nimrod's death, as Anuki, one of Nimrod's wise men, warned, "Behold, this dream foreshadows the evil which Abram and his descendants will cause the king in time to come. It foretells the day when they will rise and smite our lord the king with all his hosts, and there will none be saved except the king, with three other kings who will battle on his side." [24] Anuki continued to caution Nimrod by also recalling the prophetic sign in the heavens when Abraham was born. Anuki's revelatory warnings stirred Nimrod with great alarm and grave fear that he sent his soldiers to take Abraham's life.[25] However, Eliezer of Damascus (Gen. 15), Abraham's servant, prudently learned of the king's evil intentions and carefully warned Abraham, and he fled to safety at Noah's house.[26] Afterward, Abraham would commence his prophetic journey to the land of Canaan to receive God Almighty's eternal promise, the everlasting Abrahamic covenant, which Satan had *directly* attempted to forbid three times!

In summary, Nimrod, one of Satan's *original hunters*, relentlessly strove to have a *direct* impact on God's plan of salvation through the Abrahamic covenant by attempting to kill God's fisherman three times. However, God Almighty, not Satan, was in total control over the patriarch Abraham's life. As we continue our journey to discover Satan's *original hunters*, it is paramount to understand Nimrod's *regions* of dominance, because, in doing so, we will obtain a greater understanding of Satan's *end-of-the-age hunters,* and ultimately, his final hunter, the Antichrist.

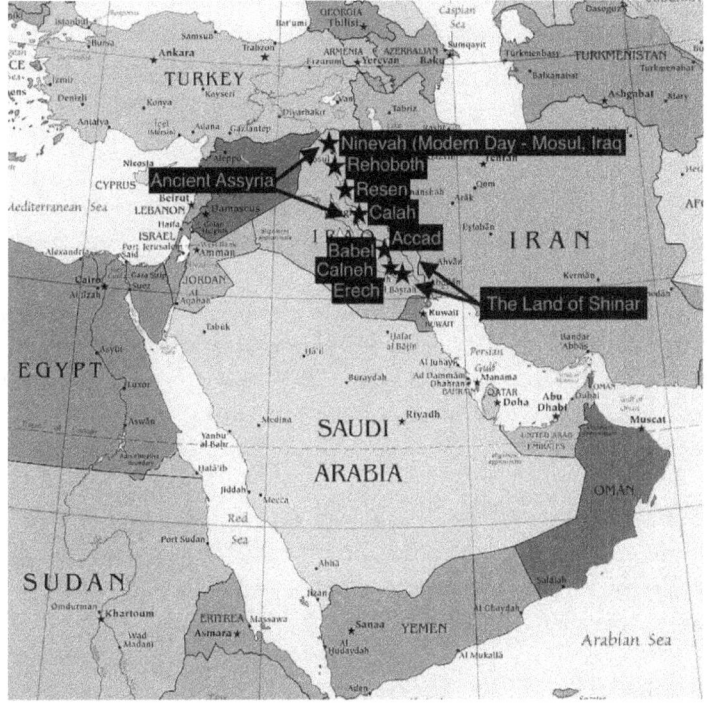

Nimrod

ISHMAEL (SATAN'S HUNTER OF ISAAC—ABRAHAMIC COVENANT)

Satan influenced his ensuing *original hunter,* Ishmael, to *directly* attempt to forbid the Abrahamic covenant from continuing through God's *pure royal lineage* from Abraham to Isaac (Luke 3:23–28). Once Abraham and Sarah traveled through the hot desert days and the cool nights of the Middle East, they arrived in the land of Canaan (Promised Land) and made an extremely poor but prophetic decision. Make no mistake: their erroneous choice has exceedingly impacted not only biblical and world history unto this day, but also the religious, social, and geopolitical landscape of the Middle East, North Africa, and frankly, the world. Assuredly, Abraham and Sarah's unwise decision will perpetually manifest until Messiah's second coming and millennial reign.

In the Abrahamic covenant, God promised Abraham a son (Isaac) through Sarah (Gen. 15, 17), who would continue the *pure royal lineage* unto Messiah. Carelessly, Sarah, who was barren at the time (Gen. 16:2), was not patient for

God's perfect timing, and she consequently provided her maidservant, Hagar, an Egyptian, to Abraham to conceive a child for her, named Ishmael (16:11). Although Ishmael was *not* God's chosen seed to continue the *pure royal lineage* unto Messiah (Gen. 17), the Angel of the Lord (Messiah) promised Hagar that she and Ishmael would become a great nation, because Ishmael was "a seed" of Abraham (Gen. 12:3), and his descendants would be exceedingly abundant.

> Genesis 16:10–12: "*Then the Angel of the* LORD *said to her, 'I will multiply your descendants exceedingly, so that they shall not be counted for multitude.'* And the Angel of the LORD said to her: 'Behold, you *are* with child, and you shall bear a son. *You shall call his name Ishmael,* because the LORD has heard your affliction. *He shall be a wild man; his hand shall be against every man [hunter], and every man's hand against him. And he shall dwell in the presence of all his brethren.*'"

> Genesis 17:20: "And as for Ishmael, I have heard you. *Behold, I have blessed him, and will make him fruitful, and will multiply him exceedingly.* He shall beget twelve princes, *and I will make him a great nation.*" (See Gen. 21:18.)

From these passages, we can see that the Angel of the Lord also emphatically declared Ishmael would be a wild man. His hand would be against everyone, and everyone would be against him. Messiah affirms Ishmael as a hunter, and Satan would influence him to *directly* attempt to prohibit the Abrahamic covenant from sustaining through Isaac (Gen. 17), who continued the *pure royal lineage* unto Messiah. In E. W. Bullinger's *Number in Scripture*, he corroborates Ishmael as a hunter as he explains the spiritual difference between his birth and Isaac's: "Oh! how great was the difference! Isaac, 'born after the spirit'; Ishmael 'born after the flesh' and therefore a *persecutor" (hunter).* (see Rom. 9:7; Gal. 4:28–31.)[27]

The Talmud records Ishmael's begrudging attempt to kill Isaac: "Ishmael, the son of Hagar and Abraham, was very fond of hunting and field sports. He carried his bow with him at all times, and upon one occasion, when Isaac was about five years of age, Ishmael aimed his arrow at the child, crying, 'Now I am going to shoot thee.'"[28] Sarah witnessed this action, and fearing for her son's life, and disliking the child of her handmaid, she made many complaints to Abraham of the boy's doings, and urged him to dismiss both

Hagar and Ishmael from his tent and send them to live somewhere else.[29] The Talmud parallels the Holy Bible's account of the primary reason why Sarah demanded that Abraham send Hagar and Ishmael away from Isaac, who was God's chosen heir of the Abrahamic covenant (Gen.21): Ishmael was caught "scoffing," or "mocking" (NIV). In other words, he was ridiculing, scorning, or belittling Isaac.

> Genesis 21:9–13: "And Sarah saw the son of Hagar the Egyptian, whom she had borne to Abraham, *scoffing*. Therefore, she said to Abraham, 'Cast out this bondwoman and her son; *for the son of this bondwoman shall not be heir with my son [pure royal lineage], namely with Isaac.*' And the matter was very displeasing in Abraham's sight because of his son. *But God said to Abraham, 'Do not let it be displeasing in your sight because of the lad or because of your bondwoman. Whatever Sarah has said to you, listen to her voice; for in Isaac your seed shall be called. Yet I will also make a nation of the son of the bondwoman, because he is your seed.'"*

> Galatians 4:29, "But, as he who was born according to the flesh then *persecuted* him who was born according to the Spirit, *even so it is now.*" (See Gal. 4:22–31.)

God Almighty clearly confirmed Sarah's demand to Abraham was correct, and He also prophesied once again that Ishmael would become a great nation, because he was Abraham's seed. And indeed, Ishmael and his descendants would become an enormously expanded nation, just as God promised Abraham. In his book *The Antiquities of the Jews*, Flavius Josephus named Ishmael as being the founder of the Arab nation, and he wrote of Ishmael's descendants (nations), "But as for the Arabians, they circumcise after the thirteenth year, *because Ishmael, the founder of their nation*, who was born of the concubine, was circumcised at that age. As for Ishmael and his twelve sons (Arabians), these inhabited all the country from Euphrates to the Red Sea, and called it Nabatene. They are an Arabian nation and name their tribes from these, both because of their own virtue and because of the dignity of Abraham their father." [30]

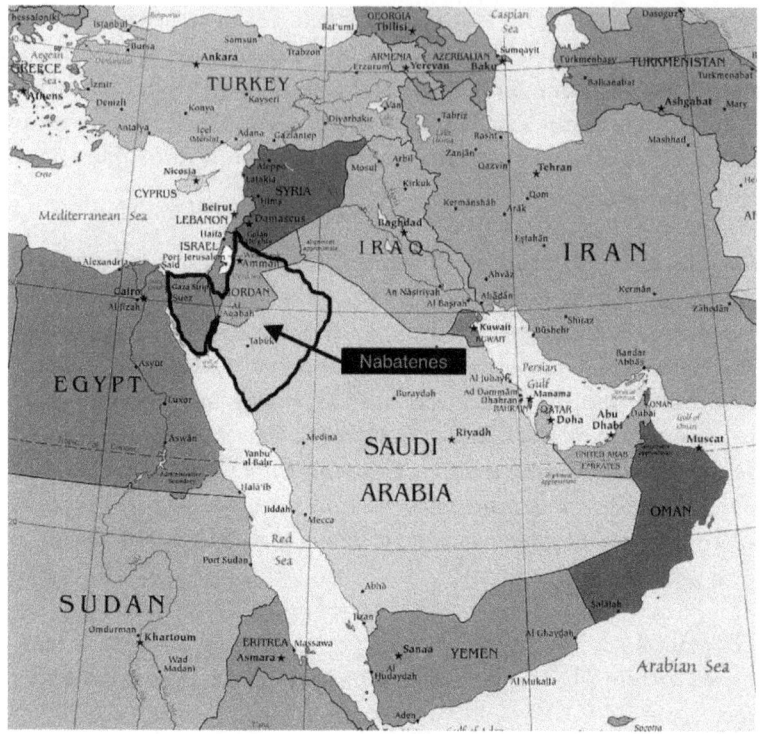

Nabatene

In summary, Ishmael was Satan's *original hunter* who *directly* attempted to forbid the Abrahamic covenant to Isaac, who continued the *pure royal lineage* unto Messiah. Once Isaac was born and reached five years of age, Ishmael, nineteen, endeavored to *hunt* Isaac until Sarah cleverly foiled his plot. Certainly, Satan influenced Ishmael's behavior, because it would have prohibited the Abrahamic covenant to eternalize through the *pure royal lineage* unto Isaac, and eventually to Messiah. This clearly substantiates God's support of Sarah's demand to Abraham and His confirmation and command to him (Gen. 21:12). As we proceed to explore Satan's *original hunters*, the regions of Hagar and Ishmael's descendants will give us great insight into Satan's *end-of-the-age hunters*, as we will discover in a later chapter.

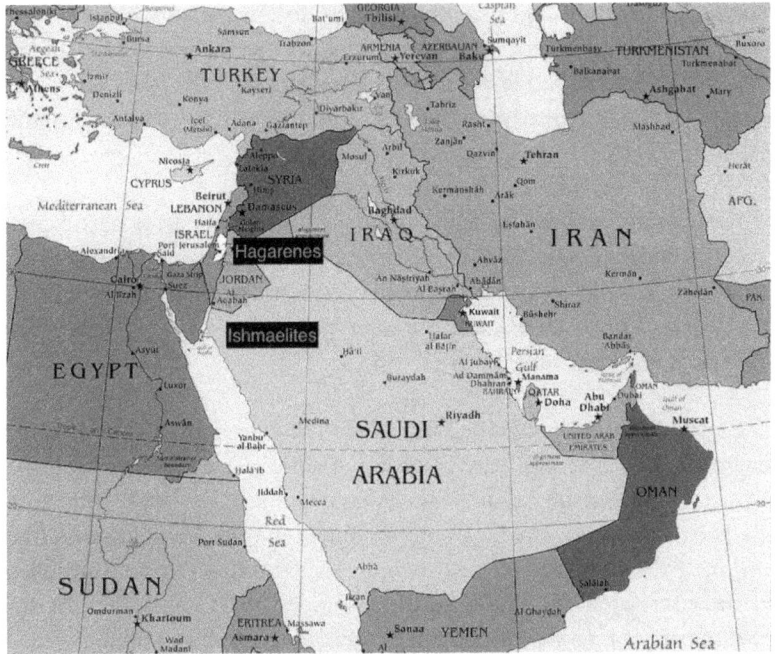

Hagar – Ishmael

ESAU (SATAN'S HUNTER OF JACOB—ABRAHAMIC COVENANT)

After Satan's unsuccessful attempt through Ishmael to destroy Isaac, he empowered another hunter, Esau, to *directly* attempt to forbid the Abrahamic covenant from continuing through the ensuing descendant of God's *pure royal lineage*, Jacob, whom God renamed Israel (Gen. 35:10). Once the patriarch Abraham succumbed, and Isaac inherited the blessings from his father (Gen. 25:5), including the promise of the Abrahamic covenant (Gen. 26:2–5), his wife, Rebekah, conceived twin sons, Esau and Jacob. During her pregnancy, the two sons *struggled* against one another inside her womb. Alarmed, she prayed to God for understanding.

> Genesis 25:23: "And the LORD said to her: '*Two nations are in your womb*, two peoples shall be separated from your body; *one people shall be stronger than the other, and the older shall serve the younger.*'"

Just as God had preordained Isaac and Ishmael to emerge as two different nations, He also predestined Jacob and Esau to evolve into separate nations, as one would become fishermen, and the other one would become hunters. As the Almighty announced His incredible prophecy to Rebekah, He sovereignly proclaimed, "*The older shall serve the younger*," which prophesies significant implications for the end of the age (Isa. 46:9–10).

> Genesis 25:24–26: "So when her days were fulfilled for her to give birth, indeed, there were twins in her womb. And the first came out red. He was like a hairy garment all over; so they called his name Esau. Afterward his brother came out, *and his hand took hold of Esau's heel; so his name was called Jacob.*"

As the twin boys were delivered into their worldly prophetic journeys, Esau came out first and Jacob second. Consequently, according to God's prophecy to Rebekah, Esau, the older, would serve Jacob, the younger. This is to say, Jacob was God's preordained, chosen heir (fisherman), who continued the *pure royal lineage* of the Abrahamic covenant unto Messiah. On the contrary, Esau would become a hunter, who continued the lineage of Satan's *original hunters* (Nimrod, Ishmael). To make this even clearer, Esau married Ishmael's daughter, Basemath (Gen. 28:9), which further validates God's sovereign plan as to which lineage would be God's fishermen (Isaac, Jacob), and who would be Satan's hunters (Ishmael, Esau).

Symbolically, yet prophetically, during the twins' birth, Jacob placed his hand on Esau's heel to prevent Esau from crushing his head (Gen. 25:26). This was Satan's first attempt to kill Jacob, because he influenced Esau as an infant to attempt to crush Jacob's head, which would have prohibited the Abrahamic covenant and the *pure royal lineage* from eternalizing through him. In a prophetic foreshadow of Jacob and Esau's struggle, we find unique symbolism in a prophecy by God Almighty to Satan, which authenticates the identity of Jacob as a fisherman, and Esau as a hunter.

> Genesis 3:15: *"And I will put enmity between you [Satan] and the woman [Jacob/Israel]*, and between your [Satan's] seed and her Seed [Messiah]; He [Messiah] shall bruise your [Satan's] head, and you [Satan] shall bruise His [Messiah's] heel."

Ultimately, God's prophecy to Satan is proclaiming Messiah's final victory over the Antichrist (Rev. 19:11-21) and the evil one (Rev. 20:7-10), because

Messiah will bruise both of their heads. Nevertheless, this symbolically correlates to Jacob and Esau's birth, because Esau (Satan's seed) attempted to "bruise" Jacob's (Israel's) head, but Jacob grabbed Esau's heel and stopped him. As we will discover in a later chapter, at the end of the age, Messiah, who is the King of Israel (Jacob), will faithfully and truly "bruise" Esau's head (region), just as Esau *directly* attempted to do to Jacob. The Holy Bible proclaims how God Almighty, Messiah, and the Holy Spirit, not mankind, will deal with this kind of evil.

> Leviticus 24:19–20: "If a man causes disfigurement of his neighbor, *as he has done, so shall it be done to him—fracture for fracture, eye for eye, tooth for tooth; as he has caused disfigurement of a man, so shall it be done to him.*" (See Ex. 22:24; Matt. 5:17–20.)

Furthermore, Jacob's strength and control over Esau's crushing heel is a prophetic sign the nation of Israel (Jacob) will ultimately become a stronger nation than Esau, just as God prophesied (Gen. 25:23), which will ultimately culminate at Messiah's second coming and during the millennial reign. Please note, just as God changed Jacob's name to Israel (Gen. 35:10), His inspired Word records Esau is the nation of Edom (Gen. 36:1).

> Romans 9:10-13: "And not only *this,* but when Rebecca also had conceived by one man, *even* by our father Isaac (for *the children* not yet being born, nor having done any good or evil, that the purpose of God according to election might stand, not of works but of Him who calls), it was said to her, "The older shall serve the younger." As it is written, "Jacob I have loved, but Esau I have hated."

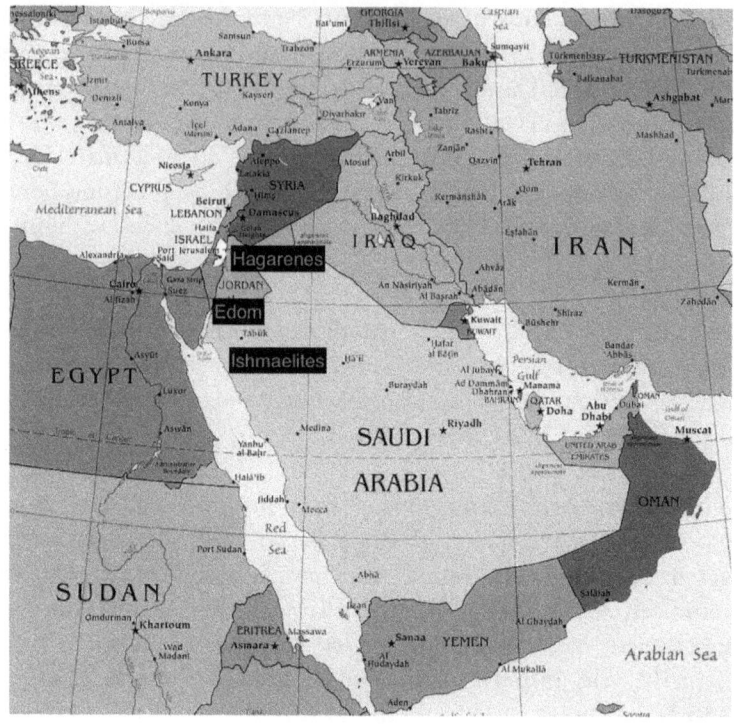

Edom

Omnisciently, God's prophetic words to Rebekah about Jacob and Esau were settled in different, unique circumstances. We will begin with Esau selling his birthright to Jacob, which substantiates God's prophecy, and also validates the Abrahamic covenant would perpetuate through Jacob (Israel).

Genesis 25:29–34: "Now Jacob cooked a stew; and Esau came in from the field, and he was weary. And Esau said to Jacob, 'Please feed me with that same red stew, for I am weary.' *Therefore, his name was called Edom.* But Jacob said, 'Sell me your birthright as of this day.' *And Esau said, 'Look, I am about to die; so what is this birthright to me?'* Then Jacob said, 'Swear to me as of this day.' *So he swore to him, and sold his birthright to Jacob.* And Jacob gave Esau bread and stew of lentils; then he ate and drank, arose, and went his way. *Thus Esau despised his birthright.*" (See Heb. 12:16.)

A birthright is a very special blessing and honor given to a firstborn son. In Isaac's and Esau's day, the firstborn son would inherit the privilege of being the family leader and receive double the inheritance. However, if the oldest son chose to foolishly sell or give away his birthright, he could exercise this right. Consequently, in betraying his blessing as the firstborn, he would be forgoing the leadership role and the double inheritance and lose both altogether. It is truly important to realize that omnipotent God understands all the decisions that we make even before we act upon them, because He has known each one of us before the foundation of the world (Jer.1:5; Eph.1:4).

The Talmud also records Jacob and Esau's birth and struggle, and it expounds the reason Esau was so hungry on that prophetic day. This event also connects to the fulfillment of Nimrod's dream that we previously discussed. The Talmud records:

> And it came to pass that Esau went hunting in the field upon a certain day, when Nimrod, too, was enraged in the same pursuit. *Both being mighty hunters*, a rivalry existed between the two, *a deadly jealousy*. Esau happened to see Nimrod when all his attendants, save two men, had left him. Esau concealed himself, and when Nimrod passed the place where he was hiding pointed his arrow, pulled the cord, and shot Nimrod through the heart. Then rushing from his concealment, Esau enraged in a deadly struggle with Nimrod's two attendants, and overcame and killed them both. *Then stripping from Nimrod's shoulders the wonderful coat, before mentioned, which God had made for Adam, Esau hastened home, reaching his father's tent weary, hungry, tired, and faint.*[31]

The Talmud's historical reference to this climatic, yet decisive event not only explains why Esau was ragingly hungry when he sold his coveted birthright to Jacob, but it also confirms the fulfillment of Nimrod's dream that a descendant of Abraham (Esau, his grandson) would kill him.[32] Although Nimrod and Esau were both Satan's evil hunters, they turned on each other, just as Satan's *end-of-the-age* hunters will turn on each other, as well (Zech. 12:4).

Before the patriarch Isaac succumbed, he blessed both sons and ratified the lineage of the two separate nations of Jacob (Israel, fisherman) and Esau (Edom, hunters). Please note that although Rebekah convinced Jacob to portray himself to Isaac as his older brother and deceive his father (Gen. 27),

God Himself had told Rebekah before the twins were born "the older [Esau] will serve the younger [Jacob]." Surely, we should not focus our attention on the perceived sin of Rebekah and Jacob, but let our faith and trust be in the Lord God of Jacob, who is sovereign, holy, and divine (Isa. 55:9). Isaac declared to Jacob the following prophetic blessing for the nation of Israel, which will be *completely* fulfilled at Messiah's second coming and millennial reign.

> Genesis 27:28–29: "Therefore may God give you of the dew of heaven, of the fatness of the earth, and plenty of grain and wine. *Let peoples serve you, and nations bow down to you. Be master over your brethren [Esau], and let your mother's sons [Esau] bow down to you.* Cursed *be* everyone who curses you, and blessed be those who bless you!" (See Gen. 12:13.)

God's fisherman Isaac also gave Esau a prophetic blessing that would extend through Jacob's and Esau's descendants throughout the generations, confirming not only God's prophecy to Rebekah (Gen. 25:23), but also Jeremiah 16, the prophecy of the fishermen and the hunters.

> Genesis 27:37, 39–40: "Then Isaac answered and said to Esau, 'Indeed I have made him [Jacob/Israel] your master, and all his [Jacob's] brethren I have given to him as servants . . . Behold, your dwelling shall be of the fatness of the earth, and of the dew of heaven from above. *By your sword you shall live [hunter], and you shall serve your brother [Jacob/Israel]; and it shall come to pass, when you become restless [hunter], that you [Esau] shall break his [Israel's] yoke from your neck.*'"

Isaac prophesied that Esau (Edom) would serve Jacob (Israel), and his nation would be Satan's hunters of God's fishermen, the children of Israel, as he proclaimed, Esau would live "by the sword." The patriarch also declared, "It shall come to pass, when you become restless, that you shall break his yoke from your neck." The Talmud expounds the meaning of Isaac's prophetic words for not only Jacob and Esau's lifetime, but throughout their descendant's lives, as well, even unto the end of the age: "Isaac also blessed the children of Esau, saying: 'The dread of you [hunters] shall be upon your enemies (Israel); your God will fill their hearts with fear." [33]

What can we conclude from this recorded history?

The nation (region) of Esau (Edom) and his descendants will provoke fear on its enemies (Jacob/Israel), and Esau's god will fill Jacob's (Israel) heart and his descendants with worry and fear. As we continue on our journey throughout this book, the god of Esau (Edom) will become very clear and unquestionable. We will also ascertain the prophetic meaning of this statement not only as it relates to Esau (Edom), but also to his descendants (hunters) and their god at the end of the age.

After Esau heard Isaac's troubling and afflicted blessing to him, he was filled with rage and evil toward Jacob.

> Genesis 27:41–42: "*So Esau hated Jacob* because of the blessing with which his father blessed him, and Esau said in his heart, 'The days of mourning for my father are at hand; *then I will kill my brother Jacob.*' And the words of Esau her older son was told to Rebekah."

Once Rebekah heard of Esau's evil (hunter) intentions, she cautiously warned Jacob and commanded him to leave and stay with her brother, Laban, in Haran (Gen. 27:43). Deviously, Esau learned of Jacob's journey, and he sent his son Eliphas and other men to *hunt* Jacob. The Talmud records, "When Jacob had departed from his father's house, Esau called to him his son Eliphas, and said to him in secrecy, 'Go follow after Jacob with thy bow in thy hand, lie in wait for him, *slay him* upon the mountains, take for thy own what treasure he has with him, and then return to me.'" [34]

As Jacob traveled to Haran, he saw Eliphas traveling toward him, so he collectedly waited on his nephew to approach, erroneously believing he was relaying a message from his father, Isaac.[35] Consequently, when Eliphas approached Jacob, he drew his sword and was ready to consummate Esau's evil plan. Nevertheless, Jacob cleverly responded to his nephew, "Take all that I have, all that my father and my mother gave into my hands, but spare my life. Your kindness will be accounted to you as righteousness."[36]

In God's amazing love and abundant grace for Jacob, and for His everlasting promise of the Abrahamic covenant to be fulfilled through the *pure royal lineage*, He granted Jacob favor in the eyes of Eliphas and the other men, and the hunters allowed him to proceed unharmed and intact for his journey. However, Eliphas did take Jacob's gold, silver, and everything of value he received from his parents, Isaac and Rebekah.[37] Once Jacob escaped death and persisted on his journey, God appeared to him in a dream on Mount Moriah (Temple Mount). God ratified the promise of the Abrahamic covenant, including the *pure royal lineage*, would continue through Jacob and not through Esau. [38]

> Genesis 28:13–15: "And behold, the LORD stood above it and said: '*I am the LORD God of Abraham your father and the God of Isaac; the land on which you lie I will give to you and your descendants.* Also your descendants shall be as the dust of the earth; you shall spread abroad to the west and the east, to the north and the south; and in you and in your seed all the families of the earth shall be blessed. *Behold, I am with you and will keep you wherever you go, and will bring you back to this land; for I will not leave you until I have done what I have spoken to you.*'"

In summary, Jacob's and Esau's prophetic births into two separate nations not only conveys great insight into God's *original fishermen* and Satan's *original hunters*, but it also provides an incredible prophetic foreshadowing of what will occur at the end of the age. As we will discover in a later chapter, the twins' births prefigure Jeremiah's prophecy of the fishermen and the hunters at the end of the age. As we proceed, remember that Jacob's (Israel) descendants are the children of Israel, and Esau (Edom) is the father of the Edomites. The prophets Obadiah and Malachi give us great understanding of God's feelings toward Jacob (Israel) and Esau (Edom).

> Obadiah 1, 8–10, 15, 17-18, 21: "Thus says the Lord God concerning Edom, '*Will I not in that day,*' says the LORD, '*even destroy the wise men from Edom, and understanding from the mountains of Esau? Then your mighty men, O Teman, shall be dismayed, to the end that everyone from the mountains of Esau may be cut off by slaughter. For violence against your brother Jacob, shame shall cover you, and you shall be cut off forever.
> . . For the day of the LORD upon all the nations is near; as you have done, it shall be done to you*; your reprisal shall return upon your own head . . . But on Mount Zion there shall be deliverance, and there shall be holiness; The house of Jacob shall possess their possessions. The house of Jacob shall be a fire, and the house of Joseph a flame; *but the house of Esau shall be stubble*; they shall kindle them and devour them, *and no survivor shall remain of the house of Esau,*' for the LORD has spoken . . . Then saviors [NIV: deliverers] shall come to Mount Zion to judge the mountains of Esau, and the kingdom shall be the LORD's." (See Joel 3:19–20; Amos 1:11–12.)

Malachi 1:2–3: "'I have loved you [Jacob],' says the LORD. 'Yet you say, "In what way have You loved us?" Was not Esau Jacob's brother?' says the LORD. 'Yet Jacob I have loved; but Esau I have hated, and laid waste his mountains and his heritage for the jackals of the wilderness.'" (See Isa. 34.)

Again, in a later chapter, we will clearly discover how Esau's lineage provides us with great understanding of Satan's *end-of-the-age hunters*, as Esau is Edom and is "the father of the Edomites in Mount Seir" (Gen. 36:1, 8–9). Esau's descendants expanded to the *regions* of Teman (Yemen) and Bozrah (Gen. 36:15, 33–34).

Edom, Ishmaelites, Bozrah

GOLIATH (SATAN'S HUNTER OF DAVID—DAVIDIC COVENANT)

Just as Satan *directly* attempted to hunt God's *original fishermen*, Abraham, Isaac, and Jacob, which would have fundamentally prohibited the everlasting promises of the Abrahamic covenant from coming to fruition, the evil murderer also endeavored to hunt and destroy King David. Nonetheless, this time, Satan influenced an ancient enemy of Israel, the Philistines, and its infamous giant champion, Goliath, in a unique and solitary way to attempt to forbid God's everlasting promise to King David (Davidic covenant).

During Saul's and David's reigns as king of Israel (1050–1012 BC, 1010–970 BC), the Philistines were one of the children of Israel's most dangerous enemies and bitter rivals. The Philistines' lineage descends from Ham's grandson, Casluhim, whose father is Mizraim. Please note: Mizraim and Cush, who begat Nimrod, are brothers, which establishes Nimrod and Casluhim as cousins (Gen. 10). Keep in mind, Noah's prophecy not only cursed Canaan and his descendants, but also Ham and his lineage (Gen. 9:24–27), who would ultimately become bitter enemies of the God of Israel, including King David.

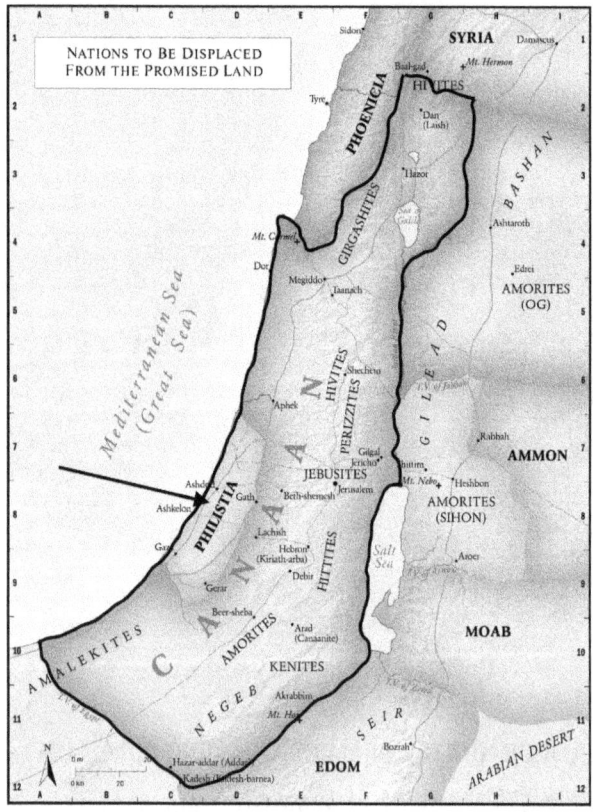

Philistines

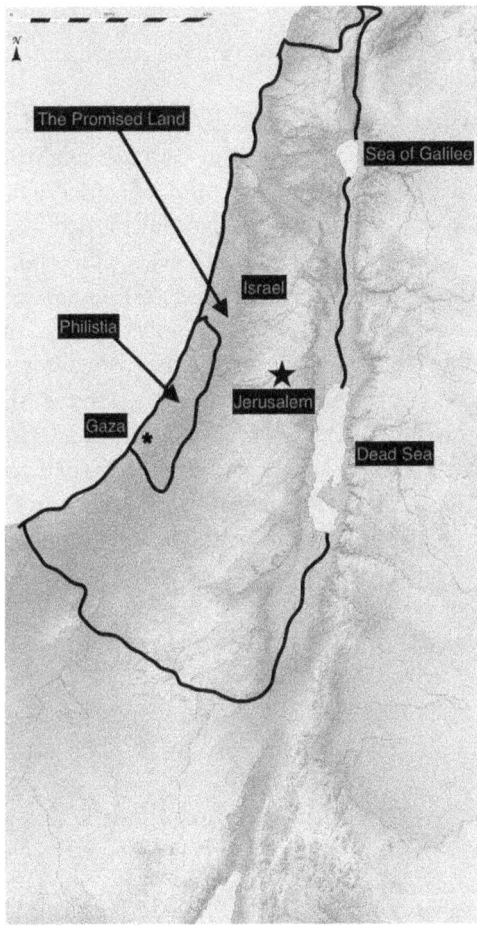
Modern Philistia

The incredible rise of David's prominence commenced as the prophet Samuel explained to Saul that the Lord had rejected him as king of Israel and had stripped away his rule over the kingdom. The two principal reasons God dethroned Saul was because of his disobedience in presenting an unlawful sacrifice and offering to Him (1 Sam. 13), and secondly, for not executing king Agag and the Amalekites for ambushing the children of Israel as they journeyed from Egypt to the Promised Land (1 Sam. 15). Once Samuel visited Saul and proclaimed the Lord's judgments upon him, the Almighty distinctly told Samuel to promptly visit Jesse in Bethlehem with a horn full of holy oil, and he anointed a man after God's own heart, David (1 Sam. 16:1–13).

Nevertheless, before David officially became king of Israel, Satan influenced the ancient Philistines, including Goliath, to assemble in the land of Judah to battle against the Israelites.

Goliath's physical presence, and all it encompassed, was exceedingly towering among the people of David's time. Goliath's height has been estimated between seven and nine feet (six cubits), and he carried weapons suitable for his massive physique. Josephus wrote that Goliath had a substantial bronze helmet upon his head and he was coated with a breastplate that weighed five thousand shekels, which is an estimated 150 pounds. He had greaves of brass completely covering his vast, bulky body, and his iron spear was not carried lightly in his right hand, but instead, he carried it lying on his massive shoulders. Goliath had an iron spearhead of six hundred shekels, and many followed him to carry his armor. [39] E. W. Bullinger confirms Goliath's role as Satan's hunter, because his height and branded armor associates with the number six, which is the number of man, and ultimately, the Antichrist (*six* cubits, *six* pieces of armor, spearhead weighed *six* hundred shekels of iron (666)—1 Sam. 17:4–7). [40]

As this biblically renowned battle approached, the Philistines were summoned on one side of the mountain and the Israelites on the other, and a shadowed valley separated the two rivals (1 Sam.17:2–3). Shortly after the two armies were assembled, Goliath, Satan's giant champion hunter mocked and shouted at the children of Israel.

> 1 Samuel 17:8–10: "'Why have you come out to line up for battle? Am I not a Philistine, and you the servants of Saul? *Choose a man for yourselves, and let him come down to me [hunter]. If he is able to fight with me and kill me, then we will be your servants. But if I [hunter] prevail against him and kill him, then you shall be our servants and serve us.*' And the Philistine said, '*I defy the armies of Israel this day; give me a man, that we may fight together.*'"

After Goliath boldly and tauntingly presented himself for forty days and forty nights to the fearful and reluctant armies of Saul, David arrived at Israel's camp to give his brethren some food (1 Sam. 17:16–19). Once David greeted his brothers, the giant champion appeared once more with the same arrogant, provoking words, and the armies of Israel dreadfully fled, except for David (1 Sam. 17:23–25). Goliath challenged the Israelites to choose a man to come down and face him one-on-one. Once David heard Goliath's challenge, he was determined to accept it. On the contrary, Saul and the children of Israel were demeaned and discredited, and they pleaded with David not to foolishly fight Goliath. Boldly, "the man after God's own heart" responded with strength and courage!

> 1 Samuel 17:34–37: "But David said to Saul, 'Your servant used to keep his father's sheep, and when a lion or a bear came and took a lamb out of the flock, I went out after it and struck it, and delivered the lamb from its mouth; and when it arose against me, I caught it by its beard, and struck and killed it. *Your servant has killed both lion and bear; and this uncircumcised Philistine will be like one of them, seeing he has defied the armies of the living God.*' Moreover, David said, 'The LORD, who delivered me from the paw of the lion and from the paw of the bear, *He will deliver me from the hand of this Philistine [hunter].*' And Saul said to David, 'Go, and the LORD be with you!'"

David approached Goliath with his staff in his hand, his sling, and *five* smooth stones. He chose five stones because the number five symbolizes *divine grace*, and he was acknowledging his own perfect weakness supplemented by God's divine strength. Yet, David only used *one* of the stones in his battle against Goliath, which signifies God's unity and holiness, as He is the one true, living God of Israel. [41]

Once Goliath drew near to David, he mocked him and blasphemed the God of Israel, just as his influencer Satan has done (1 Sam.17:42–44; see Gen. 3, Matt. 4). Accordingly, David's divine strength, faith, and courage from the Lord God of Israel became paramount, not only against Goliath and the Philistines, but also to the children of Israel, because he eventually reigned as King of Israel after his legendary, colossal victory.

> 1 Samuel 17:45–51: "Then David said to the Philistine, 'You [hunter] come to me with a sword, with a spear, and with a javelin. *But I come to you in the name of the LORD of hosts, the God of the armies of Israel, whom you have defied. This day the LORD will deliver you into my hand, and I will strike you and take your head from you. And this day I will give the carcasses of the camp of the Philistines to the birds of the air and the wild beasts of the earth, that all the earth may know that there is a God in Israel.* Then all this assembly shall know that the LORD does not save with sword and spear; *for the battle is the LORD's, and He will give you into our hands.*'

"So it was, when the Philistine arose and came and drew near to meet David, that David hurried and ran toward the army to meet the Philistine. Then David put his hand in his bag and took out a stone; and he slung it and struck the Philistine in his forehead, so that the stone sank into his forehead, and he fell on his face to the earth. So David prevailed over the Philistine with a sling and a stone, and struck the Philistine and killed him. But there was no sword in the hand of David. Therefore, David ran and stood over the Philistine, took his sword and drew it out of its sheath and killed him, and cut off his head with it. And when the Philistines saw that their champion [hunter] was dead, they fled."

In summary, God allowed Satan to influence the Philistines, including Goliath (hunter), to defy and challenge Israel in an unusual way with a one-on-one battle, instead of army against army. Satan connived the Philistines into attempting to manipulate the odds of the smaller David being killed by the giant champion Goliath, which if successful, would have forbidden the everlasting Davidic covenant from being fulfilled. Sovereignly, God orchestrated David to arrive on the battlefield at that specific, and prophetic moment in time. David, God's fisherman, arrived "in the name of the LORD of hosts, the God of the armies of Israel," and defeated Satan's hunter. (see 1 John 4:4.)

Although David was never directly pursued by Satan's hunter, as his forefathers were, Goliath's unanswered challenge by the armies of Israel provoked David's decision to battle Goliath and put his life in danger. Again, this was Satan's devious attempt to manipulate the odds to prevail against God's fisherman. David's death would have negated God's plan of salvation according to the everlasting promise of the Davidic covenant. However, David faithfully trusted the Lord God of Israel, and the Almighty was always with him (1 Sam. 16:13), including his battle against Goliath. As we proceed forward with Satan's *original hunters*, we must examine the region of the Philistines, because it will give us profound wisdom about Satan's *end-of-the-age hunters*.

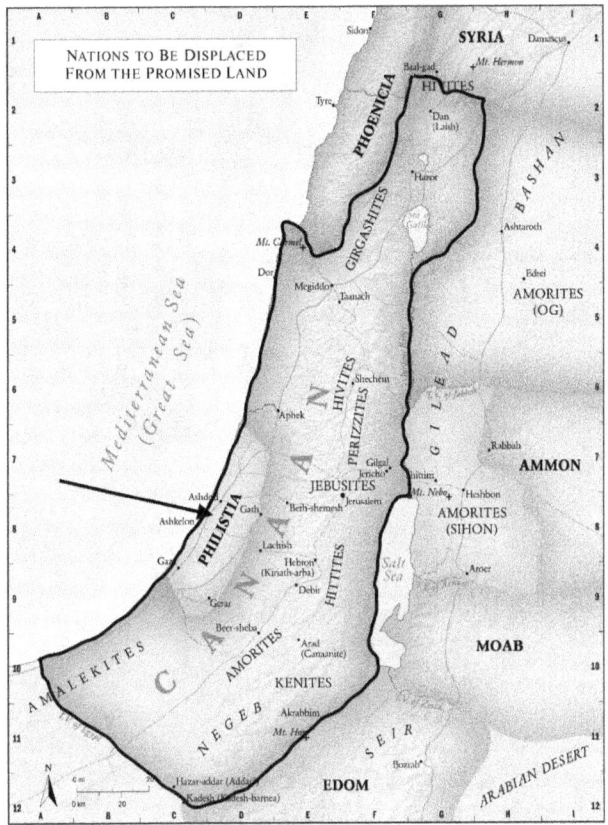

Philistines

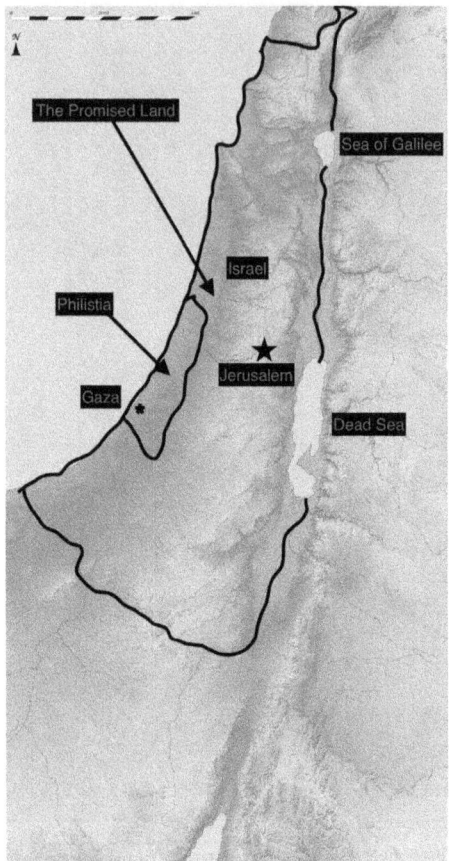

Modern Philistia

THE HERODIAN FAMILY (SATAN'S HUNTERS OF MESSIAH—NEW COVENANT)

HEROD THE GREAT (37–4 BC)

To the same degree Satan endeavored to destroy Abraham, Isaac, Jacob, and David with their respective hunters, which would have prohibited the everlasting promises of the Abrahamic and Davidic covenants, he certainly attempted to directly forbid the promised Seed, Messiah, and King of Israel, Yeshua, from becoming God's holy Vessel of the new covenant (Jer. 31, Matt. 26:27). As previously discussed, once Messiah *completely* fulfills the new covenant at His second coming and during his millennial reign, He also fulfills the Abrahamic and Davidic covenants.

Satan's first hunter of the new covenant was Herod the Great, who began the lineage of hunters through the Herodian dynasty, which occurred from 37 BC to AD 92. Herod, a Roman-appointed king of Judea (37–4BC), was born in Idumea, which is located in the *region* of Edom (Esau).

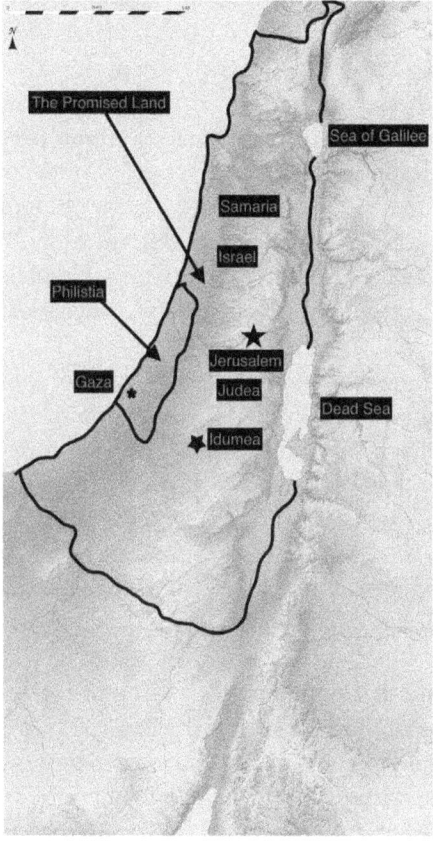

IDUMEA

Just as Esau, Herod's ancestor, *directly* attempted to forbid Jacob to eternalize the *pure royal lineage* of the Abrahamic covenant, Herod viciously and barbarically attempted to eliminate the ultimate fulfillment of the *pure royal lineage* of the everlasting covenants, Yeshua, who is the Seed, Messiah, and King of Israel. As we proceed, let us keep in mind the unequivocal words of judgment the Lord God of Israel prophesied about Esau and his descendants (hunters), which includes the Herodian family, through His prophets Obadiah and Malachi (Obad. 17–18, Mal. 1:2–3).

In world history, Herod is recognized as a distinguished builder, because He constructed and renovated magnificent, colossal building projects throughout Judea. These projects included the renovation of the Jewish temple, the construction of the port and harbor at Caesarea Maritima, and the construction of the fortresses at Masada, Heodium, Alexandrium, Hyrcania, and Machaerus. [42] Herod also implemented water supplies for Jerusalem and he is credited for the enclosure of the cave of the Patriarchs in Hebron.[43] Although Herod contributed to the infrastructure of Judea, and it is recorded he converted to Judaism, he also built heathen cities, such as Sebaste, and temples to pagan gods.[44] A great example of Herod's ideology and paganism is when he erected a golden eagle at the entrance of the Jewish temple, which is strictly forbidden by God in the Holy Bible (Ex. 20, Deut. 4). [45] Unfortunately, idolatry was not the only blasphemous abomination Herod committed, because he executed several members of his own family, including his wife, Mariamne I. [46]

Herod the Great, who declared himself "king of the Jews," vehemently endeavored to attain his self-entitled proclamation by *directly* attempting to hunt the one true, living King of the Jews, Yeshua, shortly after He was born. Ultimately, Satan influenced Herod's evil actions, because with Yeshua being born, he understood the Child was the Seed, Messiah, and King of Israel, who would fulfill God's everlasting covenants, and ultimately, doom him forever!

Herod's most infamous and abhorrent act of evil, called the Massacre of the Innocents, is recorded in the Holy Bible.

After Messiah was divinely born, wise men from the East traveled to Jerusalem to inquire of Herod where *the* King of the Jews had been born, so they could worship and adore Him (Matt. 1:1–2). Once Herod heard the wise men's requests, he was deeply troubled in his spirit and became filled with demonic outrage and jealousy. Fearfully and prophetically, Herod summoned the chief priests and scribes to acquire wisdom concerning what the biblical prophets foretold about the birth of the Jewish Messiah (vv. 3–5), and they quoted the prophet Micah.

> Micah 5:2: "But you, Bethlehem Ephrathah, though you are little among the thousands of Judah, *yet out of you shall come forth to Me the One to be Ruler in Israel, whose goings forth are from of old, from everlasting.*"

Once Herod understood the Jewish Messiah would be born in Bethlehem, he disingenuously inquired about the star the wise men followed to discern the timing of Messiah's birth. Subsequently, in Herod's conniving way, he sent the wise men to Bethlehem to confirm the Child had been born. Once validated, Herod commanded them to report Messiah's location to him, falsely claiming he would travel and "worship" Him, as well (Matt. 2:7–8). When the wise men located the anointed and prophesied King, they rejoiced with exceedingly cheerfulness, and they worshipped and presented Him with gifts. Afterward, being divinely warned in a dream, the wise men returned to their own country without reporting back to Herod (vv. 9–12). Thereafter, an angel of the Lord appeared to Joseph in a dream:

> Matthew 2:13: "Arise, take the young Child and His mother, flee to Egypt, and stay there until I bring you word; *for Herod [hunter] will seek the young Child to destroy Him.*"

After Satan's hunter Herod figured out he had been deceived by the wise men, in his furious outrage and anger, he swiftly and demonically ordered his soldiers to inexcusably commit the massacre mentioned earlier.

> Matthew 2:16–18: "*[Herod] sent forth and put to death all the male children who were in Bethlehem and in all its districts, from two years old and under, according to the time which he had determined from the wise men. Then was fulfilled what was spoken by Jeremiah the prophet, saying: 'A voice was heard in Ramah, lamentation, weeping, and great mourning, Rachel weeping for her children, refusing to be comforted, because they are no more.'*" (See Jer. 31:15.)

In summary, Herod the Great, a descendant of Esau,[47] was Satan's first hunter to *directly* attempt to forbid Yeshua from fulfilling the new covenant, through the Massacre of the Innocents. In Satan's abominable attempt, he understood it would also prohibit the *pure royal lineage* and the Abrahamic and Davidic covenants from being fulfilled, thus terminating God's plan of salvation for Jews and Gentiles though his everlasting promises. Nevertheless, God, not Satan, was in total control over His Son's life and His eternal purposes! Herod the Great's ruthlessness and barbaric reign prove he was not a man of God, but an evil hunter (Edomite) for Satan.

HEROD ANTIPATER (4 BC–AD 39)

Another one of Satan's hunters who *directly* attempted to forbid the new covenant, which fulfills the Abrahamic and Davidic covenants, was Herod the Great's son, Herod Antipater. This evil hunter is better known by his nickname, Antipas, and also by Herod the Tetrarch. Herod Antipas had a *direct* impact not only on Messiah's death, but also on John the Baptist's execution, because he was the *foreshadowing* of the Messiah (Matt. 3, John 1:6–9). Keep in mind, Herod Antipas continues Satan's lineage of hunters through the Edomites, because, like his father, he was a descendant of Esau (Edom).

After the death of Herod the Great (4 BC), Caesar Augustus sealed the legacy of the infamous Herodian dynasty by promoting Herod Antipas to rule over Galilee and Perea, which was a client state of the Roman Empire. Equivalent to his father, Antipas was a great builder, and he is credited for projects at Betharamphtha, Sepphoris, and his capital, Tiberias, which was located on the western shore of the Sea of Galilee. Antipas named the city after the Roman Emperor Tiberius, who succeeded Augustus in AD 14. [48]

Now, let us discover Antipas's climatic ascension into his role as Satan's hunter during this prophetic time, which was Messiah's first coming, by exploring his animosity toward the prophet, John the Baptist. As John began his ministry in the proximity of the Jordan River and the Sea of Galilee, which was located on the western edge of Antipas's territory of Perea, he preached a baptism of repentance for the remission of sins (Luke 3:1–9). After John boldly and unapologetically preached the message of repentance, baptism, and the coming of the Messiah (vv. 15–17), he also sternly rebuked Antipas for his incestuous marriage, because his wife, Herodias, was his brother Philip's wife (vv. 18–19). Due to Antipas's fear of and respect for John the Baptist as a holy and just man, instead of killing him, he bound him in prison in Machaerus (Jordan) for the sake of Herodias (Mark 6:17–20). Nevertheless, his incestuous wife anxiously and deviously waited for the perfect opportune time to consummate her bitter revenge on God's prophet, which occurred on Antipas's birthday.

During Antipas's birthday celebration, as all of his high officers and chief men joyfully commemorated, Herodias's daughter pleased the king by dancing for him. Subsequently, Antipas proclaimed, "Ask me whatever you want, and I will give it to you." He also swore to her, "Whatever you ask me, I will give you, up to half my kingdom" (Mark 6:22–23). Ecstatically, the young girl asked her mother what she should petition for, and Herodias vigorously and relentlessly declared, "The head of John the Baptist" (v. 24)! Once the daughter immediately demanded the wish of her mother, Antipas was exceedingly sorrowful; however, because of his oaths, he ordered the beheading of John the Baptist (vv. 25–28). Although Antipas was reluctant to kill John the Baptist, this does not acquit him of John's blood on his hands, because he was still the earthly king in charge, who could have prohibited this evil act.

In complete fulfillment of his duty as Satan's hunter, Antipas also *directly* enabled the crucifixion of Messiah. Make no mistake: God Almighty, who is the God of Israel, is in absolute control over the whole universe and understands Satan and his evil hunter's actions before they occur. This includes Messiah's death, which was *preordained* before the foundation of the world (Ps. 118:22–29; Micah 5:2; John 3:16; 1 Peter 1:19–21; Rev. 13:8). Now, with this in mind, let us review Antipas's role in Messiah's *predestined* death.

After Messiah was baptized by John the Baptist and tempted by Satan (Matthew 3–4), He began his ministry in Galilee, which was the territory of Herod Antipas. Over time, as Antipas heard great praise about Messiah, His message of salvation, and His miraculous works, he was perplexed and sought to meet Him, because rumors proliferated that John the Baptist had risen from the dead, or else the prophet Elijah had gloriously appeared. (Mark 6:14–16; Luke 9:7–9). As Messiah's holy and divine message of salvation resonated at a profound and piercing level to not only believers and unbelievers, but also to Antipas, a group of Pharisees warned Messiah that Antipas desired to kill (hunt) Him.

> Luke 13:31–33: "On that very day some Pharisees came, saying to Him, '*Get out and depart from here, for Herod wants to kill You.*' And He said to them, '*Go, tell that fox,* "Behold, I cast out demons and perform cures today and tomorrow, and the third day I shall be perfected." Nevertheless, I must journey today, tomorrow, and the day following; for it cannot be that a prophet should perish outside of Jerusalem.'" (See Matt. 23:37–39.)

When Messiah denounced Antipas by calling him a "fox," He symbolically correlated his character with his Edomite heritage, as foxes are red, hairy hunters. The Holy Bible describes Esau (Edom) in this exact manner (Gen. 25:25, 27). Interestingly enough, the Greek word for fox is *alopex,* which is *feminine,* and it advocates that Messiah was calling Antipas a vixen, which is a crafty and cunning person. Living up to Messiah's omniscient proclamation as a vixen, Antipas outspokenly mandated the death of Messiah, which obviously validates his role as Satan's hunter.

The book of Luke records Messiah was first brought before Pontius Pilate, because he was governor of Roman Judea, which encompassed Jerusalem where Messiah was arrested. Once Pilate learned Messiah was a Galilean, and therefore, under Herod Antipas's jurisdiction, he sent him to *the fox*, who was also in Jerusalem at the time (Luke 23:6–7). There are several reasons for this. First, in Messiah's day, the normal legal procedure of the early Roman Empire was for the defendants to be tried by the authorities of their local provinces. Accordingly, the trials were generally based in the location of the alleged crimes. Second, if Pilate was not required to send Messiah to Antipas, he may have been showing courtesy to *the fox*, and at the same time, avoiding the need to deal with the Jewish authorities himself. Last and foremost, Pilate's wife had warned him, "Have nothing to do with that just Man, for I have suffered many things today in a dream because of Him" (Matt. 27:19).

Initially, with Messiah in custody, Antipas was intrigued and interested in encountering Messiah in hopes of witnessing Him perform a miracle and to hear His wise teachings. Nevertheless, to Antipas's agitated disappointment, Messiah remained silent in the face of questioning, and Antipas treated Him with contempt, mocked Him, and ordered Him back to Pilate (Luke 23:8–11).

Just as Herod Antipas had commanded John the Baptist's beheading, Satan's Edomite hunter also ordered Messiah to be delivered unto Pilate, who cowardly conceded to the people's vehement desire for Him to be crucified. Without any doubt, Herod Antipas and Pontius Pilate have Messiah's blood on their hands, although Pilate did declare, "I am innocent of the blood of this just Person. You see to it" (Matt. 27:24). Obviously, Pilate cannot cleanse himself—only Messiah can—but it shows he was verbally reluctant to allow Yeshua's crucifixion. On the contrary, there is no record that Herod Antipas had any reservation or remorse for his part in Messiah's crucifixion. In fact, the opposite is true, as the Holy Bible records that *the fox* wanted to kill Him (Luke 13:31).

Contrary to God's *original fishermen*, Abraham, Isaac, Jacob, and David, the Almighty allowed Satan to influence Antipas to enable the crucifixion of His only begotten Son, Yeshua. What can we conclude from this? Why did God allow Satan to influence His Son's crucifixion? The ultimate, yet simple, but most amazing answer is . . . love! As it is written: "For God *so loved* the world that He gave His only begotten Son, that whoever believes in Him should not perish but have everlasting life" (John 3:16). The Almighty's ultimate will and purpose is for *all* of mankind to inherit everlasting life, which, assuredly, only comes through the ultimate sacrifice of Yeshua Hamashiach, Jesus the Messiah!

John 14:6: "Jesus said to him, 'I am the way, the truth, and the life. No one comes to the Father except through Me.'"

John 15:13: "Greater love has no one than this, than to lay down one's life for his friends."

Prophetically, just as Isaiah proclaimed, mankind needed an Intercessor and a Redeemer to bring salvation to the world, and God's own right Hand, His Branch of righteousness to David, Yeshua HaMashiach, Jesus the Messiah, completely fulfilled God's *preordained*, incredible, and awesome will for *all* mankind (Ps. 110:1–2; Isa. 59:15–20; Matt. 22:43–45)! Furthermore, God divinely and sovereignly shielded and protected His *original fishermen* from Satan's *original hunters* so that His everlasting promises could be covenanted with His *original fishermen*, as well as to keep *the pure royal lineage* intact and unblemished unto Messiah. Therefore, underlining God's omniscient, omnipresent, and omnipotent ways, God used Satan's jealous and raging foolishness of influencing his hunters to kill Messiah to bring salvation to all of mankind, which establishes Him as the new covenant (Matt. 26:27–29)! In other words, by Messiah being crucified and ultimately resurrected, He fulfilled the biblical requirements of the Jewish Messiah in the new covenant, which ultimately fulfills the Abrahamic and Davidic covenants!

Hebrews 10:5–7, 10, 12–14: "Therefore, when He came into the world, He said: 'Sacrifice and offering You did not desire, *but a body You have prepared for Me*. In burnt offerings and *sacrifices* for sin You had no pleasure. Then I said, *"Behold, I have come—in the volume of the book it is written of Me—to do Your will, O God."'* By that will we have been sanctified through the offering of the body of Jesus Christ once *for all*. But this Man, *after He had offered one sacrifice for sins forever, sat down at the right hand of God, from that time waiting till His enemies are made His footstool. For by one offering He has perfected forever those who are being sanctified.*" (See Ps. 40:6–8; Isa. 59:15–20; Jer. 31:31–37; Matt. 5:17–20.)

In conclusion, since the beginning, Satan has influenced specific hunters to *directly* attempt to forbid God's everlasting covenants to His *original fishermen*. From Nimrod's demonic attempts to kill Abraham, to Ishmael's diabolical effort to dethrone Isaac, to Esau's devilish actions toward Jacob, to Goliath's evil challenge to David, and concluding with the Herodian family's hellish decisions against Messiah, God has allowed Satan to use his *original hunters* according to His preordained purposes and to ultimately bring glory to Him through His everlasting covenants (Ezek. 36:22–36)!

Tellingly, *all* of Satan's *original hunters* who *directly* attempted to prohibit the everlasting covenants to God's *original fishermen* originated from specific *regions* that are today the nations that surround God's Promised Land of Israel. The ancient names of the people of these regions are the Babylonians/Chaldeans (Nimrod), Ishmaelites (Ishmael), the Hagarenes (Hagar), the Edomites (Esau), and the Philistines (Goliath). Does this not provide us great wisdom concerning Satan's *end-of-the-age hunters*, including the *final hunter*?

> Isaiah 46:9–10: "Remember the former things of old, for I am God, and there is no other; I am God, and there is none like Me, *declaring the end from the beginning, and from ancient times things that are not yet done.*"

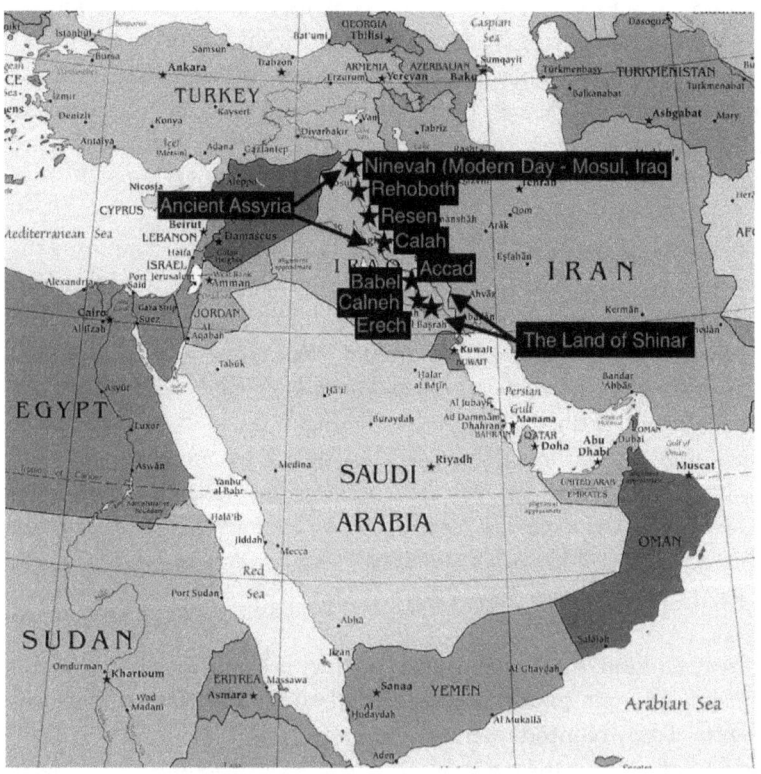

Nimrod

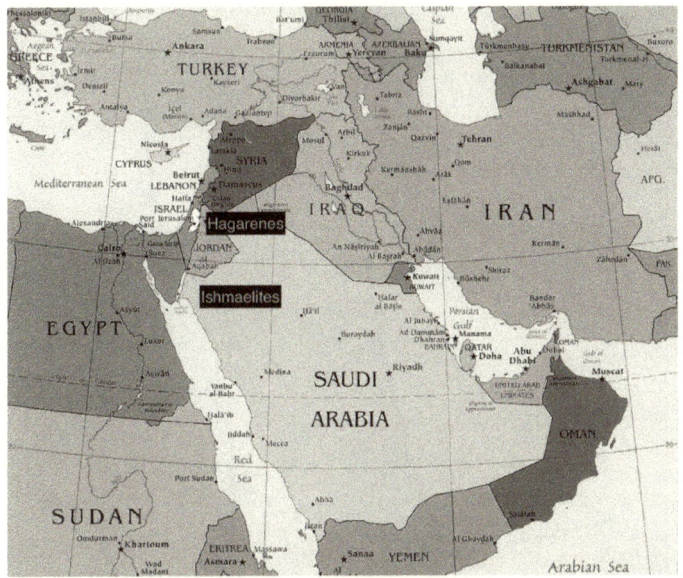
Hagar/Ishmael

Edom

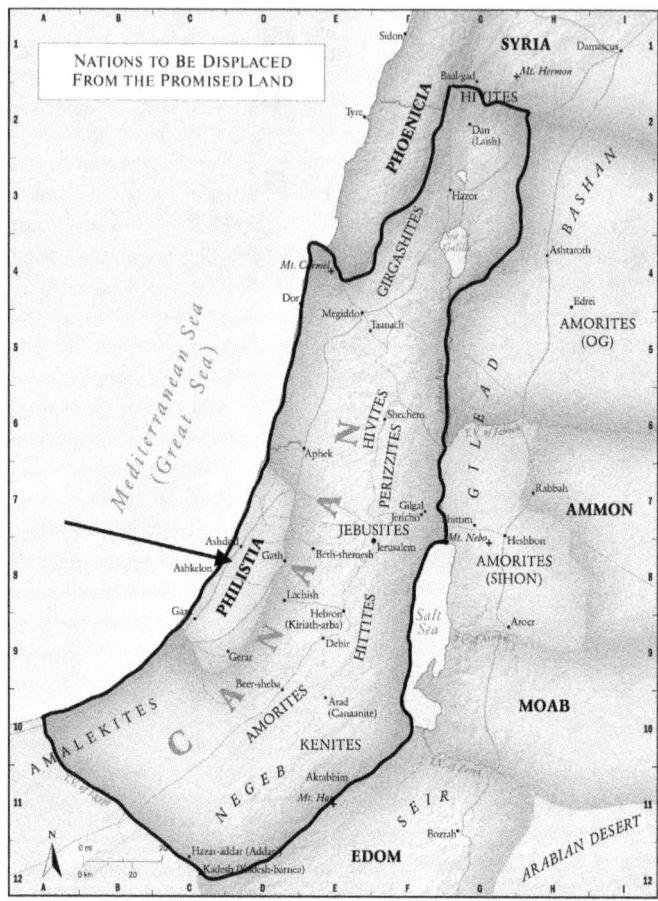

Philistines

CHAPTER 5

THE MYSTERY OF ALIYAH

As we journey from the ancient days of God's *original fishermen* and Satan's *original hunters* to modern day, let us discover the mystery of Aliyah. This extraordinary revelation will provide us with great knowledge of God's release of His *end-of-the-age* fishermen and Satan's *end-of- the-age* hunters of Jeremiah's prophecy. *Aliyah* is a term commonly used by the children of Israel, because it indicates when a person returns to the Promised Land from the diasporas. In Hebrew, *Aliyah* means to ascend, and it spiritually refers to the act of "going up" toward Jerusalem (Strong's #5944). According to the traditional Jewish ordering of books of the Tanakh (Old Testament), the very last word of the last book in the original Hebrew (2 Chr. 36:23) is veya'al, a jussive verb form derived from the same root as Aliyah, meaning "and let him go up" to Jerusalem in Judah. The late Elie Wiesel, who won the Nobel Peace Prize and was awarded the Presidential Medal of Freedom and the Congressional Gold Medal, wisely declared, "One does not go to Jerusalem, *one returns to it [Aliyah]. That's one of its mysteries.*"[1] Unequivocally, Jerusalem is God's righteous, holy city that is strategically located on His holy mountain, Mount Zion. The prophet Daniel validates Jerusalem as God's holy mountain, and Messiah commanded the children of Israel to be "the light of the world," which in essence would vastly illuminate Jerusalem as "the shining city on the mountain" (Dan. 9:16, 20; Matt. 5:14–16). Hebrew writer Elhanan Leib Lewinsky wrote, "Without Jerusalem, the land of Israel is as a body without a soul."

After the Roman Empire destroyed Jerusalem and exiled the children of Israel from the Promised Land in AD 70, which fulfilled Messiah's grave prophecy (Luke 19:41–44), Aliyah was only a national hope, aspiration, and prayer for the children of Israel. Throughout the centuries, as the Lord God prophetically scattered the Jewish people among the nations, they absorbed severe trials and tribulations, and Aliyah seemed more delusive and futile than ever before. It certainly seemed there was not a prophetic sign, revelation, or glimmer of hope that shined upon God's chosen people to make Aliyah to the Promised Land.

Does the mystery of Aliyah present us with unique patterns and markers of migrations of the children of Israel, and also an extraordinary template for their return to the Promised Land? Does this mystery directly correlate with the everlasting covenants and the prophecy of the fishermen and the hunters? Has the Lord God used celestial signs in the heavenly realm to warn the children of Israel of His appointed times of Aliyah? Have we witnessed these spectacular, but dire warnings in recent years? Let us commence to answer these profound questions by first understanding how the Lord God communicates to His people in the heavens, His heavenly billboard.

> Genesis 1:14: "Then God said, 'Let there be lights in the firmament of the heavens to divide the day from the night; and let them be for *signs and seasons*, and for days and years.'"

One of the primary reasons God created the heavens was for *signs* and *seasons*. The Hebrew word for *signs* is *owth*, which means "to signal warnings" or "an omen" (Strong's #226). The Hebrew word for *seasons* is *mo'ed*, which is defined as "an appointed feast" or "a divine appointment" (Strong's #4150). The Almighty is proclaiming He will use His celestial bodies to signal warnings on His heavenly billboard to interact with mankind for His divine appointments or appointed times. This is to say, God will communicate His divine appointments or appointed times with us through the sun, moon, and stars, which He sovereignly ordained during His creation of the world (Genesis. 1). In Psalms 19:1, King David prophetically announces, "The heavens declare the glory of God; and the firmament shows His handiwork," which clearly emphasizes God's ultimate and complete control over the universe (See Ps. 147:4–5; Prov. 3:19–20; Jer. 51:15–16). Messiah also gives us a great example of God's divine appointments or appointed times in His Olivet Discourse (Matt. 24–25).

> Matthew 24:29–30: "Immediately after the tribulation of those days the *sun will be darkened, and the moon will not give its light; the stars will fall from heaven, and the powers of the heavens will be*

shaken. Then the sign of the Son of Man will appear in heaven, and then all the tribes of the earth will mourn, and they will see the Son of Man coming on the clouds of heaven with power and great glory." (See Isa. 13:10; Ezek. 32:7–8; Joel 2:30–31; Luke 21:25–28; Rev. 6:12.)

Unequivocally, Messiah is prophesying about the celestial signs and signals before His second coming, which is certainly a divine appointment or an appointed time. Obviously, this is *the* supreme example of what God is referring to in Genesis, which is a divine appointment, or an appointed time, on His prophetic timeline.

Genesis 1:14 directly corroborates with the Lord's seven feasts in Leviticus 23, as the Hebrew word, *mo'ed*, appears in both Scriptures. Keep in mind: *mo'ed* is defined as both *seasons* and *feasts*. The preeminent example of how these Scriptures perfectly correlate with one another is when Messiah, the Passover Lamb, was crucified on the Feast of Passover (John 18:39–40), buried on the Feast of Unleavened Bread (Mark 15:42–47), resurrected on the Feast of Firstfruits (Luke 24:1–12), and poured out His holy spirit on the Feast of Shavuot/Pentecost (Acts 2). Remarkably, these were God's preordained divine appointments (seasons) that occurred on His predetermined appointed times (feasts). Amazingly, Messiah fulfilled His Father's first four feasts in Leviticus 23—Passover, Unleavened Bread, Firstfruits, and Shavuot—to the exact day, hour, and detail of the ceremony (Matt. 27–28; Mark 15–16; Luke 23–24; John 18–20; Acts 1–2)! Since Messiah is the same yesterday, today, and forever (Heb. 13:8), and He does not change (Mal. 3:6), and there is no shadow of turning with Him (James 1:17), at His second coming, *He will fulfill the unfulfilled three fall feasts: Trumpets, Yom Kippur, and Tabernacles (Leviticus 23).* In our book *God's Prophetic Timeline: Messiah's Final Warning*, we thoroughly explain the tremendous impact of the Lord's seven feasts as they directly coincide with Messiah's first and second coming events (www.wndsuperstore.com/ www.amazon.com, www.faithfulperformance.com).

Without any doubt, God uses the sun, moon, and stars to signal and warn mankind of His divine appointments at His appointed times. By studying astronomy and history, we can observe specific patterns that help us to understand if there is a parallel between God's divine appointments and celestial occurrences. Note that there is a major difference between astronomy and astrology. Astronomy is about the Creator of the universe, God Almighty, and astrology is about mankind worshipping "the created," instead of the Creator (see Rom. 1:25). As long as we focus on God (astronomy), and not ourselves (astrology), we will not fall into error.

The mystery of Aliyah is directly connected to a phenomenon of celestial occurrences of what is known as a *blood moon tetrad*. This phenomenon consists of four consecutive total lunar eclipses (blood moons) with no partial lunar eclipses in between them. Each of the blood moons is separated from the other by six lunar months for two consecutive years. In other words, the four blood moons occur six months apart in two consecutive years. To obtain a more in-depth understanding of blood moon tetrads, I would strongly recommend Mark Biltz's book *Blood Moons: Decoding the Imminent Heavenly Signs*, as his expertise and research on this phenomenon is impeccable.

In Psalms 89, the psalmist declares the moon is God's "faithful witness in the sky" (v.37). Interestingly enough, the Talmud records that when a blood moon (lunar eclipse) occurs on the *Lord's holy feast days (Lev. 23)*, it indicates God's warning to Israel, because its calendar months are based on the moon (Hebrew calendar). On the contrary, the occurrence of a solar eclipse signifies His warning to the nations, as its calendar months are only based on the sun (Gregorian calendar). Also, the rabbinical thinking is, as the sun is larger than the moon, so are the nations in size compared to Israel. [2]

According to NASA, from 1999 BC to AD 3000 (five thousand years), there will be 3,479 total lunar eclipses (blood moons), but only 142 of them will be tetrads. Over the last two thousand years (since Messiah), there have been 62 tetrads, *but only nine of them fell on the Lord's feast days, with the last one occurring in 2014–2015.* [3] In this chapter, we will explore the prominent significance of *four* blood moon tetrads, which have occurred in the last five hundred years.

Since 1492, a tetrad of blood moons has only occurred *four* times on the Lord's feast days (divine appointments). In *all* four instances, and in both years of the tetrad, the blood moons appeared on the Feast of Passover and the Feast of Tabernacles. The mathematical odds of this occurring is overwhelmingly astronomical, *unless* the Almighty desired to directly communicate with mankind by signaling warnings from His heavenly billboard. Extraordinary, yet prophetically, in *all* four divine appointments, the essential significance of the tetrads has resulted in a Jewish migration, with the last three tetrads resulting in an Aliyah to the Promised Land and Jerusalem! Now, let us review the four blood moon tetrads and how they connect with the mystery of Aliyah, the everlasting covenants, and the prophecy of the fishermen and the hunters.

THE BLOOD MOON TETRAD OF 1493–1494

1. April 2, 1493—Feast of Passover
2. September 25, 1493—Feast of Tabernacles
3. March 22, 1494—Feast of Passover
4. September 15, 1494—Feast of Tabernacles

For most Americans, the historical year of 1492 is remembered and celebrated as the incredible time Christopher Columbus "sailed the ocean blue" and founded America. On the contrary, for the children of Israel, it commemorates the Spanish Inquisition, which is one of the most horrific periods in Jewish history, because their ancestors were tragically expelled from Spain. After the Jewish expulsion from Spain in 1492, a tetrad of blood moons appeared on the Lord's feast days of Passover and Tabernacles (1493–1494).

The Spanish Inquisition, also known as the Tribunal of the Holy Office of the Inquisition, was established in 1480 by King Ferdinand and Queen Isabella of Spain. The main purpose of the inquisition was to preserve the Catholic orthodoxy in Spain by eliminating all heresies of Christianity, which, in their minds, were the Jewish people and the Jewish roots of the Christian faith. Professor Benzion Netanyahu, a hawkish Judaic scholar, who is the father of current prime minister of Israel Benjamin Netanyahu, wrote in his book *The Origins of the Inquisition*: "The royal decree explicitly stated that the Inquisition was instituted to search out and punish converts from Judaism who transgressed Christianity by secretly adhering to Jewish beliefs and performing rites and ceremonies of the Jews. No other group was mentioned, no other purpose indicated, which is a fact that in itself suggest a close relationship between the creation of the Inquisition and Jewish life in Spain. Other facts, too, attest to that relationship." [4]

Ultimately, the Spanish Inquisition became an authoritarian dictatorship towards the Jewish people living in Spain and its controlled territories. The children of Israel were singlehandedly discriminated against by the supposedly "religious monarchs." Historian Henry Kamen provides evidence of the extreme anti-Semitism toward the children of Israel, also called Marranos (pigs), during the Spanish Inquisition. In quoting the expulsion edict itself, he writes, "The great harm suffered by Christians from the contact, intercourse, and communication which they have with the Jews, who always attempt in various ways to seduce faithful Christians from our Holy Catholic Faith . . . The only solution to all these ills is to separate the said Jews completely from contact with the Christians, and expel them all from our realms." [5]

On March 31, 1492, King Ferdinand and Queen Isabella of Spain issued the Alhambra Decree (Edict of Expulsion), which ordered the expulsion of the children of Israel from Spain and its territories by July 31, 1492, *unless* they converted to Catholicism. The Edict of Expulsion declared: "Whereas, having been informed that in these kingdoms, there were some bad Christians who Judaized and apostatized from our holy Catholic faith, the chief cause of which was the communication of Jews with Christians . . . We ordered the said Jews in all cities, towns, and places in our kingdoms and dominions to separate into Jewries [ghettos] and place apart . . . hoping by their separation alone to remedy this evil . . . But we are informed that neither that, not the execution of some of the said Jews . . . has been sufficient for a complete remedy . . . Therefore, we . . . resolve to order all the said Jews and Jewesses to quit our kingdoms and never return . . . *by the end of the month of July next, of the present year 1492 . . . if they do not perform and execute the same, and are found to reside in our kingdoms . . . they incur the penalty of death . . . We likewise grant permission and authority to said Jews . . . to export their wealth and property . . . provided they do not take away gold, silver, money, or other articles prohibited by the laws of the kingdom.*" [6]

During the Spanish Inquisition, the monarchs allowed the Jewish people to leave with their possessions, except for their gold, silver, minted money, or other things prohibited by the laws of their kingdom. Many scholars and historians believe the tremendous fortune that was stolen and confiscated from the children of Israel during the Spanish Inquisition financed Christopher Columbus's voyage to America.

The Edict of Expulsion, issued on March 31, 1492, allowed the Jewish people only four months to convert, exile, or be executed, culminating on July 31, 1492. Professor Netanyahu recorded an eyewitness to the persecution of the Spanish Inquisition. He writes, "Those of them who refused to accept baptism were immediately slain, and their corpses stretched in the streets and the squares, offered a horrendous spectacle." [7] Astonishingly, according to historian Joseph Perez, as a result of the Alhambra Decree and the extreme persecution of prior years, more than two hundred thousand Jews converted to Catholicism, and as many as one hundred thousand of them were expelled from Spain. [8]

The original date of the Jewish expulsion was July 31, 1492, but it was extended by Grand Inquisitor Torquemada until August 2, 1492, which fell on the cursed Jewish date of the ninth of Av on the Hebrew calendar. In Christopher Columbus's diary, he confirmed the extension of the Alhambra decree, as the extended date coincided with the same month his voyage sailed to the New World, which was August 3, 1492: "*In the same month* in which their Majesties *issued the edict* that all Jews should be driven out of the kingdom and its territories, *in the same month*, they gave me the order to undertake with sufficient men my expedition of discovery of the Indies." [9] The ninth of Av became a cursed date throughout Jewish history in consequence of the ten spies who returned to Moses from the land of Canaan with a bad report. Only Joshua and Caleb had true faith in the Lord God of Israel to conquer the Promised Land (Num. 13–14). Here are some of the major events in Jewish history that have occurred on the infamous, cursed ninth of Av.

- The first temple was destroyed in 586 BC.
- The second temple was destroyed in AD 70.
- England expelled all Jews from the country in 1290.
- On August 2, 1941, SS commander Heinrich Himmler formally received approval from the Nazi Party for "The Final Solution." As a result, the Holocaust began and almost one-third of the world's Jewish population perished.
- In 1942, Hitler's proclamation to kill the Jewish people occurred on this cursed day. Nazism, World War II, and the Holocaust killed Polish Jews from the Warsaw Ghetto. Eight hundred thousand innocent Jewish people were exterminated at Treblinka, and six million overall in the Holocaust.
- In 2005, the Jewish people were forced to evacuate Gaza because of the pressure from the Bush administration and the United Nations. Twenty-four hours later, America was evacuating Louisiana (Hurricane Katrina) (Gen. 12:3).

On August 3, 1492, in God's ultimate love and amazing grace, He provided a beacon of light in the form of Christopher Columbus (there is significant evidence that he was a Messianic Jew—a Jewish believer), who set sail for the New World the day after the deadline of the Alhambra Decree, which spiritually linked the two together. In Columbus's *Book of Prophecies*, he wrote:

At an early age, I began to sail upon the ocean. For more than forty years, I have sailed everywhere that people go. I prayed to the merciful Lord about my heart's desire, and He gave me the spirit and the intelligence for the task: seafaring, astronomy, geography, arithmetic, skill in drafting, spherical maps . . . It was the Lord who put in my mind (I could feel his hand upon me) to sail from here to the Indies. All who heard of my project rejected it with laughter, ridiculing me. *There was no question that the inspiration was from the Holy Spirit, because He comforted me with rays of marvelous illumination from the Holy Scriptures . . . encouraging me continually to press forward.* It is possible that those who see this book will accuse me of being unlearned in literature, of being a layman and a sailor. *I reply with the words of Matthew 11:25: "Lord . . . because Thou hast hid these things from the wise and prudent, and has revealed them unto babes."* The Holy Scriptures testify in the Old Testament by the prophets and in the New Testament by our Redeemer Jesus Christ that this world must come to an end. The signs of when this must happen are given by Matthew, Mark, and Luke. The prophets also predicted many things about it. Our Redeemer Jesus Christ said that before the end of the world, all things must come to pass that had been written by the prophets. Isaiah goes into great detail describing future events. **(*Editor: Forgive him for not using Hebraic terminology. His life would have been endangered.*)** [10]

Columbus also recorded in his book, "No one should fear to undertake any task in the name of our Savior, if it is just and the intention is purely for His service . . . Day and night, moment by moment, everyone should express to Him their devoted gratitude. These are great and wonderful things on the earth, and the signs are that the Lord is hastening the end. *The fact that the Gospel must still be preached in so many lands in such a short time—this is what convinces me.*"[11]

Columbus's voyage from Spain would eventually consummate in the establishment of the safest refuge in the history of the world for the children of Israel, which is known as America! Nevertheless, during and after the horrific Spanish Inquisition, the Jewish people migrated and settled into all parts of the world, including Europe (Italy, Portugal, Greece, Bulgaria, Serbia, Bosnia), the Ottoman Empire, North Africa (Morocco, Algeria, Tunisia, and Libya), and eventually, America. Approximately five-hundred years after the proclamation of the Alhambra Decree, it was formally rescinded on December 16, 1968. Unfortunately, the tragic history and scar tissue had already been accumulated within the Jewish community by this time. To this day, Spain has never been the dominant power it once was, because of its anti-Semitism during the Spanish Inquisition (see Gen. 12:3).

In summary, the Jewish migration from Spain in 1492 encored with a blood moon tetrad in 1493–1494 on the Feast of Passover (April 2, 1493, and March 22, 1494) and the Feast of Tabernacles (September 25, 1493, and September 15, 1494). This divine occurrence of the blood moon tetrad on the Lord's feast days would be the *first of four phenomenal occurrences* on the holy feast days that would align with a *Jewish migration caused by persecution*.

THE BLOOD MOON TETRAD OF 1949–1950

1. April 13, 1949—the Feast of Passover
2. October 7, 1949—the Feast of Tabernacles
3. April 2, 1950—the Feast of Passover
4. September 26, 1950—the Feast of Tabernacles

After World War II (1939–1945), which perpetuated with the decline and nonexistence of Hitler's evil Nazi regime, which murdered more than six million Jewish people, there was a migration (Aliyah) to the Promised Land three years later in 1948. These prophetic events followed the exact same pattern of the Spanish Inquisition events and blood moon tetrads, as *persecution led to a migration of the children of Israel*. However, this time, it was an Aliyah to Israel! Most people are familiar with Hitler's anti-Semitic beliefs and rhetoric during that gruesome, unspeakable time, but if not, here are some quotes from this evil dictator about the children of Israel, taken from his repugnant two-volume work, *Mein Kampf*.

- "The black-haired Jewish youth lies in wait for hours on end, satanically glaring at and spying on the unsuspicious girl whom he plans to seduce, adulterating her blood and removing her from the bosom of her own people. The Jew uses every possible means to undermine the racial foundations of a subjugated people."
- "The personification of the devil as the symbol of all evil assumes the living shape of the Jew."

- "And so he [the Jew] advances on his fatal road until another force comes forth to oppose him, and in a mighty struggle hurls the heaven-stormer back to Lucifer. Germany is today the next great war aim of Bolshevism. It requires all the force of a young missionary idea to raise our people up again, to free them from the snares of this international serpent."
- "Hence today I believe that I am acting in accordance with the will of the Almighty Creator: 'by defending myself against the Jew, I am fighting for the work of the Lord.'"

After the horrific atrocities of Hitler's Nazi regime, the Lord God of Israel provided another glimmer of hope, just as He did after the Spanish Inquisition, by ordaining the establishment of His heritage, His land, Israel again as nation!

On May 14, 1948, the nation of Israel was "born again," which provoked an enormous Jewish Aliyah to the Promised Land, fulfilling biblical prophecy (Isa. 66:8). Subsequently, a tetrad of blood moons occurred in 1949 and 1950 on the Lord's feast days, continuing the mystery of Aliyah. How did Israel become a nation again in 1948?

On November 5, 1914, during World War I, the British Empire declared war on the Ottoman Empire (Muslim), who controlled Jerusalem and occupied the Promised Land (Israel). On November 2, 1917, the British Empire's foreign secretary, Arthur James Balfour, sent a letter to Walter Rothschild, who was one of the leaders of the British Jewish community. Rothschild submitted the declaration to the Zionist Federation of Great Britain and Ireland, and it became known as the Balfour Declaration. In 1917, which was a jubilee year (see Lev. 25), the Balfour Declaration became the first official step in fulfilling the 1948 prophecy (Isa. 66:8).

In 1917, at the pinnacle of World War I, General Allenby of the British Empire captured a region of the Promised Land from the Ottoman Empire, which ended four hundred years of Muslim control. As the war concluded and the Ottoman Empire declined in power, the League of Nations divided the Promised Land between Israel and the Arabs. Regrettably, once the declaration was executed, the children of Israel were allocated approximately 20 percent of the land God promised to them in the Abrahamic covenant (Gen. 15), *excluding Jerusalem*. The remainder of the Promised Land was given to the Arabs. Now, although the children of Israel will not inherit *all* of the Promised Land until Messiah returns for His second coming and millennial reign, 20 percent was an inconsiderable portion compared to what the Arabs received (80 percent). Nevertheless, the 1917 Balfour Declaration was the first official step for the children of Israel to regain control over the Promised Land in 1948.

Israel becoming a nation again in 1948 was a major fulfillment of biblical prophecy (Isa. 66:8), because it is the "key that opens the door" for *all* of the other end-of-the-age prophecies to be fulfilled, including the prophecy of the fishermen and the hunters (Jer. 16). Keep in mind, Jeremiah's prophecy will be *completely* fulfilled during the time of Jacob's trouble, which we will discuss in a later chapter. Of course, there will be perpetual fulfillments of Jeremiah's prophecy (Aliyah) from 1948 until the climatic pinnacle, however, the *ultimate* fulfillment will occur at the end of the age.

From 1948, the children of Israel's hope, aspirations, and prayers of Aliyah have become a reality in record-setting numbers to the Promised Land. Israel's first prime minister, David Ben-Gurion stated, "Suffering makes people greater, and we (Jewish people) have suffered much. We had a message to give the world, but we were overwhelmed, and the message was cut off in the middle. In time there will be millions of us – becoming stronger and stronger – and we will complete the message." In 1950, the Law of Return was established, which granted every Jewish person the automatic right to immigrate to Israel and become a citizen of the nation. [12] From 1948 to 1950, more than 500,000 Jewish people made Aliyah to the Promised Land. By 1951, the consensus of the children of Israel had nearly doubled the overall population of 800,000 in 1948. From 1948 through 2016, the number of the children of Israel who have made Aliyah to the Promised Land is over 3.2 million. When Israel officially became a nation again in 1948, there were approximately 800,000 Jewish people living in the country, and by 2017, an incredible 6,484,000, which accounts for 43 percent of the world's total Jewry, as the mystery continues to fulfill biblical prophecy. We will explore these amazing statistics in more detail in the next chapter.

In summary, after the proclamation of the Balfour Declaration in 1917, and after the diabolic persecution of the Jewish people during World War II by Adolf Hitler (1939-1945), the nation of Israel was "born again" in 1948. Equivalent to the children of Israel's migration to other nations after the atrocious persecution of the Spanish Inquisition (1492), the result from the Nazi persecution culminated with the rebirth of Israel as a nation in 1948 that provoked a record-setting Jewish Aliyah to the Promised Land.

Incredibly, yet divinely, it was encored with a tetrad of blood moons on the Feast of Passover (April 13, 1949, and April 2, 1950) and the Feast of Tabernacles (October 7, 1949, and September 26, 1950). The Aliyah of this blood moon tetrad is paramount, because it enabled the children of Israel to perpetually make Aliyah to the Promised Land, which God promised their forefathers (Abrahamic covenant). From 1948 unto today, there has been an enormous Aliyah of the children of Israel to the Promised Land (3.2M), validating and continuing this incredible mystery. As we proceed, keep in mind that once again, the Lord God redeemed the children of Israel from *persecution* (Hitler) by "rebirthing" Israel as a nation again in 1948.

BLOOD MOON TETRAD OF 1967–1968

1. April 24, 1967—the Feast of Passover
2. October 18, 1967—the Feast of Tabernacles
3. April 13, 1968—the Feast of Passover
4. October 6, 1968—the Feast of Tabernacles

During the climatic pinnacle and culmination of the Six-Day War (June 5–10, 1967), another divine appointment on God's prophetic timeline was fulfilled when the children of Israel recaptured Jerusalem for the first time in approximately nineteen hundred years. Amazingly, a blood moon tetrad occurred on the Lord's feast days in 1967–1968, as the Jewish people were making Aliyah into the holy city of Jerusalem. The fulfillment of the 1967 prophecy is monumental, because the children of Israel have to control Jerusalem before Messiah returns for His second coming and millennial reign.

> Psalm 102:16: "For the Lord shall build up Zion [Jerusalem]; He shall appear in His glory [Second Coming]."

> Isaiah 66:8–9: "'For as soon as Zion [Jerusalem] was in labor, she gave birth to her children. Shall I bring to the time of birth, and not cause delivery?' says the Lord. 'Shall I who cause delivery shut up *the womb?*' says your God."

As we have discovered, although the 1917 Balfour Declaration was the first official step for Israel to become a nation again in 1948, the League of Nations did not allocate the holy city of Jerusalem to the Jewish people. The children of Israel were only allotted 20 percent of the land promised by God in the Abrahamic covenant, *excluding Jerusalem*. Therefore, once Israel became a nation again in 1948, Israeli-Arab relations became exceedingly strained, which escalated into dangerous levels of persecution and ignited the Six-Day War in 1967. It is worth noting that the 1967 conflict between the Jewish people and the Arabs derived from the Abrahamic covenant and the question of who had the rights to the land: Isaac and Jacob's descendants or Ishmael and Esau's descendants.

On June 7, 1967 (Jubilee Year, Leviticus 25), fifty years after the 1917 Balfour Declaration (Jubilee Year), Israeli soldiers entered the Lion's Gate (eastern gate) and recaptured Jerusalem as its capital for the first time in approximately nineteen hundred years! Israel defeated five countries in order to win the Six-Day War: Egypt, Jordan, Syria, Iraq, and Lebanon. These five countries had the additional support of Algeria, Saudi Arabia, Libya, Kuwait, Pakistan, Morocco, Sudan, the PLO, and Tunisia. Astonishingly, yet prophetically, nineteen short years after becoming a nation again (1948), Israel recaptured Jerusalem in the Six-Day War and rested on the Sabbath, fulfilling the 1967 prophecy (see Ps. 102:16; Isa. 66:8–9) on God's prophetic timeline. Only by God Almighty's divine intervention can a nation that only had nineteen years to establish itself and train its own military, defeat all five of those countries and its allies. Hallelujah!

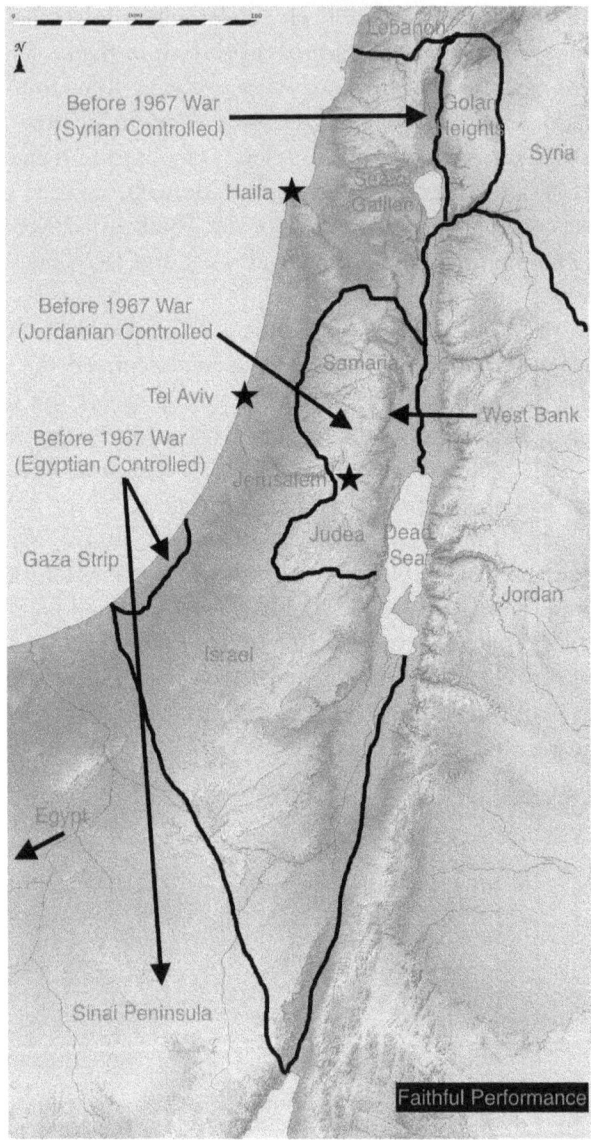

Israel Pre-1967

THE MYSTERY OF ALIYAH

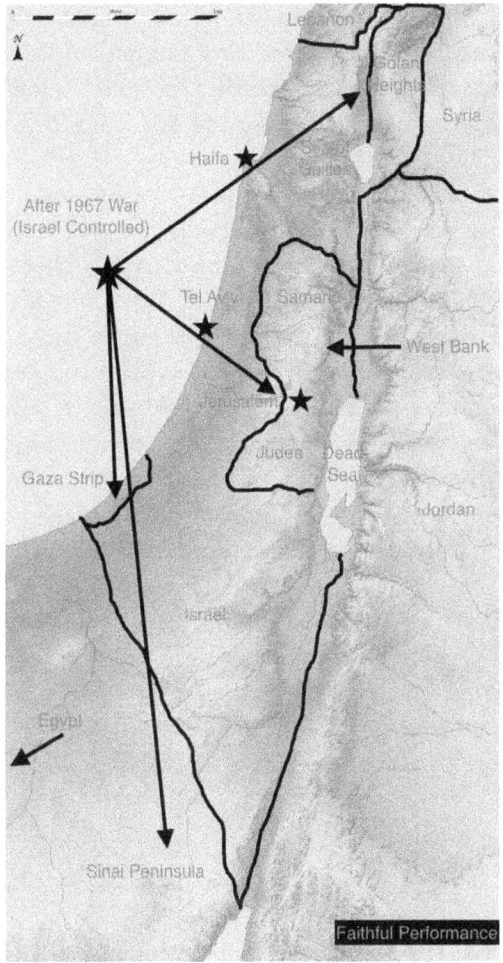

Israel Post 1967

Tensions and relations between the children of Israel and the Arabs (Ishmael, Esau) have been gravely strained for more than four thousand years, due to the interpretation of the Abrahamic covenant. Just as we have discovered in chapter 1, the Holy Bible clearly proclaims that Abraham's *seed* would be a blessing to *all* the families of the earth (Gen. 12:3). This is the reason all three monotheistic religions, Judaism, Judeo-Christianity, and Islam, respectively, recognize him as the "father" of their religion. However, God Almighty boldly and distinctively declared to Abraham that He specifically chose Isaac as the *only seed* to continue the *pure royal lineage* that would propagate Messiah

(Gen. 15, 17, 21). This is to say, although Abraham and Sarah sinned against God, which resulted in Abraham begotten a son named Ishmael, God clearly told Abraham that Isaac, who was born after the Spirit, is the chosen seed of the *pure royal lineage*, not Ishmael, who was born after the flesh (Gen. 17, Gal. 4:21–31).

Accordingly, from Abraham's days until Messiah's second coming and millennial reign, the lineage of the children of Israel (Jews) is from Isaac, Jacob (Gen. 25), and David, and their descendants (Matt. 1, Luke 3). The lineage of the Muslims continues through Ishmael, Esau, and their descendants (Muslims). Interestingly enough, Isaac and Ishmael were stepbrothers, and Jacob and Esau were twins. The Abrahamic covenant is the foremost reason the Jews and Muslims have been in a generational, yet biblical war with one another for thousands of years. Each nation believes their forefather, Isaac (Jews) and Ishmael (Muslims), received the eternal promise through Abraham from God to inherit the Promised Land. Make no mistake: this generational family feud will perpetuate until Messiah's second coming and millennial reign.

In summary, the Six-Day War culminated with the children of Israel recapturing Jerusalem as their capital, which was a major fulfillment of biblical prophecy. As the children of Israel overcame *persecution* and *war* to make Aliyah to Jerusalem for the first time in nearly nineteen hundred years, the mystery of Aliyah was confirmed once again with a blood moon tetrad in 1967–1968.

BLOOD MOON TETRAD OF 2014–2015

1. April 15, 2014—the Feast of Passover
2. October 8, 2014—the Feast of Tabernacles
3. April 4, 2015—the Feast of Passover
4. September 28, 2015—the Feast of Tabernacles

In 2014 and 2015, the fourth blood moon tetrad in the last five hundred years occurred on the Lord's feast days. As previously discussed, the blood moon tetrads, which fall on the Lord's feast days, are exceptionally unique and do not manifest very often. In fact, from 1492 until 2014, there have only been *three* occurrences of a blood moon tetrad on the Lord's feast days. The first phenomenon resulted in a Jewish migration from Spain (1493–1494), and the last two culminated with the children of Israel making Aliyah to Israel (1949–1950) and Jerusalem (1967–1968). Please note, all three of the migrations were the result of *persecution and/or war*. The 2014–2015 tetrad was the *ninth overall* blood moon tetrad in the last two thousand years. In other words, there were a total of *nine* blood moon tetrads that occurred at nonspecific times, not just on the Lord's feast days.

In Bullinger's *Number in Scripture*, he explains how prophetically colossal the number nine is as it correlates to the mystery of Aliyah. He writes, "The number nine . . . is the last of the [single] digits, *and thus marks the end;* and is significant of the *conclusion of a matter*. It is akin to the number six, six being the sum of its factors (3 × 3 = 9, and 3 + 3 = 6), and is thus significant of *the end of man,* and the summation of all man's works. Nine is, therefore, *The Number of Finality or Judgment* . . . *It marks the completeness, the end and issue of all things as to man—the judgment of man and all his works.* It is a factor of 666, which is 9 times 74 . . . The sum of the 22 letters of the Hebrew alphabet is 4995 (5 × 999). *It is stamped, therefore, with the numbers of grace and finality.*" [13]

To summarize Bullinger's account, the number nine is preeminent because it represents the *finality or judgment of all things*. If this is the case, the *ninth* blood moon tetrad's (2014-2015) importance cannot be overstated. Now, let us review what the apostle Peter proclaimed about the mystery of God's prophetic timeline.

> 2 Peter 3:8 (NIV): "But do not forget this one thing, dear friends; *with the Lord a day is like a thousand years, and a thousand years are like a day.*"

What is Peter declaring in this Scripture? This mystery journeys us back to a pattern at the beginning of creation. In the beginning, the Almighty created the earth in *six days* and rested on the *seventh day* (Gen. 2:1–3). Additionally, in Leviticus 25, the Lord commanded the children of Israel to work *six years* and rest on every *seventh year (Shemitah, Lev. 25:1–7)*. So, just as the Lord rested on the *seventh day*, and the children of Israel were commanded to rest on the *seventh year*, the saints (you and me) will rest on the *seven thousandth year*, which is Messiah's millennial reign!

Let us calculate this mystery: The period between Adam and Yeshua was 4,000 years (4 days completed), and from Yeshua (AD 30) until now almost 2,000 years have passed (almost 2 days completed), for a grand total of approximately 6,000 years (6 days completed). Just as the Lord worked *6 days* and rested on the *7th*, and the children of Israel were commanded to work *6 years* and rest on every *7th*, the earth will rest on the *7,000th year (7th day)*, which will be Messiah's millennial reign (1,000-year reign). My friend, according to these prophetic tabulations, we are about to enter the 7th day, or 7,000th year. After the completion of Messiah's 1,000-year reign on earth, it will be the 8,000th year, the *8th day*, which represents eternity, the New Jerusalem (Shmini Atzeret, the 8th day of the Feast of Tabernacles)!

According to the Holy Bible, after Messiah's first coming events, which completed 4,000 years (4 days), the next two thousand years (2 days) before His millennial reign (7,000th year–7th day) would bring major fulfillments of the end-of-the-age prophecies. Assuredly, this encompasses the 1948 and 1967 prophecies, as well as Jeremiah's prophecy of the fishermen and the hunters, which will ultimately consummate into Messiah's second coming events.

In conclusion, since 1492, four blood moon tetrads have occurred on the Lord's feast days of Passover and Tabernacles. In the first three of the phenomenal displays, the prophetic result has been a migration of the children of Israel because of *persecution/war*, with the last two consummating in an Aliyah to the Promised Land and Jerusalem (1948, 1967). As we proceed, let us consider a few questions. Are God's celestial bodies divine markers that commence Jeremiah's prophecy of the fishermen and the hunters? Did the fulfillment of the 1948 prophecy, along with the blood moon tetrads of 1949–50, signify the release of God's fishermen? Who are God's *end-of-the-age* fishermen to Jeremiah's prophecy? We will address those next.

CHAPTER 6

GOD'S END-OF-THE-AGE FISHERMEN

B efore the foundation of the world, the Almighty preordained a specific appointed time and event that would serve as a *marker*, which would "open the door" for *all* of His end-of-the-age prophecies to be consummated, including Jeremiah's prophecy of the fishermen and the hunters. The distinct *sign* for *all* of the end-of-the-age events to be fulfilled was that Israel *had* to become a nation again (Isa. 66:8). Clearly, without the fulfillment of this spectacular event, which happened in 1948, there would not be any hope or reason for a massive Jewish Aliyah to the Promised Land, which is a major prerequisite for God's everlasting covenants to be fulfilled (Jer. 31). What further emphasizes its profound importance is that the rebirth of Israel was encored with a blood moon tetrad (marker). Now let us recall Jeremiah's prophecy of the fishermen and the hunters to understand the *proper order* in which they would be released.

> Jeremiah 16:14–16: "'Therefore behold, the days are coming,' says the LORD, 'that it shall no more be said, "The LORD lives who brought up the children of Israel from the land of Egypt," but, "The LORD lives who brought up the children of Israel from the land of the north and from all the lands where He had driven them." For I will bring them back into their land which I gave to their fathers. Behold, I will send for many fishermen,' says the LORD, 'and they shall fish them; *and afterward* I will send for many hunters, and they shall hunt them from every mountain and every hill, and out of the holes of the rocks.'"

Jeremiah prophesied that the Lord God will *first* send His fishermen to "fish" the children of Israel back to the Promised Land. *Afterward*, He will send Satan's hunters to *hunt* those who did not heed His fishermen's call to make Aliyah to Israel. Keep in mind, the hunters will hunt the children of Israel from every hill and mountain, and from the holes of the rocks of *all* lands. Thus, for Jeremiah's prophecy to initiate, Israel had to become a nation again, because it is the land the fishermen and the hunters will prompt the Jewish people to make Aliyah to. Although there have been Aliyahs to the Promised Land before 1948, which predominantly occurred from 1882 to 1948, Israel was not "born again" as a nation. Therefore, once Israel became a nation again in 1948, God's *end-of-the-age* fishermen *began* their prophetic calling of Jeremiah's prophecy. In fact, just as we briefly discussed in the previous chapter, the Jewish Aliyah from 1948 unto today has been the largest Aliyah ever!

1882–1948 IMMIGRATION CHART

1882-1903	35,000
1904-1914	40,000
1919-1923	40,000
1924-1929	82,000
1939-1948	110,000
TOTAL	**307,000**

1948 TO 2016 IMMIGRATION CHART

Year	Count	Year	Count
1948	101,828	1983	16,906
1949	239,954	1984	19,981
1950	170,563	1985	10,642
1951	175,279	1986	9,505
1952	24,610	1987	12,965
1953	11,575	1988	13,034
1954	18,491	1989	24,050
1955	37,528	1990	199,516
1956	56,330	1991	176,100
1957	72,634	1992	77,057
1958	27,290	1993	76,805
1959	23,988	1994	79,844
1960	24,692	1995	76,361
1961	47,735	1996	70,919
1962	61,533	1997	66,221
1963	64,489	1998	56,730
1964	55,036	1999	76,766
1965	31,115	2000	60,201
1966	15,957	2001	43,473
1967	14,469	2002	33,570
1968	20,703	2003	23,273
1969	38,111	2004	20,899
1970	36,750	2005	21,183
1971	41,930	2006	19,269
1972	55,888	2007	18,131
1973	54,886	2008	13,701
1974	31,979	2009	14,574
1975	20,028	2010	16,633
1976	19,754	2011	16,892
1977	21,429	2012	16,557
1978	26,394	2013	16,968
1979	37,222	2014	26,500
1980	20,428	2015	31,013
1981	12,599	2016	27,000
1982	13,723		
		TOTAL	**3,210,159**

As shown in the charts, during the sixty-six years from 1882 to 1948, 307,000 Jewish people made Aliyah to the Promised Land. However, during the sixty-eight years from 1948 to 2016, more than 3.2 million Jewish people made Aliyah! Clearly, these statistics validate the great impact and importance of Israel's rebirth as a nation again in 1948, which ignited the activity of God's *end-of-the-age* fishermen of Jeremiah's prophecy.

So, who are God's *end-of-the-age* fishermen described in Jeremiah's prophecy? Do God's *original fishermen*—Abraham, Isaac, Jacob, and David, and their descendants—provide great insight into who God's *end-of-the-age* fishermen are? The prophet Isaiah revealed great wisdom concerning this mystery.

> Isaiah 46:9–10: "Remember the former things of old, for I am God, and there is no other; I am God, and there is none like Me, *declaring the end from the beginning, and from ancient times things that are not yet done*, saying, 'My counsel shall stand, and I will do all My pleasure.'"

The Lord God of Israel is "declaring the end from the beginning, and from ancient times things that are not yet done," which certainly includes His *end-of-the-age* fishermen of Jeremiah's prophecy. We have discovered that God's *original fishermen* were the patriarchs, from whom the Jewish lineage descends. Accordingly, God's *end-of-the-age* fishermen (from 1948 until Messiah's second coming) referred to in Jeremiah's prophecy will be the children of Israel (Jews). This includes prime ministers and presidents of Israel, government leaders, and all Jewish organizations, agencies, and charities who encourage and support the Jewish people around the world to make Aliyah to the Promised Land. Keep in mind: the role of Jeremiah's fishermen is to "fish" the Jewish people back to the Promised Land, and obviously, Israel's government leaders, organizations, agencies, and charities are the *predominant* advocates for fulfilling this extraordinary prophecy.

You might be thinking, "How could the Jewish people, of which the majority do not even believe in Yeshua, be God's end-of-the-age fishermen? Do not God's fishermen have to believe in Messiah to become "fishers of men"? (see Matt. 4:19). In Romans 11, the apostle Paul sheds light on this mystery.

> Romans 11:28-29: "Concerning the Gospel they [Jews] are enemies for your sake, *but concerning the election they [Jews] are beloved for the*

sake of the fathers. For the gifts and the calling of God are irrevocable" (everlasting covenants).

Paul explained that although the majority of the Jewish people are enemies to the gospel (Yeshua), they are still the *elect* of the everlasting covenants, because of Abraham, Isaac, Jacob, David. Remember: God made an *everlasting promise, a sworn oath*, to the Patriarchs and their descendants, which include the Jewish people of today. Just like His *original fishermen*, He will use His *end-of-the-age* fishermen, Israel's leaders, organizations, agencies, and charities, to "fish" the Jewish people to make Aliyah to the Promised Land. Of course, many Gentile believers (fishermen) have been and will continue to be *secondary* fishermen to the Jewish Aliyah, but God's *end-of-the-age* fishermen *in Jeremiah's prophecy* are the children of Israel. Additionally, it is only logical that the Jewish people, not Gentiles, "fish" their brethren to the Promised Land. At the end of the age, Messiah Himself will remove the veil from their hearts and pour out His Holy Spirit upon them, and they will no longer be "enemies of the gospel." At that amazing, prophetic moment, they will be His people, and He will be their God!

> Jeremiah 32:37–41: "Behold, I will gather them out of all countries where I have driven them in My anger, in My fury, and in great wrath; I will bring them back to this place, and I will cause them to dwell safely. *They shall be My people, and I will be their God*; *then I will give them one heart and one way, that they may fear Me forever, for the good of them and their children after them. And I will make an everlasting covenant with them [new covenant], that I will not turn away from doing them good; but I will put My fear in their hearts so that they will not depart from Me. Yes, I will rejoice over them to do them good, and I will assuredly plant them in this land, with all My heart and with all My soul* . . . *I will bring on them all the good that I have promised them [everlasting covenants]."*

> Ezekiel 36:24–28: "For I will take you from among the nations, gather you out of all countries, and bring you into your own land. *Then I will sprinkle clean water on you, and you shall be clean; I will cleanse you from all your filthiness and from all your idols. I will give you a new heart and put a new spirit within you; I will take the heart of stone out of your flesh and give you a heart of flesh. I will put My Spirit within you and cause you to walk in My statutes, and you will keep My judgments and*

do them. Then you shall dwell in the land that I gave to your fathers; you shall be My people, and I will be your God."

Now, let us proceed by exploring God's primary *end-of-the-age* fishermen of Jeremiah's prophecy, which have "fished" the children of Israel since 1948, and the awesome results of the Jewish Aliyah to the Promised Land since that prophetic time.

DAVID BEN-GURION

David Ben-Gurion was the principal founder of the State of Israel in 1948, and later, he became known as its "founding father." [1] Ben-Gurion was the first prime minister of the Jewish State (1955–1963), and he harbored a deep and burning passion for Zionism and Aliyah, which substantiates him as a fisherman. He famously proclaimed, "No city in the world, not even Athens or Rome, ever played as great a role in the life of a nation for so long a time, as Jerusalem has done in the life of the Jewish people." [2] In 1935, Ben-Gurion became the leader of the Jewish Agency, and years after, president of the Jewish Agency Executive. In 1946, he became the executive head of the World Zionist Organization. After 1948, these two organizations became the foremost fishermen of the Jewish Aliyah to the Promised Land, and Ben-Gurion was the leader of both. On May 14, 1948, David Ben-Gurion formally declared the existence and establishment of the State of Israel, and he was the first to sign its Declaration of Independence.[3] Afterward, he famously proclaimed, "In Israel, in order to be a realist you must believe in miracles."

As prime minister, Ben-Gurion oversaw the Jewish Aliyah from all countries of the world to the Promised Land, including Operation Magic Carpet, which airlifted Jews from Arab countries. God's fisherman envisioned an exceedingly great and hopeful manifestation of an enormous Jewish Aliyah to Israel, declaring, "There are eleven million Jews in the world. I don't say that all of them will come here, but I expect several million, and with natural increase I can quite imagine a Jewish state of ten million." [4] From 1948 unto 1963, under David Ben-Gurion's leadership in many facets of government, agencies, and organizations, the Jewish Aliyah to the Promised Land exploded, as he proclaimed, "Their faith is their passport." [5] Following is a chart outlining the Jewish Aliyah under his leadership.

1948-1963 IMMIGRATION CHART

1948	101,828
1949	239,954
1950	170,563
1951	175,279
1952	24,610
1953	11,575
1954	18,491
1955	37,528
1956	56,330
1957	72,634
1958	27,290
1959	23,988
1960	24,692
1961	47,735
1962	61,533
1963	64,489
TOTAL	**1,158,519**

After the Six-Day War (1967), Ben-Gurion strongly advocated for a vast Jewish settlement program for the Old City and its surrounding areas, as well as the establishment of large industries in Jerusalem, which would give the Jewish people an incentive to make Aliyah. [6] David Ben-Gurion passed away on December 1, 1973, shortly after Israel's military victory in the Yom Kippur War. During Ben-Gurion's leadership as prime minister of Israel, the World Zionist Organization, and the Jewish Agency, he was one of God's primary *end-of-the-age* fishermen.

THE JEWISH AGENCY FOR ISRAEL

The Jewish Agency for Israel is the largest Jewish nonprofit organization in the world, and it is renown as the predominant agency for the Jewish Aliyah to the Promised Land. Since the rebirth of Israel in 1948, the Jewish Agency for Israel has "fished" *three million* Jewish people back to the Promised Land. [7] During the beginning years of Israel's rebirth, this fishermen organization has also overseen approximately one thousand towns and villages in the Promised Land, as it helps and supports the people who make Aliyah.[8] In 1949, one year after Israel's rebirth, God's fishermen brought 239,000 Holocaust survivors from Europe and Cyprus to Israel. [9] Shortly thereafter, the Jewish Agency also airlifted 50,000 Yemenite Jews to the Promised Land via Operation Magic Carpet, and over the next few years, they assisted hundreds of thousands of Jewish people to make Aliyah to Israel from North Africa, Turkey, Iraq, and Iran. [10] Between 1948 and 1952, God's fishermen helped an estimated 700,000 Jewish immigrants to make Aliyah to the Promised Land. [11]

In the 1980s, the Jewish Agency began to "fish" the Ethiopian Jewish community back to Israel via Operation Moses and Operation Joshua, and 8,000 immigrants were airlifted out of Ethiopia. [12] As the Soviet Union collapsed in the 1980s, Russian and Eastern European Jews commenced Aliyah to Israel by the tens of thousands, and the Jewish Agency, God's fishermen, assisted them. [13] After the fall of the Berlin Wall in 1989, an estimated one million Jews from the former Soviet Union have made Aliyah to the Promised Land, with the arbitrary help stemming from the Jewish Agency. [14] In 1990, an estimated 185,000 immigrants made Aliyah to the Promised Land, and in 1991, approximately 150,000 followed suit, and the Jewish agency were the predominant fishermen. [15]From 1991 to 2000, an average of 60,000 Russian and Eastern European Jews made Aliyah to Israel every year. [16] In 1991, an estimated 14,400 Ethiopian Jews were *fished* back to the Promised Land over thirty-six hours in Operation Solomon. [17] Since the 1960s, 92,800 Ethiopian Jews have made Aliyah to Israel.

In 2014, the first year of the blood moons, the Jewish Agency assisted an estimated 26,500 Jewish people in making Aliyah to Israel, *which was the highest number in thirteen years.* [18] Without any doubt, from 1948 until today, the Jewish agency is one of God's premier *end-of-the-age* fishermen.

THE WORLD ZIONIST ORGANIZATION

The World Zionist Organization (ZO) is a brother fisherman organization with the same goals, attributes, and ideals as the Jewish Agency, and its leadership was closely intertwined during the early years of the rebirth of the State of Israel. The ZO served as an umbrella organization for the Zionist movement, which includes the principal objective of a Jewish Aliyah. The following are brother organizations or associations with the ZO and the

Jewish Agency for Israel: the Jewish Colonial Trust, the Jewish National Fund, United Israel Appeal (Keren Hayesod), World Zionist Congress, the Jerusalem Program, the Jewish Federations of North America, the Ministry of Immigrant Absorption, and Partnership2gether.[19] Certainly, with the direct association to the Jewish Agency for Israel, the World Zionist Organization, along with its sister organizations and associations under its umbrella, are God's *end-of-the-age* fishermen of Jeremiah's prophecy.[20]

In conclusion, God appointed a specific time and event that would serve as a marker or sign to initiate His end-of-the-age events. This divine appointment was fulfilled when Israel became a nation again in 1948 (closely preceding the blood moons of 1949 and 1950), and it opened the door for the beginning of the fulfillment of all end-of-the-age prophecies, including Jeremiah's prophecy of the fishermen and the hunters. Without a doubt, God's *end-of-the-age* fishermen ignited their activity in 1948, resulting in more than 3.2 million Jewish people making Aliyah to the Promised Land, as the mystery perpetuates to its ultimate fulfillment. God's *end-of-the-age* fishermen of Jeremiah's prophecy are the children of Israel, who, through government leadership, organizations, agencies, and charities, will prophetically call upon their brethren to make Aliyah to the Promised Land, just as we have previously discovered. Most certainly, the end will be like the beginning, and from ancient times things not yet fulfilled (Isa. 46:9–10).

But what about Satan's *end-of-the-age* hunters of Jeremiah's prophecy? Have they been released into their prophetic calling at the end of the age, also resulting in an Aliyah to the Promised Land? In 2014–2015, did the *ninth* blood moon tetrad of the last two thousand years, which indicates "finality, completeness, conclusion, and the end of a matter," [21] *mark* the release of Satan's *end-of-the-age* hunters? Who are Satan's *end-of-the-age* hunters? Has current Israeli prime minister Benjamin Netanyahu prophetically called the children of Israel to make Aliyah to the Promised Land, validating his role as God's fisherman?

CHAPTER 7

SATAN'S END-OF-THE-AGE HUNTERS AND THE ALIYAH OF 2014–2015 FROM EUROPE

To understand the Aliyah from Europe that initiated in 2014–2015 (blood moon tetrads), and how it corroborates with Jeremiah's prophecy of the fishermen and the hunters, let us first explore the volatile, chaotic, and lawless climate of the Middle East and North Africa, the main regions referenced in the Holy Bible. Afterward, we will explore the imperative, yet tragic effects of the major geopolitical decisions in these regions. Of course, the Middle East and North African regions have always been a very tense and fragile environment where Israel and its surrounding neighbors are concerned, and they will continue to be until Messiah's second coming. As we have discussed, the reason for the generational tension between them is the Abrahamic covenant, or the God-given rights to the land of Canaan.

With that being said, according to the biblical prophets, including Messiah, there will be a *specific* time when the regions of the Middle East and North Africa will reach their final apocalyptic pinnacle. Assuredly, our generation is currently witnessing the *beginning of sorrows* of the "final pinnacle," which will journey us through the fulfillment of the end-of-the-age prophecies, including Messiah's second coming and millennial reign. In our book *God's Prophetic Timeline: Messiah's Final Warning*, we thoroughly explain, in great detail, how, according to the biblical prophets, the current kingdoms and events of today perfectly align with Daniel's four prophesied kingdoms (Dan. 2,7,8), which will rise to power before Messiah's second coming events. As of 2017, our generation is currently living in the period represented by the Medo-Persian Empire, or modern-day Iran, which is the second of Daniel's four kingdoms (Dan. 2, 7). Here is a quote from the book:

"If we take into account what Jesus and the biblical prophets foretold in the Holy Bible, and align the prophecies with the current events of today, then we are definitely living at the end of the age. Furthermore, we are also witnessing the fulfillment of the four kingdoms that Daniel prophesied about before Messiah's second coming and millennial reign." [1]

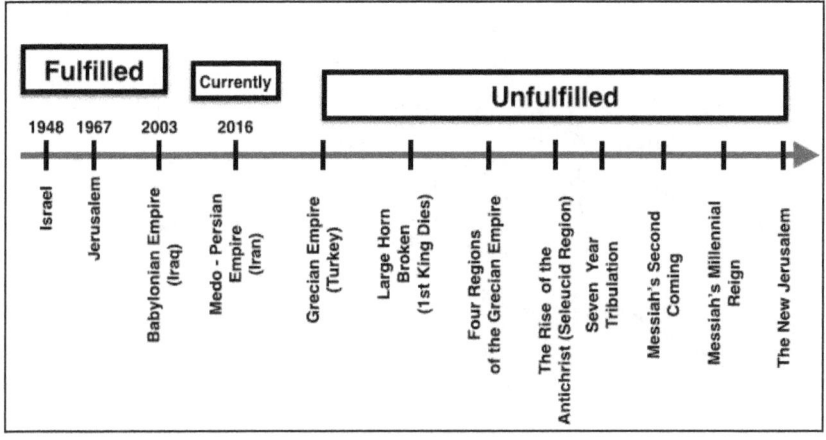

God's Prophetic Timeline

From 2003 unto the blood moon tetrad of 2014–2015, the Middle East and North African regions have significantly transformed, as kingdoms conquered kingdoms, and nations began to collapse with governmental anarchy, civil war, terrorism, and civil unrest (Iraq, Libya, Egypt, Lebanon, Sudan, Syria, Yemen, Turkey, etc.). These prophetic events in the Middle East and North Africa have created tremendous instability, chaos, and *migration*, as the overall region has deteriorated into a tumultuous war zone that is unprecedented in history. As we briefly review the recent history of these countries, I want to be very clear that I am not advocating for the dictatorships that were removed from power. I am only presenting the facts of each country's tremendous insecurity and instability, which have resulted in escalated tyranny, war, and terror in the region.

IRAQ (BABYLONIAN EMPIRE)

The Middle East commenced its *final* prophetic implosion in 2003, when international allies led by the United States accused Saddam Hussein of harboring weapons of mass destruction. Subsequently, the international allies forcefully removed the dictator from power in Iraq (the site of the biblical Babylonian Empire), fulfilling Daniel's first kingdom of his *latter-day* prophecies (Dan. 2:28–44; 7:2–4). Once God weighed Saddam's kingdom in the balances, numbered its days, and found him wanting ("Mene, Mene, Tekel, Upharsin"; see Dan. 5), Iraq became a grueling pivotal battleground primarily between the Iraqi government, Iran, and ISIS, as they battle for the country's soul.

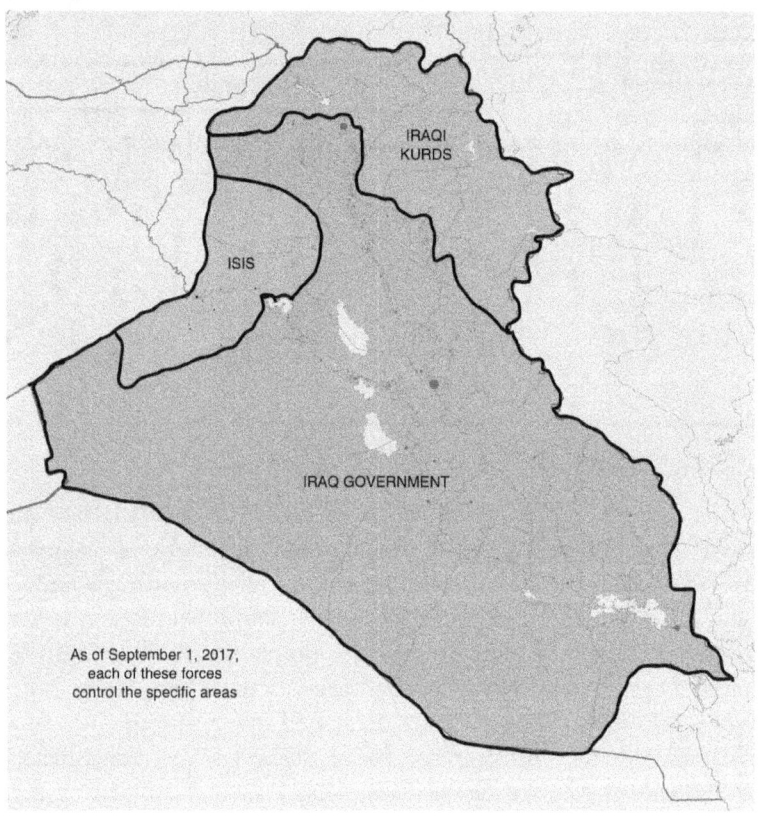

Iraq

On April 14, 2003, the capital city of Baghdad fell to the United States and its allies. This resulted in a relentless governmental cataclysm. From that essential time in history, political and religious turmoil, terror, and civilian unrest and insecurity have reached a dangerous pinnacle of no return, as political parties, nations, and terror groups have pursued supreme power for this strategic piece of real estate in the Middle East. The United States and its allies established a transitional government to govern Iraq, known as the Coalition Provisional Authority, which excluded the Baath Party members and other government officials of Saddam Hussein. [2] Consequently, forty thousand schoolteachers who joined the Baath Party simply to keep their jobs under Saddam Hussein lost them. [3] The U.S.-led alliance also dissolved the fragmented remains of the Iraqi Army, further escalating the climatic tensions of a post-Saddam environment. [4] The governmental instability of Iraq created different Sunni and Shia militias and terrorist organizations to fight the coalition forces and one another, as each strove for ultimate control over the fertile crescent country. Before Saddam's removal, Iraq was Sunni governed, but once the dictator was extracted, anarchy persisted between the Sunni and Shia Muslims, the two largest sects of Islam, with both fighting against the new Iraqi government (Shia).[5] From 2003 unto 2011, it is reported approximately 500,000 people have died in Iraq as a result of war-terror related causes.[6]

In 2011, once the United States and its allies receded from Iraq, the ancient country continued to struggle in political, religious, and cultural uncertainty as the Arab Spring (2011) protest spread through its borders. [7] From late 2011 to early 2012, the Iraqi National Movement, which represents the majority of Iraqi Sunnis, boycotted Iraq's parliament, upholding the predominantly Shia government's desire to remove the Sunnis from power over the country. Throughout 2012–2013 (Arab Spring), protests and violence intensified and raged throughout Iraq, as Sunnis and Shias continued to battle over governmental control and power. [8] Sunni militants persistently attacked the Iraqi Shia population to damage the people's trust in the Shia leadership of Nouri al-Maliki,[9] who succeeded the Iraqi Transitional Government and is allied with and supported by Iran (Shia).[10] In fact, the late King Abdullah of Saudi Arabia (Sunni) declared Nouri al-Maliki "an Iranian agent, who opened the door for Iranian (Shia) influence in Iraq." [11] He continued, "I have no confidence whatsoever in Maliki to stabilize Iraq, and how could I meet with someone I don't trust?" [12] Abdullah expressed his frustration and disgruntlement with the political situation in Iraq because it is one of the major barriers between Saudi Arabia and Iran. Saudi Arabia (Sunni) and Iran (Shia), by the way, are ancient, bitter enemies who profoundly hate each other. Their hatred will conclude with Iran destroying Saudi Arabia at the end of the age (Isa. 21).

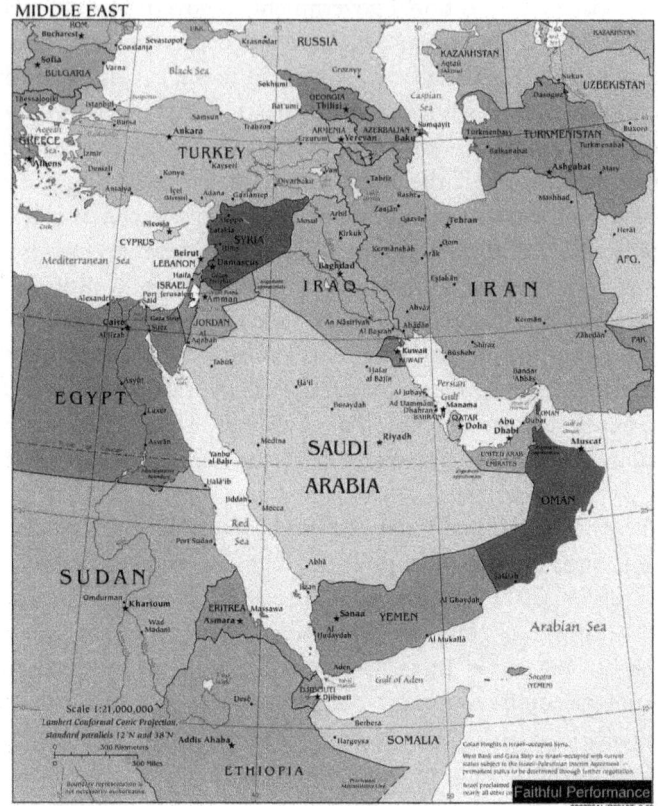

ME Map

Middle East journalist Michael Weiss confirms Abdullah's proclamations about the Iranian influence in Iraq. He writes, "Iranian strategy was designed to prevent the Iraqi government from functioning *so that Iran could exert greater control over the country under the guise of providing stability.*" [13] Weiss also provides insight into the terror group al-Qaeda's strategic impact in Iraq when Saddam Hussein was in power. He wrote that al-Qaeda allied with the Iranians in covert operations in order to destabilize Saddam's government.

Just as the prophet Daniel prophesied, once the Babylonian Empire (Iraq) succumbed to its prophetic calling at the end of the age (Dan. 2:28–44; 7), which occurred in 2003, the Medo-Persian Empire (Iran), the second kingdom, will become the dominant superpower in the region. Iraq and Iran have been supreme rivals for the past several decades, as each country has pompously striven to be the absolute leader and dominant nation of the Middle East. Therefore, once Iraq (Babylonian Empire) was dethroned from power, it was just a matter of time before Iran (Medo-Persian Empire) would march across the border and exert its influence and power over the chaotic and volatile nation (Dan. 8:3–4, 20). As mentioned earlier, our generation is currently living in the period represented by the second of Daniel's four Middle Eastern kingdoms, which is Iran, the Medo-Persian Empire. The next Middle Eastern kingdom that will rise to power is the Grecian Empire, which is Turkey (Dan. 2, 7, 8:5–8, 21). For more information, see *God's Prophetic Timeline: Messiah's Final Warning.*

In 2014, Iraq became even more unstable with the rise of ISIS, as the terror group seized control over large areas of Iraqi land, including Tikrit, Fallujah, and Mosul, which dislodged hundreds of thousands of Iraqi citizens. [14] On June 4, 2014, the barbaric group attacked Mosul (ancient Nineveh) and completely subdued the city on June 10. [15] The aftermath of the ISIS invasion of Mosul forced more than a hundred thousand Christians from their treasured land, which they had called home for more than five thousand years. [16] The terrorists also vandalized and burned down their churches and monasteries, including heritage sites and artifacts. [17]

However, on October 16, 2016, Iraqi, Kurdish, American, Turkish, and French armed forces launched a cohesive military venture to recapture Mosul from ISIS. [18] Subsequently, under the largest deployment of Iraqi forces by U.S. and coalition forces, a massive military offensive liberated the ancient city of Mosul from the barbaric group ISIS. [19] On July 9, 2017, Iraqi Prime Minister Haider Al-Abadi arrived in Mosul to declare the liberation of Mosul and reclaim it after three years of ISIS control. [20] The next day, a formal declaration made the liberation of Mosul official. [21]

In summary, the fall of Iraq in 2003 not only destabilized the country with violence and death, but it also created a domino effect of instability and lawlessness throughout the region, as terrorist nations and organizations filled the vacuum it created. The fall of Iraq also began an enormous refugee migration pandemic in the region, when 1.5 million Iraqi citizens departed to Syria, which eventually would have its own refugee crisis. It also paved the way for Iran (Medo-Persia) to begin fulfilling its prophetic calling, which is the second biblical Middle Eastern kingdom to rise to power at the end of the age (Dan. 2, 7, 8). As of this writing, Iran (Medo-Persia) is currently the kingdom our generation is living in.

IRAN (MEDO-PERSIAN EMPIRE)

As we briefly discussed, after the nation represented by Daniel's Babylonian Empire (Iraq) fell in 2003, the prophet declared that Iran (Medo-Persia) would rise to power to fulfill its prophetic destiny (Dan. 2,7,8). Since 2003, Iran, which is the ram depicted in Daniel 8, began its push "westward, northward, and southward, so that no [one] could withstand him, nor was there any that could deliver from his hand, but he did according to his will and became great" (Dan. 8:4). As of 2017, Iran continues to fulfill its prophetic calling by also financing and advocating terrorism and governmental anarchy throughout the region, which has consummated with regional chaos and civilian unrest across the Middle East (Iraq, Yemen, Lebanon, Syria). Prime Minister Benjamin Netanyahu, when questioned about Iran and their behavior since the catastrophic nuclear deal by the Obama administration (2015), compared the terrorist nation to "a hungry tiger that is unleashed." [22] I strongly concur with Netanyahu's analysis, because Iran will proceed to fulfill its prophetic calling by forming a "Shia Crescent" from Iran to the Mediterranean Sea (Dan. 2,7,8:4).

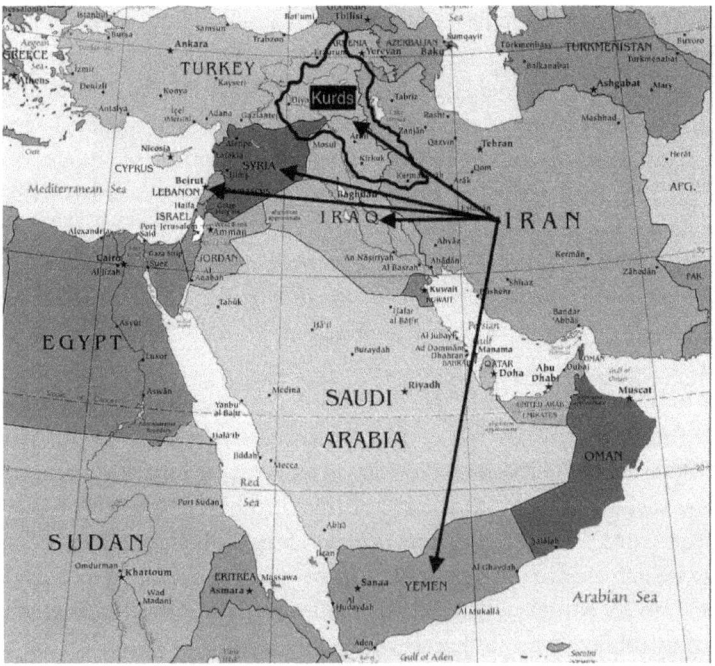

Iran

As Iran perpetually spews out its evil proclamations toward the United States and Israel, referring to them as "Big Satan" and "Little Satan," respectively, and declaring "Death to Israel and America," the Shia nation persists in marching across the Middle East, financing and supporting terror. Since the fall of Iraq in 2003, Iran's dominance of the Middle East has resulted in war, terror, devastation, and civil unrest and instability. In the past decade, as war and terrorism has perpetuated over the oil-enriched land of Iraq, Iran has marched into it and financed and controlled Iraqi leaders such as al-Maliki, an Iranian agent. Additionally, Iran directly controls terrorist groups such as Hezbollah, which has dominance over approximately half of Lebanon, and Hamas, which resides in the Gaza Strip, by supporting them financially and militarily. [23] In fact, Hezbollah leader Hasan Nasrallah declared, "Hezbollah gets its money and arms from Iran, as long as Iran has money, so does Hezbollah." [24] Keep in mind that Iran, along with Hezbollah and Hamas, has proclaimed their ultimate goal is to "wipe Israel off the face of the earth." [25]

Furthermore, Iran (Shia) has also invaded Yemen to battle Saudi Arabia (Sunni) for regional power, resulting in governmental anarchy, civilian unrest, and terror. Iran has major influence and control over leaders and groups in Yemen, which is located on Saudi Arabia's southern border, which surely poses a national security issue for Arabia. This is the prominent reason for the Yemen conflict, as Iran is strategically setting up a biblical showdown with Saudi Arabia in the future (Isa. 21). From March 2015 to March 2017, the Yemen conflict resulted in 7,600 deaths and 42,000 injured, as 180,000 people have fled the tumultuous, war zone country. [26]

In its most recent march of war, Iran has ground troops in Syria, where, as of 2014–2015 (the time of the blood moons), the tragic civil war had escalated in horrific intensity. Iran directly supports Syria and its president, Bashar al-Assad, and it provides a tremendous amount of financial and military support. Labib al-Nahas, the chief of foreign relations for Ahrar al-Sham, who leads the principal organization of the Syrian Islamic Front, declared that Iran is viciously seeking to create areas it can control. "Iran was very ready to make a full swap between the north and south. *They wanted a geographical continuation into Lebanon (from Iran). Full sectarian segregation is at the heart of the Iranian project in Syria. They are looking for geographical zones that they can fully dominate and influence. This will have repercussions on the entire region.*" [27] He continued, "This is not just altering the demographic balance. *This is altering the balance of influence in all of these areas and across Syria itself.* Whole communities will be vulnerable. *War with Iran is becoming an identity war. They want a country in their likeness, serving their interests. The region can't tolerate that.*" [28] Without a doubt, Iran is fulfilling its prophetic calling of Daniel 2, 7, and 8, as it marches across the Middle East, "northward, westward, and southward" (Dan. 8:4), attempting to establish a "Shia Crescent" to the Mediterranean Sea.

In summary, after reviewing the map, Iran (Medo-Persia, Ram, Daniel's second kingdom) has marched across the Middle East, just as Daniel 8 prophesies, which will also fulfill Daniel 2 and 7's second kingdom. After the fall of Iraq (Babylonian Empire) in 2003 (Daniel's first kingdom), Iran has waged a regional, political, cultural, and religious war across the Middle East, creating governmental anarchy, terror, civilian unrest, and catastrophic fragility in the region. In doing so, Iran has obtained major influence and control over Iraq, Lebanon, Yemen, and Syria, as it continues to fulfill its prophetic calling.

ISIS

Since the catastrophic emergence of ISIS in 2014, the Middle East and North African regions have become extremely barbaric and gruesome. This demonic group has publicly displayed their abominations on television and social media while it quests to obliterate any and all historical artifacts and civilization that does not assimilate to their fundamentalist Islamic beliefs (Sunni). Throughout Iraq, Syria, Libya, Yemen, and other nations, ISIS has established a brutal identity for their ultimate aspiration: an Islamic caliphate. However, although ISIS, world leaders, and the mainstream (lame-stream) media, speak of an ISIS caliphate in the Middle East, it is not biblical, because, according to the Holy Bible, Turkey will rise to power and form a caliphate and reign supreme in the Middle East. Turkey (Grecian Empire), as noted earlier, is the third of Daniel's four prophesied kingdoms (Dan. 2,7,8), and it will rise to power and defeat Iran (Medo-Persia), which again, is the second kingdom (Dan. 8). We will discuss this more in a later chapter.

In fact, in July 2015, as the United States special forces raided a compound housing Abu Sayyaf, the ISIS chief financial officer, they produced evidence that Turkish officials directly dealt with ranking ISIS (also known as ISIL) members. [29] There are also actual copies of transcripts of Turkey providing direct military aid to ISIS, [30] as well as, president Erdogan's own son-in-law, Berat Albayrak, directly facilitating the sale and acquisition of assets between ISIS and the Turkish government. [31] Certainly, Turkey is supporting and helping ISIS stay in power for their own evil agenda. Therefore, make no mistake: Turkey will be the leader of the Islamic caliphate, just as the biblical prophets foretold (Dan. 2, 7, 8, Ezek. 38–39).

This is also validated by ISIS itself, because the terror group displays symbols that pay homage and allegiance to the ancient Ottoman Empire (Turkey). A certain Arabic source writes, "The use of *Dabiq* by Isis is symbolic of the major historical event at *Dabiq* (1516), as it is the name of the battle the Ottomans (Turkey) won which paved the way for their occupation of Iraq and the Levant for more than four centuries, as well as being the springboard for the Islamic armies to fight the Rum (Romans/Europeans) in their quest for world domination." [32] Additionally, ISIS's television station is called Dabiq, and the evil group calls its magazine Dabiq in order to honor the Ottoman (Turkey) victory at Dabiq, Syria (1516). Even the ISIS flag is an Ottoman (Turkish) insignia, which is the insignia of Islam's prophet, Muhammad's ring, which comes from the Turkish Topkapi museum; everything about ISIS pays homage and allegiance to the Ottoman (Turkey) Empire's victory in Dabiq, Syria, in 1516. Certainly, ISIS is Turkey's "little brother," or as a recent president declared, "the JV team," [33] and this demonic group will continue to manifest terror, fear, and instability across the region while Turkey and Iran, the "varsity teams," rises to fulfill their prophetic callings in Daniel 2, 7, and 8.

To authenticate, we have previously discovered that ISIS is no longer in power and control of one of its two "self proclaimed" capitals, Mosul, Iraq. [34] As of October 17, 2017, ISIS has also been defeated in Raqqa, Syria, its other self-proclaimed capital. Talal Salo, spokesman for the U.S.-backed Syrian Democratic Forces (SDF), stated, "Major military operations in Raqqa are finished but they are now clearing the city of sleeper cells—if they exist—and mines." He continued, "The situation in Raqqa is under control and soon there will be an official statement declaring the liberation of the city." The SDF is a coalition of Arab and Kurdish fighters. U.S. President Trump also substantiated that Raqqa's liberation from ISIS is a major pivotal point in the Middle East, declaring it as a "critical breakthrough" in the worldwide campaign to defeat the barbaric group and its "wicked ideology." Along with the Islamic State's defeat in Mosul, Iraq (July 10, 2017), the president emphasized, "The end of the ISIS caliphate is in sight." [35]

ISIS losing its power and control over Mosul (Iraq) and Raqqa (Syria) is very substantial in two ways. First, the barbaric group is now reduced to a terrorist organization only, since their self-proclaimed caliphate is destroyed. Second, ISIS's collapse will *eventually* encore with a supreme biblical battle between Iran and Turkey over this coveted real estate (Iraq, Syria) for regional dominance and superiority, just as Daniel 8 prophesied. However, ISIS will continue as a terrorist organization that will ignite terror, anarchy, and civil unrest across the world.

LIBYA (ONE OF THE THREE KINGS CONQUERED BY THE ANTICHRIST)

During the Arab Spring of 2011, a governmental revolution developed in Libya, and Libyan dictator Muammar Gaddafi was removed from office by the United States and its allies after forty-two years in power (1969–2011). The aftermath of this prophetic event fueled more lawlessness, violence, and tumult across the North African and Middle Eastern regions, which evolved into another Libyan civil war in 2014. Once again, I am not advocating for Gaddafi's dictatorship, or any other dictatorship; however, the removal of any dictator after forty-two years of power would create massive instability, just as the removal of Saddam Hussein caused in Iraq.

On February 17, 2011, major protests in Libya broke out against Gaddafi's government, because the majority of the Libyans were disgruntled with the political and governmental corruption. [36] On February 27, 2011, the National Transitional Council, an anti-Gaddafi group, formed to act as the intermediate government in the rebel controlled areas, and they govern the eastern cities of Benghazi, Misrata, al-Bayda, and Tobruk. [37]

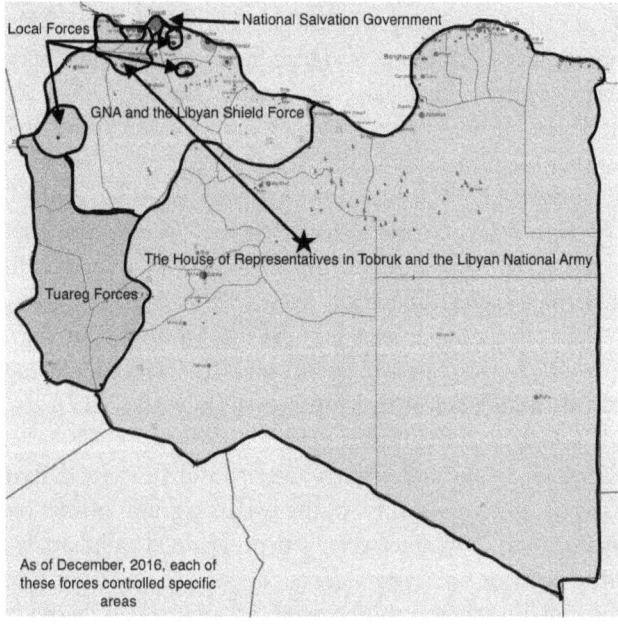

Libya

On March 21, 2011, as the civil war reached its violent and atrocious pinnacle, which included numerous civilian deaths, a multinational coalition led by NATO intervened to protect the Libyan citizens. [38] Subsequently, on August 20, 2011, the International Criminal Court issued an arrest warrant for Gaddafi and his government officials. On October 20, 2011, the evil dictator was killed, ending his forty-two year dictatorship over Libya. [39] Gaddafi's void in Libya was filled with complete lawlessness, war, terror, insecurity, and instability. Interestingly enough, prior to the 2011 revolution, Gaddafi warned Europe, America, and the international community by stating, "If you kill me, Libya will descend into chaos and become like Somalia, with warlords running the country." [40] Unfortunately, the evil dictator was correct on his prediction. Several military regimes, militias, revolutionary brigades, and terrorist organizations strategically formed in separate sections of Libya, none united with the other, as violence extended throughout its borders. [41] The National Transitional Council of Libya (NTC), the interim government, was not adequately prepared to succeed after the first civil war in 2011. Former president Barack Obama admitted this was his "worst mistake," which alludes to the failed preparation of Libya's government after the removal of Gaddafi. [42] The 2011 civil war and revolution progressively escalated and intensified into the 2014 civil war, which is ongoing as of 2017.

In 2014, the second Libyan War accelerated when the government of the Council of Deputies was democratically elected and internationally recognized as the Libyan government. Other groups, such as the Tobruk government (east Libya) and the Islamist government of the General National Congress (GNC, West Libya), also known as the National Salvation Government, desired control over Libyan soil, as well. The GNC is led by the Muslim Brotherhood, and is backed by a group of Islamic fundamentalists, including Qatar, Sudan, and Turkey. [43]

In late 2015, the General National Congress and Tobruk government agreed to unite, in principle, as the Government of National Accord. To this day, it is uncertain as to the specific details of the unification. Of course, with the perpetual warfare and instability of the country, other revolutionaries and terrorist groups are also fighting for power and control over this ancient land, including ISIS, the Shura Council of Bengazi Revolutionaries, and the Tuareg militias of Ghat. [44] From 2016 unto today, although many political developments have called for a "unified government," Libya is still at the height of a political, cultural, and religious crossroads. [45]

In summary, the removal of Gaddafi in 2011 began a civil war that has perpetuated into a second civil war and caused devastation and uncertainty for the citizens of Libya. The oil-enriched nation is embedded in terror, chaos, and instability, which continues to certify the final implosion of the North Africa and Middle Eastern regions. Consequently, this has resulted in a vast migration of its citizens to other parts of North Africa, the Middle East, and also Europe. Interestingly enough, Libya is one of the three countries the Antichrist conquers when he rises to his prophetic calling (Dan. 11:42–43). Is Libya primed for his taking?

EGYPT (ONE OF THE THREE KINGS CONQUERED BY THE ANTICHRIST)

During the Arab Spring of 2011, another revolutionary crisis of governmental anarchy and civilian protests evolved in Egypt, and culminated with two dramatic changes in the Egyptian government. In the 2000s, Hosni Mubarak was under tremendous scrutiny by the citizens of Egypt for a lackadaisical economy, police brutality, corruption, food-price inflation, lack of free elections, and freedom of speech, among other violations. [46] The international community was also investigating Mubarak for his human rights violations, which included torture and unfair arbitrary detentions and trials. [47] In fact, in 2007, Amnesty International alleged Egypt had become an international headquarters for torture, and a place where other countries consigned suspects for interrogation. [48]

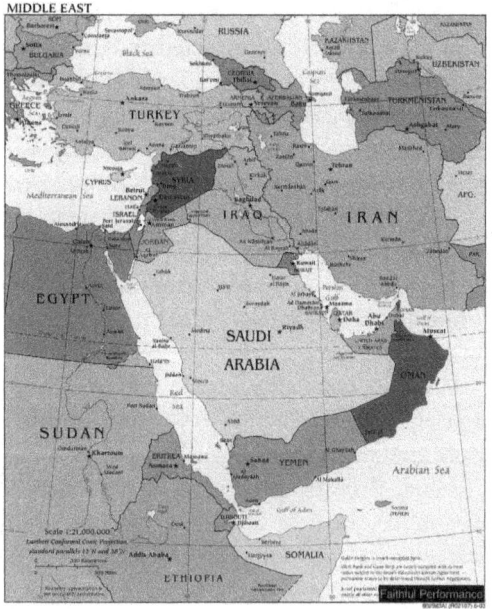

Egypt

On January 25, 2011, as civilian demonstrations, chaos, and violence soared across the ancient land of Egypt against Mubarak's government, Cairo became a "war zone." [49] In less than one month, on February 11, 2011, Mubarak resigned, ending his thirty years of rule over Egypt. [50] The Egyptian military assumed power, suspended the constitution, and dissolved the parliament. [51] On November 28, 2011, the first parliamentary election was held since Mubarak held office, and Mohamed Morsi was elected president, backed by the Muslim Brotherhood, a terrorist organization. [52] Morsi's election ushered in radical Islamic change to Egypt, including the oppressive and brutal practice of Sharia law.

These unpopular events provoked massive protests, violence, and civil unrest throughout Egypt. On December 5, 2012, hundreds of thousands of people in opposition to Morsi clashed with his supporters, in what some described as the largest and most violent civil battle in Egypt since the revolution began. [53] On July 3, 2013, as public dissensions escalated and intensified because of the fundamentalist Muslim Brotherhood government, the Egyptian military removed Mohamed Morsi from power via a coup d'état.[54]

On January 18, 2014, the Egyptian interim government instituted a new constitution, which was supported by 98 percent of the Egyptian citizens in a referendum. [55] On March 26, 2014, Abdel Fattah el-Sisi, who was at the time the head of the Egyptian armed forces that was controlling the country, announced his candidacy for president. [56] On June 8, 2014, el-Sisi, who won by a landslide, was sworn into office as president of Egypt, and he currently holds this position. [57]

In summary, the Egyptian Revolution produced two government regime changes, because the Egyptian citizens asserted their God-given rights and protested for freedom, dignity, and justice. However, in the aftermath of the brutal military coup in July 2013, and during president el-Sisi's reign, the Egyptian government has imprisoned forty thousand political opponents, participated in hundreds of alleged extrajudicial killings, and continued multiple mass killings of protestors. [58] Terror attacks have also intensified in Egypt during Sisi's reign. On April 9, 2017, two ISIS suicide bombers attacked two Coptic Christian churches at Palm Sunday services in Alexandria and Tanta, leaving forty-six people dead. [59] On May 26, 2017, ten Islamic gunmen opened fire on a bus and killed twenty-eight Coptic Christians, as the civil unrest continues its course.[60] Since Mubarak's reign in 2011 (Arab Spring), persecution and discrimination against Egypt's Coptic Christians has tremendously spiked, causing great concern of the current government's stability under el-Sisi. Interestingly enough, Egypt is one of the three kings that Daniel prophesied the Antichrist would conquer (Dan. 11:42–43). Is Egypt primed for his taking?

> Isaiah 19:4, "And the Egyptians I will give into the hand of a cruel master [Antichrist], and a fierce king [Antichrist] will rule over them."

SUDAN (ONE OF THE THREE KINGS CONQUERED BY THE ANTICHRIST)

Since 1955, Sudan has been submerged in three civil wars, the first from 1955 to 1972; the second from 1983 to 2005; which is one of the longest civil wars on record, and the latest battle began in 2013 and it continues today. Needless to say, a country in such volatility and bedlam will continue to have major problems with governmental anarchy, civilian unrest, and terrorism. The Second Sudanese Civil War, which basically was a continuation of the First Sudanese Civil War, rivaled the central Sudanese government and the Sudan People's Liberation Army against one another. Although the war originated in South Sudan, it expanded to the Nuba mountains and Blue Nile, and it culminated with the independence of South Sudan six years after the war ended. Now, let us fast-forward to the most recent civil war in Sudan.

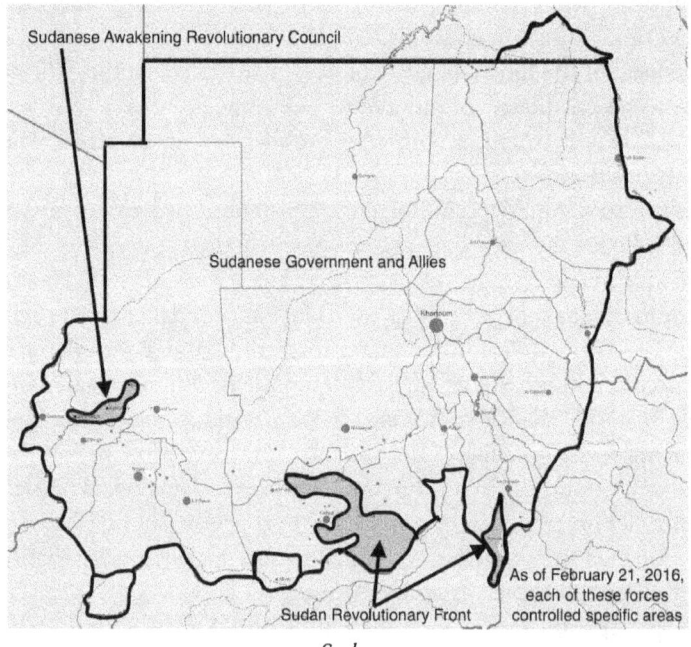

Sudan

In December 2013, during the Arab Spring, a conflict developed within the Sudan People's Liberation Movement when President Kiir accused former deputy Riek Machar and others of attempting a coup d'etat. [61] Eventually, Machar started an opposition movement against the Sudan People's Liberation Movement, which was referred to as the Sudan People's Liberation Movement-In Opposition. [62] It was also known as the anti-governmental forces (AGF). As tensions escalated and intensified, South Sudan became ignited in yet another civil war. [63] Although there have been ceasefire and peace agreements signed, the South Sudanese civil war has continued its bloody path. [64] An estimated 300,000 people have been killed in this war, and more than 3.5 million people out of 12 million have been dislodged from their homes. [65] [66] Approximately 2.1 million have found refuge within the borders of Sudan, while 1.5 million have fled to neighboring countries. [67] The Sudanese refugees account for the world's third largest refugee population (Syria, Afghanistan). As the civil war rages in the agricultural fields of South Sudan, approximately six million people are facing starvation, because famine has devoured the land. [68] In fact, in February 2017, the Unity State by the government and the United Nations declared Sudan a famine country. [69]

In summary, the South Sudanese Civil War continues to validate the escalated anarchy, instability, and chaos of the Middle East and North African regions, which is the principal focus of the end-of-the-age events. The prophet Daniel specifically mentions Sudan, along with Egypt and Libya, as the three countries the Antichrist conquers at the end of the age (Dan. 11:42–43). Please note, in Daniel 11, ancient Ethiopia is modern-day Sudan (Cush). Is Sudan primed for his taking?

LEBANON (HEZBOLLAH)

As Lebanon is a bitter rival and enemy of its southern neighbor, Israel, it is paramount to understand their past wars in order to give us knowledge of the current geopolitical and religious climate of the country. In 1982, Israel invaded Lebanon after the Palestinian Liberation Organization (PLO), which operated in southern Lebanon, made several attacks on civilians in both Israel and Lebanon. [70] Additionally, after a failed attempt to assassinate Shlomo Argov, Israel's ambassador to the United Kingdom, an Israeli military operation was launched into Lebanon. [71] After the invasion, the Israeli Defense Forces (IDF), in cooperation with the Free Lebanon State and Maronite allies, occupied southern Lebanon. Subsequently, the PLO relocated its headquarters to Tripoli, Libya. Once the PLO was expunged from Lebanon, and with the implementation of a pro-Israeli Christian government under the leadership of President Bachir Gemayel, Israel optimistically hoped to sign a forty-year peace treaty. [72]

Lebanon

However, with the emergence of Hezbollah, a Shia Islamist terror group, who was conceived by Muslim clerics to harass Israeli occupation of southern Lebanon, the forty-year peace treaty was suspended. [73] Former Israeli prime minister Ehud Barak declared, "When we entered Lebanon . . . there was no Hezbollah. We were accepted with perfumed rice and flowers by the Shia in the south. It was our presence there that created Hezbollah." [74] During the war, Hezbollah not only used guerilla warfare tactics, but they also performed suicide attacks against Israeli Defense Forces (IDF) and Israeli targets outside of Lebanon. [75] Once Israeli-ally President Gemayel was assassinated in September 1982, Israel's position in Lebanon became unsustainable, which culminated in the eventual withdrawal of Israeli soldiers from Lebanon on May 24, 2000. Afterward, Hezbollah held a victory parade and celebrated, proclaiming this as a great moment for its movement.[76] Unfortunately, since that time, the militant group's popularity has soared in Lebanon.

In 2006, Hezbollah paramilitary forces and the IDF battled once again for thirty-four days (July 12–August 14). The conflict ensued after Hezbollah precipitated a cross border raid, where they kidnapped and killed Israeli soldiers. The terror group also fired rockets into the Israeli border, killing three, injuring two, and seizing two Israeli soldiers.[77] Israel responded with airstrikes on targets in Lebanon that damaged Lebanese infrastructure with an air and naval blockade,[78] a ground invasion in southern Lebanon, and an attack on Beirut's airport, which Israel believed Hezbollah used to import weapons and supplies from Iran and others.[79] Hezbollah responded by launching more rockets into northern Israel and engaging the IDF in guerilla warfare.[80] A ceasefire agreement ended the war on August 14, 2006.

From Hezbollah's prominent rise to power in the 1980's unto today, the terror group proceeds to persistently forge its political, military, and religious dominance in Lebanon, which is described as the "Lebanonisation of Hezbollah." The extreme militant group has also consistently participated in elections, and they won all twelve seats on its electoral list in 1992. Clearly, as of today, Hezbollah has supreme influence over Lebanon. In an interview during the 2006 Lebanon War, then Lebanese president Emile Lahoud proclaimed, "Hezbollah enjoys utmost prestige in Lebanon, because it freed our country . . . Even though it is very small, it stands up to Israel."[81] Hezbollah has been described as a "state within a state," and its organization has political seats in the Lebanese government, a satellite TV station, radio, and a military.[82]

Hezbollah receives their weapons, financial support, and military training mostly from Iran (Shia), as it follows the Shia fundamentalist theology of the late Ayatollah Khomeini (Iran) in order to spread the Islamic revolution.[83] Iran has invested billions of dollars in restructuring Hezbollah (Lebanon) to limit the power of current leader Hassan Nasrallah.[84] In 2010, Iran's parliamentary speaker, Ali Larijani, stated, "Iran takes pride in Lebanon's Islamic resistance movement for its steadfast Islamic stance. Hezbollah nurtures the original ideas of Islamic Jihad." It is reported Iran invested $400 million in Hezbollah between 1983 and 1989, and in 2010 alone, it gave Hezbollah an astonishing $400 million. Other estimates declare Iran gives Hezbollah an average of $100–200 million a year.[85] Former Israeli defense minister Moshe Ya'alon declares, "There is no nation called Lebanon, the decisions are made by Iran and not by the president or Nasrallah," [86] which again, validates Iran's dominance over the region, including Lebanon (Hezbollah), as it is spreads its "Shia Crescent."

In summary, from the birth of Hezbollah, its prominent and ultimate goal has been to exterminate Israel. In fact, Hezbollah's 1985 charter proclaims, "Our struggle will end only when this entity [Israel] is obliterated."[87] According to Hezbollah's deputy-general, Na'im Qasim, the destruction of Israel is the core belief and the central principle of Hezbollah's existence. [88] In 2017, Hezbollah chief Hassan Nasrallah called for a "cleansing of Jews from Israel," and continued to declare "the Jews should leave Israel as they will have no secure place in occupied Palestine." [89] Most certainly, Hezbollah has assisted Iran, and others, in the regional chaos, terror, and war that has engulfed the Middle East region.

SYRIA

On March 15, 2011 (Arab Spring), the Syrian civil war ignited and feverishly escalated and intensified in 2014–2015 (blood moon tetrad). As of 2017, the civil war continues its bloody path of war, terror, chaos, and civilian unrest and displacement. The Syrian civil war manifested as its citizen's discontentment for their basic human rights of expression, association, and assembly, continued to heighten with the Assad regime. [90] The massive uprising of protestors and demonstrators alleged Assad failed to substantially improve the state of human rights since taking power in 2000. [91] Eventually, the citizen's protests and demonstrations accelerated into a perpetual military conflict that has decimated the historical enriched land of Syria. The conflict primarily rivals Syrian president Bashar al-Assad's government, along with his major allies, Russia, Iran, Hezbollah, and Hamas, against various rebels and countries, including, the United States, Saudi Arabia, Turkey, ISIS, the Kurds (SDF), and the Free Syrian Army (FSA).

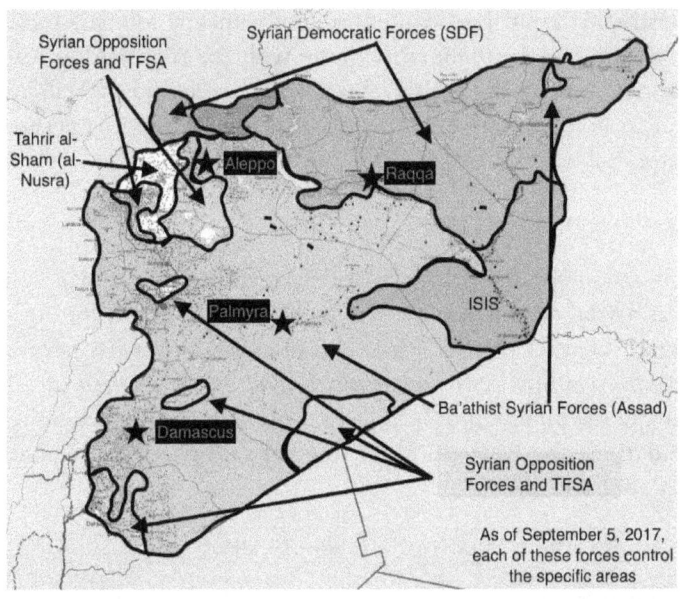

Syria

The Syrian civil war has inflicted brutal living conditions on its citizens, inspiring international organizations to accuse Assad's government, ISIS, and the rebel groups of severe human rights violations. [92] In fact, the Syrian conflict holds the world record for the largest sum of money ever requested for a single humanitarian emergency, which reached an astonishing $6.5 billion as of December 2013. [93] However, with the perpetuation of vicious warfare throughout the country, along with the dislodgement of its citizens, it has been a critical challenge to connect humanitarian aid workers with those who are in desperate need. As of February 2016, the accumulated death toll was estimated at 500,000. [94]

The consequential, tragic results of the massive bloodshed, violence, and lawlessness in Syria has produced an exceedingly great refugee movement from the bloodthirsty country. Keep in mind, after the fall of Iraq, 1.5 million Iraqi refugees migrated to Syria. As of March 2015 (blood moon tetrad), an estimated 10.9 million Syrians, almost half of the population, have been dislodged, as an estimated 3.8 million became refugees. [95] Lebanon has received approximately 700,000 refugees, and Turkey has been the most hospitable, accepting 1.7 million in 2015. [96]

In summary, the Syrian civil war has decimated the country into lawlessness, war, and terrorism, as the country's soul hangs in the balance.

This catastrophic event has resulted in approximately four million refugees seeking asylum in other countries. Along with the Arab Spring refugees in neighboring countries, the Syrian refugee crisis has created an Arab migration like no other in recent history, as many escape the horrors of a persistent and destructive civil war.

TURKEY

Turkey is a transcontinental country that is strategically and prophetically located as a vital centerpiece betwixt the Middle East and Europe. Turkey is a natural gateway between the two continents, and it has been an open and clear passage for the Syrian refugees, *and others*, to *flood* into Europe. According to the biblical prophets, Turkey plays an extremely significant role at the end of the age, which includes Jeremiah's prophecy of the hunters (See Dan. 2, 7, 8, Ezek. 38–39).

Turkey

After the fall of the Ottoman Empire in 1923, under the leadership of Mustafa Kemal Ataturk, the Republic of Turkey instituted radical reforms from its tyrannical constitutional monarchy, including the transformation of its fundamentalist Islamic rule. Unfortunately, approximately eighty years later, under the leadership of former prime minister and current president Recep Tayyip Erdogan and his party, the AKP Party (2001–), Turkey has been revolutionized into its former authoritarian state. Erdogan has reversed many of the secular reforms implemented by Ataturk since the founding of the Republic of Turkey (1923), such as limiting freedom of speech, freedom of the press, a legislative system of checks and balances, and a set of standards for secularism in government. [97] The AKP Party and Erdogan's leadership has been described as becoming increasingly authoritarian, which has led to governmental anarchy, chaos, and civilian unrest and insecurity in the onetime secular nation. [98] In fact, before Turkey's constitutional referendum of April 2017, which was a vote to change the parliamentary system to a presidential system (dictatorship), the Council of Europe warned of a "dramatic regression of its democratic order." [99] Erdogan won the 2017 referendum, and he now has "sweeping executive powers" in Turkey, which will lead to the fall of Turkish democracy and the birth of a dictator. [100] Many critics have accused Erdogan of striving to become an Ottoman sultan (dictator) and eliminate the secular and democratic principles of the republic, which suggests democracy cannot flourish under Erdogan. [101] On June 22, 2016, the Parliamentary Assembly of the Council of Europe warned in its resolution, "the functioning of democratic institutions in Turkey, recent developments in Turkey pertaining to freedom of the media and of expression, erosion of the rule of law and the human rights violations in relation to anti-terrorism security operations in south-east Turkey have . . . raised serious questions about the functioning of its democratic institutions." [102] In 2016, as he spoke about his constitutional reforms, Erdogan used Hitler and Nazi Germany as a great example of a model the sultan desires. [103] Furthermore, under Erdogan and the AKP Party, the old role of the Diyanet has been revived, which maintains control over Islam in Turkey, and it promotes a very conservative strict Sunni doctrine. [104] Erdogan's tyrannical rule has resulted in governmental anarchy, terror, chaos, and civilian unrest.

On May 27, 2013, in Istanbul, Turkish citizens summoned at Taksim Square during the Gezi Park demonstrations, protesting against Erdogan's authoritarianism and policies, which resulted in Turkey's largest protest in a decade, as it spread across the country. An estimated 3.5 million people protested, and approximately five thousand demonstrations escalated throughout Turkey. [105] Eleven people were killed; more than 8,000 were injured, many critically; and 3,000 were arrested. [106] After weeks of clashes between police and protestors, the Turkish government at first apologized to the protestors, but afterward ordered a crackdown on them. [107]

In July 2015, an ISIS suicide bomber killed thirty-three people in the Turkish town of Suruc, near Turkey's border with Syria. [108] In October 2015, two Muslim suicide bombers detonated explosives that killed more than one hundred people outside of Ankara's main train station. [109] On January 12, 2016, a Muslim suicide bomber in Istanbul's historic Sultanahmet district, near Blue Mosque and the Hagia Sophia, killed thirteen people, and injured fourteen others. [110] On June 28, 2016, at Ataturk Airport in Istanbul, three Muslim gunmen staged shootings and suicide bombings that killed forty-five people, injuring 230 others, as terror has become substantial in Turkey, as well. [111] In August 2017, three Muslim gunmen killed eighteen people at a Turkish restaurant in Burkina Faso. [112]

On July 15, 2016, a coup d'etat was attempted by the military to remove Erdogan from power. Nonetheless, by the following day, Erdogan's government had successfully reasserted itself with effective and total control over Turkey. [113] During the coup, more than 300 people were killed, 179 civilians, and more than 2,100 injured. [114] Many government buildings, including the Turkish Parliament and the presidential palace, were bombed from the air. [115] There is widespread suspicion that Erdogan staged the event for complete control and authority over Turkey, because no government official was arrested, which, among other factors, raised suspicion of a false flag event. [116] Erdogan and other government officials have alleged exiled cleric and former ally of Erdogan, Fethullah Gulen, for staging the coup. [117] Whatever the case may be, in the aftermath of the coup, Erdogan has striven to purged all perceived enemies from all aspects of Turkish society: the judicial and education systems, the media, civil groups, Gulen followers, and so on. [118] Just one year after the coup, Erdogan's government has arrested over 123,000 citizens, has fired over 145,000, removed nearly 9,000 academics, closed over 2,000 schools, arrested nearly 300 journalists, shut down an estimated 200 media outlets, and dismissed approximately 5,000 judges. [119] Without question, this is unparalleled in world history! Many of the world media have described the purges as a "counter-coup," expecting Erdogan to "become vengeful and obsessed with control more than ever, exploiting the crisis not just to punish mutinous soldiers but to further quash whatever dissent is left in Turkey." [120] Clearly, Erdogan and the AKP Party "is the biggest media boss in Turkey." [121]

On June 15, 2017, the leader of Turkey's largest opposition party to Erdogan, Kemal Kilicdaroglu, organized a twenty-three-day, 250-mile walk from Ankara to Istanbul, in protest of the dictator's widening crackdown on the Turkish people. [122] Kilicdaroglu declared, "Let the whole world hear, we are facing a dictatorial regime in Turkey, in our own land." Erdogan responded, "Everyone should know their place, no one wins a thing when they, on the one hand, say they respect the law and then go on the path of breaking the law . . . They won't win anything with this and on the contrary, it will make them lose." [123]

Since the commencement of the Syrian refugee crisis, Turkey has accepted approximately 3.4 million refugees from its southern neighbor, making it the host country with the largest refugee population in the world. [124] Unfortunately, 90 percent of the Syrian refugees in Turkey remain outside of camp settings, with limited access to basic services. The influx of Syrian refugees into Turkey, along with the lack of camps and services for their daily needs, have caused a tragic humanitarian crisis, which has resulted in millions of refugees leaving the country for Europe, via the "natural gateway of Turkey."

Cunningly, Erdogan has exploited the refugee crisis as a tool for negotiating deals against Europe, including Turkey's EU accession. In February 2016, the dictator threatened to send millions of refugees from Turkey to EU member states, declaring, "We're not idiots . . . We can open the doors to Greece and Bulgaria anytime and we can put the refugees on buses . . . So how will you deal with refugees if you don't get a deal? Kill the refugees?" [125] In response, on March 11, 2016, the German minister of defense, Ursula von der Leyen, stated the refugee crisis had made good cooperation between the EU and Turkey an "existentially important" issue. "Therefore it is right to advance now negotiations on Turkey's EU accession." [126] Furthermore, since Erdogan obtained power in Turkey, he has built 17,000 Islamic prayer sites in Germany, and Turkey controls 900 mosques in the infamous Nazi country. [127]

In summary, the once-secular Turkey is being tragically transformed into its old tyrannical Ottoman Empire ways, resulting in governmental anarchy, civilian protests, terror, and overall chaos and insecurity. Regardless of Erdogan's "leverage" with the Syrian and Iraqi refugees, millions of Muslim refugees have already infiltrated Europe, by way of ships and boats from North Africa, or via Turkey's natural gateway. If Turkey's refugee camps do not become effective and sufficient enough for the refugees to live and participate in everyday activities, along with Erdogan's diabolic plans, we can have confidence they will continue to migrate through the natural passage of Turkey into Europe.

Turkey, which is Daniel's third prophesied kingdom that will follow Medo-Persia (Iran), is tremendously rising to fulfill its prophetic calling (Dan. 2,7,8). In an article on the Gatestone Institute website, Uzay Bulut, a journalist who was born in Turkey and raised Muslim, wrote: "Given the political developments in Turkey for more than a decade, the country seems to be fast-forwarding to be the second – and possibly even more dangerous version of – the Islamic Republic of Iran." [128]

THE CATACLYSMIC AFTERMATH OF THE FINAL IMPLOSION OF THE MIDDLE EAST AND NORTH AFRICA

Have the chaos, terror, and war in the Middle East and North African regions ignited Satan's *end-of-the-age* hunters? Has the refugee migration from the Middle East and North African regions into Europe been infiltrated with Satan's *end-of-the-age* hunters? Was the 2014–2015 blood moon tetrad a warning sign and marker that Satan's *end-of-the-age* hunters have been released into Europe? If so, has it resulted in a Jewish Aliyah to the Promised Land, continuing to fulfill the mystery of Aliyah (blood moon tetrads), Jeremiah's prophecy of the fishermen and the hunters, and ultimately, God's everlasting covenants?

Since 2003 (Iraq) through 2011–2014 (Arab Spring), and beyond, the cataclysmic aftermath of the governmental anarchy, civilian unrest, war, terror, and lawlessness in the Middle East and North African regions continues to be very substantial and extreme in all aspects. These prophetic events have created great uncertainty of stable leadership in both regions that has allowed terrorist organizations such as ISIS, Hamas, Hezbollah, al-Qaeda, and others, to significantly organize, stabilize, and terrorize the region.

As previously discussed, as ISIS's caliphate has become inexistent, the terror group still remains a substantial threat in Europe. According to a recent report in 2017, the barbaric group has sent a vast number of extremists into Europe to carry out deadly attacks: [129]

- According to an unnamed report, a secretive unit of the Islamic State has been training British fighters to carry out terror attacks in the UK. This is the same unit that trained the jihadists behind the Paris and Brussels attacks.
- A fighter of the Islamic State—also known as IS, ISIS, ISIL, or Daesh—captured by Kurdish forces in Syria "revealed that a group known as the al-Kharsa brigade has inducted European would-be suicide bombers and subjected them to a grueling training program at a secret camp in Syria before sending them home to carry out attacks," according to the *London Times*. "It takes seven months to be trained in al-Kharsa brigade," the

fighter explained. "It is very hard. Every European who crosses the border to Syria, they are offered [the opportunity] to join. If 20 start the training, only five finish it. Then after that they go back to Europe and attack." About four dozen people from countries, including the UK, Belgium, France, and Germany, have gone through the training, he said. Recruits learn bomb-making skills, along with training in ISIS religious ideology and physical endurance. All recruits must be willing to die for the ISIS cause.

- According to Gilles de Kerchove, the EU's counterterrorism coordinator, one-third of an estimated five thousand European jihadists who were trained in Syria and Iraq have returned to their home countries. Authorities have not been able to detect many of them. In May 2017, British intelligence officers said the UK is home to twenty-three thousand jihadist extremists, all of whom are potential attackers.[130]

Additionally, Iran, a terrorist nation, which supports Hamas (Gaza) and Hezbollah (Lebanon), and Turkey and Saudi Arabia, which supports ISIS, as well as other militant organizations, have seized this opportunity to proliferate propaganda and terror not only across the Middle East and North African regions, but also into Europe in a horrific and devastating way. Make no mistake: The Middle East and North African regions have ignited their final implosion before the return of Yeshua the Messiah at His second coming, and the *aftershocks* have tremored into Europe.

THE ALIYAH OF 2014–2015 (BLOOD MOONS) FROM EUROPE

From this point forward and through chapter 8, we will explore the consequential aftermath of the final implosion of the Middle East and North Africa as it pertains to Europe and America, as they inhabit the second (America) and third (Europe) largest populations of Jewish people in the world.

Now, let us remember that in 2014–2015, the *ninth* blood moon tetrad of the last two thousand years appeared on the Lord's feast days, which indicates "finality, completeness, conclusion, and the end of a matter." Did the 2014–2015 blood moon tetrad follow the pattern of the previous three blood moon tetrads in the last five hundred years (1493–1494, 1949–1950, 1967–1968), which resulted in an Aliyah of the children of Israel because of *persecution*? Was the blood moon tetrad a *marker and sign* for the release of Satan's *end-of-the-age hunters*, just as the 1949–1950 tetrad released God's *end-of-the-age* fishermen?

Before we commence, let me be very clear that I am not suggesting or implying that *all* Muslim refugees have bad intentions, because many are kind, loving, and gracious people. I am using the phrase "Islamic flood" in reference to the Islamic extremists who have infiltrated the refugee migration into Europe.

Since 2014, as approximately 2.5 million Middle Eastern and North African refugees flooded into Europe, many of whom were truly seeking asylum from war and terror in their respective countries, many Islamic extremists have infiltrated the migration, as well. [131] The barbaric group ISIS claims it has sent thousands of jihadists into Europe posing as refugees, while they patiently wait for their leader's command to attack. In fact, an ISIS leader, speaking on the condition of anonymity, declared, "There are now more than 4,000 covert ISIS gunmen ready across the European Union." [132] We can have confidence that other militant Islamic groups have also infiltrated the "open borders" of the European countries as they eagerly wait for the opportune time to attack.

Regrettably, the old anti-Semitic ghost is also rising again in Europe, but this time, it is compounded by the Islamic refugees' hatred for the Jewish people. Since the Islamic flood into Europe (2014–2015—blood moons), there has been a clear, yet disturbing rise in anti-Semitic behavior against the children of Israel. According to a study by Hanns Seidel Foundation, "more than half of Muslim asylum seekers showed clear tendencies of an anti-Semitic attitude pattern, which is anchored in the educational system of the refugees' countries of origin." [133]

In several European countries, there have been numerous terrorist attacks on each country's soil, including vigorous verbal and physical assaults on the Jewish people, as Europe breathes life into its dark and gloomy past. Dieter Graumann, president of Germany's Central Council of Jews, exasperatedly stated, "These are the worst times since the Nazi era," and, "It's an outbreak of hatred against Jews so intense that it's very clear indeed." [134] The Islamic flood into Europe has transformed and will continue to transform the continent into a persistent cultural, political, and religious debacle. In 2014, Philip Carmel, European policy director for the European Jewish Congress, declared, "The Middle East is being imported into Europe." [135]

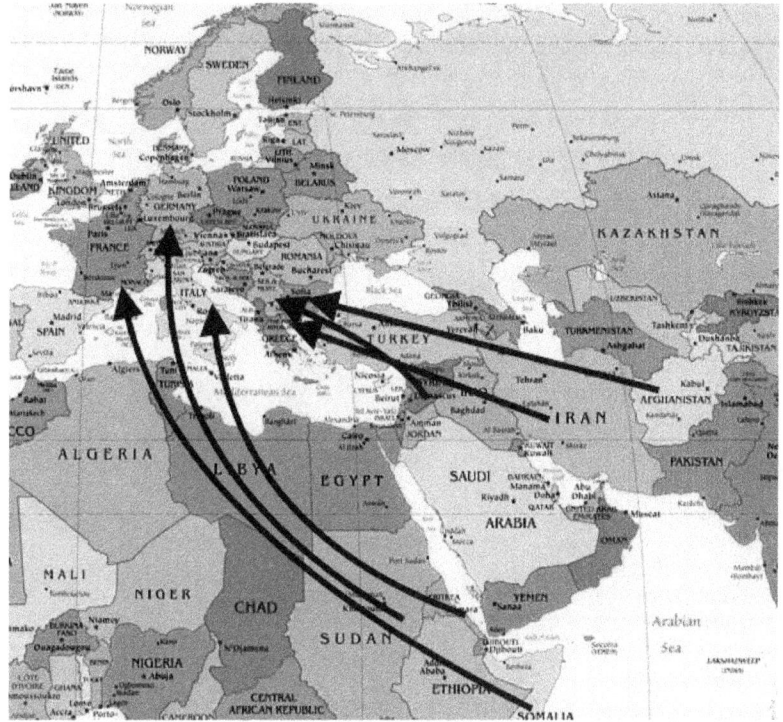

Islamic Flood

A report by researchers at Tel Aviv University showed a 40 percent increase in anti-Semitic attacks across the world in 2014 (blood moons), with European countries headlining the list. [136] The country with the most transgressions was France, who inhabits the third largest Jewish population in the world, but there were also sharp rises in anti-Semitic violence in the United Kingdom, Germany, Austria, Italy, and Sweden. It is not by chance or coincidence that these six countries are in the top ten places where the Muslim refugees sought asylum in Europe.

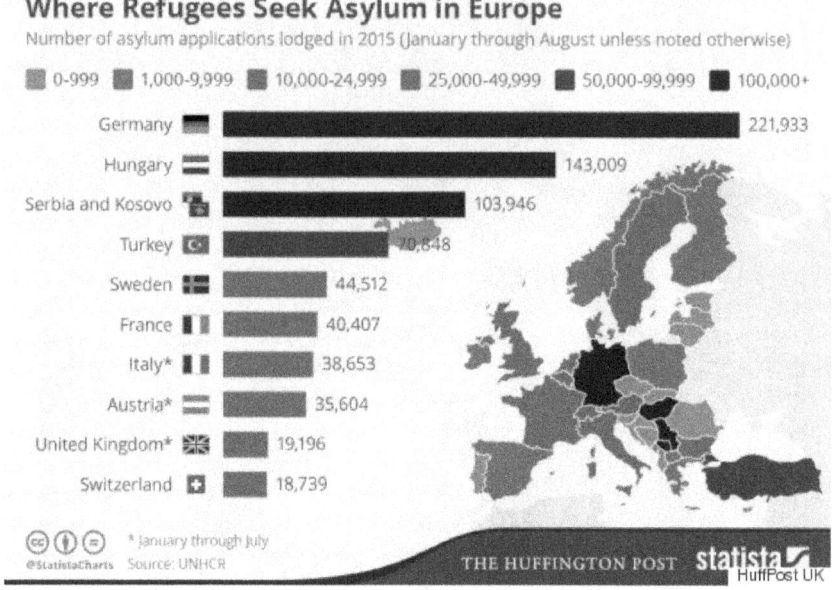

Top Ten Places

Israel's U.N. envoy Danny Danon proclaimed to the United Nations that hatred of Jews and the demonization of Israel are at "the highest level of our lifetimes," and "over one-third of European Jews are afraid to wear a yarmulke or Star of David in public." Danon finished by declaring, "Today we hear things about Jews and the Jewish people that we thought belonged to the pages of history . . . Anti-Semitism is returning to everyday life without shame." [137]

Now, let us explore the Islamic pandemic in Europe by discovering some of the major attacks in the countries, beginning with France, which is the country that has endured the majority of the terrorist attacks since 2014 (blood moons), as Satan's *end-of-the-age* hunters were released.

FRANCE

On July, 20, 2014 (blood moons), in Sarcelles, France, a riot broke out at a pro-Palestinian (Muslim) protest only a few blocks away from a Jewish synagogue. A Jewish pharmacy was destroyed by Muslims, who were protesting Israel's military campaign in Gaza. [138] On January 7, 2015 (blood moons), a shooting massacre occurred at the offices of satirical magazine *Charlie Hebdo* in Paris, which published a cartoon depicting Islam's prophet, Muhammad, naked and crouching. The Muslim gunmen shouted, "We have avenged the prophet Muhammad," and also screamed, "Allahu Akbar" (Allah is great), as twelve people were being shot and killed. [139] The shooting spree continued into the Paris suburb of Montrouge when one of the connected gunmen killed a policewoman. The "three-day wave of terror" in Paris concluded at the Jewish Hyper Cacher supermarket, where four Jewish people were killed by Muslim extremists.[140]

On November 13, 2015, one of the largest terrorist attacks in recent European history occurred in "the city of love." Three groups of Muslims, one with a Syrian passport, inflicted carnage upon Paris, killing 129 people and wounding another 352, of which 99 of these were critical. [141] These tragic events took place at a concert hall, in cafés, in restaurants, and in the open streets, all in the name of Islamic jihad.[142]

On July 14, 2016, in Nice, France, a Tunisian Muslim plowed a nineteen–ton refrigerated truck into a massive crowd of people along a span of 1.4 miles, killing 86 people and injuring 434. [143] On February 3, 2017, Paris was the recipient of another terrorist attack on its soil, but this time at the renowned Louvre Museum. While attempting to enter the Louvre, an Egyptian Muslim man raged toward a group of French soldiers, shouting, "Allahu Akbar," attacking and injuring one soldier with a machete. [144] On October 1, 2017, French police killed a Muslim man who stabbed two innocent young women after shouting "Allahu Akbar" in Marseille's train station. [145]

Since 2014 (blood moons), sixty-two terrorist attacks have occurred in France, resulting in 251 deaths and 625 injured people. All of these evil acts were perpetrated by Muslims, who have stabbed, shot, beheaded, and used vehicles and explosives to commit jihad against not only the Jewish people, but also Christians and anyone who does not follow their demonic theology of Islam. Have these horrendous events in France provoked a Jewish Aliyah to the Promised Land, validating Jeremiah's prophecy of the hunters?

After the Paris terror attacks in 2014, a Jewish Agency affiliated think tank prepared a plan to help 120,000 French Jews emigrate to Israel. According to the Jewish Agency, in 2014, which was the first year of the blood moon tetrad, 7,239 Jews made Aliyah to Israel, compared to just 1,893 in 2011, 1,918 in 2012, and 3,298 in 2013. In 2015, the second year of the blood moon tetrad, 7,876 Jews made Aliyah to the Promised Land, followed by an additional 5,118 in 2016.[146] Please note, France has the third-largest Jewish population in the world (460,000), behind Israel and America.[147] Therefore, since the blood moon tetrad of 2014–2015, the Islamic invasion, terrorism, and anti-

Semitism that has occurred in France is consummating into the *beginning* of an enormous Jewish Aliyah to the Promised Land, which substantiates the everlasting covenants and Jeremiah's prophecy of the fishermen and hunters.

GERMANY

Germany has been one of the largest advocates for the resettlement of Middle Eastern and North African refugees into Europe, and it has received an estimated one million into their country. [148] Alarmingly, Germany's Muslim population surpassed 6 million in 2016 for the first time, predominantly fueled by the country's open border refugee policy. [149] Leo Hohmann, author of *Stealth Invasion: Muslim Conquest Through Immigration and the Resettlement Jihad*, states, "Germany's future is an Islamic state that will be completed within the next 10 to 20 years." He continued, "In many ways, Germany is already conquered by Islam, as Islam is afforded special favor that other religions do not enjoy."[150] Historian Walter Laqueur wrote in his book The Last Days of Europe that "Germany had some 700 little mosques and prayer rooms in the 1980s, but there are more than 2,500 at the present time." [151]As of 2017, the consequences of the Islamic flood and refugee absorption have been grim and disastrous, to say the least.

In June 2014, three Muslims carried out an arson attack (firebombs) on a Jewish synagogue in Wuppertal, Germany. [152] In July 2014, in response to Israeli operations in Gaza, Muslims attacked Jewish synagogues in Berlin, Germany. [153] The extremists also smashed windows of Jewish-owned businesses and torched others, while chanting, "Jews to the gas chambers," and "Jew! We'll get you," and "Hamas, Hamas, Jews to the Gas." [154] On December 22, 2014, a Muslim man shouting, "Allahu Akbar," purposely hit ten innocent pedestrians in his van at the Christmas market of Nantes, killing one person and injuring ten. [155]

In the country infamously known for its Nazism, anti-Semitic Muslims have also attacked Jewish people on the streets. These evil acts coincided with a sermon of an imam in a Berlin mosque who allegedly called on Muslims to murder Jews in 2014. [156] On July 22, 2016, an Iranian Muslim killed nine people and injured thirty-six in a mass shooting attack in Munich, Germany. [157] On December 19, 2016, a Tunisian Muslim stole a semi-trailer truck, killed its driver, and drove into a crowd of people at Breitscheidplatz in Berlin, killing twelve and injuring fifty-six others. [158] On July 28, 2017, a Muslim man shouting "Allahu Akbar" used a machete to kill a man and injure six other people at a supermarket in Hamburg, Germany. [159] On July 30, 2017, an Iraqi Muslim shot and killed one person and injured three others at the grey nightclub in Konstanz, Germany. [160]

Since 2014 (blood moon tetrad), the horrendous carnage in Germany has prompted German chancellor Angela Merkel to regretfully state, "If it was possible, I would go back in time many, many years in order to be able to better prepare myself, the government and those who are responsible for this situation which struck us relatively unexpected last summer" (2015). [161] Unfortunately, hindsight is twenty-twenty.

Sadly, German women have also been under extreme duress as a result of the Islamic flood. During the 2015–2016 New Year Eve celebrations, Germany had twenty-four alleged rapes and 1,200 women were sexually assaulted by an estimated 2,000 Muslim men. [162] Please note, in some Arab countries, this sickening behavior is called *"taharrush jamai/gamea,"* or group sexual harassment. [163] German chief prosecutor Ulrich Bremer declared, "The overwhelming majority" of suspects were illegal immigrants and asylum seekers who had recently arrived in Germany. [164]

The anti-Semitic overtone in Germany has even reached Angela Merkel's political party (CDU), as Werner Mroz had to resign from his position after declaring, "Jews are crap" (expletive removed). [165] Additionally, in June 2017, Berlin mayor Michael Muller permitted approximately six hundred Hezbollah members and supporters to march and protest at the al-Quds Day rally, which calls for the destruction of Israel, in the heart of Berlin. A spokesman for the cowardly mayor stated, "The mayor does not comment on representatives of foreign groups," which raises red flags to the government's tolerance of anti-Semitism of Islamic terrorist groups.[166]

Interestingly enough, Muslim "no-go zones" have been established in Germany all the way back to 1991. Charles Sasser, author of *Crushing the Collective: The Last Chance to Keep America Free and Self-Governing*, states, "There were no-go zones *then [1991]*, now imagine what's happened since then. I mean, [1991] was a long time ago. Now they've got no-go zones everywhere." [167]

Without question, all of the German citizens are reaping the aftermath of the reckless and irresponsible decisions of the German government to open its borders, while only using elementary vetting procedures on the refugees to distinguish the good asylum seekers from the evildoers. Anti-Semitism in Germany is dangerously rising again from its dark shadows of old, and it will vastly increase with the influx of Muslim refugees into the country. Although not all of the attacks have been directed towards the Jewish people, there is a clear and overall anti-Semitic attitude and behavior in Germany, which will continue to escalate the Jewish Aliyah from the country and continue to fulfill Jeremiah's prophecy and the everlasting covenants.

BELGIUM

Belgium is another country in the European Union that has witnessed anti-Semitic violence and terrorist attacks as a result of the Islamic flood into Europe. On May 24, 2014 (blood moon), in the beautiful city of Brussels, a Muslim who fought as a jihadist in Syria, shot four Jewish people at a Jewish museum. [168] On July 16, 2014, at a Palestinian rally, Muslims chanted, "Death to the Jews!" and "Gas the Jews!" which sustains the anti-Semitic chant that has recently echoed throughout Europe. [169] On March 22, 2016, three coordinated suicide bombings by Muslim terrorists occurred in Belgium. One was at Maalbeek metro station in Brussels, and two were at the Brussels airport in Zaventem, which killed 32 people and injured 340 (62 critically), as the wave of terror relentlessly extends across the continent. [170]

AUSTRIA

Austria, which is the southern neighbor of Germany, and the country who gave the world Adolf Hitler, has seen its old anti-Semitic ghost begin to rise again, as well. Since the blood moon tetrad of 2014–2015 and the Islamic invasion, anti-Semitic incidents have drastically increased throughout the historically rich country. According to the Austrian Forum Against Anti-Semitism, which was presented by the Jewish Communities of Austria, anti-Semitic incidents have steadily increased 82 percent, with 255 incidents occurring in 2014, 465 in 2015, and 477 in 2016. [171] Amber Weinber, of the Austrian Forum Against Anti-Semitism, stated, "What we see is that racism [and anti-Semitism have become] more socially acceptable in Austria," and continued, "Since it has become more socially acceptable, people increasingly are posting [anti-Semitic messages] in their own name or sending letters with return addresses on them." [172]

On July 24, 2014, a friendly football match between Israel's Maccabi Haifa and a French team had to be called off after Muslim protestors stormed the field and fought with Israeli players. Afterwards, the Haifa captain, Yossi Benayoun, stated, "We had no choice but to defend ourselves." [173] The Muslims were protesting Israel's Operation Protective Edge against Gaza.

In 2017, a study published by the University of Teacher Education in Vienna revealed that almost 50 percent of young Austrian Muslims hold anti-Semitic views. Vienna sociologist Kenan Gungor declared there is an "imported anti-Semitism among Muslims in Austria with an established narrative toward Jews." The article continues to state that Austrian Muslims do not differentiate between Austrian Jews and Israeli Jews." [174]

SPAIN

As Islamic terrorism spreads like fire across the European continent, this evil doctrine has also directly impacted Europe's southwest country of Spain. On August 17, 2017, a Muslim man drove a van into pedestrians in Barcelona, Spain, killing thirteen people and injuring at least 130 others, one of whom died ten days later. [175] A few hours after the Barcelona attack, five Muslim men drove a vehicle into pedestrians in nearby Cambrils, killing one woman and injuring six others. [176] The terrorist attacks were the deadliest in Spain since the 2004 Madrid train bombings and the deadliest in Barcelona since the 1987 Hipercor bombing. [177]

These Islamic terror events inclined Barcelona's chief rabbi, Meir Bar-Hen, to emphasize to the Jewish people: "*Do not think we are here for good, buy property in Israel.*" He continued to declare, "This place is lost. Do not repeat the mistake of the Algerian Jews, of Venezuelan Jews. Better get out early than late. Europe is lost, go to Israel [Aliyah]." [178] Meir Bar-Hen has a very valid point, because demographically, the Muslim population in Spain has exponentially increased from one hundred thousand in 1990 to two million in 2017. [179] Just by pure statistics, there is a highly calculated chance that Islamic terrorism will continue to explode in Spain.

UNITED KINGDOM

The United Kingdom, which is located in the far northwest of Europe, has also witnessed the devastating effects of the refugee flood during the blood moon tetrad of 2014–2015, which confirms the widespread effects of the Islamic pandemic. In 2016, the Campaign Against Anti-Semitism published a report stating anti-Semitic crime in the United Kingdom had reached a record level in 2015. [180] It reported there was a 26 percent increase in anti-Semitic crime, and a 51 percent increase in violent anti-Semitic attacks, surpassing the previous record in 2014 (blood moon tetrad). [181] The Community Security Trust also published a report that indicated a significant increase in anti-Semitic incidents during 2014 in the United Kingdom, more than twice as many than the previous year. [182]

In the first half of 2017, it was reported that 767 anti-Semitic incidents occurred, a 30 percent increase from 589 in the first six months of 2016, the highest total ever recorded, leading chief executive of the Community Security Trust David Delew to proclaim, "It is sadly clear that the overall situation has deteriorated." He continued, "Anti-Semitism is having an increasing impact on the lives of British Jews and the hatred and anger that lies behind is spreading." [183] Since the extreme rise of anti-Semitism in the United Kingdom, according to a new survey by the Campaign Against Anti-Semitism, it is documented that one in three British Jews have considered leaving the country (Aliyah) over safety concerns. Additionally, four out of ten of them hide their faith due to fear of getting attacked for being Jewish. [184] Now let us review some of the terror attacks that have recently occurred in the United Kingdom.

On August 4, 2016, a Somali Muslim killed a woman and injured five in a knife attack near a British museum. [185] On March 22, 2017, in the vicinity of the Palace of Westminster in London, a Muslim man drove a car into pedestrians along the south side of Westminster Bridge, killing 5 people, and injuring 50. [186] In the wave of these anti-Semitic crime reports and terror attacks, Mark Raoli, head of Britain's counterterrorism unit, declared, "The picture of global terror is cause for concern for the Jewish neighborhoods in Britain. We are witnessing continuous anti-Semitic rhetoric from the extremists, as well as attacks against the Jews." [187]

On May 22, 2017, a Muslim man detonated a bomb following a concert at the Manchester Arena in Manchester, England, killing 23 people and injuring 119 (23 critically). [188] [189] On June 3, 2017, three Muslim men killed 8 people and injured dozens more when they plowed a rented van into pedestrians on the London Bridge, and afterward, stabbed people at the Borough Market area. [190] On September 15, 2017, ISIS claimed responsibility for a terror attack on the London metro, which injured 22 people. [191] Most certainly, the United Kingdom's trials and tribulations with anti-Semitic behavior and terrorist attacks perpetuates the cataclysmic trend of the Islamic flood into Europe.

It is worthy to note as of May 9, 2016, London received its first Muslim mayor, Sadiq Khan (British Pakistani), who is also the first Muslim mayor of a major Western capital. Amazingly enough, Khan held the largest personal mandate of any politician within the United Kingdom, and he had the third-largest mandate in Europe (France, Portugal) [192] Khan has been described as a center-left social democrat and a moderate Muslim. [193]

Nevertheless, you cannot judge a book by its cover, and Sadiq Khan could be dire kryptonite for the city of London. According to an investigation by Disobedient Media, they discovered Khan has ties to ISIS, Hamas, Al-Nusra, Al-Qaeda, the Taliban, the Muslim Brotherhood, and to prominent, but radical Muslim imams and leaders. [194] In fact, the Muslim mayor of London faced deep criticism for refusing to designate Hezbollah as a terrorist organization. [195] After reluctantly wavering and buckling to political pressure, Khan did finally support Hezbollah's full designation as a terrorist organization. [196] Interestingly enough, the Muslim mayor did set up a task force to jail those who "annoy" Muslims online. [197]

Disturbingly, Khan also served as a consultant for convicted 9/11 plotter Zacarius Moussaoui, and it was later reported that he was the only practicing Muslim on Moussaoui's defense team.[198] In 2009, as Khan was interviewed by Iranian Press TV, he referred to moderate Muslims and groups who commonly lead the fight against Islamic extremism as "Uncle Toms." [199] In September 2016, after the New York and New Jersey bombings that injured 35 people, Khan stated the threats of terrorist attacks are "part and parcel of life in a big city," and, "western civilization must live with terrorism as part of daily life." [200] During his time as mayor, London has seen an increase in terror incidents, especially in 2017. With Britain hopefully seceding from the European Union by April 2019 (Brexit), and as terror persists its dark and tragic course in London and the United Kingdom, it will be very interesting to watch how the Brits respond in the voting booth in regard to Sadiq Khan.

OTHER EUROPEAN COUNTRIES THAT HAVE SEEN A RISE IN ANTI-SEMITISM

As the Islamic flood expands throughout the four corners of Europe, other countries have been tremendously affected with this pandemic, as well. Denmark, Sweden, Finland, Italy, Ukraine, Poland, the Netherlands, and others, have reported anti-Semitic attacks and incidents on Jewish people, synagogues, businesses, sporting events, and schools. This evil behavior has resulted in the closing of some of the Jewish synagogues, businesses, and schools. Anti-Semitic incidents have included hate speech, threatening emails, social media bullying, Nazi Swastika graffiti on public walls, and the list goes on and on. Incredibly, there are also "no-go zones" for non-Muslims on full display in Germany, France, Belgium, Italy, Spain, Sweden, and the United Kingdom. [201]

Without question, Europe's soul is hanging in the balance, while its leaders decide how to strategically resolve the Islamic flood and the horrific increase of terror resulting from the cultural implementation. Needless to say, if European leaders keep bowing down to Islam and do not correct this pandemic expeditiously, Europe's soul, including the deterioration of its unique historical culture, will be decimated and overshadowed by Islamic culture. With that being said, we can have total confidence that Jeremiah's prophecy of the hunters will proceed to manifest into a massive Jewish Aliyah from Europe to the Promised Land.

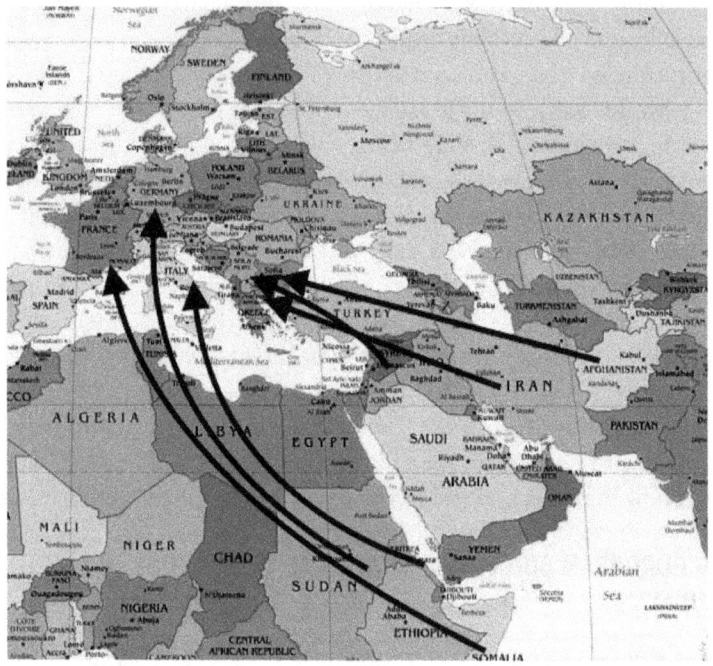

Islamic Flood

GOD'S FISHERMEN OF THE MYSTERY OF ALIYAH IN 2014–2015 (BLOOD MOON TETRAD)

Since 2014–2015, as anti-Semitism, persecution, and terror attacks continued to escalate across Europe, Israeli prime minister Benjamin Netanyahu and other prominent Israeli leaders, prophetically *fished*, or called upon the Jewish people to make Aliyah to Israel, establishing them as God's fishermen of Jeremiah's prophecy. On February 15, 2015, which was the second year of the blood moon tetrad, Netanyahu announced the Israeli government would discuss a $46 million plan to encourage Aliyah from Belgium, France, and

Ukraine.²⁰² God's fisherman also passionately urged a massive Aliyah from Europe to Israel by declaring, "We are preparing for a wave of mass Aliyah [Jewish immigration] from Europe; we are calling for a wave of mass Aliyah from Europe. *I want to tell all the Jews of Europe, and Jews wherever they may be: 'Israel is the home of every Jew . . . Israel awaits you with open arms.*" ²⁰³ Prime Minister Netanyahu is prophetically fulfilling his part as a fisherman of Jeremiah's prophecy, because he openly advocates and pleads with the Jewish community in Europe to make Aliyah to the Promised Land. Below are some other remarks Netanyahu made during the 2014–2015 blood moon tetrad.

- "Jews have been murdered again in European soil, and Israel is your home." ²⁰⁴
- "Israel is the only place where Jews can truly feel safe." ²⁰⁵
- "Extremist Islamic terrorism has struck Europe again, this time in Denmark. Jews have been murdered again on European soil only because they were Jews, and this wave of terrorist's attacks, including murderous anti-Semitic attacks, *is expected to continue.*" ²⁰⁶
- "To the Jews of Europe and to the Jews of the world, I say that Israel is waiting for you with open arms." ²⁰⁷

Prime Minister Netanyahu was not the only Israeli leader (fisherman) prophetically calling the children of Israel to the Promised Land. Defense Minister Moshe Ya'alon also supported the idea of more Jews making Aliyah to Israel, which highlights the dangers the Jewish community is facing abroad. He said, "The Jewish community, not just in France, [also in] Belgium and other places, Sweden, is under attack, a combined Islamist, anti-Semitic attack. *We knew that if [radical] Islam raised its head in Europe, the Jews would be the first to be harmed. The safest place for Jews is in the national home of Jews.*" ²⁰⁸

Additionally, Eitan Uri Bakhar, from the World Zionist organization (fishermen) proclaimed, "Europe is waking up to a new era, a new reality, to which we in Israel and around the Jewish world have been pointing out for the last 10 years. *We are witnessing a rise of anti-Semitic attacks and expressions.*" ²⁰⁹ With all three of these leaders advocating a Jewish Aliyah from Europe, it should be noted, "by the mouth of two or three witnesses the matter shall be established" (Deut. 19:15; 2 Cor. 13:1).

During 2014 (blood moons), the Aliyah of the Jewish people *from Europe* to the Promised Land increased by 84 percent with the arrival of 9,156 immigrants compared to approximately 4,973 in 2013, higher than any year since 1970! [210] In 2015, it surpassed 2014, with 10,118 Jewish people making Aliyah to Israel.[211] The European countries with the largest surges were Italy and France. [212]

SATAN'S END-OF-THE-AGE HUNTERS ARE PRIMARILY RADICAL ISLAMIC MUSLIMS

As the vigorous anti-Semitism and vicious terrorist attacks continue to escalate and intensify in the Middle East, North Africa, and Europe, we can have confidence that radical Muslims are Satan's *end-of-the-age* hunters. Again, this is not to declare that *all* Muslims are terrorists or radical jihadists, because many are peaceful, moderate people who want to live in peace and harmony. With that being said, it would be highly irresponsible and frankly ignorant if we do not recognize and proclaim the absolute facts about the widespread pandemic of Islamic terrorism, anti-Semitism, and the increasing acceptance of their demonic theology. Therefore, do Satan's *end-of-the-age* hunters, who are radical Muslims, absolutely correlate with Satan's *original hunters*? Do both originate from the same *regions* of the world? Let us recall what the prophet Isaiah proclaimed about the end of the age.

> Isaiah 46:9–10: "Remember the former things of old, for I am God, and there is no other; I am God, and there is none like Me, *declaring the end from the beginning, and from ancient times things that are not yet done*, saying, 'My counsel shall stand, and I will do all My pleasure.'" (See Ecclesiastes 1:9-10)

Assuredly, the Lord God declares the end from the beginning and from ancient times things that are not yet done. Accordingly, if believers would like to understand the end of the age, it is a prerequisite to understand the beginning, which not only includes the Torah and the biblical prophets, but also Satan's *original hunters*. In other words, the *regions* of Satan's *original hunters* will be the exact same *regions* that his *end-of-the-age* hunters will primarily rise from, which is the Middle East and North Africa.

Satan's *original hunters*, Nimrod, Ishmael, Esau (Edom), Goliath (Philistines), and the Herodian family (Esau descendants), *all* originated from the Middle East, which today, are *regions* controlled and dominated by fundamentalist Islamic leadership. Additionally, Cush (Sudan), who was Nimrod's father, had three brothers, Mizraim (Egypt), Put (Libya), and

Canaan, which makes them Nimrod's uncles, whose regions are in North Africa. Therefore, since the end will be like the beginning, and Satan's *original hunters* emerged from today's Islamic countries of the Middle East, then Satan's *end-of-the-age* hunters, including the final hunter (Antichrist), will rise from these nations, as well. In fact, when we review a current map of the Middle East, it emphatically affirms this point, because *all* of the nations that surround Israel are Islamic nations, who are the ancient, generational enemies that perpetually and vehemently hate the God of Israel and His people. Interestingly enough, most of these countries forbid admission to Jewish passport holders, including Iran, Iraq, Kuwait, Lebanon, Libya, Saudi Arabia, Sudan, Syria, UAE, and Yemen. Is this by coincidence?

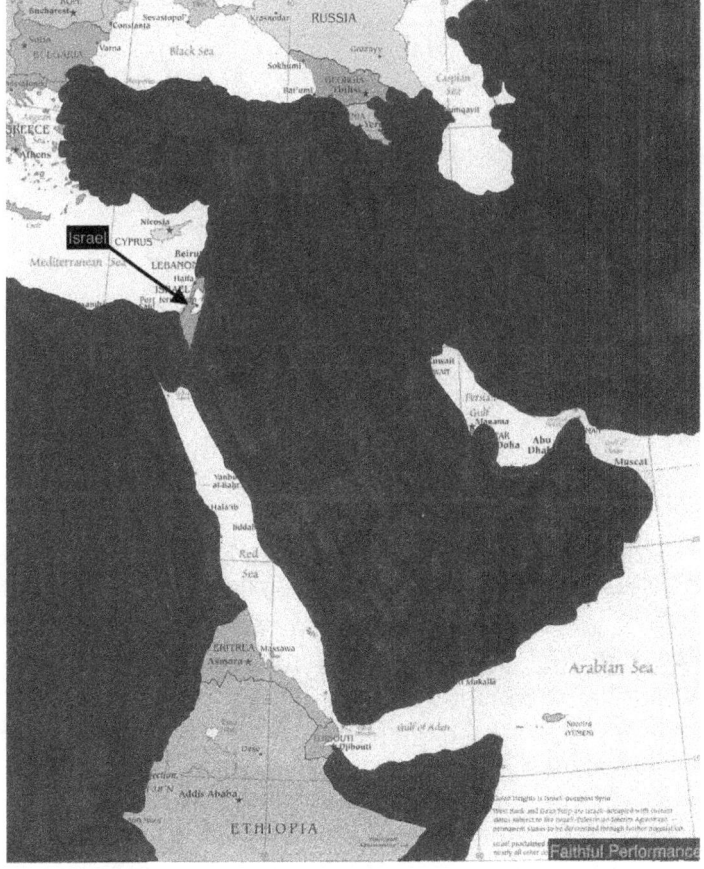

Israel Surrounded by Islamic Nations

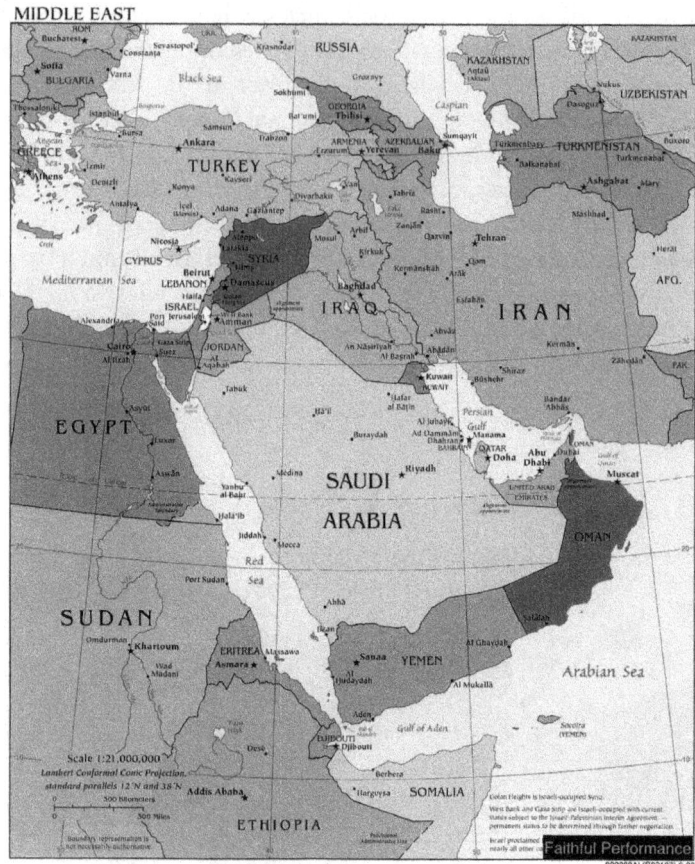

Israel Surrounded by Islamic Nations #2

In conclusion, as a direct, yet consequential result of governmental anarchy, war, terror, and civilian unrest in the Middle East and North Africa, millions of refugees flooded into Europe during the 2014–2015 blood moon tetrad. Once the rise of Islamic anti-Semitism and terror attacks kindled in Europe, it provoked an Aliyah to the Promised Land, as Satan's *end-of-the-age* hunters perpetuated fear and chaos across the continent. These evil actions have led Prime Minister Netanyahu and others to prophetically *fish* the children of Israel back to the Promised Land. Please note, just as the year 1948 released God's *end-of-the-age* fishermen, the blood moon tetrad years of 2014–2015 *commenced* the release of Satan's *end-of-the-age* hunters, who are primarily radical Muslims. Unfortunately, Europe will continue to witness an escalation of terror and violence as we journey towards the end of the age unto Messiah's second coming, resulting in a massive Jewish Aliyah to the Promised Land.

What about the United States, which harbors over six million Jewish people and has been the safest refuge for them in world history? Have the warning signs of Satan's *end-of-the-age* hunters appeared in America? Have Satan's hunters been released in the land of the free?

Read on to find out.

CHAPTER 8

THE ALIYAH FROM THE UNITED STATES

Throughout America's unrivaled prosperous history, the land of the free has been the safest refuge in the world for the children of Israel. From 1492, when Columbus sailed the ocean blue from Spain to America during the Spanish Inquisition, unto today, the God of Israel has sovereignly preordained America to be a protective harbor for His chosen people, until their prophetic calling to make Aliyah to the Promised Land.

Beginning in the 1500s, upon its prayers and hopes of peace, prosperity, and security, a perpetual Jewish migration sailed from the Eastern world to the shores of America. In the late 1700s to 1800s, as anti-Semitism and persecution tragically increased and expanded throughout the Middle East and Europe, the Jewish population in America exponentially compounded, from approximately 2,000 residents in 1790 to 15,000 by 1840. Amazingly, in 1880, which was only four decades later, the Jewish population increased to an estimated 250,000. [1] From 1880 to 1914, which was the beginning of World War I, approximately 1.5 million Jewish people immigrated to America from Eastern Europe, as anti-Semitism and persecution continued its demonic rise in the twentieth century. In 1942, the Jewish population in America was an estimated 4.3 million, and in 1970, 5.4 million. As of 2017, the Jewish population in America is an estimated 5.7 million, which is second largest in the world to Israel (6.3M). [2]

In the twentieth century, the children of Israel rose to significant affluence in America, and by the end of the century, they were relatively wealthy among the citizens of America. In 1983, economist Thomas Sowell wrote, "Jewish family incomes are the highest of any large ethnic group in the U.S., 72% above the national average," and, "the social and economic distance covered in a relatively short time makes the Jewish experience in America unique."[3]

In the 1980s, *Forbes* magazine reported that of the four hundred richest Americans, more than one hundred were Jewish, which was nine times greater than expectations based on the overall population. Historian Edward Shapiro estimates over 30 percent of American billionaires are Jewish.[4] He also cites a 1986 issue of *Financial World* that listed the top 100 money makers in 1985, and half the people mentioned were Jewish.[5] Incredibly, 37 percent of all American Nobel Prize winners are Jewish. [6]

According to financial experts, historians, and statistics, America has not only been a safe refuge for the children of Israel, but also a great financial blessing, as well. Certainly, the children of Israel are a cornerstone fabric in American exceptionalism. Although America was not perfect when it came to massive immigration for Jewish refugees during the diabolical Nazi-Germany regime, or the rise of anti-Semitic groups within its borders during the 1900s, overall, it clearly has given the Jewish people freedom, security, and prosperity.[7]

Additionally, America has been the greatest ally to the State of Israel since its rebirth in 1948 (see Isa. 66:8), and the red, white, and blue has been enormously blessed and rewarded by God for its loyalty to His heritage, His land, and His people (see Gen. 12:3). In fact, one could argue that America's incredible, expeditious ascent to the greatest superpower in world history is directly linked to its support of the Jewish state in 1948 and thereafter.

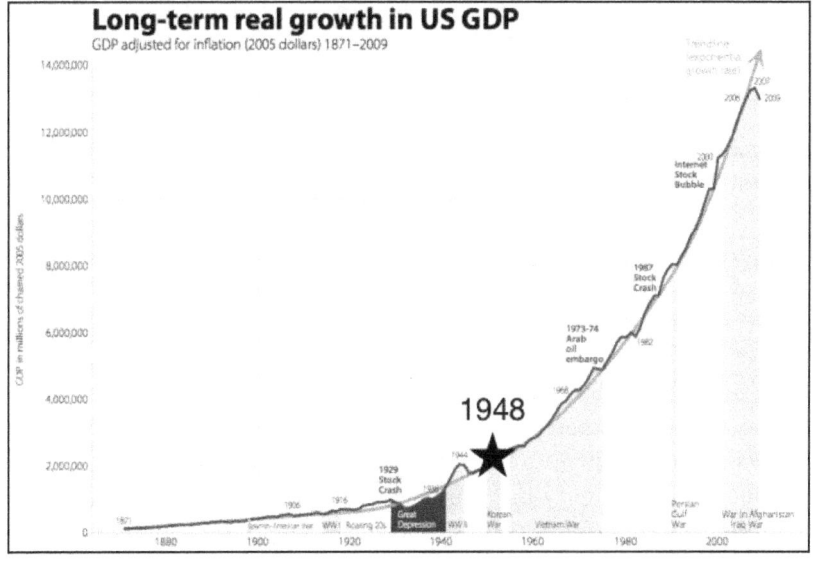

U.S. GDP

As the chart validates, since America's bold and unwavering recognition and support of the State of Israel in 1948 and beyond, it has not only been a beacon of freedom, but also the land of financial dreams and prosperity for all of mankind, including the children of Israel.

Without question, America has been a profound blessing by God Almighty in *all* aspects to the children of Israel. Since this is the case, why would the Jewish people leave America to make Aliyah to Israel? Why would they make Aliyah to Israel if they are richly blessed in every way in America? What would provoke and encourage them to leave the land of the free? The resounding, yet somber answer is found in Jeremiah's prophecy that will occur at the end of the age.

> Jeremiah 16:14–17: "'Therefore behold, the days are coming,' says the LORD, 'that it shall no more be said, "The LORD lives who brought up the children of Israel from the land of Egypt," but, "The LORD lives who brought up the children of Israel from the land of the north *and from all the lands [including America] where He had driven them." For I will bring them back into their land which I gave to their fathers. Behold, I will send for many fishermen,' says the LORD, 'and they shall fish them; and afterward I will send for many hunters, and they shall hunt them from every mountain and every hill, and out of the holes of the rocks. For My eyes are on all their ways; they are not hidden from My face, nor is their iniquity hidden from My eyes.'"*

According to God's prophet Jeremiah, the children of Israel will make Aliyah to the Promised Land from *all nations, including America, via God's fishermen and Satan's hunters*. Remember: God's *end-of-the-age* fishermen have been released since 1948, and they will continue to "fish" the Jewish people from America to Israel. From 1973 to 2016, an average of 2,500 Jewish people a year made Aliyah from America to the Promised Land. [8] However, it is a substantially small amount compared to the 5.7 million that is living in America today, which confirms why God will allow Satan's hunters to invade America in all capacities. This is to say, the children of Israel who reside in America have no reason to make Aliyah to Israel, which is surrounded by the cataclysmic warfare of the Middle East and North Africa, if America is safe and prosperous. Therefore, have Satan's hunters initiated their prophetic calling in America? Has the U.S. government been infiltrated with Islamic fundamentalist groups and lobbyists, which has escalated anti-

Semitism across the country? Has the Islamic doctrine infiltrated America's education system and universities? Is America witnessing the manifestation of anti-Semitic rhetoric, protests, incidents, and violence in the land of the free? Are we witnessing the *beginning* of the fulfillment of Jeremiah's prophecy in America before our very eyes?

To completely understand the prophetic calling of Satan's *end-of-the-age* hunters in America, let us first review how Islamic extremists has infiltrated the United States government, deceptively cunning its way to the highest office in the world, the presidency of the United States.

ISLAMIC INFILTRATION IN THE U.S. GOVERNMENT
SAUDI ARABIA

The ultimate conspirator of Islam's ideological and financial influence in America, and frankly the world, is the kingdom of Saudi Arabia, which is the region of Ishmael and Esau (Satan's *original* and *end-of-the-age* hunters). Saudi Arabia is a theocratic monarchy with a legal system based on the strictest form of Islamic Sharia law, where citizens can receive harsh punishments, including death, for apostasy and blasphemy. [9] Make no mistake: Islam is the greatest false religion and abomination the world has ever known, and Saudi Arabia is the womb where its evil roots originated in the seventh century (AD 610). In the next chapter, we will thoroughly discuss how Islam is the primary religion Satan has used and will use to directly defy and blaspheme the Holy Bible, as it sadly deceives billions of people (Muslims). Regrettably, Islam is the world's second-largest religion, and it is the fastest-growing one, with over 1.8 billion followers (Muslims), or 24 percent of the global population. [10] Interestingly enough, in 2017, Saudi Arabia was ranked as the *most* religious country in the world, and ninth among the world's most powerful countries. [11] Saudi Arabia is the home to Islam's two most holy cities, Mecca and Medina. Mecca exhibits the most sacred site in Islam, the blasphemous Kaaba shrine, where 15 million Muslims visit annually, which unfortunately makes it one of the most visited locations on planet Earth. [12]

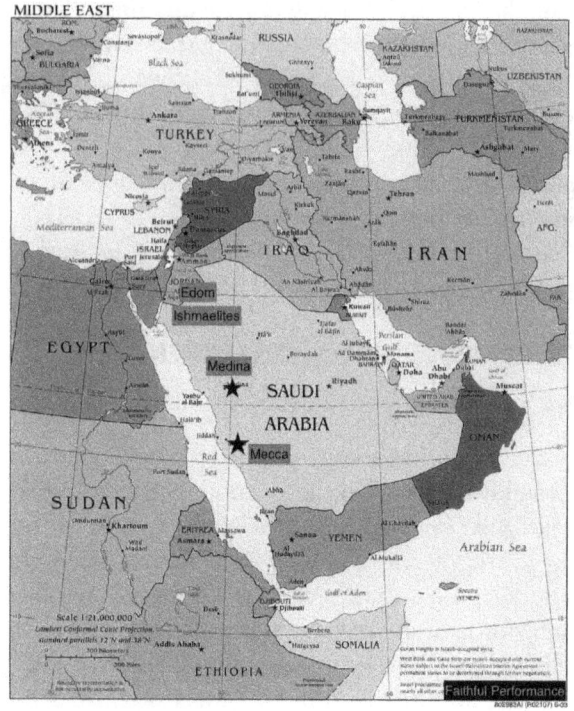

Saudi Arabia, Mecca, Medina

Kaaba Shrine

In our book *God's Prophetic Timeline, Messiah's Final Warning*, we thoroughly explore Revelation 17–18 (Mystery Babylon), confirming Mecca, Saudi Arabia, as Mystery Babylon, or the great harlot. In these two prophetic chapters, John describes a great harlot who sits in a desert (wilderness), with whom the kings of the earth commit fornication and its inhabitants are made drunk with the *wine of her fornication* (Rev. 17:1–2). The prophet uses wine as symbolism for the one product in the world the kings of the earth and its inhabitants require every day for occupations and activities in our society, which is oil. John also uses fornication as symbolism, because he is speaking of the most adulterous false religion in the history of the world, which certainly is Islam. In other words, John is prophesying about a specific city and kingdom, which will leverage a product (oil) to deceive the kings and the inhabitants of the earth to spread its evil, blasphemous religion.

Without any doubt, Saudi Arabia has leveraged its oil (wine), and also the abundance of its luxury (Rev.18:3), to spread its harlot propaganda and tyranny of Islam, the mother of all abominations (false religion), across the world. Unfortunately, the luxurious abundance and influential power of the harlot's oil has infiltrated the U.S. government, buying politicians' souls, including presidents, which has enabled its radical Sunni Islamic doctrine to infiltrate America's borders in *all* major capacities. Accordingly, how did Saudi Arabia rise to power and leverage its oil with America, which has culminated with them buying major influence within the U.S. government and education systems to spread its harlot ideology?

Before the Ottoman Empire (Turkey) collapsed in 1923, it controlled most of the Arabian Peninsula, with the Arabians (Ishmaelites) occupying the other areas of the region. After the Ottoman Empire collapsed, King Abdul Aziz (Ibn Saud) gained power and control over the region, including its capital, Riyadh, Saudi Arabia. In 1932, the region was named "the kingdom of Saud," and by the time of his death in 1953, it stretched from the Persian Gulf to the Red Sea, and from Iraq to Yemen.

Ottoman Empire

In the 1930s, as Saud obtained complete power and control over Saudi Arabia, the Saudi's discovered massive oil reserves in their land, which would eventually change the geopolitical and religious landscape of the world. Subsequently, Aramco, an *Arabian-American oil company*, was formed, and the great harlot began to spew its fundamentalist ideology and financial perversion all over the world, including America. Saudi Arabia would come to have the largest proven crude oil reserves and largest daily oil production in the world until 2011 (overtaken by Venezuela). [13] As of recent years, Aramco's value has been estimated between $1.25 trillion and $10 trillion, making it the *world's most valuable company*. [14] Although the Saudi government obtained complete control of Aramco in 1980 by acquiring 100 percent stake in the company, America's soul had already been sold to the great harlot. [15] As of this writing, the Saudi's perpetual adulterous influence in the U.S. government, federal agencies, and politicians, including presidents, has significantly increased since their total control over Aramco.

The kingdom of Saudi Arabia is the originator, manufacturer, and major financer and supporter of the world's most fundamentalist form of Sunni Islam, called Wahhabism. During Saud's reign (1932–1953), he instituted Wahhabism, which was agreed upon by the dynastic alliance between his family and Muhammad ibn Abd al-Wahhab, the father of Wahhabism. Wahhabism is the strictest form of Sunni Islam. [16] It controls and neglects the basic human rights of society, including women, in the form of freedom of speech and expression, controlled prayer and behavior, conformity of dress code, business and leisure activities, lifestyle choices, and many other God-given rights. [17] The Saudi government forces excessive and extreme measures in establishing obedience to the strict rules of Wahhabism, which includes public beatings, executions, and imprisonment for breaking one of the least of its requirements. Saudi Arabia's human rights record is a clear indicator of its inhumane governing, because, according to the International Human Rights Rank Indicator, it poorly ranks 205 out of 216 countries. [18]

Nevertheless, the Wahhabi fundamentalism continues in Saudi Arabia unto this day, as al-Ash-Sheikh, Saudi Arabia's leading religious family, are descendants of Wahhab. In fact, Salman bin Abdul Aziz, who is the current king of Saudi Arabia, proclaims Wahhabism is "pure Islam." [19] In the past few decades, it is estimated the great harlot has spent upward of $100 billion of their petrodollars to spread Wahhabi Sunni Islam, between $2 billion and $3 billion per year since 1975, and at least $87 billion from 1987 to 2007. [20] Tens of billions of dollars were also spent in non-Islamic nations: 200 universities, 210 Islamic centers, 1,500 mosques, 4,000 preachers and missionaries, 2,000 schools for Muslim children, book materials, media, and subsidies to reward journalists and Islamic scholars. All of these petrodollars were spent in Asia, Africa, Europe, and North America for the widespread regard of Wahhabi Sunni Islam. [21] The tens of billions of dollars in "petro-Islam" funded an estimated "90% of the expenses of the entire faith," which is staggering, and it includes funding terrorist organizations. During this time, Wahhabism procured a preeminent position of strength in the global expression of Islam, which in its strictest form commands Muslims to "hate infidels for their religion . . . for Allah's sake," [22] and it declares, "Democracy is responsible for all the horrible wars in the 20th century." [23]

Does this doctrine sound like a lovely and wonderful, peaceful religion that the U.S. government needs to be in alliance with? Does Saudi Arabia's doctrine of Wahhabism align with our Judeo-Christian values that America was built upon?

The kingdom of Saudi Arabia is not only the womb where Islam was birthed, but with its Wahhabi Sunni doctrine, it is also the predominant theological and ideological fountain and financier of Islamic terrorist groups, such as al-Qaeda, ISIS, Al-Shabaab, Boko Haram, Al-Nusra Front, the Taliban, and others. These extremist groups, along with other terrorist nations, are guilty of the escalated and widespread violence that we have witnessed in the Middle East, North Africa, and Europe since 2003 (Iraq). Saudi Arabia finances and supports *all* of these terrorist groups, which makes it arguably the most prolific sponsor of Islamic terrorism across the globe. [24] Just as the apostle John describes, "I saw the woman [harlot], drunk with the blood of the saints and with the blood of the martyrs of Jesus" (Rev. 17:6). Therefore, when we witness or read about the martyred believers and Jews by Satan's hunters in the Middle East, Africa, and Europe, more than likely, Saudi Arabia's petro dollars are funding or at least associated with these evil groups, perpetually fulfilling John's prophecy. As we have discovered, Saudi Arabia is the region of Ishmael and Esau (Edom), which, *as a region*, are *generational enemies* to the Jewish people. Former Florida Senator Bob Graham stated, "Saudi Arabia has not stopped its interest in spreading extreme Wahhabism. ISIS . . . is a product of Saudi ideals, Saudi money and Saudi organizational support, although now they are making a pretense of being very anti-ISIS." [25] Former CIA director James Woolsey described Saudi Arabia as "the soil in which al-Qaeda and its sister terrorist organizations are flourishing." [26] In 2015, the vice chancellor of Germany, Sigmar Gabriel, accused Saudi Arabia of supporting religious extremism, proclaiming, "Wahhabi mosques are financed all over the world by Saudi Arabia." [27]

SAUDI ARABIAN INFLUENCE IN THE UNITED STATES GOVERNMENT

Since the American-Saudi partnership in Aramco was formed (1930s), it has perpetuated through the lineage of U.S. presidents, as the Saudi's petrodollars and the abundance of its luxury has infiltrated the land of the free in *all* capacities of American society. Most certainly, as the apostle Paul proclaimed, "The love of money is the root of all evil," and this truth definitely describes Saudi Arabia and the U.S. government (1 Tim. 6:10). Following is a list of Saudi influence over recent U.S. presidents.

- Jimmy Carter—King Saud, founding member of the Carter Center—tens of millions donated over the years. In 1993 alone, the late King Fahd gifted $7.6 million, while more recently, the

king's nephew, Prince Alwaleed Bin Talal, donated at least $5 million to the Carter Center. [28]
- The Bush Family (including allied companies and institutions)—at least $1.476 billion donated. [29]
- Clintons—$10-25 million in donations to the Clinton Foundation [30]

Would not Saudi Arabia expect a return on their investment from this enormous amount of money donated to these greedy presidents, obtaining favor within the borders of the land of the free? Would not the Saudis leverage their money to implement their evil agenda for America? The resounding answer is absolutely yes!

Throughout the twentieth century, the benefits of the partnership were basically one-sided, to say the least. The great harlot has sold oil to America at prices of its own discretion, and in exchange, the U.S. government foolishly provides them with military support and ignorantly turns a blind eye to their inhumane and abysmal religious atrocities. [31] Saudi Arabian petrodollars and lobbyists have also endangered America's sovereignty, which ultimately will release Satan's hunters in America. The most effective Saudi lobbyist was Prince Bandar, Saudi Arabia's ambassador to the U.S. from 1983 to 2005, who was fundamentally influential for the great harlot. He effectively joined the Bush administration as a virtual member of the cabinet.[32] The *Economist* reported, "No Arab ambassador, perhaps no ambassador, has come close to matching Prince Bandar's influence in the American capital." At the height of his powers he was indispensable to both sides: in Mr. Ottaway's words, "at once the king's exclusive messenger and the White House's errand boy." [33] This should be absolutely alarming for American citizens for any foreign lobbyist to have this much influence and power in the U.S. government, much less a representative of a country who faithfully practices Wahhabism.

Just in the first decade of the twenty-first century (2000–2010), the Saudis paid an estimated $100 million to American firms to lobby the U.S. government for the great harlot's agenda for America, which is "to transform America into a Wahhabi-style Islamic state." [34] What is even more disturbing about the "drunkenness of the U.S. government," is the Saudi lobbying mostly occurred *after* the 9/11 attacks, which is absolutely astonishing, insulting, and reckless, because fifteen of the nineteen hijackers of the four airliners on 9/11 originated from Saudi Arabia. [35] This is treason at its highest level, because 9/11 was an act of war, and it should have the American people protesting and demanding answers from the U.S. government, including presidents, who have sold America's soul to the great harlot. Since 2015, Saudi Arabia has paid $18 million to 145 registered lobbyists to influence the U.S. government for its propaganda and agenda. [36] Clearly, the U.S. government has cowardly bowed down to the "almighty petrodollar" and the consequential aftermath will not be in favor of the children of Israel, and frankly, all believers in Messiah, because Satan's hunters will be released in America.

What has been the overall result of the Saudi's oil, petrodollars, luxury, and lobbying in America? What has America received in return? Since 2001, which again, was *after* the devastating 9/11 attacks, more than nine hundred mosques have been erected in America, which is an 80 percent *increase* from approximately three hundred mosques *before* 2001, and the overwhelming majority were financed by Saudi Arabia. [37] Again, this is extremely careless, irresponsible, and repulsive.

The great harlot also finances the majority of imams (preachers) of the mosques in America, and the "peaceful curriculum" in these mosques is Wahhabi Sunni Islam. According to a report by Freedom House, a Washington based nongovernmental organization (NGO), "Wahhabi influence over Islamic institutions in the U.S. was considerable by 2003," which was reported from a testimony before the U.S. Senate. [38] To support this testimony, on July 25, 2017, Imam Ammar Shahin of the Islamic Center of David in Northern California was caught on camera encouraging American Muslims to eliminate Jewish people, and he prayed for their death. The Wahhabi Sunni Islam teacher also led a prayer in response to the metal detectors being placed at the Temple Mount in response to a Muslim terrorist attack, declaring, "Liberate the Al-Aqsa Mosque from the filth of the Jews," and, "Annihilate them to the very last one." [39]

Since 2004, Saudi Arabia has been designated as a "country of particular concern" under the International Religious Freedom Act of 1998 for participating in "severe violations of religious freedom." [40] According to a report by Freedom House, "The Saudi government and its affiliates published hundreds of publications filled with hatred and intolerance toward Christians, Jews, and other Americans, which was disseminated across the country by 2006." [41] The report concluded, "The Saudi government propaganda examined reflects a totalitarian ideology of hatred that can incite to violence," and, "It is being mainstreamed within our borders through the efforts of a foreign government, namely Saudi Arabia, and it demands our urgent attention." [42]

By 2013, 75 percent of North American Islamic mosques and centers relied on Wahhabi preachers (imams), who promote anti-American ideas in person and online through sermons of Saudi-produced literature." [43] According to U.S. intelligence officials, in September 2013, hundreds of millions of dollars were still flowing to Muslim terrorists from private donors in the kingdom of Saud. [44] In May 2016, it was reported the kingdom of Saudi Arabia had "spent untold millions promoting Wahhabism, the radical form of Sunni Islam that inspired the 9/11 hijackers and that now inflames the Islamic State (ISIS)." [45] Furthermore, Saudi Prince Ben-Talah has invested $27 million petrodollars to support Palestinian suicide bombers, and ironically, he just happens to be the largest shareholder in Newscorp, the parent company of Fox News.

How could the U.S. government allow such a hate-filled, evil, and blasphemous ideology to infiltrate America's borders, especially *after* the 9/11 attacks? Why would they enable the great harlot to continue to expand their demonic bondage doctrine, including an 80 percent increase in mosques since 2001, across the land of the free? How could they allow an ancient enemy to the children of Israel, Saudi Arabia, who is located in Satan's *original and end-of-the-age hunter's regions* of Ishmael and Esau, to plant its evil roots deep into the four corners of America?

As we have discovered, John provides the answer: the "kings of the earth committed fornication, and the inhabitants of the earth were made drunk with the wine [oil] of her fornication [false religion]," while the harlot is "drunk with the blood of the saints and . . . the martyrs of Jesus" (Rev. 17:2, 6). Assuredly, the U.S. government's irresponsible, careless, and reckless behavior will only escalate and intensify the climatic and ultimate release of Satan's *end-of-the-age* hunters in America against the children of Israel, fulfilling Jeremiah's prophecy.

MUSLIM BROTHERHOOD

Another Sunni Islamic fundamentalist organization that has astonishingly obtained significant status within the U.S. government is the Muslim Brotherhood. This political, religious, yet terrorist organization was founded by Hassan al-Banna in Egypt in 1928. Hassan al-Banna was extremely clear on the brotherhood's ultimate goals for not only America, but for the whole world. He declared, "It is in the nature of Islam to dominate, not to be dominated, to impose its law on all nations and to extend its power to the entire planet." [46] Please note, the terrorist group Hamas is directly associated with the Muslim Brotherhood, and its charter calls for the murder of Jews, the obliteration of Israel, and Israel's replacement with an Islamist theocracy.[47]

The Muslim Brotherhood unequivocally believes in the establishment of Sharia law based on the Qur'an and the Sunnah, which is the oral account of the teachings, deeds, and sayings of the Islamic prophet Muhammad. [48] The terrorist organization believes the Qur'an and the Sunnah are the "sole reference point for . . . ordering the life of a Muslim family, individual, community . . . and state." [49] The Muslim Brotherhood's motto and slogans include, "Islam is the Solution, Allah is our objective, the Prophet is our leader [Muhammad], *the Qur'an is our law, Jihad is our way. Dying in the way of God is our highest hope.* God is greater!" [50]

The Muslim Brotherhood's initial goal was to build a transnational organization, as groups were founded in Lebanon (1936), Syria (1937), and Transjordan (1946), with its strategic headquarters for the whole Muslim world located in Cairo, Egypt. [51] Other Brotherhood organizations were founded in Tunisia, Morocco, Algeria, Afghanistan, and Malaysia. [52] As of 1994, an international agency of the terrorist organization "assures the cooperation of the ensemble" of its national organizations. [53]

To understand how the Muslim Brotherhood infiltrates governments with the sole intent and purpose of overthrowing them, let us review its history in Egypt, which eventually culminated with the Brotherhood's successful conquest of the Egyptian government. From 1936 to 1938, the Muslim Brotherhood grew from 800 members to 200,000, and by 1948, it had over two million members. [54] After several years of revolting against the Egyptian government, assassinating the Egyptian prime minister, and being accused of several bombings and brutal killings, the Egyptian government banned the Muslim Brotherhood from Egypt. [55] Shortly thereafter, on February 12, 1949, the Brotherhood's leader, Hassan al-Banna, was assassinated in what many concluded was retaliation of the assassination of Egypt's prime minister.

In the 1950s to 1960s, after the Muslim Brotherhood revolted once again over Egypt's monarchy, the organization was banned, thousands of its members were imprisoned, many were tortured in holding camps, while others sought asylum in Saudi Arabia. [56] It is worthy to note that for a half century, Saudi Arabia financed the Muslim Brotherhood, because the two shared similar doctrine and interests. [57]

In the 1970s, under new Egyptian president Anwar Sadat, the Muslim Brotherhood was welcomed back to Egypt, members were released from Egyptian prisons, and its organization was overall tolerated. Subsequently, the Brotherhood launched into Egyptian politics, in order to overthrow the current government in favor of their fundamentalist theology. [58]

From 1981 to 2011, under the Hosni Mubarak regime, the Muslim Brotherhood consistently called for "Islamic reform" and a "democratic system" in Egypt. During Mubarak's era, the brotherhood was the largest opposition group, and it built a profound network of support and admiration through charities, social work, and social media. [59] In the 2005 Egyptian parliamentary elections, the Muslim Brotherhood was victorious in its infiltration of the Egyptian government, because it won eighty-eight seats compared to fourteen seats for the opposition. [60] During the Brotherhood's term in parliament, there were grave concerns about its commitment to democracy, equal rights, and freedom of expression and belief, because these were the principles the organization politicked on. [61] In October 2007, the Muslim Brotherhood released a detailed political platform. One of the two essential issues it called for was a board of Muslim clerics to oversee the government, and the other was limiting the office of the presidency to Muslim men only. [62] Additionally, a deputy leader of the organization declared it would seek dissolution of the 32-year peace treaty with Israel. [63]

After the Egyptian Revolution of 2011, which removed Hosni Mubarak from power, the Muslim Brotherhood was legalized in Egypt. [64] In the 2011 parliamentary elections, the Brotherhood dominated by winning 235 out of 498 seats, far more than any other party. [65] The Muslim Brotherhood finalized its infiltration of the Egyptian government by winning the 2012 presidential election with Mohamed Morsi. [66] However, the terrorist organization's giant victory was short-lived due to its radical legislation, referendums, prosecution of journalists, pro–Muslim Brotherhood gang attacks, and persecution of Egypt's Coptic Christians. On July 3, 2013, in response to one of the largest protests in human history, the Egyptian military arrested and detained Morsi.[67] In response to Morsi's arrest, Muslim Brotherhood supporters looted and burned police stations and dozens of churches, as they escalated violence throughout Egypt, resulting in the death of over 600 people and the injury of 4,000. [68] Consequently, the Egyptian military cracked down on the Muslim Brotherhood, which many called the worst in eight decades, because most of its leaders were held in custody, including its supreme leader, Mohammad Badie.[69]

On September 23, 2013, an Egyptian court outlawed the Muslim Brotherhood and seized its assets, and on December 21, Prime Minister Hazem Al Beblawi proclaimed the Muslim Brotherhood as a terrorist organization.[70] On March 24, 2014, an Egyptian court sentenced 529 members of the Muslim Brotherhood to death. [71] In the following months, an estimated 16,000 to 40,000 members and supporters were arrested by

Egyptian police. [72] In February 2015, an Egyptian court sentenced another 183 members of the Muslim Brotherhood to death, [73] and former president Mohamed Morsi, was sentenced to death, along with 120 others, on May 16, 2015. [74]

Is this the kind of Islamic doctrine that the U.S. government needs to be infiltrated and associated with?

The Muslim Brotherhood has approximately eighty chapters and organizations across the world, including the following countries: Bahrain, Iran, [75] Turkey, [76] Iraq, [77] Israel, [78] Gaza Strip, [79] Jordan, [80] Qatar, [81] Kuwait, [82] Lebanon (1964), Syria, [83] United Arab Emirates, [84] Yemen, [85] Algeria, Libya, [86] Mauritania, [87] Morocco, [88] Somalia, [89] Sudan, [90] Tunisia (1981), Indonesia, [91] Malaysia (1951), Maldives (2005), Tajikistan (1990), and Saudi Arabia. [92]

As of 2015, the Muslim Brotherhood has been labeled a terrorist organization by Egypt,[93] Russia, [94] Syria, the UAE, [95] and ironically, the great harlot, Saudi Arabia. [96] Although Saudi Arabia financed the Muslim Brotherhood for over a half century, the two extremists became estranged during the Gulf War and after the election of Mohamed Morsi in Egypt in 2012. Saudi Arabia opposed Iraq's invasion of Kuwait by Saddam Hussein, but the Muslim Brotherhood supported it. The Brotherhood also took offense with Saudi Arabia because it allowed U.S. troops to be based in the kingdom of Saud to fight Iraq during the Gulf War. [97] The tensions escalated between the two during the Arab Spring, because the Saudis' royal family was alarmed by the example set by the Muslim Brotherhood in Egypt's revolution and elections with Mohamed Morsi.[98] What compounded the matter was the Muslim Brotherhood acquired many supporters inside the kingdom of Saud, because the Saudis used many of the Brotherhood as teachers, and they "methodically . . . took control of Saudi Arabia's intellectual life." [99] Consequently, the Muslim Brotherhood was labeled a threat to the royal family's control, because its members became "entrenched both in Saudi society and in the Saudi state, taking a lead role in key governmental ministries." [100] Stephane Lacroix, an expert on Saudi affairs, declared, "The education system is so controlled by the Muslim Brotherhood, it will take 20 years to change, if at all." [101]

Now that we have explored the Muslim Brotherhood's infiltration and eventual collapse of the Egyptian government, and the cataclysmic effects that resulted, let us explore the Brotherhood's infiltration and influence in the U.S. government.

THE MUSLIM BROTHERHOOD'S INFILTRATION OF THE U.S. GOVERNMENT

Since 1953, after the Muslim Brotherhood met with U.S. President Dwight D. Eisenhower in the Oval Office, the terrorist group has received a false reputation of credibility and tolerance in America. In 1963, the United States chapter of the Muslim Brotherhood was created through the Muslim Students Association (MSA). [102] In the following decades, other "front organizations" were specifically created in America for the Muslim Brotherhood to infiltrate the U.S. government and the education system:

- North America Islamic Trust (NAIT) (1971)
- International Institute of Islamic Thought (IIIT) (1980s)
- Islamic Society of North America (ISNA) (1981)
- The American Muslim Council (1990)
- Muslim American Society (MSA) (1992)
- The Council on American-Islamic Relations (CAIR) (1994)

Without any doubt, the Muslim Brotherhood wants to infiltrate the U.S. government and politically collapse America's current constitution and laws, thereby implementing Sharia law, which is Islam's evil doctrine. In 1988, an FBI informant inside the U.S. Muslim Brotherhood reported, "The Muslim Brotherhood was in the first of six phases to institute the Islamic Revolution in the United States." The overall objective is to "peacefully get inside the United States government and also American universities," and ultimately, "change the Constitution of America." [103] Omar Ahmed, who is chairman of the board of CAIR, a Muslim Brotherhood front organization, declared, "Islam isn't in America to be equal to any other faith, but to become dominant. The Qur'an should be the highest authority in America, and Islam the only accepted religion on earth." [104]

The Brotherhood believes America is an apostate nation with infidels that does not champion moral and human values and cannot lead humanity. [105] The Muslim Brotherhood calls for political and religious jihad against its enemies—Israel and America—because "waging Jihad against both of these infidels is a commandment of Allah that cannot be disregarded." [106]

In 1982, a document titled "The Muslim Brotherhood Project" was discovered in Switzerland. In 2005, Scott Burgess translated it into English. It outlined in detail "a global vision of a worldwide strategy for Islamic policy [or political Islam]." [107] In 2007, during the Holy Land Foundation trial, which was a terror-financing trial, a 1991 document written by Mohamed Akram Adlouni, the "Explanatory Memorandum on the General Strategic Goal for the Group in North America," was discovered in a 2004 FBI raid of a Virginia home and admitted as an exhibit. [108] This document outlined in detail the strategy and intentions of the Muslim Brotherhood in America, which included "eliminating and destroying the Western civilization from within." [109] This clearly explains to all Americans, including the intoxicated U.S. government, the Muslim Brotherhood's plans to infiltrate the political system and attempt to overthrow the American constitution (political Islam).

In the U.S. Congress, there have been attempts to pass legislation to criminalize and label the Muslim Brotherhood as a terrorist organization, but to no avail. U.S. Senator Ted Cruz and U.S. Representative Mario Diaz-Balart introduced the Muslim Brotherhood Terrorist Designation Act of 2015, but unfortunately, the bill did not pass. [110] Interestingly enough, this bill was introduced *after* Egypt, Russia, Syria, UAE, and even the great harlot, Saudi Arabia, designated the Muslim Brotherhood as a terrorist organization. Why did the U.S. Congress, including former presidents George W. Bush and Barack H. Obama, not proclaim the Muslim Brotherhood as a terrorist organization, especially after the governmental anarchy, chaos, and civilian unrest the Muslim Brotherhood instigated in Egypt, along with the detailed documents of the Brotherhood's intentions for America? Does the Muslim Brotherhood have influence in the U.S. Congress and the presidency of the United States?

Clare Lopez, a former CIA officer, claims the Muslim Brotherhood achieved "information dominance" during the George W. Bush presidency, and it escalated in the Barack H. Obama administration. At the Gatestone Institute, she wrote, "The careful insinuation of Muslim Brothers into positions from which they can exercise influence on U.S. policy began long before the attacks of 9/11, although their success has accelerated dramatically under the administration of President Barack Obama." [111]

Throughout former President Barack Obama's eight years, many critics have wondered if he had any anti-American connections in the Islamic world, especially with a terrorist organization such as the Muslim Brotherhood. Regrettably, Obama's half brother, Malik Obama, is directly linked to the Egyptian Muslim Brotherhood, which validates why the former president supported Mohamed Morsi's (MB) election in Egypt. Malik Obama oversees the Muslim Brotherhood's international investments, and according to an Egyptian report, which cites the vice president of the Supreme Constitutional Court of Egypt, Tehani al-Gebali, Malik Obama "is one of the architects of the major investments of the Muslim Brotherhood." [112] Although a few of the mainstream media covered and announced this troubling connection with the Obamas before the former president was elected, most of the mainstream (lame-stream) media, politicians, and Americans foolishly disregarded these indicting connections and remained *politically correct*. This is why former president Barack H. Obama was so adamant about defending and protecting Islam during his eight-year term. According to former Department of Homeland Security officer Philip Haney, who worked under the Obama administration, he was ordered to eliminate all information that incriminated the Muslim Brotherhood as a terrorist organization. Haney stated, "I can't explain to you the ideology or the worldview of this [Obama] administration that makes them so adamant to protect Islam from harm by addressing it in its true nature." [113] Haney believes "if we don't find the wherewithal to address the nature of the threat we face realistically, courageously, and honestly, we're going to find ourselves confronted with a dragon who will become capable of devouring us if we're not careful." [114]

The Muslim Brotherhood's influence in the U.S. government's policies has been thoroughly documented in *New York Times* best-selling authors Aaron Klein and Brenda J. Elliott's book, *Impeachable Offenses: The Case to Remove Barack Obama from Office*. It documents that Obama assisted Islamic extremist groups rise to power in the Middle East (Arab Spring), including the Muslim Brotherhood, because its members were allowed to serve on important American antiterrorism security advisory boards. [115] In fact, Mohamed Elibiary, an Egyptian-born Muslim Brotherhood operative, and former senior advisor to Obama, *unbelievably* served five years on the former president's Homeland Security Advisory Council. [116] The book also substantiates the Obama administration could have leaked out and exposed national security and classified information through Hillary Clinton's deputy chief of staff, Huma Abedin, who has personal and family associations to the Muslim Brotherhood and Saudi Arabia. [117] As of March 29, 2017, Judicial Watch released 1,184 pages of State Department records, including previously unreleased Hillary Clinton email exchanges, revealing additional instances of Abedin and Clinton sending classified information through unsecured email accounts and contributors being given special access to the former secretary of state. [118]

Abedin was on the executive board of the Muslim Student Association (MSA), which is a front group for the Muslim Brotherhood. [119] In the Holy Land Foundation trial in 2007, there was an additional document introduced that confirmed the Muslim Brotherhood's association with the MSA, and it also authenticates its overall goal for the land of the free. It states, "Muslim Brotherhood members must understand that their work in America is a kind of grand jihad in eliminating and destroying the Western civilization from within and 'sabotaging' its miserable house by their hands and by the hands of the believers so that it is eliminated and Allah's religion is made victorious over all other religions." [120]

From 1995 through 2008, Abedin worked at the *Journal of Muslim Minority Affairs*, which is a Sharia law journal whose editor in chief was her own mother, Saleha Abedin. [121] Additionally, Saleha Abedin sits on the Presidency Staff Council of the International Islamic Council for Da'wa and Relief, an organization chaired by the leader of the Muslim Brotherhood.[122] Abedin's father, Syed Zaynul Abedin, was a professor in Saudi Arabia, who founded the Institute for Muslim Minority Affairs, which Saudi Arabia supported along with the Muslim World League. According to former federal prosecutor Andrew McCarthy, the Muslim World League is "perhaps the most significant Muslim Brotherhood organization in the world."[123] A Saudi government document, inspired by Huma Abedin's father, explains the concept and goal of Muslim Minority Affairs is "to establish global Sharia in our modern times."[124] Do not forget, this is a person who was Hillary Clinton's confidante for several years, which is very disturbing, to say the least.

Can you believe these people were working on behalf of the American people for several years? It is time for America to wake up from its delusional sleep and tranquility. Without any doubt, America's soul has been sold to the Islamic agenda of Saudi Arabia and the Muslim Brotherhood by greedy, corrupt presidents and politicians, and they have defiantly infiltrated the U.S. government with their demonic, fundamentalist Wahhabi doctrine. Former defense secretary Robert Gates, who worked under the Obama administration (2009–2011), emphatically proclaims, "We've got Muslim Brotherhood in the U.S. government today, at least 10 or 15 of them in the U.S. government." [125] The Islamic infiltration of the U.S. government will only enable Satan's hunters to be released in America, ultimately, provoking the Jewish people to make Aliyah to the Promised Land.

ISLAMIC INFILTRATION OF AMERICA'S EDUCATION SYSTEM

Another troubling sign of the Islamic invasion of America is in the education system, including universities, colleges, and schools. As previously discussed, the Muslim Brotherhood has "front organizations" for the specific and sole purpose of infiltrating not only the U.S. government, but also the education system, from top to bottom. The Muslim Students Association (MSA) was the first Muslim Brotherhood entity formed in America (1962), and it has chapters at nearly every major college and university campus. The MSA is a point of recruitment for the Muslim Brotherhood, and it promotes a Sharia-based agenda, which is dedicated to spreading fundamentalist Islam among American youth. This is to say, the MSA is in alliance with the "global Islamic movement." The MSA aggressively promotes anti-Semitic operations on many campuses, such as the anti-Zionist "Israel Apartheid Week." MSA has several offshoots, including, the IMA, the MAYA, the ICNA, and the ISNA.[126]

The International Institute of Islamic Thought (IIIT) is another Muslim Brotherhood front organization that has dangerously infiltrated the education system in America. Their objective is to infiltrate not only the U.S. government, but also American universities. [127] The IIIT is the same organization that Mohamed Morsi (MB) welcomed to reform the education system during his short rule over Egypt.[128] Unfortunately, the IIIT has donated massive amounts of money to several universities and colleges to establish its radical Islamic education, or Sharia-based doctrine to America's young adults, perpetuating the ultimate Islamic takeover of America. The universities and colleges include, but are not limited to: George Mason University, Nazareth College, Shenandoah University, Hartford Seminary, United States Naval Academy, Binghamton University, Eastern Mennonite University, University of Delaware, American University, University of Maryland, Manhattanville College, Georgetown University, University of Virginia, and Middle Tennessee State University.[129]

In 1988, a source for the FBI reported, "In phase one of the Islamic revolution as followed by the Muslim Brotherhood, the IIIT leadership has indicated that in this phase their organization needs to peacefully get inside the U.S. government and also *American universities*." [130] Most certainly, in the past few decades, the Muslim Brotherhood under their "front organizations" have achieved their goal, which is to infiltrate all capacities of American society and proceed with the Islamic invasion of America.

Saudi Arabia has also pumped their petrodollars into colleges and universities to appoint radical Islamic professors and teachers in departments of history, political science, Middle East studies, and so on. Basically, these professors connive and brainwash American students with an anti-American and anti-Zionist point of view. They deceivingly convince the young adults that America, its people, and its foreign policy, are the global problem, and that America's wealth, lifestyle, and success are oppressing all of the other countries in the world.

In recent years, American public schools have been indoctrinated with Islam, as well. Research and studies have reported more than five hundred historical errors in the public-school textbooks on Islam, clearly showing a biased and favorable view of Islamic doctrine.[131] Clearly, the U.S. government, which is infiltrated by Islamic extremists and their petrodollars, is to blame for this atrocity, because of its legislative influence and implementation of Common Core, a national curriculum. Consequently, America's youth are being deceived, and they are in danger of being indoctrinated into following or defending Islam's radical teachings and practices. The Islamic indoctrination has reached such insanity that a school in California, and in other states, taught its students a course that essentially requires them to become Muslims for three weeks. The schools ask them to dress as Muslims, change their names to Muslim names, memorize verses from the Qur'an, and make Islamic faith declarations such as "Allah is the One True God." [132] Certainly, all of the madness in the public school system has ensued because of the U.S. government's bowing down to radical Islamic groups such as the Council on American-Islamic Relations (CAIR) and the American Muslim Council, who have direct connections to terrorist organizations associated with Saudi Arabia and the Muslim Brotherhood. In fact, American Muslim Council representative Abdul Rahman Al-Amoudi, is serving a twenty-three–year prison sentence for being a top fund-raiser for al-Qaeda in America.[133]

Furthermore, there are more than 225 Muslim schools in the United States that indoctrinate an estimated fifty thousand children with Islamic education.[134] Again, the overall financier of these schools is Saudi Arabia and the Muslim Brotherhood, which certainly will be teaching and grooming these children in strict Wahhabi Sunni Islam. Bridgette Gabriel, founder of *ACT! for America* and the American Congress of Truth, summarizes the Islamic indoctrination of children very well by proclaiming, "They foster an environment of hate, loathing, and resentment toward Western culture, Christians, Jews, Shiites, secular Muslims, and non-Muslims."[135]

ANTI-SEMITISM ON UNIVERSITY CAMPUSES

As the petrodollars perpetually pump anti-Semitic doctrine into America's colleges and universities, it has resulted in a significant rise in anti-Semitism. The Anti-Defamation League released data that reports, "In 2015, anti-

Semitic attacks significantly rose by 3 %, with a 50% increase in violent assaults than in the previous year. On college campuses, it nearly doubled in 2015 compared to 2014" (years of blood moons). [136] In 2014, a study by Trinity College found over half of Jewish college students have experienced anti-Semitism on their campus. [137] In 2016, the AMCHA Initiative, an organization that fights anti-Semitism on college campuses, reported the number of incidents involving the suppression of Jewish students' freedom of speech and assembly *doubled* from 2015.[138] The AMCHA study reported campuses that have an active "Students for Justice in Palestine" chapter are *seven times* more likely to have incidents targeting Jewish students.[139]

ANTI-SEMITISM IN AMERICA

America has not only seen a rise in anti-Semitism at its colleges and universities, but it also has become widespread in all aspects of society. There are clear and disturbing statistics and trends of anti-Semitism that are occurring in the land of the free. In 2014 (a blood moons year), according to the Anti-Defamation League's Audits of Anti-Semitic Incidents (ADL), the total number of incidents increased by 21 percent from 2013. [140] There were 912 anti-Semitic incidents throughout America in 2014, which was the first time *in a decade* the overall number significantly rose. Abraham H. Foxman, the ADL national director, stated, "2014 was a particularly violent year for Jews both oversees and in the United States."[141] Barry Curtiss-Lusher, the ADL national chairman, stated, "The reported increase in U.S. anti-Semitic incidents coincided with a huge upsurge in anti-Semitic attacks *in Europe and elsewhere around the globe.*"[142] The states with the highest numbers of anti-Semitic attacks were the ones with the largest Jewish populations, New York, California, New Jersey, Florida, Pennsylvania, and Massachusetts.[143]

In 2015, according to the ADL, the number of violent anti-Semitic assaults in America rose 3 percent from 2014. [144] The ADL's annual audit recorded a total of 941 incidents in America compared to 912 incidents in 2014.[145] On university and college campuses, a total of 90 incidents were reported on 60 campuses, nearly doubling the 47 incidents reported on 43 campuses in 2014.[146] ADL CEO Jonathan A. Greenblatt stated, "We are disturbed that violent anti-Semitic incidents are rising. And we know that for every incident reported, there's likely another that goes unreported. The trend toward anti-Semitic violence is very concerning."[147] In 2015, the ADL also reported a great outburst of hate through online social media platforms. Greenblatt declared, "Online hate is particularly disturbing because of the ubiquity of social media and its deep penetration into our daily lives, plus the anonymity offered by certain platforms which facilitates this phenomenon. This issue has grown exponentially in recent years because the Internet provides racists and bigots with an outlet to reach a potential audience of millions." [148] In 2015, the states with the largest Jewish population were once again those with the highest anti-Semitic incidents, New York, California, New Jersey, Florida, and Massachusetts.[149]

In 2016, according to the ADL, anti-Semitic incidents in America rose *34 percent*, exploding by the numbers of 2015. [150] There were 1,266 reported acts targeting Jewish people and institutions. Jonathan Greenblatt stated, "There's been a significant, sustained increase in anti-Semitic activity since the start of 2016, and what's most concerning is the fact that the number has accelerated over the past five months. Clearly, we have work to do and need to bring more urgency to the fight."[151]

In the first quarter of 2017, a wave of bomb threats hit twenty-nine Jewish Centers in America with evacuations occurring in Phoenix, Palo Alto, San Diego, Long Beach, Seattle, North Carolina, Michigan, Rhode Island, Florida, Pennsylvania, Indiana, New York, New Jersey, Alabama, Delaware, Maryland, and Virginia.[152] In general, in the first quarter of 2017, anti-Semitic incidents jumped *86 percent*, with 541 reported incidents, which was on pace for more than 2,000 incidents in the year.

Anti-Semitic incidents at nondenominational elementary, middle, and high schools increased *106 percent*, from 114 in 2015 to 235 in 2016.[153] This increase accelerated *in the first quarter of 2017*, when 95 incidents were reported. Greenblatt stated, "Schools are a microcosm of the country. Children absorb messages from their parents and the media, and bring them into their schools and playgrounds. We are very concerned the next generation is internalizing messages of intolerance and bigotry."[154] We can have total confidence the Islamic infiltration of their wicked agenda in public schools have also been a major factor in these troubling statistics. Once again, the states with the most incidents continues among the states with the largest Jewish populations, California, New York, New Jersey, Florida, and Massachusetts.

AMERICA'S OPEN BORDERS

In the past several years, especially this past U.S. presidential election year, America's southern border with Mexico has hit fever-pitched levels among political, social, and religious realms. Republicans and Democrats, who both have had tremendous opportunities to protect our borders from the entry of terrorists, have failed. Although elected President Donald J. Trump has boldly and sternly pledged to build an impenetrable wall and crack down on Islamic terrorism, it could be too late, because the negligent open border policy for several decades has allowed Satan's hunters to enter America. In 2006, a House Committee on Homeland Security report stated, "Each year, hundreds of illegal aliens from countries known to harbor terrorists or promote terrorism are found trying to cross the border along the Rio Grande Valley." The report acknowledged that "members of Hezbollah have already entered the United States across the border prior to 2005." [155] In 2012, a report from the House Committee on Homeland Security showed "1,918 '*special interest aliens*' were stopped at the border from fiscal years 2006–2011." [156] By the way, "special interest aliens" is code for terrorists, or Satan's hunters. Once again, this clearly points to the recklessness and stupidity of the U.S. government's policies, which have been allowed by Republicans, Democrats, and presidents from both parties.

On March 23, 2016, at a House Oversight Committee, National Security Subcommittee hearing, U.S. Representative Ron DeSantis declared, "Recent reports state that the U.S. Customs and Border Protection has apprehended several members of known Islamist terrorist organizations crossing the southern border in recent years." [157] The *Houston Chronicle* validates DeSantis's statement from a report it inappropriately obtained from the State Department of Public Safety who distributed it to Texas elected officials, which acknowledged that border security agents have apprehended several Somali terrorists, who are known members of al-Shabaab, an Islamic extremist group that was once funded by Osama Bin Laden (al-Qaeda). Other "special interest aliens" who have been arrested while attempting to cross the porous southern border and who have known connections to terrorist groups include Afghans, Iranians, Iraqis, Syrians, Libyans, and Pakistanis.[158]

It is reported that immigrants who have been arrested over the past few years have terrorist associations, and they originate from thirty-five countries in the Middle East, North Africa, and Asia. [159] From November 2013 to July 2014, authorities reported 143 land border crossing encounters with watch-listed individuals from these countries in southwest border states.[160] What is even more disgraceful is the Department of Homeland Security's terrorist "hands off list," which was revealed when Senator Charles Grassley released internal DHS emails in 2014. The emails included a 2012 communication between the U.S. Immigration and Customs Enforcement (ICE) and U.S. Customs and Border Protection about whether officials would give a visa to a person who was believed to be a Muslim Brotherhood member and associated with Hamas and Hezbollah. [161] Why would a terrorist be "hands off"?

Positively, the Islamic infiltration of the U.S. government impacted this ridiculous and insane list, because of our corrupt, bought-off politicians in Washington D.C. To put this in perspective, in 2017, the GOP Congress *killed* a legislation bill banning taxpayer funding of Hamas, a sworn enemy of America and Israel. [162] Therefore, if our greedy and ignorant politicians killed a bill to stop the funding of a terror group with our tax dollars, do you think they will stop them from entering our country?

MUSLIM REFUGEE IMMIGRATION IN THE UNITED STATES

America has been one of the most compassionate and accepting nations in the world, if not the most, when it comes to foreign immigration. After all, the land of the free was built upon immigrants from *all* lands of the world. It is the very fabric that makes America such a great phenomenon, because of its acceptance of all people from all ethnicities, religions, and backgrounds. Without any doubt, the majority of people who immigrate to America have fallen in love with its ideas: liberty, freedom, and prosperity. Most immigrants treasure the opportunity to *assimilate* into the American dream, including its society, and contribute to the greatness of it. However, just as we have discovered, Islam, and the extremists who defiantly support and advocate its dominance of the world, directly defies the liberties and freedoms that America was built upon by its founding fathers. As previously mentioned, Islam's ultimate goal is complete global domination, which includes domination over America, culminating with the eradication of its constitution and laws in favor of Islamic Sharia law.

Please note: I love the diversity of America, with neighborhoods such as Chinatown, Little Havana, Little Italy, and so forth, but I am definitely opposed to any culture or "religion" that wants to completely eradicate what America was built upon, which is Judeo-Christian values that protect and support the constitution of freedom of speech, religion, and liberty. Make no mistake: Islam will *never* coexist with these God-given principles.

In 1992, according to the Pew Research Center, 41 percent of green card holders arrived from the Middle East, North Africa, sub-Saharan Africa, and the Asia Pacific region, where fundamentalist Islam dominates. [163] Since 1992, an estimated two million Muslims have immigrated to the United

States.[164] On the contrary, before 1990, fewer than 5 percent of foreigners who took up residence in the United States came from Muslim countries.[165] In 2002, the percentage increased to 53 percent for these regions. Over that same period, the number of Muslim immigrants coming to America annually has doubled, from an estimated fifty thousand to one hundred thousand each year.[166] Of course, there is not an official estimate of Muslims in America because the Census Bureau does not track religious affiliation. Nevertheless, Pew estimates there were 2.75 million Muslims living in America in 2011, with only 1.7 million of them holding legal permanent residency status. On the contrary, CAIR states there are approximately 7 million Muslims in America.[167]

In the past decade, under former president Barack H. Obama's administration, immigration for Muslim immigrants from terrorist countries escalated at an alarming pace. The *Investor's Business Daily* (IBD) reported that between 2010 and 2013, the Obama administration imported approximately three hundred thousand new immigrants from Muslim nations known for Islamic fundamentalism—more than from Central America and Mexico combined in that same period.[168] Many of the 41,094 immigrants were from terrorist hot spots, like Iraq, where ISIS operates. House Homeland Security committee chairman Mike McCaul proclaimed that Obama's new policy is "a federally sanctioned welcome party to potential terrorists."[169] The IBD also reported that ISIS claimed to have released a huge wave of hunters from Libya across the Mediterranean Sea disguised as refugees to enter and cause destruction in Europe.[170] We can have confidence that ISIS and other terror groups have taken advantage of America's open border policies, as well as other lackadaisical, politically correct immigration policies, and they have cleverly, but legally, entered America to promote their agenda. In fact, it is reported that American authorities are not able to estimate the number of "homegrown" terrorist jihadists, much less the infiltration of the refugee immigration.

In Pew's report, "The Future of the Global Muslim Population, Projections for 2010–2030," it projects that if the current trend continues, the Muslim population in America will vastly increase in the next twenty years, from 2.6 million to 6.2 million in 2030.[171] This massive wave of Muslim immigrants has resulted in some of America's towns and cities being "Islamized," which means city governments and councils are being overtaken by Muslim leadership. This will only lead to drastic changes within the cities in order to be in compliance with the Qur'an and Sharia law.

EXAMPLES OF THE ISLAMIC INVASION OF AMERICA

In Islam, the term *Hijrah* is used when Muslims migrate to populate non-Muslim nations to impose Sharia law in the name of Allah. Without question, America is witnessing the *beginning* of "Hijrah" in the land of the free. Let us explore how the Islamic Hijrah has affected some cities and towns in America.

Dearborn, Michigan, has an estimated 100,000 people, and 40 percent of them are Muslims. [172] In 2013, a leaked government document revealed that more Muslims living in Dearborn were on the federal terror watch list than from any other city except New York, and several of them have been arrested after attempting to leave America to join terrorist organizations.[173] Even more troubling, author Steve Tarani declared that he has witnessed "no-go zones" where Dearborn Police cannot enter while riding with a member of the Detroit Metro SWAT Police.[174] He also states that in certain areas of Dearborn, "street signs suddenly go from English to Arabic." One could conclude that Dearborn is being transformed into operating as an Islamic Sharia city.

Another example of the Islamic invasion of U.S. towns and cities is Hamtramck, Michigan, which became the first jurisdiction in the nation to elect a majority Muslim council in 2013.[175] In the past decade, the Muslim population exploded with the arrival of thousands of Muslim immigrants, and in 2004, the town's culture shifted, because the city council gave permission to a downtown Islamic center to broadcast its call to prayer from the speakers atop its roof.[176] Hamtramck is approximately 23 percent Muslim, and unless there is a change in politics, it will continue to transform into an Islamic city within America. (Since the outbreak of the Syrian Civil War in 2011, over 2,100 Syrian refugees have entered Michigan, and the results will continue to dangerously manifest as they have in Hamtramck and Dearborn).

The Islamic invasion has also reshaped Minneapolis, Minnesota. U.S. Representative Michele Bachmann, who has been one of the few outspoken political leaders against Islam, proclaimed, "Minnesota is no longer the state I moved to in the mid 1960s, then, we were a well-ordered society with a high-functioning population." Today, Minnesota has the largest Somali (mostly Muslim) community in America, with a population of approximately forty thousand. [177] As a whole, the Somali refugees have not assimilated into American society, which has led to the denigration of the culture of Minnesota and a large number of social problems, including terrorism. Bachmann declared, "Parallel societies kill assimilation from the Third World and create havoc in American societies," continuing, "This is a failed multicultural experiment that is killing people and destroying the future of the West." [178] She is referring to the following events: a recent shooting of a man by a Somali-refugee cop, Muslims being found with bomb-making devices, Somali women clothed from head to toe with Muslim clothing, the Sharia mind-set of female genital mutilation, domestic abuse of women, Sharia-controlled zones, the refusal to assimilate into American culture and ways, and Islamic terrorism in the state. [179] Representative Bachmann sums up the refugee immigration process best, declaring, "Immigrants must know it is a condition of entry to the U.S. to assimilate into Western society by adopting allegiance to Western law. Immigrants should also be required to adopt Western dress, and be informed they must abandon the illegal aspects of following Sharia law."

In a small southern town in Tennessee, the Islamic invasion has also resulted in devastating results, as Muslim refugees refuse to assimilate into it. Residents of Shelbyville, Tennessee, have witnessed firsthand the culture clash of the Islamic refugees and American values. According to a local reporter for the *Shelbyville Times-Gazette*, "The Somalis are very, very rude, inconsiderate, very demanding. They would go into a store and haggle over prices. They would also demand to see a male salesperson, would not deal with women in stores. Their culture is totally alien to anything the residents are used to."[180] Regrettably, the culture clash has also led to a series of violent crimes by the Somali migrants. On September 27–29, 2016, three churches were shot up by Muslims with AK47s. Jihad Watch, the only "media" to report the heinous crime, reported, "A Muslim shoots up three churches and nothing is said about his motive or his Islamic identity. Would the same courtesy be shown a Christian who shot up three mosques? Why the cover-up? Who is responsible for it?" [181]

What compounds the Islamic refugee crisis in Tennessee is that Nashville is preparing to become the most liberal sanctuary city in the United States. Two ordinances filed by Metro councilmen Bob Mendes and Colby Sledge, drafted with the assistance of the Tennessee Immigrant and Refugee Rights Coalition (TIRRC) and cheered on by Mayor Megan Barry, will make Davidson County and Metro Nashville the most liberal sanctuary for refugees; in fact, even more liberal in its policies than New York City or San Francisco.[182] The citizens of Nashville should demand that these incompetent liberal politicians kill this legislation, because Metro Nashville and its surrounding counties will only continue to witness an increase in violence and crime.

The last example we will discuss of the Islamic invasion of American cities and towns is Utica, New York. In a piece titled "My Hometown is

Gone," Loretta the Prole, a former citizen of Utica and a blogger, conveyed her experience of living in an Islamizing area where there is a 25 percent (or more) refugee, mainly Muslim population. She witnessed two major changes: "Churches have been turned into mosques and Muslim immigrants placed into local positions of bureaucratic power," which replaces Americans with Islamic refugees. [183] Who are these refugees, and who is their allegiance to? Before Loretta moved to North Carolina, she went to meetings in upstate New York and was told that Utica was "full of ISIS and the local police were really worried."

These are just a few of many examples of how American towns and cities are being infiltrated by Muslim refugees who refuse to assimilate to American values and culture. Instead, they would like the implementation of Islamic Sharia law. In the words of president Teddy Roosevelt, the American people "must demand for migrants to assimilate, because there is no room for them to be American and something else." Without question, the U.S. refugee program for Muslims has failed, as towns, cities, churches, and ultimately, people, are being tremendously affected by the Islamic invasion of America. This invasion has been stained by hundreds of brutal attacks across the nation,[184] on which, I suppose, one could write a whole series of books. The U.S. government's reckless and ignorant refugee policies and its bowing down to Islam will ultimately release Satan's hunters into America. Pamela Geller, president of the American Freedom Defense Initiative warns, "[Legislators] are bent on keeping America on a path that will only bring civil strife and bloodshed on a massive scale—and sooner than anyone expects."[185] I completely concur with Geller's analysis because of what the prophet Jeremiah prophesied more than twenty-five hundred years ago about Satan's hunters (Jer. 16:16).

TERRORIST ATTACKS IN AMERICA

With Saudi Arabia and the Muslim Brotherhood's infiltration of the U.S. government and education systems, combined with decades-long Muslim migration in America, including open borders, we need to ask ourselves, "Have Satan's *end-of-the-age* hunters been released in the land of the free? Are we witnessing the devastating effects of the Islamic infiltration of the United States government and the greedy, politically correct politicians and media? Does America have active terrorist cells training inside its borders?"

Throughout the past several decades, and especially since the horrific terrorist attacks of 9/11, there have been numerous major terrorist attacks on American soil from Islamic extremists, including the Fort Hood (2009) and Boston Marathon attacks (2013). Since the blood moon tetrad of 2014–2015, which was the *sign and marker* for the release of Satan's *end-of-the-age* hunters, these extremists have caused terror inside the borders of America. Following is a list of the *major terrorist attacks* since the blood moon marker of 2014–2015.

- Chattanooga, Tennessee, July 16, 2015—A Kuwaiti Muslim immigrant opened fire on two military facilities, a U.S. Naval Reserve Center and a military recruiting office, killing 5 U.S. service members.[186]
- San Bernardino, California, December 2, 2015—A Muslim couple who had pledged allegiance to ISIS killed 14 people, seriously injuring 22 others. Until recently, it was the deadliest mass shooting in the United States since the 2012 Sandy Hook school shooting, and the deadliest terrorist attack to occur in the United States since 9/11. [187]
- Orlando, Florida, June 12, 2016 – A Muslim man who called 911 and proclaimed allegiance to ISIS, killed 49 people, wounding 58 others, in a nightclub. At the time, it was the deadliest mass shooting in United States history, and the deadliest terrorist attack on American soil since 9/11. [188]
- Las Vegas, Nevada, October 1, 2017 – It is the deadliest mass shooting in U.S. history, as 58 people were killed and 546 injured. There is major controversy and several conspiracy theories surrounding this horrendous event because the investigation and statements of the federal and local authorities have major faults, to say the least. In my personal opinion, this was an Islamic terrorist attack. How could this be? *Let us follow the money.* The CEO of Mandalay Bay, James Murren, has donated millions to organizations tied to Islamic terrorism, including CAIR. The U.S. Justice department has labeled CAIR "an unindicted co-conspirator to Muslim terrorism." Even liberal Democrat Senator Chuck Shumer said, "CAIR has ties to terrorism and intimate links with Hamas." Additionally, and quite revealing, Murren sold off most of his company shares (13.7 million worth) of the company's stock *prior* to the Las Vegas shooting. Coincidence?

Of course not, but rather indicting. Even more astonishing and troubling, *Murren is a sitting member of the Homeland Security National Infrastructure Advisory Council, which raises major red flags.* So, let us get this straight … The CEO of Mandalay Bay, the site of the deadliest mass shooting in U.S. history, is a sitting member of the Homeland Security National Infrastructure Advisory Council, and has donated millions to Islamic terror groups? I believe we can connect the dots.[189]

- New York City, New York, October 31, 2017 – A Muslim man drove a flatbed pickup truck and rammed into runners and cyclists on a bike path in Lower Manhattan, New York City, killing 8 people, and injuring at least 11 others.[190] Combined with Europe, this was the 15th vehicular ramming-attack by Islamic jihadists since 2014 (blood moons). In total, these attacks have killed 142 people, in which seems like the Islamist's "new method" of causing terror.

Following is a map of Jihad training camps in America. This information was provided by Steven Emerson of American Jihad and independent investigators.

THE ALIYAH FROM THE UNITED STATES

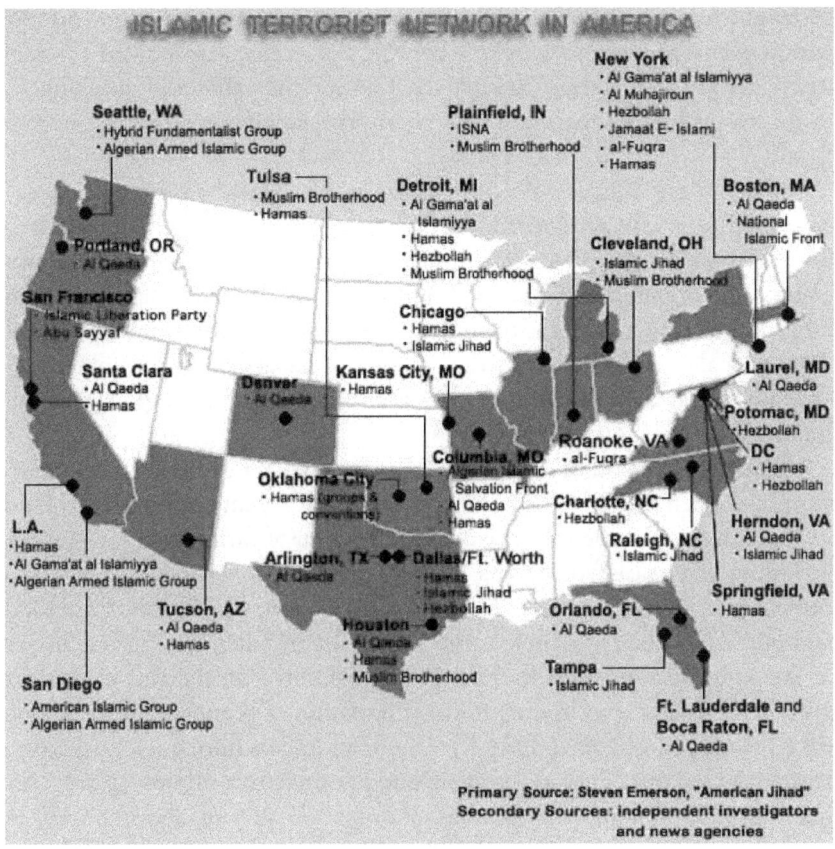

Terrorist Training Camps

THE GREAT AMERICAN ECLIPSE

Before we conclude, let us discuss a fascinating celestial occurrence that happened in America. On August 21, 2017, the "Great American Eclipse," a *total* solar eclipse, transpired *only* over the United States in totality. In chapter 5, we discussed the unique phenomenon of another one of God's celestial bodies, the blood moons, and how they *directly* correlate as *signs and markers* to the children of Israel. The occurrence of a solar eclipse signifies His warning to the nations, *or in this case, America*, because the *total eclipse only* occurred over the land of the free in *totality*. Remember: the blood moons indicate God's warning to Israel, because its calendar months are based on the moon (Hebrew calendar). On the contrary, the occurrence of a solar eclipse signifies His warning to the nations, or the nation over which the solar eclipse beckons, as its calendar months are only based on the sun (Gregorian calendar). Also, the rabbinical thinking is, as the sun is larger than the moon, so are the nations in size compared to Israel. [191]

What many believers did not realize is the "Great American Eclipse" coincided at a very specific and humble time on God's calendar, which is the Hebrew calendar. The total eclipse befell on the beginning of the month of Elul, the month of *repentance*. This month holds supreme significance in biblical history, because it is the exact time (Elul 1) Moses ascended Mount Sinai to make "atonement" for the children of Israel's sin of the golden calf (Exodus 32). It is also the precise time that Satan began to tempt Messiah in the wilderness for forty days (Matt. 4).

Therefore, instead of America celebrating the "Great American Eclipse" as a good omen, it should be humbly praying and repenting to the Lord God for its sins, because the total solar eclipse is a sign of forthcoming judgment, including the release of Satan's hunters. Without question, America has turned from its first love and what it was built upon, which is the Lord God and His Word, the Holy Bible. America has deeply fallen into great apostasy in the past several decades, including but not limited to: aborting more than 60 million little lambs, leading in the exportation of pornography, removing prayer from our schools and the Ten Commandments from our courthouses, removing God out of our government and personal lives, approving same-sex marriage (the Supreme Court), abusing drugs and alcohol, and so on. All in all, America has called evil good and good evil (see Isa. 5:20). Accordingly, why would the Almighty keep His hand of protection upon America while it keeps abominating and blaspheming His law and commandments? Did He not destroy Israel, His promised land, *twice*, for the same adulterous and wicked ways? Believe me: if the Lord God destroyed His heritage, His covenanted land, *twice* for their disobedience and stiff-necked ways, we can be sure that He will allow war and terrorism to come upon the shores of America.

THE AFTERMATH OF THE GREAT AMERICAN ECLIPSE

Since the *sign or marker* of the "Great American Eclipse," America has witnessed and endured major cataclysmic events that, if calculated, would be astronomical in coincidental nature. In other words, it is not by coincidence these major tragic events have occurred *since* the total eclipse over America.

Following is a list of just a few of the major events. *Keep in mind, the total eclipse occurred on August 21,* and within the first *three months*, these major events occurred on American soil:

- three major hurricanes, Harvey, Irma, and Maria, which were the costliest on record at that point in history ($317 billion) [192]
- more than two thousand earthquakes, the strongest at the time being in Hennessey, Oklahoma (3.4); Lompoc, California (4.9); and Anchor Point, Alaska (4.9) [193]
- the worst mass shooting in American history, with 58 people killed and 546 injured (Las Vegas, Nevada). [194]

Is this a coincidence? There is a wise saying that coincidence is God's way of being anomalous. Let us remember what America's first president, George Washington, warned its citizens about God's hand of protection.

An Excerpt of George Washington's Inaugural address of 1789:

> Such being the impressions under which I have, in obedience to the public summons, repaired to the present station; it would be peculiarly improper to omit in this first official Act, my fervent supplications to that Almighty Being who rules over the Universe, who presides in the Councils of Nations, and whose providential aids can supply every human defect, that his benediction may consecrate to the liberties and happiness of the People of the United States, a Government instituted by themselves for these essential purposes: and may enable every instrument employed in its administration to execute with success, the functions allotted to his charge. In tendering this homage to the Great Author of every public and private good I assure myself that it expresses your sentiments not less than my own; nor those of my fellow-citizens at large, less than either. No People can be bound to acknowledge and adore the invisible hand, which conducts the Affairs of men more than the People of the United States. Every step, by which they have advanced to the character of an independent nation, seems to have been distinguished by some token of providential agency. And in the important revolution just accomplished in the system of their United Government, the tranquil deliberations and voluntary consent of so many distinct communities, from which the

event has resulted, cannot be compared with the means by which most Governments have been established, without some return of pious gratitude along with a humble anticipation of the future blessings which the past seem to presage. These reflections, arising out of the present crisis, have forced themselves too strongly on my mind to be suppressed. You will join with me I trust in thinking, that there are none under the influence of which, the proceedings of a new and free Government can more auspiciously commence . . . I dwell on this prospect with every satisfaction which an ardent love for my Country can inspire: since there is no truth more thoroughly established, than that there exists in the economy and course of nature, an indissoluble union between virtue and happiness, between duty and advantage, between the genuine maxims of an honest and magnanimous policy, and the solid rewards of public prosperity and felicity: *Since we ought to be no less persuaded that the propitious smiles of Heaven, can never be expected on a nation that disregards the eternal rules of order and right, which Heaven itself has ordained: And since the preservation of the sacred fire of liberty, and the destiny of the Republican model of Government, are justly considered as deeply, perhaps as finally staked, on the experiment entrusted to the hands of the American people.*

America . . . the sword is coming . . .

In conclusion, the ultimate goal of Islam is to dominate the world through the governing of Sharia law. The Saudis and the Muslim Brotherhood's goal to Islamize America begins with immigration, and perpetuates through the infiltration of the U.S. government, the education system, and the invasion of U.S. cities and towns. It is certain the U.S. government has been infiltrated with Islamic influence, which has pierced the highest offices of the United States. Not only has the Islamic invasion infiltrated the U.S. government and the education system, but Muslims have also built hundreds of Wahhabi Sunni mosques throughout America. Just as we have discovered in the previous chapter with Europe, America is journeying down the same bloody death path of Islamization. Ultimately, the Islamic invasion of Satan's hunters in America will fulfill Jeremiah's prophecy (Jer. 16:16), because approximately half of the world's Jewry lives in America. According to Jeremiah's prophecy, which will fulfill the everlasting covenants, the Jewish people will make Aliyah to the Promised Land at the end of the age—the period in which our generation is living. Europe will continue to be terrorized on a regular basis by

Satan's hunters, and the years ahead for America will look the same. Although Donald J. Trump and his administration are taking bold actions against allowing Satan's hunters into America, much more is needed to eliminate the Islamic invasion. He is one man, with one team, fighting decades of greedy corruption by Washington politicians. Additionally, the president will only have four, possibly eight years, to resolve the decades-long Islamic invasion. In my opinion, and according to God's prophetic timeline, the damage has been done, and Satan's hunters are rooted within America's borders. Make no mistake: Jeremiah's prophecy of the hunters will continue to manifest until its complete fulfillment in all nations, including America, which will culminate with a massive Aliyah from America to the Promised Land. I pray that just as the God of Israel protected Abraham, Isaac, Jacob, and David from Satan's *original hunters*, He will protect His faithful remnant, Jews and Gentiles, from Satan's *end-of-the-age* hunters in America from this time forth and forevermore. Amen, Amen, and Amen!

CHAPTER 9

SATAN'S FINAL HUNTER

At the end of the age, Satan will *directly* attempt to forbid God's everlasting covenants from being *completely* fulfilled by Messiah at His second coming and during His millennial reign, as he demonically influences his *final hunter*, the Antichrist. Assuredly, just as Satan conspired against God's *original fishermen* by attacking them individually through his *original hunters*, he will desperately attempt to thwart Messiah's fulfillment of the everlasting covenants by possessing and inspiring the Antichrist to battle against Him at His second coming (Isa. 46:9–10; Rev. 19:11–21). Additionally, at the last three and one-half years of the age, Satan will influence his *final hunter*, the Antichrist, to inundate and spew out his wrath, terror, and destruction on *all* of God's people, Jews and Gentiles, because he will understand his time is short (Rev. 12:12-17). As we have discussed, Satan certainly understands biblical prophecy, which includes the everlasting covenants, the prophecy of the fishermen and the hunters, the time of Jacob's trouble, and Messiah's second coming, and it is the premier reason he inspires these horrendous and gruesome acts during this prophetic period.

Could Satan's *original hunters*, who *directly* attempted to forbid God's everlasting covenants to His *original fishermen*, bestow indispensable knowledge of Satan's *final hunter* at the end of the age? Do Satan's *original hunters*, along with the biblical prophets, validate the *region* from which the final hunter will rise? Do the biblical prophets call the Antichrist, who is Satan's *final hunter*, by the *literal* name of this *region*? Let us review the maps of Satan's *original hunters*.

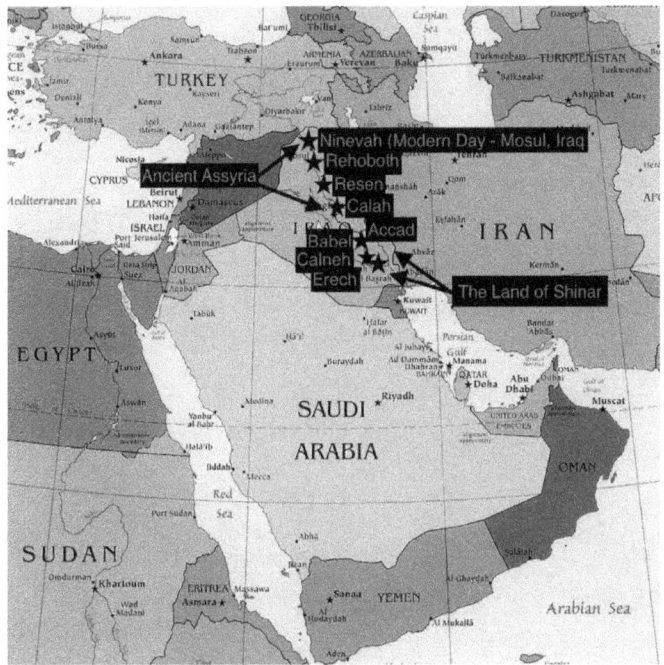

Nimrod

Hagar – Ishmael

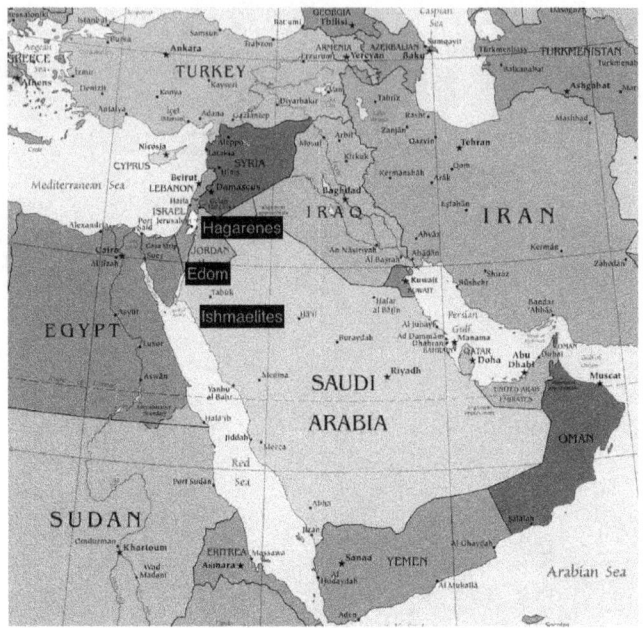
Esau-Edom

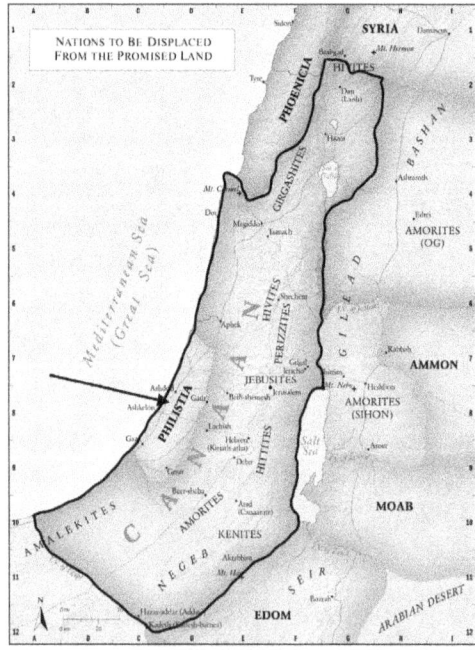
Philistines

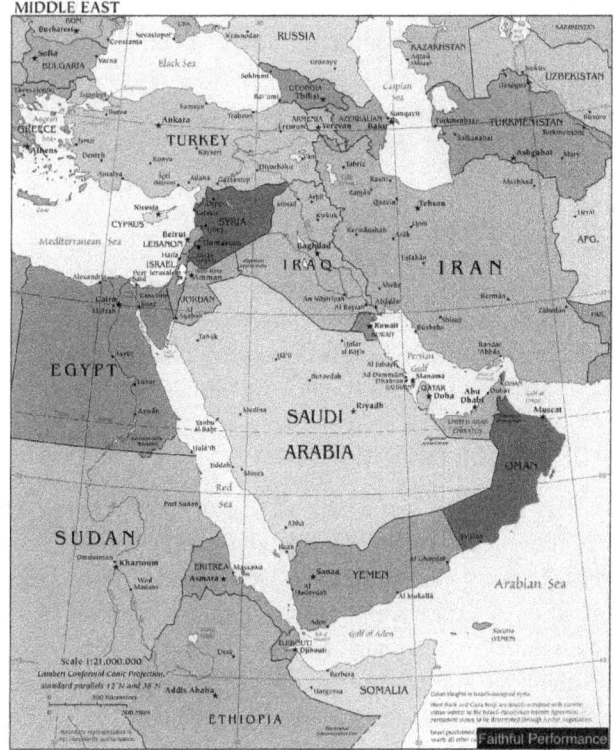

Middle East

After reviewing the maps, it is clear that *all* of Satan's *original hunters*, who *directly* attempted to forbid God's everlasting covenants, originated from a specific location and primary *region*: The Middle East. What is even more incredible is Satan's *original hunters* inhabited the exact region that is currently being ruled by radical Islamic countries (Muslims), who vehemently hate the nation of Israel. Understand, of course, that this book is focused on *regions* and not specific people, as there are millions of Arabs in the Middle East and North African regions who are faithful, fervent believers in Yeshua the Messiah (Isa. 17, 19). Hallelujah! Accordingly, what conclusions can we draw regarding the Middle Eastern *region* as it correlates with Satan's *final hunter*?

Isaiah 46:9–10: "Remember the former things of old, for I am God, and there is no other; I am God, and there is none like Me, *declaring the end from the beginning, and from ancient times things that are not yet done*, saying, 'My counsel shall stand, and I will do all My pleasure.'"

Ecclesiastes 1:9–10: "*That which has been is what will be, that which is done is what will be done, and there is nothing new under the sun. Is there anything of which it may be said, 'See this is new?' It has already been in ancient times before us.*"

Clearly, since the living Word proclaims that God "declares the end from the beginning, and from ancient times things not yet done," and, "that which has been is what will be, that which is done is what will be done, and there is nothing new under the sun," this should also pertain to Satan's *final hunter*.

THE ORIGIN OF SATAN'S FINAL HUNTER

In our book, *God's Prophetic Timeline, Messiah's Final Warning* (mentioned earlier), we thoroughly explain in great detail Daniel's visions and prophecies (Dan. 2, 7–9, 11), along with Revelation 13, 17, and 18, which confirms the *region* the Antichrist will rise from, as well as the *region* of his ten kings. For the sake of redundancy, in summary, we will examine Daniel 7 and Revelation 13, because these awesome, prophetic chapters validate where the *final hunter* will rise from and the identity of the ten kings of his "conglomerate kingdom."

Daniel 7 proclaims there will be four *different* kingdoms (beasts) that will rise out of the earth before Messiah's second coming (vv. 1–8). Before we begin exploring this prophecy, let us recall that Daniel was commanded to "shut up the words, and seal his book *until the time of the end*" (Dan. 12:4), which includes *all* of his prophetic visions in his book. In Daniel 7, we can also validate this vision as an end-of-the-age prophecy, because it prophesies about the same "little horn" that is prophesied in Daniel 8, which God's messenger Gabriel repeatedly declared to Daniel was a vision for the end of the age (Dan. 8:16–19). Therefore, if Daniel 8 is an end-of-the-age prophecy that prophesies about the "little horn" (Antichrist), then so is Daniel 7, because it foretells about the same "little horn." Furthermore, Daniel literally names the empires in Daniel 2 and 8 that will rise to power at the end of the age, which perfectly correlates with Daniel 7 (Dan. 2:28, 38–44; 8:16–22). With the knowledge of these empires, along with their prophetic foreshadows in history, here are Daniel 7's four kingdoms in exact order:

DANIEL 7'S FOUR BEASTS (KINGDOMS) (DAN. 7:3–8)

Lion—Babylon (Iraq)
Bear—Medo-Persia (Iran)
Leopard—Grecian (Turkey)
Antichrist kingdom (Ten kings)

Babylonian Empire

Medo-Persian Empire

Grecian Empire

After reviewing the maps, it is clear the first three kingdoms, the Babylonian, Medo-Persian, and Grecian Empires, ruled over the *same* land area, because they conquered one another. Now, let us review the ancient maps to surmise if the Babylonian, Medo-Persian, and Grecian Empires ruled over the exact same *region* that Satan's *original hunters* emerged from and are named after.

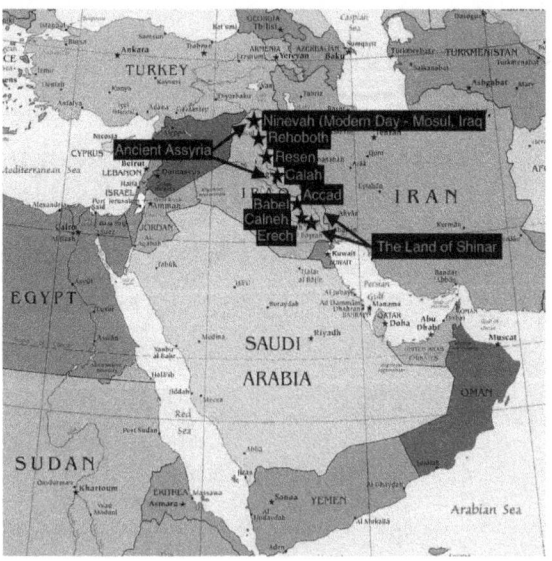

Nimrod

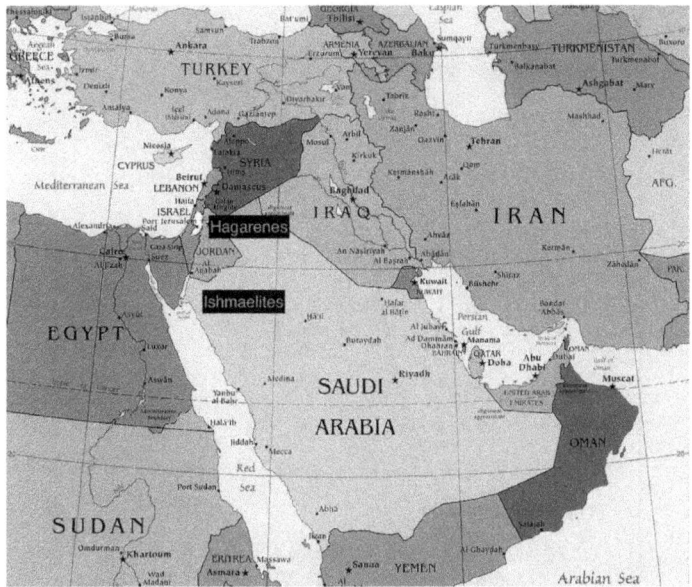
Hagar – Ishmael

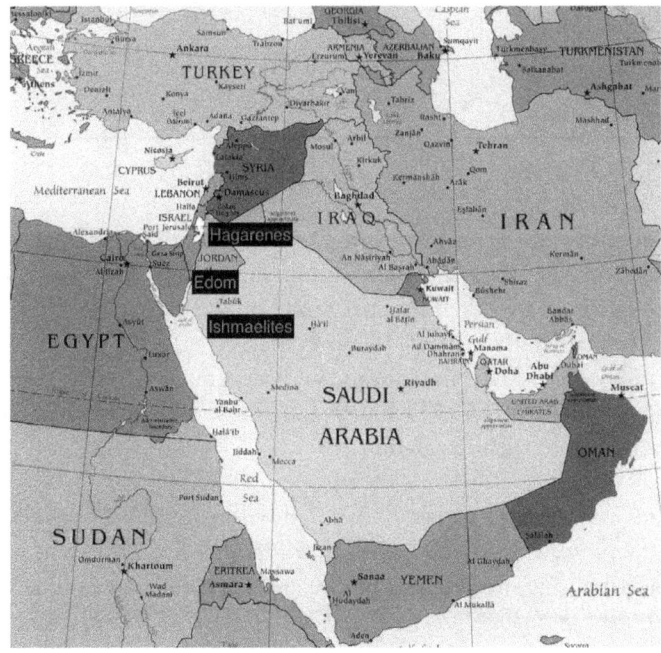
Esau-Edom

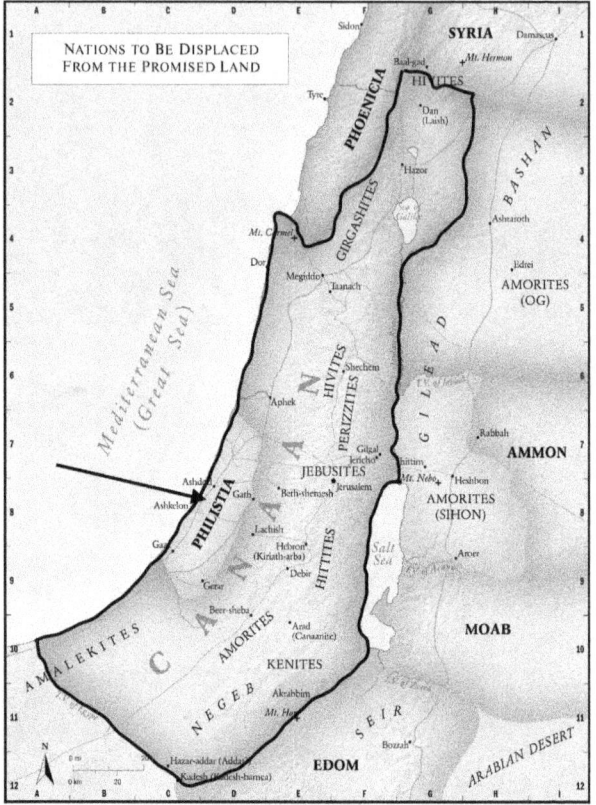

Philistines

Although the three kingdoms in Daniel 7 ruled over a larger *region* of land than Nimrod, Ishmael, Esau (Edom), and the Philistines, *all* three kingdoms encompassed the principal *region* of Satan's *original hunters*. Keep in mind, the Babylonian (Iraq), Medo-Persian (Iran), and Grecian (Turkey) empires today are *all* Islamic nations, with dominant Muslim populations. What can we make of Daniel's fourth kingdom, the Antichrist's kingdom? Does it corroborate with Revelation 13?

> Daniel 7:7: "After this I saw in the night visions, and behold, *a fourth beast, dreadful and terrible, exceedingly strong.* It had huge iron teeth; it was devouring, breaking in pieces, and trampling the residue with its feet. *It was different from all the beasts that were before it, and it had **ten horns**.*"

In Revelation 13:1–2, John describes *one* beast that absolutely parallels with the fourth beast in Daniel 7, which substantiates what *region* the Antichrist and his kingdom will rise from:

> "Then I stood on the sand of the sea. *And I saw a beast rising up out of the sea, having seven heads and **ten horns**, and on his horns ten crowns, and on his heads a blasphemous name. Now the beast which I saw was like a **leopard**, his feet were like the feet of a **bear**, and his mouth like the mouth of a **lion**.*"

Daniel 7's fourth beast and Revelation 13's *one* beast both have *ten horns*, which accurately aligns the empires. Now, let us take a closer examination of the conglomerate beast of Revelation 13, and how it exactly matches with the first three beasts of Daniel 7.

John's vision in Revelation 13 describes *one beast* who looked like a lion, a bear, and a leopard. Sound familiar? Daniel 7 prophesied about *three separate beasts*: a lion, a bear, and a leopard (vv. 2–8). What conclusions can we draw from Daniel 7 and Revelation 13?

In Daniel 7, the *three separate* beasts represent the three different kingdoms in the exact order they will occur at the end of the age; lion (Iraq), bear (Iran), and leopard (Turkey). What does this mean for the *one* beast in Revelation 13? John's vision describes *one* beast instead of three, and it perfectly corroborates with Daniel 7's fourth beast. The *one* beast in Revelation 13 will be a "conglomerate" of *all* three of Daniel 7's kingdoms: lion (Iraq), bear (Iran), and leopard (Turkey).

DANIEL 7'S BEASTS (KINGDOMS)

1. Lion—Iraq
2. Bear—Iran
3. Leopard—Turkey

REVELATION 13 (ONE BEAST/KINGDOM) (DANIEL 7'S 4TH BEAST)

1. Lion (Iraq), Bear (Iran), Leopard (Turkey)

In other words, the final hunter and his kingdom, the beast kingdom, will consist of the "conglomerated *region*" of *all* three of these empires, because it is a lion, bear, and leopard combined into *one* beast (kingdom). Remember: these three empires (lion—Iraq, bear—Iran, and leopard—Turkey) primarily ruled over the same *region* that is located in the Middle East, which is the exact same *region* from which Satan's *original hunters* emerged. The prophet Hosea also gives us confirmation, as he prophesied to the children of Israel about the time of Jacob's trouble.

> Hosea 13:7–8: "So I will be to them like a *lion [Babylonian]*; like a *leopard [Grecian]* by the road I will lurk; I will meet them like a *bear [Medo-Persia]* deprived of her cubs; I will tear open their rib cage, and there I will devour them like a lion [Babylonian]. *The wild beast [Revelation 13] shall tear them.*"

Daniel, John, and Hosea are clearly explaining the Antichrist's kingdom (lion, bear, leopard) will consist of Islamic countries, which are located in the exact same *region* that Satan's *original hunters* originated from and inhabited. As the prophet proclaimed, the end will be like the beginning, and from ancient times things not yet fulfilled (Isa. 46:9–10). Now, since we understand the specific *region* where the Antichrist's kingdom (ten kings) will be located, what particular area does the *final hunter* rise from?

> Daniel 7:8: "I was considering the [ten] horns [of the fourth beast], and there was another horn, *a little one*, coming up among them, before whom three of the first [ten] horns were plucked out by the roots. *And there, in this horn, were eyes like the eyes of a man [Antichrist], and a mouth, speaking pompous words.*"

Once Daniel finished describing the fourth beast in Daniel 7, he continues to explain the *region* the Antichrist will rise from. He declares the "little horn" will rise from among the ten horns (kings), which Daniel 7 and Revelation 13 prove is the *conglomerated region* of the Babylonian—Iraq (lion), Medo-Persian—Iran (bear), and Grecian—Turkey (leopard) Empires. Amazingly, Daniel 8 also prophesies very specific details of the *region* the *final hunter* will rise from.

In Daniel 8, the prophet foretells of a future war that will occur at the end of the age between a ram and a goat (vv. 17–19). The angel Gabriel explains the ram is Persia (Iran) and the goat is Greece (Turkey) (vv. 20–21). In Hebrew, the word used for Greece in this text is *Javan*, which is western Turkey. Greece was not yet a country when Daniel wrote this prophecy (536 BC), and wouldn't be until 1830.

Daniel prophesies that Turkey (goat) will "confront the ram [Iran] with rage, attack him, and cast him to the ground, trampling him" (Dan. 8:6–7). Once Turkey accomplishes its prophetic destiny, the tyrannical Islamic country will become great (v.8), and then its leader, the first king, will die (v.v. 8,21). Subsequently, Turkey (goat) will be divided into four regions (v.v. 8,22) just like the ancient Grecian Empire eventually did after the death of Alexander the Great.

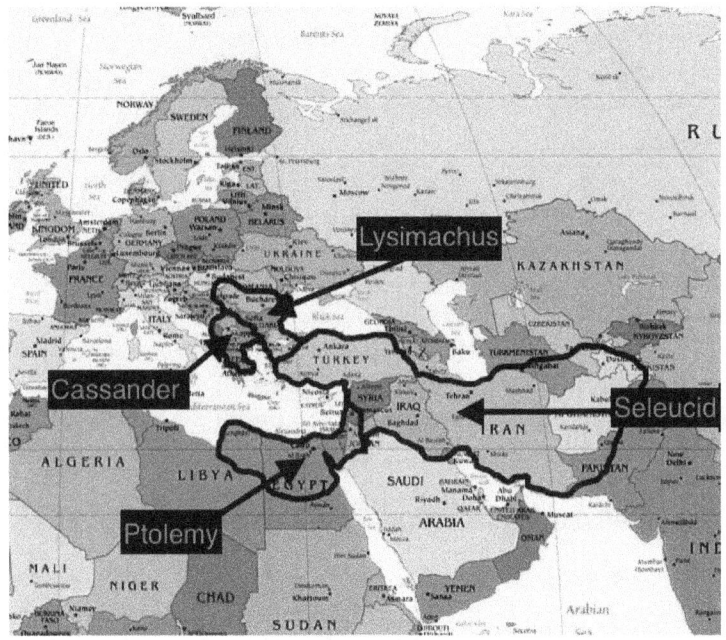

Four Divisions

Daniel continues to explain that after the four regions are established, a "little horn"— the same "little horn" as in Daniel 7—who is the Antichrist, will rise from one of the four regions of Turkey (Dan. 8:9). Which of the four regions will Satan's *final hunter* rise from?

> Daniel 8:9: "And out of one of them came a little horn *which grew exceedingly great toward the south*, toward the east, and toward the Glorious Land."

If the little horn (Antichrist) "grows exceedingly toward the south," then he must be coming from the north, which is the Seleucid (north) division of the Grecian Empire (Turkey), which again, is the same *region* of Satan's *original hunters.*

In the book of Revelation, Messiah also validates the Antichrist's rise out of the Seleucid division. Pay close attention to the present-tense nature of His words.

> Revelation 2:12–13, "And to the angel of the church in Pergamum write, 'These things says He who has the sharp two-edged sword: "I know your works, and where you dwell, *where Satan's throne is.* And you hold fast to My name, and did not deny My faith even in the days in which Antipas was My faithful martyr, who was killed among you, *where Satan dwells."*

Messiah is speaking to the church at Pergamum, which was located in the ancient Seleucid division of modern-day Turkey. Note that He prophesies where Satan's throne *is* located, not *was* located, so this is where Satan "dwells," not "dwelled." Of course, Satan runs to and fro all over the earth (Job 1:7; John 12:31; 14:30), but Messiah clearly emphasizes Satan's (Antichrist) throne is located in the Seleucid region. Therefore, as the Scriptures clearly declare, Satan will expand his territory "toward the south, toward the east, and toward the Glorious Land (Dan. 8:9–12).

THE TEN KINGS OF THE ANTICHRIST'S KINGDOM

Now, let us explore the ten kings of the Antichrist's kingdom, as it will progressively validate the prophetic correlation of the Middle East and North Africa, Satan's *original hunters*, his *end-of-the-age* hunters, and his *final hunter.* In chapter 1, we discussed Noah's prophetic curse on Ham and Canaan because of their sin against him, which culminated with God promising the children of Israel (Shem's lineage) the land of Canaan (Abrahamic covenant). The Almighty will also judge Ham's other descendant's *regions*, Mizraim (Egypt), Put (Libya), and Cush (Sudan), by allowing the Antichrist to conquer them during the time of Jacob's trouble. In Daniel 7, he prophesies the Antichrist will conquer three of the ten kings when he acquires full power and authority of his kingdom at the end of the age (Dan. 7:8, 24). In Daniel 11, he declares who these three kings are.

> Daniel 11:42–43: "He shall stretch out his hand against the countries, and the land of *Egypt* shall not escape. *He shall have power*

over the treasures of gold and silver, and over all the precious things of Egypt; also the Libyans and Ethiopians [Sudan] shall follow at his heels."

Three of the ten kings of the Antichrist's kingdom will be Egypt, Libya, and Sudan. Ethiopia in the text is modern-day Sudan (Cush). By naming three of the ten kings, Daniel confirms the conglomerated *region* of the Babylonian (lion), Medo-Persian (bear), and Grecian (leopard) Empires, and also the *region* of Satan's *original hunters,* as these three countries are located in the *region.*

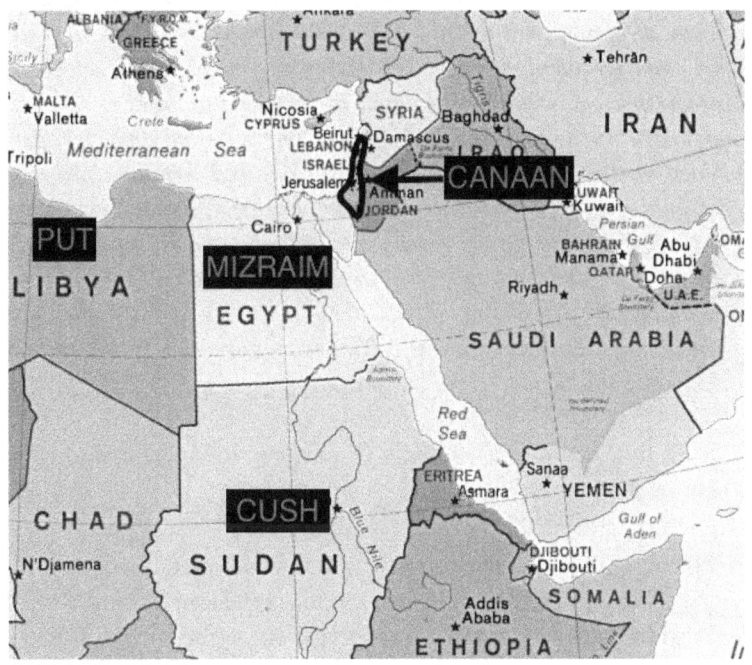

Hamites

The Egyptians are descendants of Mizraim (Nimrod's uncle), the son of Ham, who was cursed by Noah and became the "father of the Egyptians." Isaiah prophesied about the *final hunter's* rule over Egypt at the end of the age, as he records, "And the Egyptians I [God] will give into the hand of a cruel master. And a fierce king will rule over them" (Isa. 19:4). The Libyans are descendants of Put (Nimrod's uncle), son of Ham, and the Sudanese are descendants of Cush (Nimrod's father), who is the son of Ham, as well.

All four of Ham's sons, Cush, Mizraim, Put, and Canaan, were judged because of their father's sin towards Noah. The Talmud substantiates Ham's descendants as evil men, as Cush (Sudan), Mizraim (Egypt), Put (Libya), and Canaan's (land of Canaan) descendants played a major role with their relative Nimrod in respect to the rebellious and blasphemous Tower of Babel:

> And it came to pass about this time that the officers of Nimrod and *the descendants of Phut [Libya], Mitzrayim [Egypt], Cush [Sudan], and Canaan [Canaanites] took counsel together, and they said to one another:* "Let us build a city and also in its midst a tall tower for a stronghold, a tower the top of which shall reach even to the heavens. Then shall we truly make for ourselves a great city and mighty name, before which all our enemies shall tremble. None will then be able to harm us, and no wars may disperse our ranks." And while they were building, rebellion budded in their hearts, rebellion against God, and they imagined that they could scale the heavens and war with Him. They divided into three groups and the first group stated, *"We will ascend to heaven and place there our gods, and worship them."* The second group said, *"We will pour into the heavens of the Lord and match our strength with His."* The third group stated, *"Yea, we will smite Him with arrow and with spear."*[1] (See Gen. 11:1–9)

Doesn't this sound like the Holy Bible's description of Satan, who will incarnate the *final hunter*?

- Isaiah 14:13–14, "For you have said in your heart: 'I will ascend into heaven, I will exalt my throne above the stars of God; I will also sit on the mount of the congregation on the farthest side of the north; I will ascend above the heights of the clouds, I will be like the Most High.'" (See 2 Thess. 2:3–4.)
- Ezekiel 28:2, "Because your heart is lifted up, and you say, 'I am god, I sit in the seats of gods, in the midst of the seas . . .'"
- Revelation 12:4, "His tail drew a third of the stars of heaven and threw them to the earth."

Egypt, Libya, and Sudan will be three of the ten kings. Accordingly, who are the other seven kings? Four of the kings will be revealed when the Grecian

Empire (Turkey) divides into four regions, or "horns" (symbolic for kings), after its leader dies, which authenticates seven of the ten kings in the conglomerated *region* (Dan. 8:21–22). However, only time will tell who the remaining three kings (horns) will be. Nevertheless, just as with the other seven kings, they will be specifically located in the conglomerate *region* of the Babylonian (lion), Medo-Persian (bear), and Grecian Empires (leopard), which is the exact same *region* of Satan's *original hunters*. This is to say, these ten kings will form the Antichrist's kingdom, which perfectly aligns with the *region* of Satan's *original hunters and the Babylonian, Medo-Persian, and Grecian Empires*. As we discovered in previous chapters, this prophetic *region* has been the lightning rod of Satan's *end-of-the-age* hunters, and it will ultimately consummate in his *final hunter*, the Antichrist.

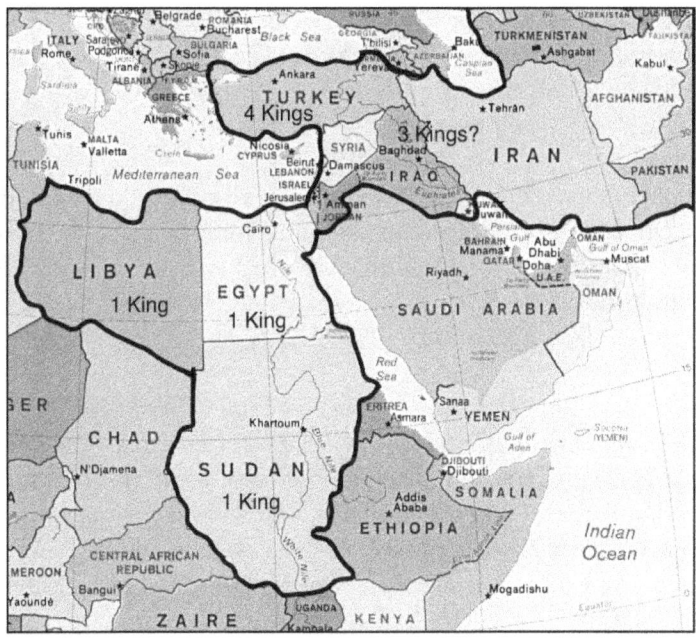

Ten kings

THE LITERAL NAMES OF THE FINAL HUNTER

Now that we have ascertained the correlation of the *regions* of Satan's *original hunters* to his *end-of-the-age* hunters, including his *final hunter*, let us proceed in corroborating the Antichrist with the biblical prophet's literal references of him. This authentication will affirm not only the identity of the Antichrist and his kingdom, but also the *region* of Satan's *original hunters* that journeys back to Noah's prophetic curse of Ham and Canaan.

The Lord God prophesied through the biblical prophets the *literal names and countries* that directly align with the Antichrist and his kingdom. Although the biblical names have changed throughout history, the *region* has remained exactly the same. We just have to correlate the ancient names to their modern-day names. Just as Yeshua is referred to by several names (Prince of Peace, Lamb of God, Lion of Judah, the Branch of Righteousness, Rabbi, Messiah, Immanuel, Wonderful Counselor, Son of Man, Mighty One, Son of God, Teacher, etc.), the final hunter is also called by several names, as well.

1. THE KING OF ASSYRIA AND THE ASSYRIAN (SYRIA)

> Isaiah 10:12: "Therefore it shall come to pass, *when the Lord has performed all His work on Mount Zion and on Jerusalem*, that He will say, '*I will punish the fruit of the arrogant heart of the king of Assyria, and the glory of his haughty looks.*'"

Isaiah is prophesying about Messiah's second coming, and he confirms Messiah will then perform all of His work on Mount Zion and on Jerusalem, which obviously has not been fulfilled yet. Once this is accomplished, Messiah will "punish the arrogant, haughty looking king of Assyria," who is Satan's *final hunter* (see Rev. 19:17–21).

> Isaiah 10:24–26: "Therefore thus says the Lord GOD of hosts: 'O My people, who dwell in Zion, do not be afraid of *the Assyrian*. He shall strike you with a rod and lift up his staff against you, *in the manner of Egypt*. For yet a very little while and the *indignation will cease, as will My anger in their destruction.*' And the LORD of hosts will stir up a scourge for him like the slaughter of Midian at the rock of Oreb; *as* His rod was on the sea, *so will He lift it up in the manner of Egypt.*"

The prophet places Messiah on earth at His second coming, because the text substantiates the "indignation," or Great Tribulation period, will end when Messiah "ceases from His anger in their destruction." Please note, Daniel also records the Antichrist's journey from Egypt to the Promised Land (Dan. 11:40–45), which corroborates the timeframe of this event. Messiah's scourge of the final hunter (the Assyrian) will parallel "the slaughter of Midian at Oreb" (Judg. 6–8), as He rides on a swift cloud into Egypt (Isa. 19).

Isaiah 14:24–25: "*The LORD of hosts has sworn, saying, 'Surely, as I have thought, so it shall come to pass, and as I have purposed, so it shall stand: that I will break the Assyrian in My land, and on My mountains tread him underfoot.* Then his yoke shall be removed from them, and his burden removed from their shoulders.'"

Once again, Isaiah references the Antichrist as being *the Assyrian* when he quotes the Lord God proclaiming, *"I will break the Assyrian in My land [Promised Land], and on My mountains tread him underfoot."* Certainly, this puts Messiah on earth at His second coming, and at that point, He will remove the Antichrist's yoke and burden from the children of Israel. This prophecy coincides with the prophet Micah's literal reference to Satan's *final hunter*.

Micah 5:5–6: "*When the Assyrian comes into our land, and when he treads in our palaces,* then we will raise against him seven shepherds and eight princely men. *They shall waste with the sword the land of Assyria, and the land of Nimrod* at its entrances; *thus He [Messiah] shall deliver us from the Assyrian,* when he comes into our land and when he treads within our borders."

Micah is prophesying about Messiah's second coming, because when the Assyrian (Antichrist) enters the Promised Land (Dan. 11:40–45), Messiah will deliver the children of Israel out of his hand. Additionally, at that time, seven shepherds and eight princely men will lay to waste the land of Assyria, *including the land of Nimrod at its entrances,* which validates the correlation of the *regions* of Satan's *original hunters*, his *end-of-the-age* hunters, and his *final hunter*. These extraordinary prophecies not only refer to Satan's *original hunter*, Nimrod, but they also affiliate the Assyrian Empire (900–609 BC) with the Seleucid king, Antiochus Epiphanes IV (175–164 BC), who ruled in Assyria and is the main prophetic foreshadow of Satan's *final hunter* (Dan. 11). These end-of-the-age, literal references about the king of Assyria and the Assyrian is a direct reference to the Antichrist, and these prophecies will be fulfilled at Messiah's second coming. As the prophet declared, "the end will be like the beginning, and from ancient times things not yet done" (Isa. 46:9–10).

2. THE KING OF BABYLON (IRAQ)

In Isaiah 14, after he prophesies about the king of Babylon, which is another name for the Antichrist, he continues to write about Lucifer (Satan) and his fall from heaven (Isa. 14:12–15). Afterward, Isaiah prophesies again about the *final hunter* (Isa. 14:16–21), because Satan will incarnate him.

> Isaiah 14:3–6, 9, 11: "*It shall come to pass in the day the* LORD *gives you rest from your sorrow, that you will take up this proverb against the king of Babylon,* and say: 'How the oppressor has ceased, the golden city ceased! *The* LORD *has broken the staff of the wicked, the scepter of the rulers*; He who struck the people in wrath with a continual stroke, *He who ruled the nations in anger, is persecuted and no one hinders . . . Hell from beneath is excited about you, to meet you at your coming*; It stirs up the dead for you, all the chief ones of the earth; it has raised up from their thrones all the *kings of the nations . . . They all shall speak and say to you: "Have you also become as weak as we? Have you become like us?* Your pomp is brought down to Sheol [hell], *and* the sound of your stringed instruments; the maggot is spread under you, and worms cover you.'""

When Isaiah declares, "It shall come to pass in the day the LORD gives you rest from your sorrow," he is referring to the Day of the Lord, which is Messiah's second coming. At that time, Israel will "take up the proverb against the king of Babylon," who is Satan's *final hunter*, and they will declare *all* of Isaiah's proclamations that he foretells in this prophecy. Isaiah's prophetic, end-of-the-age words about the Antichrist, which includes "hell from beneath is excited about you, to meet you at your coming, and the kings of the nation's questions and pronouncements," parallel Revelation 19:11–21, which prophesies Messiah's second coming. This is the moment of truth for the king of Babylon (Antichrist) and the false prophet, as both will be cast *alive* into the lake of fire and brimstone, and their armies will be destroyed by Messiah at His second coming (Rev. 19:11–21)! Remember: Babylon (Iraq) is the *region* where Satan's *original hunter*, Nimrod, began his reign. Once again, "the end will be like the beginning, and from ancient times things not yet done" (Isa. 46:9–10).

3. PRINCE OF TYRE (LEBANON)

Before we explore the prophecy of the prince of Tyre, which is another name for Satan's *final hunter*, let us first grasp the context of Ezekiel's revelation. In Ezekiel 28, he first prophesies about the prince of Tyre (Antichrist). Subsequently, he prophesies against the king of Tyre, who is Satan

(Ezek. 28:11–19). Ezekiel wrote this prophecy in a specific way in order for us to understand the diabolic relationship between Satan and the Antichrist, as Satan will indwell his *final hunter* (Rev. 13:4). With this context in mind, let us review the prince of Tyre.

> Ezekiel 28:1–10: "The word of the LORD came to me again, saying, 'Son of man, say to the prince of Tyre, "Thus says the Lord GOD: *'Because your heart is lifted up, and you say, "I am a god, I sit in the seat of gods, in the midst of the seas," yet you are a man, and not a god, though you set your heart as the heart of a god* (Behold, you are wiser than Daniel! *There is no secret that can be hidden from you!* With your wisdom and your understanding you have gained riches for yourself, and gathered gold and silver into your treasuries; by your great wisdom in trade you have increased your riches, and your heart is lifted up because of your riches),' "therefore thus says the Lord GOD: *'Because you have set your heart as the heart of a god, behold, therefore, I will bring strangers against you, the most terrible of the nations; And they shall draw their swords against the beauty of your wisdom, and defile your splendor. They shall throw you down into the Pit, and you shall die the death of the slain in the midst of the seas.* Will you still say before him who slays you, "I *am* a god"? *But you shall be a man, and not a god, in the hand of him who slays you. You shall die the death of the uncircumcised by the hand of aliens; for I have spoken,'* says the Lord GOD.""""

The eerie descriptions in this prophecy *directly* align with the other biblical prophets' rebellious characteristics of the Antichrist, who is called the prince of Tyre:

- His heart is lifted up and exalted (Dan. 8:10–11, 24–25; 11:36).
- He declares that he is a god and sits in the seats of gods (Isa. 14:13; Dan. 11:37).
- He gathers gold, silver, and treasures (Dan. 11:28, 38, 43).
- The most powerful nations come against him (Dan. 11:30, 39–40).

These vivid descriptions of Satan's *final hunter* authenticate Ezekiel's characteristics of him, which places the prince of Tyre at the end of the age, when Messiah will return for His second coming and cast him into the pit (lake of fire).

4. PHARAOH, KING OF EGYPT

> Ezekiel 29:3–5: "Behold, I *am* against you, *O Pharaoh king of Egypt, O great monster who lies in the midst of his rivers*, who has said, 'My River is my own; I have made *it* for myself.' *But I will put hooks in your jaws, and cause the fish [armies] of your rivers to stick to your scales*; I will bring you up out of the midst of your rivers, and all the fish in your rivers [armies] will stick to your scales. *I will leave you in the wilderness, you and all the fish of your rivers [armies]; You shall fall on the open field; You shall not be picked up or gathered. I have given you as food to the beasts of the field and to the birds of the heavens.*"

Pharaoh, king of Egypt is another name that references Satan's *final hunter*. This is an end-of-the-age prophecy about the Antichrist, because, as we discovered, he invades and conquers Egypt. However, the Lord God will hear the cry of His remnant in Egypt, and He will send them "a Savior and a Mighty One," who will rescue them from the Antichrist at His second coming (Isa. 19:19–22). Furthermore, Ezekiel uses the same language in this text as he does when he refers to the Antichrist (Gog) in Ezekiel 38–39. Ezekiel prophesies that the Lord God will "put hooks into Antichrist's jaws, and his armies, leaving them in the wilderness [desert], as they fall on the open field, and the beasts of the field and the birds of the heavens will feed upon them," which is the exact same language in Ezekiel 38:4; 39:4–5, 17–20. Both prophecies in Ezekiel will be fulfilled at Messiah's second coming and during His millennial reign.

5. THE KING OF THE NORTH

Satan's *final hunter* is also called the king of the north, and Daniel 11 presents a very detailed road map of his actions and deeds when he rises to power at the end of the age, which includes the abomination of desolation (Dan. 11:21–45). Although Antiochus Epiphanes IV fulfilled some of the events in Daniel 11, which includes the abomination of desolation, he was a prophetic foreshadow of Satan's *final hunter*, who will ultimately and *completely* fulfill Daniel 11:21–45. Messiah validates this, as He warned about the Antichrist's abomination of desolation spoken of by Daniel the prophet (Matt. 24), which Antiochus could not have fulfilled, because he was already deceased when Messiah lived on earth. Clearly, "the king of the north" is a reference to Satan's *final hunter*.

In summary, the context of these *literal* references to Satan's *final hunter* are for the end of the age. They specifically align with Messiah's second coming, when He will destroy the Antichrist. In the Holy Bible, Satan's final hunter is called the king of Babylon (Iraq), the Assyrian (Syria), the king of Assyria (Syria), the prince of Tyre (Lebanon), pharaoh king of Egypt (Egypt), and the king of the north (Turkey—Seleucid). Satan is also referenced by other names, including, Lucifer, the serpent of old, the evil one, the son of perdition, the devil, and others. However, Satan's *final hunter* is specifically called by these *literal* names in order to provide us with profound wisdom, knowledge, and understanding of what the biblical prophets were forewarning about him. All of the Antichrist's *literal* names have one thing in common; they are *all* Islamic nations (Muslim) that consummately align with the *region* of Satan's *original hunters* (Isa. 46:9–10).

THE LITERAL REFERENCES TO SPECIFIC COUNTRIES MESSIAH BATTLES AT HIS SECOND COMING

Now that we have discovered the *literal* names of Satan's *final hunter* and aligned them with the *region* of his *original hunters*, let us explore in summary the *specific* countries that Messiah will battle at His second coming. Amazingly, these countries also align with the *region* of Satan's *original hunters*. Of course, on the Day of the Lord, other evil nations will join the Antichrist in the final battle of the age; however, it is impossible to neglect the biblical prophet's *literal* references to these *specific* individual countries. The context of these prophecies culminate at Messiah's second coming.

1. Babylon (Iraq), **Nimrod**—Isa. 13; 14:1–11, 22–23; 21:1–10; Jer. 50–51
2. Assyria (Syria), **Nimrod** – Isa. 14:24–27; 17; 30:27–33; 31:6–9; Jer. 49:23–27; Amos 1:3–5; Mic. 5:5–6; Zeph. 2:13
3. Dedan, Teman, Kedar (Saudi Arabia), **Ishmael**—Isa. 21:13–17; Jer. 25:23–24
4. Teman, Midian, Cushan (Saudi Arabia/Sudan), **Ishmael**—Hab. 2:3; 3:3–7
5. Idumea, Bozrah (Jordan), **Ishmael/Esau**—Isa. 34:3–10; 63:1–6

6. Edom (Jordan/Saudi Arabia), **Ishmael/Esau**—Isa.34; Jer. 49:7–22; Ezek. 25:12–14; 35:15; Joel 3:19; Amos 1:11–12; Obad. 8–9, 21
7. Moab (Edom, Jordan), **Esau**—Num. 24:17–19; Isa. 11:14; 15–16; Jer. 25:21; 48; Ezek. 25:8–11; Amos 2:1–3; Zeph. 2:8–9
8. Philistia (Gaza Strip), **Goliath**—Isa. 14:28–32; Jer. 25:20; 47; Ezek. 25:15–17; Amos 1:6–8; Zeph. 2:4–7
9. Tyre/Sidon (Lebanon), **Nimrod/Antichrist** – Isa. 2:12–13; 10:33–34; 14:28–32; 23; Jer. 25:22; Ezek. 28; Amos 1:9–10; Joel 3:1–6
10. Egypt—**Mizraim (Nimrod's uncle)**—Isa. 11:15, 19; 19; Jer. 25:19; 46; Ezek. 29:1–16; 30–31; Joel 3:19
11. Libya—**Put (Nimrod's uncle)**—Jer. 46:9–10; Ezek. 30; 38–39
12. Sudan—**Cush (Nimrod's father)**—Isa. 18; Jer. 46:9–10; Ezek. 30, 38–39; Zeph. 2:12
13. Lydia (Turkey) **Antichrist**—Jer. 46:9–10; Ezek. 30, 38–39

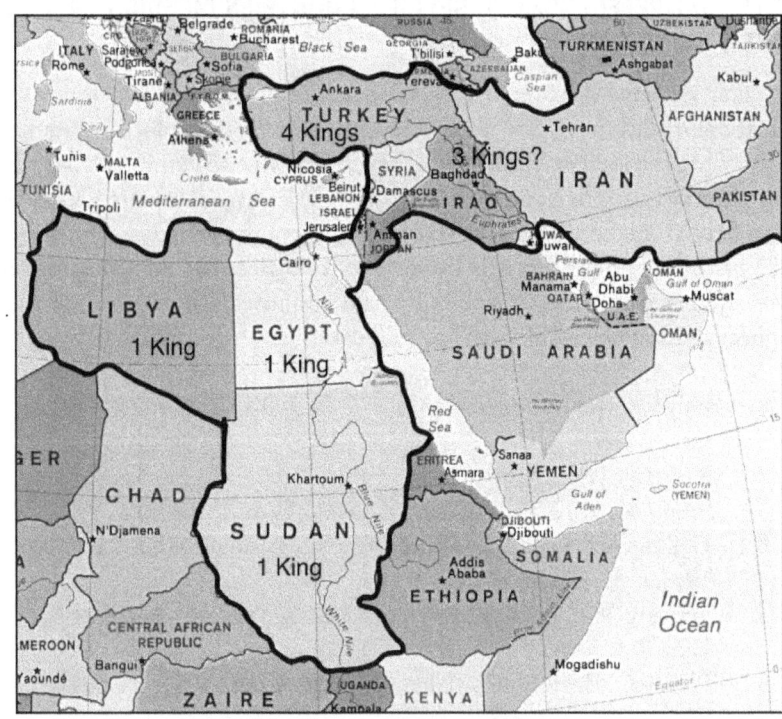

Ten Kings

THE LITERAL REFERENCES TO THE SPECIFIC COUNTRIES THAT ARE CONSIGNED TO THE PIT

In Ezekiel 25–32, Ezekiel prophesies about the *specific* nations that are consigned to the pit (hell) with Satan and the Antichrist. This exciting and long-awaited event will consummate at Messiah's second coming, when He pours out His vengeance upon His enemies (Rev. 19:19–21). According to the Scriptures, these are the *specific* nations that will be cast into the pit on the Day of the Lord: Iraq (Babylon), Syria, Saudi Arabia (Ishmael/Edom), Jordan (Edom), Turkey (Meshech, Tubal, Lydia), Egypt (Mizraim), Libya (Put), Sudan (Ethiopia), Lebanon (Tyre/Sidon), and Iran (Elam). Do we see a pattern of who Satan's hunters are from the beginning to the end?

Today, *all* of these countries are dictated and governed by Islamic leadership and are *specifically* located in the *regions* of Satan's *original hunters*. This is not to say that other evil nations and people will not be thrown into hell (Matt. 25:31–46), but Ezekiel is very specific as to which countries, as a nation, will surely perish. Once again, this echoes Isaiah's prophetic words that God is "declaring the end from the beginning, and from ancient times things not yet done" (Isa. 46:9–10).

THE FINAL HUNTER'S PRIMARY RELIGION

Now let us authenticate the primary religion that Satan will utilize at the end of the age, which coincides with the information we have discussed to this point. Before we begin, remember that Satan is the ultimate hunter and deceiver, who connives with evil men in order to execute his diabolical schemes. He is the father of lies and has been a murderer from the beginning (John 8:44). Therefore, it is not surprising that Satan would influence and create a brutal and counterfeit religion that *directly* defies the Holy Bible. As of today, there is certainly one such religion that is deceiving 1.9 billion people with its demonic and totalitarian system, and that tyrannical system is Islam. Islam is the greatest blasphemy and false religion the world has ever known because it directly and vehemently attacks everything that is holy, righteous, divine, and sovereign in the Holy Bible.

> 2 John 1:7 (KJV): "For many deceivers are entered into the world, who confess not that Jesus Christ is come in the flesh. *This is a deceiver and an antichrist.*"

For a deeper understanding of the Qur'an, Islam's holy book, and its direct defiance to the Holy Bible, I would suggest reading *New York Times* best-selling author Joel Richardson's book *The Islamic Antichrist*. I highly recommend Richardson's book because it gives its readers a clear understanding of the dangerous and emphatic deceptions of Islam (Joelstrumpet.com).

Before we proceed, it is essential to understand that when the Antichrist (Satan incarnate) rises to power at the last seven years of the age, he will not regard any god, but instead, he will exalt and magnify himself above all gods and become *a god of war or fortresses* (Dan. 11:36–39). Daniel's description of "war and fortresses" is the cornerstone of the Qur'an, which is jihad (war). In fact, 164 verses in the Qur'an advocate war, and one-third of Sharia law is in the cause of jihad against all non-Muslims. This is the reason Winston Churchill called Islam "the most retrograde force in the world," and why he compared Hitler's Mein Kampf to the Qur'an. [2] The Antichrist will use Islam, and all of its wicked doctrines (Qur'an), as the predominant deceptive tool over Muslims, as well as to oppose and defy the Holy Bible.

> 1 John 2:18: "Little children, it is the last hour: and as you have heard that the Antichrist is coming, even now, many antichrists have come, by which we know that it is the last hour."

As previously discussed, Satan understands the Holy Bible extremely well, including the timetable for God's everlasting covenants and the fulfillment of His end-of-the-age prophecies. This is why Satan influenced his *original hunters* to *directly* attempt to kill Abraham, Isaac, Jacob, and David. Satan desperately and viciously wanted to forbid God's everlasting covenants from being established with His *original fishermen*, because ultimately, Messiah will *completely* fulfill them at His second coming, and Satan will be doomed (Rev. 20). This is a war between the divine, sovereign righteousness of God's eternal promises and Satan's evil, perpetual deception. Since the beginning, Satan has been cleverly scheming to *directly* attempt to terminate God's plan of salvation for His fishermen (you and me) through His everlasting covenants.

> Genesis 3:15 ESV: "And I will put enmity between you and the woman, and between your offspring and her offspring; he [Messiah] shall bruise your [Satan's] head, and you [Satan] shall bruise His [Messiah's] heel."

In this ancient prophecy, God prophesied about the spiritual war between the woman (Israel) and her "seed," and Satan, and his "seed" (Rev. 12). In other words, God is proclaiming there will be perpetual animosity and war between His fishermen—Abraham, Isaac, Jacob, David, *and their descendants (region)*--and Satan's hunters, Nimrod, Ishmael, Esau, Goliath (Philistines), *and their descendants (regions)*. The Almighty prophesied that Satan would "bruise Messiah's heel," which occurred at Messiah's first coming (Matt. 27), and Messiah would "bruise Satan's head," which will be *ultimately* fulfilled *after* Messiah's second coming and millennial (thousand-year) reign, when Satan is cast into the lake of fire and brimstone forever and ever (Rev. 20:10). Messiah will "bruise the head" of the Antichrist at His second coming (Rev. 19:11–21).

In the Qur'an, Islam's holy book, Satan inspired Muhammad to directly contrast and defy the holiest things in the Holy Bible. By doing this, Satan undeniably blasphemes the holiest principles of Judeo-Christianity and denounces them as unholy. The Qur'an also reveals eerie and staggering similarities between the Holy Bible's Antichrist and its Mahdi (Messiah), and its disturbing alignment in regard to the last seven years of the age.

1 John 2:22–23: "Who is a liar but he who denies that Jesus is the Christ? *He is antichrist who denies the Father and the Son. Whoever denies the Son does not have the Father either*; he who acknowledges the Son has the Father also."

The apostle John declares that anyone who denies the Father (God) and the Son (Jesus) is a liar, and therefore, an antichrist. Certainly, Satan is the father of lies and definitively denies and rejects Yeshua, because God's everlasting covenants will be *completely* fulfilled through Him. Respectively, it goes without saying, Satan's *end-of-the-age* hunters, including their religion (Islam), will reject Yeshua as the Son of God, and therefore, deny the Father.

Qur'an 5:17: *"In blasphemy indeed are those that say that God is Christ the son of Mary."*

John 14:6: "Jesus said to him, 'I am the way, the truth, and the life. No one comes to the Father except through Me.'"

1 John 2:23, "Whoever denies the Son does not have the Father either; he who acknowledges the Son has the Father also."

The most basic fundamental theology and most principal commandment in the Qur'an is to deny that Yeshua is the Son of God. This blasphemous abomination is the cornerstone of the Islamic faith, and all of its other heresies are built upon this premise. This singular contrast confirms Satan's influence over the Qur'an, and his perpetual deception that overshadows nearly 2 billion people.

The Qur'an also directly blasphemes one of the holiest principles in the Holy Bible: the virgin birth of Yeshua, who is the Son of God and Messiah of the world (Isa. 7:14; Luke 1:26–38). The Qur'an claims that God does not have a Son, therefore, denying Yeshua's holy virgin birth, death, and resurrection. By rejecting Messiah's holy, divine events, this evil doctrine is also repudiating the Holy Trinity, of which Yeshua is the second person. This is the heretical and deceptive foundation that Islam is built upon, which directly denounces the most supreme revelation of the Holy Bible, Yeshua the Messiah!

> Qur'an 19:88–92: *"They said, 'The Most Gracious has begotten a son!' You have uttered a gross blasphemy.* The heavens are about to shatter, the earth is about to tear asunder, and the mountains are about to crumble. Because they claim that the Most Gracious has begotten a son. *It is not befitting the Most Gracious that He should beget a son.'"*

Clearly, the Qur'an was directly inspired by Satan to blaspheme and war against the testimony of Messiah, thus, defying and denying the Holy Trinity, the Father, the Son, and the Holy Spirit. If one of the three members is denounced, *all* are rejected (1 John 5:7). The Qur'an also ostracizes the holy crucifixion and resurrection of Messiah (Ps. 118:22–29; Luke 23–24).

> Qur'an 4:157–58: *"That they said, 'We killed Christ Jesus the son of Mary, the Messenger of Allah;' but they killed him not, nor crucified him,* but so it was made to appear to them, and those who differ therein are full of doubts, with no certain knowledge, but only conjecture to follow, for of a surety they killed him not: *Nay, Allah raised him up unto Himself; and Allah is Exalted in Power, Wise."*

Obviously, this is a direct heresy towards Messiah and His holy crucifixion and resurrection. Most certainly, Messiah's sovereign, holy, righteous, and divine crucifixion and resurrection are what constitute the Judeo-Christian faith, yet the Qur'an blasphemes and rejects these events. Islam is the only religion that directs such extreme defiance and vigorous opposition towards God Almighty and His only begotten Son.

> 1 John 4:2–3: "By this you know the Spirit of God: Every Spirit that confesses that Jesus Christ has come in the flesh is of God, *and every spirit that does not confess that Jesus Christ has come in the flesh is not of God. And this is the spirit of the Antichrist,* which you have heard was coming, and is now already in the world."

The Qur'an also defiantly disparages the blessed Holy Trinity, as it proclaims that God is *not* three persons in One. On the contrary, the Holy Bible clearly defines the Holy Trinity: God, Yeshua (the Word), and the Holy Spirit are indeed One.

> Qur'an 5:73: *"They blaspheme who say that Allah is the third of three."*

> 1 John 5:7: "For there are three that bear witness in heaven; the Father, the Word [Jesus], and the Holy Spirit; *and these three are one."*

Obviously, there are major irresolvable, fundamental differences between the commandments of the Holy Bible and what is commanded in the Qur'an. From these few comparisons, it is sufficient to conclude that what is holy in the Holy Bible—the Virgin Birth, the Crucifixion, the Resurrection, and the Holy Trinity—is unholy in the Qur'an, because these things are considered heresy and blasphemy to the Islamic faith. Is this a coincidence? How could Islam be the only religion in *direct* contrast to the Holy Bible? We will completely understand this perpetual deception from Satan as we proceed with the eerie comparisons between the Holy Bible's Antichrist and Islam's Mahdi (Messiah), which includes the eschatology of both at the end of the age.

ISLAMIC ESCHATOLOGY

Now that we have established that Satan has created a religion in direct defiance to God Almighty, let us review the end-of-the-age eschatology of the Holy Bible and the Qur'an. Eerily, and not by coincidence, both books record a seven-year period at the end of the age when a particular man rises to power. The Holy Bible proclaims this man to be Satan's *final hunter,* or the Antichrist, and the Qur'an declares him as its Mahdi or Messiah.

ISLAMIC ESCHATOLOGY CONCERNING YESHUA (JESUS) [3]

Following are Islam's beliefs concerning the person of Yeshua (whom they call Īsā):

- Yeshua was a prophet, but He did *not* die on the cross, rise from the dead, or provide atonement for mankind's sins.
- Yeshua is standing beside Allah in heaven, and He will return to Damascus on the wings of two angels.
- When Yeshua returns, He will get married, have children, die, and be buried next to Muhammad.
- Yeshua will proclaim to all Jews and Christians that He is a faithful, radical Muslim, and He will make pilgrimage to Mecca.
- Yeshua will establish worldwide Sharia law and abolish Judeo-Christianity.
- Yeshua will kill the Dajjal, or Islam's false Mahdi and his followers (Jews).
- Yeshua is a prophet of their messiah, the Mahdi (Antichrist).
- Yeshua will pray and worship the Mahdi (Antichrist).

COMPARISONS OF THE HOLY BIBLE'S ANTICHRIST AND THE ISLAMIC MAHDI ACCORDING TO BOTH BOOKS [4]

- He is an unparalleled political, military, and religious leader that will emerge in the last days.
- He has a secondary prominent figure that will emerge in the last days who will support him (false prophet).
- He will have a powerful army that will cause tremendous damage to the earth in an effort to conquer every nation and dominate the world.
- He establishes a new world order, institutes new laws, and changes the times.
- He will be a powerful leader who will attempt to institute a universal world religion.
- He will execute any person who does not submit to his world religion.
- He will specifically use beheading as the predominant tool of execution.

- He will prioritize the killing of the Jewish people.
- He will vehemently attack Jerusalem to subdue it.
- He will set himself up in the Jewish temple as his seat of authority and worship.
- He will "ride on a white horse" at the time of his arrival.
- He will confirm a peace treaty with Israel and others for seven years.
- He denies the most sacred and paramount doctrines of Judeo-Christianity

The Holy Bible's Antichrist and Islam's Mahdi coincide in the succeeding infamous characteristics, as well. Both:

- deny the Holy Trinity and the Cross
- deny the Father and the Son
- are blasphemous
- are called "deceiver"
- claim to be the Messiah
- (kingdoms) suffer a "head wound"
- work false miracles
- rule over ten kings
- use military force
- honor their god with gold and silver
- honor a god of war
- lack of respect for women and their desires
- make a seven-year peace agreement
- deceive and destroy by peace
- break treaties
- love war for booty
- desire world domination
- lead a Turkish invasion
- ascend to heaven
- are beings of light
- are pride-filled

- are called "the son of the dawn"
- are cast out of heaven
- occupy the Temple Mount
- desire Israel's destruction. [5]

This comparison between the Holy Bible's description of the Antichrist, and the Qur'an's description of their Mahdi is uncanny and undeniable.

THE HOLY BIBLE'S ANTICHRIST IS ISLAM'S MAHDI

Astonishingly, the Holy Bible's Antichrist is without a doubt the Qur'an's Mahdi (Messiah). Islam is the only religion that parallels its Messiah with the Holy Bible's Antichrist. For those who believe Christians and Muslims worship the same God, please understand this could not be further from the truth, as it is an evil, blasphemous lie. Make no mistake: Allah is not the same god as the God of Abraham, Isaac, Jacob, and David. Allah and his followers want to kill the Jews and Christians, and Yeshua the Messiah, who is the God of Abraham, Isaac, Jacob, and David, and His followers, do not want to kill the Jews and Christians—or anyone, for that matter, including Muslims. In fact, "God so loved the world that He gave His only begotten Son, that *whoever* believes in Him should not perish but have everlasting life" (John 3:16)! A great example of the supreme difference between the God of Israel and Allah (Satan) is found in the Islamic Hadith, which is a narrative of the words, actions, and habits of Muhammad. It records an eerie and frightening prophecy that parallels Jeremiah's prophecy of the hunters.

> Hadith Book 041, Number 6985: "Abu Huraira reported Allah's Messenger (may peace be upon him) as saying: *The last hour [last seven years] would not come unless the Muslims will fight against the Jews and the Muslims would kill them until the Jews would hide themselves behind a stone [rock] or a tree and a stone (rock) or a tree would say: Muslim, or the servant of Allah, there is a Jew behind me; come and kill him; but the tree Gharqad would not say, for it is the tree of the Jews."

This Islamic eschatological verse clearly illustrates Muslims, as a whole, are Satan's *end-of-the-age* hunters, and the Jewish people will be their primary prey during the last seven years. Why? Because of the interpretation of the Abrahamic covenant, which includes who has the rights to the

Promised Land. Ironically, the eerie Islamic prophecy aligns with Jeremiah's prophecy of the hunters, as the Lord will "send for many hunters, and they shall hunt them from every mountain and every hill, *and out of the holes of the rocks*" (Jer. 16:16). However, after Messiah's second coming and during His millennial reign, this anti-Semitic attitude will be profoundly different!

> Zechariah 8:22–23, "Yes, many peoples and strong nations shall come to seek the LORD of hosts in Jerusalem and to pray before the LORD. Thus says the LORD of hosts: '*In those days ten men from every language of the nations shall grasp the sleeve of a Jewish man, saying, "Let us go with you, for we have heard that God is with you."*'"

Let us summon to mind that Satan wants to be God; that's why he sinned and rebelled against the Almighty (Isa. 14:12–15; Ezek. 28:11–19). Satan has used and will continue to use Islam for his perpetual lie in order to deceive as many people as possible. When Satan's *final hunter* rises to power for the last seven years of the age, Muslims will believe their Mahdi has arrived. Unfortunately, most of them will proceed under the diabolic deception of Satan's *final hunter* (Mahdi) and not comprehend that Satan (Antichrist) is leading them to their destruction at Messiah's second coming.

Assuredly, Satan desires all of God's power and glory, as he is jealous of the Almighty. Therefore, through perpetual deception, he attempts to emulate God in all aspects. The most preeminent example of this is Israel. It is one of the smallest countries in the world, so why would Satan want to conquer and control it? The resounding answer is because the God of Israel has promised and sworn by His almighty name that the Abrahamic, Davidic, and new covenants will be fulfilled in the Promised Land—Israel—and specifically, in the holy city of Jerusalem! My friends, the Lord dwells in Jerusalem, and it is exactly where Messiah will place His feet on the earth when He arrives for His second coming and millennial reign (Ps. 9:11; Joel 3:21; Zech. 14:4; Rev. 19:11–21)! Therefore, Satan will *directly* attempt through his final hunter to prohibit the everlasting covenants from being ultimately fulfilled by Messiah, just as he did with his original hunters. Unquestionably, this is a spiritual war between God and Satan, Messiah and Antichrist, and Judeo-Christianity and Islam.

In conclusion, the Antichrist will be Satan's *final hunter*, who will rise from the Seleucid division of the Grecian Empire, the *region* of Satan's *original hunters*. The Antichrist's kingdom will be a conglomerate of the ancient Babylonian, Medo-Persian, and Grecian empires (land area), which again, perfectly aligns with the *region* of Satan's *original hunters*. The biblical prophets forewarned us about the *region* in which Islam is dominant and supreme today. They prophesied the specific, literal names of the Antichrist, as well as the exact Islamic nations that Messiah will personally fight at His second coming. The Antichrist will use Islam as his chosen religion to deceive and murder as many people as possible, as it directly blasphemes and contradicts the Holy Bible. Clearly, the holiest principles in the Holy Bible—the Virgin Birth, the Crucifixion, the Resurrection, and the Holy Trinity—are the *un*holiest things in Islam. Without a doubt, the Holy Bible's Antichrist is Islam's Mahdi and Satan's *final hunter*. I hope you will join me in prayer for the 1.9 billion Muslims to have a "Paul moment" (see Acts 9) and come to faith and salvation through Yeshua the Messiah.[6]

CHAPTER 10

THE TIME OF JACOB'S TROUBLE

To this climatic pinnacle, we have covered the supreme importance of God's everlasting covenants, the prophecy of the fishermen and the hunters, who God's *original fishermen* and Satan's *original hunters* were, the mystery of Aliyah, who God's *end-of-the-age* fishermen and Satan's *end-of-the-age* hunters are of Jeremiah's prophecy, the Aliyah from Europe, the eventual Aliyah from America, and who Satan's *final hunter* will be. Is there an appointed time for *all* of these biblical prophecies and prophetic foreshadows and events to consummate in *the main event?* Who are God's fishermen at this pivotal but crucial moment in time? Will Messiah destroy the *regions* of Satan's *original hunters,* his *end-of-the-age* hunters, *and* his *final hunter* at the exact same time? Is this when Jeremiah's prophecy of the fishermen and the hunters will be *completely* fulfilled? Is this when the *final* Aliyah will occur? Does the Holy Bible provide us with a prophecy of this appointed time in the future?

In this chapter, we will answer these questions and pinpoint the appointed biblical time when *all* of these prophetic events will be *completely* fulfilled. According to the Holy Bible, the *birth pangs* of these events will escalate and intensify at the end of the age and during the *time of Jacob's trouble,* or better known today as the seven-year tribulation period. To corroborate the timeframe and length of this devastating and horrific period in the future, let us review the story and events of the patriarch *Jacob's time of trouble.*

In the Torah, this prophetic story commences as Jacob journeys into the land of the people of the East (Gen. 29:1). Upon his arrival into the land, he sought his uncle Laban, who was his mother, Rebekah's, brother (vv. 2–6). Once he asked the men from Haran about Laban's whereabouts, he divinely met a beautiful woman, Rachel, who would eventually become his bride, albeit through *a time of trouble* (vv. 9–12). Once Laban and Jacob connected, embraced, and exchanged pleasantries, Jacob stayed with Laban for a month (vv. 13–14). During that time, Jacob constructed an agreement with Laban to marry Rachel.

> Genesis 29:15–18, 20: "Then Laban said to Jacob, 'Because you *are* my relative, should you therefore serve me for nothing? Tell me, what should your wages be?' Now Laban had two daughters: the name of the elder was Leah, and the name of the younger was Rachel. Leah's eyes were delicate, but Rachel was beautiful of form and appearance. *Now Jacob loved Rachel; so he said, 'I will serve you seven years for Rachel your younger daughter'* . . . So Jacob served *seven years* for Rachel, and they seemed only a few days to him because of the love he had for her."

As we can see, when Laban asked Jacob what his wages should be for Rachel's hand in marriage, Jacob proclaimed he would serve Laban *seven years*. Once Jacob fulfilled the *seven years* of the bridal labor agreement, he asked Laban for his beautiful bride (Gen. 29:21). But once the bridal feast had been prepared, Laban deceitfully awarded Jacob his eldest daughter, Leah, instead of Rachel (vv. 22–25).

> Genesis 29:25–28: "And [Jacob] said to Laban, 'What is this you have done to me? Was it not for Rachel that I served you? Why then have you deceived me?' And Laban said, 'It must not be done so in our country, to give the younger before the firstborn. *Fulfill her week*, and we will give you this one also for the service which you will serve with me still *another seven years.*' *Then Jacob did so and fulfilled her week.* So he gave him his daughter Rachel as wife also."

Astonished, Jacob realized Laban had outwitted him into serving an *additional seven years (week)*, which is known as *the time of Jacob's trouble*, in order to marry Rachel, his ultimate desire and true love. Jacob's additional *seven* years is a prophetic foreshadowing of *the time of Jacob's trouble* at the end of the age. This is also known as the seven-year tribulation period, because the nation of Israel (Jacob) will endure *seven years of trouble to receive their Bridegroom, the Jewish Messiah and King of Israel, Yeshua*! This prophetic time also corroborates to Daniel's 70th week, which is the last seven years of the age (seven-year tribulation) (Dan. 9:2), further authenticating its time and length.

Jeremiah, who is called the "weeping prophet," prophesied about this appointed, apocalyptic time. Before we proceed, let us remember that God changed Jacob's name to Israel, and his children are the twelve tribes of Israel (Gen. 32:28). Accordingly, God uses Jacob's time of trouble to represent the State of Israel's time of trouble at the end of the age (Gen. 32:28; 35:23–26).

THE TIME OF JACOB'S TROUBLE

> Jeremiah 30:7: "Alas! For that day is great, so that none is like it; *and it is the time of Jacob's trouble, but he shall be saved out of it.*" (See Joel 1:15.)

Jeremiah not only prophesied about the fishermen and the hunters (Jer. 16); he also proclaimed the specific time this sobering but candid prophecy would be *ultimately* fulfilled. The weeping prophet declares Israel (Jacob) will endure great tribulation during this time, "but he [Israel] will be saved out of it," at Messiah's second coming.

The everlasting covenants, the prophecy of the fishermen and the hunters, the mystery of Aliyah, and the time of Jacob's trouble are directly and cohesively correlated with one another. Keep in mind: God's promises are eternal, and the children of Israel are prophesied to make Aliyah to the Promised Land to receive their sworn inheritance. This will ultimately escalate and intensify to its highest pinnacle during the *time of Jacob's trouble* and culminate at Messiah's second coming and during His millennial reign, as we will discuss later. Consequently, Satan understands biblical prophecy, including God's prophetic timeline; hence, he has raged and always will viciously battle against God's people and the Promised Land. Please note: *all* of the biblical prophecies in the Holy Bible, absolutely every single one of them, are based upon the concrete foundation of Messiah returning to Jerusalem to fulfill the everlasting covenants!

In Jeremiah 30, the weeping prophet begins his prophecy about the *time of Jacob's trouble* by proclaiming, "'For behold, the days are coming,' says the LORD, 'that I will bring back from captivity My people Israel and Judah,' says the LORD. *'And I will cause them to return to the land that I gave to their fathers, and they shall possess it"* (Jer. 30:1–3). The terminology in Jeremiah 30 parallels the phraseology in Jeremiah 16:14–15, which declares, "'*Therefore behold, the days are coming,' says the LORD, 'that it shall no more be said, "The*

Lord lives who brought up the children of Israel from the land of Egypt," but, "The Lord lives who brought up the children of Israel from the land of the north and from all the lands where He had driven them." *For I will bring them back into their land which I gave to their fathers.*'"

Although Jeremiah's terminology in chapters 16 and 30 both corroborate and overlap at the end of the age, and specifically, at the *time of Jacob's trouble*, both prophecies present indicators of when each will reach its *ultimate* fulfillment, as we will discover. Nonetheless, until that appointed time, the Lord God will continue to influence the children of Israel to perpetually make Aliyah to the Promised Land, which *partially* fulfills both prophecies. Let us review how the Lord God of Israel will perpetuate this Aliyah until the appointed time is fulfilled.

> Jeremiah 16:16: "'*Behold, I will send for many fishermen,*' says the Lord, '*and they shall fish them; and afterward I will send for many hunters, and they shall hunt them from every mountain and every hill, and out of the holes of the rocks.*'"

Just as we discussed in previous chapters (6–9), Jeremiah's prophecy of the fishermen and the hunters is fulfilling a portion of Israel's "birth pangs," perpetuating until it reaches its *ultimate* fulfillment during the *time of Jacob's trouble*.

As we proceed in Jeremiah 30, the weeping prophet declares that during the *time of Jacob's trouble*, there will be no peace, only anguish and fear for the house of Israel and the house of Judah (vv. 4–6). Nevertheless, at Messiah's second coming, which is the last day of the *time of Jacob's trouble (Yom Kippur)*, the children of Israel will shout, "Baruch Haba b'Shem Adonai!" or "Blessed is He who comes in the name of the Lord" (Matt. 23:39). Simultaneously, the Branch of Righteousness to David (Messiah) will "break the Antichrist's yoke from Israel's neck, and foreigners shall no more enslave them" (v. 8). Subsequently, "they shall serve the Lord their God, and David their king, whom I will raise up for them" (v.9).

> Jeremiah 23:5–6: "'Behold, the days are coming,' says the Lord, '*that I will raise to David a Branch of righteousness; a King shall reign and prosper,* and execute judgment and righteousness in the earth. *In His days Judah will be saved, and Israel will dwell safely*; now this is His name by which He will be called: THE LORD OUR RIGHTEOUSNESS.'" (See Isa. 4:2; 11:1–5, Zech. 3:8, Rev. 19:11–16.)

Jeremiah 30:10–11, 14–15: "'*Therefore do not fear, O My servant Jacob,*' says the LORD, '*Nor be dismayed, O Israel; for behold, I will save you from afar, and your seed from the land of their captivity. Jacob shall return, have rest and be quiet, and no one shall make him afraid. For I am with you,*' says the LORD, '*to save you though I make a full end of all nations where I have scattered you, yet I will not make a complete end of you. But I will correct you in justice, and will not let you go altogether unpunished* . . . For I have wounded you with the wound of an enemy, with *the chastisement of a cruel one [Antichrist]*, for the multitude of your iniquities, because your sins have increased. I have done these things to you.'"

The terminology used to describe Satan's *final hunter* as a "cruel one" is also portrayed in Isaiah 19, as the Lord will also relinquish the Egyptians to him before He saves them at His glorious return (Isa. 19:4, 19–22). The Lord God will allow the Antichrist to chastise the children of Israel because of their "multitude of sins and iniquities." This parallels Jeremiah 16:17, as the Lord sends out many hunters for the Jewish people, because "His eyes are on all of their ways; they are not hidden from His face, nor is their iniquity hidden from His eyes." Jeremiah concludes his prophecy of *the time of Jacob's trouble* with hope, encouragement, grace, mercy, and ultimate love for the house of Israel and house of Judah, by describing the King of Israel's second coming!

Jeremiah 30:16–20, 22–24: "'*Therefore all those who devour you shall be devoured;* and all your adversaries, every one of them, shall go into captivity; *those who plunder you shall become plunder, and all who prey upon you I will make a prey. For I will restore health to you and heal you of your wounds,*' says the LORD, 'Because they called you an outcast saying*:* "This *is* Zion; No one seeks her."' *Thus says the* LORD*: 'Behold, I will bring back the captivity of Jacob's tents, and have mercy on his dwelling places; The city shall be built upon its own mound, and the palace shall remain according to its own plan. Then out of them shall proceed thanksgiving and the voice of those who make merry*; I will multiply them, and they shall not diminish; *I will also glorify them, and they shall not be small. Their children also shall be as before, and their congregation shall be established before Me; and I will punish all who oppress them* . . . *You shall be My people, and I will be your God.*' Behold, the whirlwind of the LORD goes forth with fury, a continuing whirlwind; It will fall violently on the head of the wicked. The fierce anger of the LORD will not return until He has done it, and until He has performed the intents of His heart. *In the latter days [time of Jacob's trouble] you will consider it."* (See Jer. 16:21, 23:3–4, 7–8.)

In summary, the patriarch Jacob's *time of trouble* is a prophetic foreshadow of the *time of Jacob's trouble* at the end of the age, which is known as the seven-year tribulation period. The *birth pangs* of Jeremiah's prophecy of the fishermen (1948) and the hunters (2014) have certainly ignited, and they will rapidly escalate and intensify the Jewish Aliyah to the Promised Land in the years to come. Nevertheless, the ultimate culmination of Jeremiah's prophecy of the fishermen and the hunters (Jer. 16) will reach its climatic pinnacle during the *first* three and one-half years of the *time of Jacob's trouble.* Yes, there will be a massive Jewish Aliyah to the Promised Land at the end of the age and *during the first three and one-half years of the time of Jacob's trouble.* This is the reason why Jeremiah proclaims the Lord will no longer be called the God who brought the children of Israel from Egypt, but the God who brought them *from the land of the north and all lands,* because the Aliyah will be much larger than the Exodus from Egypt. However, during the *last* three and one-half years of the age, the Antichrist will rage against and invade Jerusalem, defile the sanctuary, take away the daily sacrifices, and abominate the temple, causing desolation (Dan. 8:11; 11:30–31; 12:11; Matt. 24). Satan's *final hunter* will also war against the children of Israel, and many shall fall by the sword and flame, *while others are taken into captivity away from Jerusalem during the last three and one-half years* (Dan. 8:24; 11:33; Rev. 12–13). This is when Messiah commands the Jewish people to "flee to the mountains" (Matt. 24:16). This is to say, although Jeremiah's prophecy of the fishermen and the hunters foretells of an enormous Jewish Aliyah to the Promised Land through the *first* three and one-half years of the tribulation period, the Antichrist will battle against Jerusalem during the *last* three and one-half years of the tribulation and take half of the city as captives, but God's faithful remnant will remain (Zech. 14:1–2). Subsequently, *after* the final three and one-half years are completed, which will conclude upon Messiah's second coming (Yom Kippur), He will save His remnant from destruction, and the Lord God will bring His people back from their captivity to dwell in the Promised Land (Jer. 23; 30:3, 7). As we proceed, the timeline for these events will continue to become clear.

THE FINAL HUNTER AND THE COVENANT OF DEATH

As we have discovered, just as Satan influenced Nimrod, Ishmael, Esau, Goliath, and the Herodian family to *directly* attempt to forbid God's everlasting covenants to His *original fishermen* from coming to fruition, he will also utilize his *final hunter* to *directly* attempt to prohibit the eternal promises from being *completely* fulfilled at Messiah's second coming and during His millennial reign. (Isa. 46:9–10). In Satan's last major rebellion of the *current age*, which will occur during the *time of Jacob's trouble* (seven years), he will incarnate the Antichrist and demonically influence him to *directly* attempt to forbid the *ultimate* fulfillment of God's eternal promises in the Abrahamic, Davidic, and new covenants.

At God's appointed time, Satan's *final hunter* will ratify or enforce a *seven-year "peace covenant"* with Israel and other nations, which will initiate the *time of Jacob's trouble*, or the seven-year tribulation period. In other words, the execution or enforcement of the seven-year "peace treaty" will trigger the *time of Jacob's trouble (seven years)*.

> Daniel 9:27: "Then he [Antichrist] shall confirm a covenant with many for *one week [seven years]*."

"One week" in this prophecy actually means seven years, just as the prophetic foreshadowing of the time of Jacob's trouble over Rachel lasted "one week" (seven years), as well (Gen. 29:27–30). Although the Antichrist will deceptively certify, or enforce, a seven-year "peace treaty" with Israel and other countries, the covenant will actually become a covenant of death.

> Isaiah 28:15: "Because you have said, '*We have made a covenant with death, and with Sheol we are in agreement.*'"

> Hosea 13:11: "I gave you a king [Antichrist] in My anger, and took him away in My wrath" (Second Coming).

How are the children of Israel, as a nation, deceived by the Antichrist? How is Satan's *final hunter* able to earn Israel's trust? Daniel prophesies the Antichrist will be cunning and flattering, and he will proclaim peace as he deceives Israel and other nations with the covenant of death (Dan. 8:25; 11:21–25, 32). During the *first* three and one-half years, the covenant of death *could* allow the Jewish people to rebuild the temple and reinstitute the ancient laws and ceremonies of the Torah, which include, but are not limited to, the levitical priesthood, the daily sacrifices and offerings, worshipping on the Temple Mount, and so on. From Satan's perspective, what would be a superior way to entice the Jewish people than to allow these long-awaited ceremonies and traditions to be reinstated?

The apostle Paul sternly warned believers against the false proclamation of peace and safety at the end of the age, because this cunning deception will eventually become a vivid and clear realization of the worst persecution and destruction in world history (1 Thess. 5:3). Accordingly, at the midpoint of the *time of Jacob's trouble* (three and a half years), the *final hunter* will renege on the "peace covenant," and he will pour out his terror, wrath, and destruction upon the children of Israel and *all* believers in Messiah, fulfilling the covenant of death (Isa. 28:15).

> Daniel 9:27: "*But in the middle of the week [seven years],* He shall bring an end to sacrifice and offering and on the wings of abominations shall be one who makes desolate even until the consumption, which is determined, is poured out on the desolate." (See Matt. 24:15, 21–22.)

> Revelation 12:13–17: "Now when the dragon [Satan] saw that he had been cast to the earth, he persecuted the woman [Israel] who gave birth to the male *Child [Messiah].* But the woman [Israel] was given two wings of a great eagle, that she might fly into the wilderness to her place, *where she is nourished for a time and times and half a time [three and a half years], from the presence of the serpent.* So the serpent spewed water out of his mouth like a flood after the woman [Israel], that he might cause her to be carried away by the flood. But the earth helped the woman [Israel], and the earth opened its mouth and swallowed up the flood which the dragon had spewed out of his mouth. *And the dragon was enraged with the woman* [Israel], *and he went to make war with the rest of her offspring [Gentile believers], who keep the commandments of God and have the testimony of Jesus Christ.*" (See Dan. 11:31–39.)

GOD'S FISHERMEN DURING THE TIME OF JACOB'S TROUBLE

Once Satan's *final hunter* authenticates the seven-year covenant with Israel and other nations, the *time of Jacob's trouble* will begin, which is the last seven years of the age before Messiah's second coming and millennial reign. At the commencement of this prophetic, apocalyptic time, God will send His "tribulation fishermen," the two witnesses, to testify the righteous testimony of Yeshua the Messiah. The fishermen will also prophesy judgments on the earth for the *first* three and one-half years of the time of Jacob's trouble (1,260 days).

> Revelation 11:3–6: "'*And I will give power to my two witnesses, and they will prophesy one thousand two hundred and sixty days, clothed in sackcloth.*' These are the two olive trees and the two lampstands standing before the God of the earth. And if anyone wants to harm them, fire proceeds from their mouth and devours their enemies. And if anyone wants to harm them, he must be killed in this manner. These have power to shut heaven, so that no rain falls in the days of their prophecy; and they have power over waters to turn them to blood, and to strike the earth with all plagues, as often as they desire."

Who are God's two fishermen at this perilous appointed time? In the book of Malachi, the prophet prophesies and substantiates Elijah as one of God's "tribulation fishermen," who is sent by Him before the coming of the great and dreadful Day of the Lord (4:5). Elijah is commissioned to Jerusalem to testify the divine testimony of Messiah, and to *fish* "the hearts of the fathers to the children, and the hearts of the children to their fathers" (4:6). According to Malachi's prophecy, Elijah will be one of the two witnesses during the *first* three and one-half years of the *time of Jacob's trouble*. Who is God's other "tribulation fisherman"?

In the Holy Bible, there are two people, Enoch and Elijah, who were "caught away" or "raptured" *without* dying in the flesh (Gen. 5:24; 2 Kings 2:11). In Hebrews 9, Paul explains, "It is appointed for men to die once," and in 1 Corinthians 15, he declares, "Flesh and blood cannot inherit the kingdom of God" (1 Cor. 15:50). Paul's declarations *could* be indicating that Enoch will join Elijah as God's fishermen at this cataclysmic time, because both "were flesh and blood and did not die." Whatever the case may be, at the end of the appointed time for God's two fishermen, which will occur at the midpoint of the tribulation period, the *final hunter* will kill them, and their dead bodies will lie in the streets of Jerusalem for three and one-half days. Subsequently, God will resurrect them with His breath of life, and both prophets will ascend to heaven in a cloud. In the same hour, a great earthquake will devastate a tenth of the city, killing seven thousand people (Rev. 11:7–13).

THE 144,000 FISHERMEN DURING THE TIME OF JACOB'S TROUBLE

During the time of Jacob's trouble, the Lord God will *seal* 144,000 fishermen and they will proclaim the good news of Messiah to people in hopes of "fishing" them into the kingdom. Along with the two tribulation witnesses (fishermen), the 144,000 will be monumental for a massive revival during the time of Jacob's trouble. We can only imagine what the dynamic relationship, if any, will be like between the two tribulation fishermen and the 144,000 sealed fishermen.

> Revelation 7:1–8: "After these things I saw four angels standing at the four corners of the earth, holding the four winds of the earth, that the wind should not blow on the earth, on the sea, or on any tree. Then I saw another angel ascending from the east, having the seal of the living God. And he cried with a loud voice to the four angels to whom it was granted to harm the earth and the sea, saying, "*Do not harm the earth, the sea, or the trees till we have sealed the servants of our God on their foreheads.*" And I heard the number of those who were sealed. One hundred and forty-four thousand of all the tribes of the children of Israel were sealed:
>
>> of the tribe of Judah twelve thousand were sealed;
>> of the tribe of Reuben twelve thousand were sealed;
>> of the tribe of Gad twelve thousand were sealed;
>> of the tribe of Asher twelve thousand were sealed;
>> of the tribe of Naphtali twelve thousand were sealed;
>> of the tribe of Manasseh twelve thousand were sealed;
>> of the tribe of Simeon twelve thousand were sealed;
>> of the tribe of Levi twelve thousand were sealed;
>> of the tribe of Issachar twelve thousand were sealed;
>> of the tribe of Zebulun twelve thousand were sealed;
>> of the tribe of Joseph twelve thousand were sealed;
>> of the tribe of Benjamin twelve thousand were sealed."

The apostle John described in detail the twelve tribes that will be sealed from *the children of Israel*. As we have discussed, the end will be like the beginning, and from ancient times things not yet fulfilled (Isa. 46:9–10). With that being said, there is much debate as to whether or not Gentiles are included in this "divine sealing." Whatever the case may be, it is certain the 144,000 will be God's fishermen who will spread the good news of Yeshua (Great Commission). John authenticated this in Revelation 14, as the 144,000 "will sing a song only they can learn before the throne, and they will follow the Lamb wherever He goes (Rev. 14:3–5).

THE MIDPOINT OF THE TIME OF JACOB'S TROUBLE (THREE AND A HALF YEARS)

The prophecy of the fishermen and the hunters will increasingly precipitate the Jewish Aliyah into the Promised Land until the midpoint of the *time of Jacob's trouble*. Remember: for the *first* three and one-half years of the *time of Jacob's trouble*, the Antichrist glorifies himself in the name of "peace." Therefore, as a whole, the children of Israel will be deceived, and they will continue to make Aliyah to Jerusalem, believing they will be secure from Satan's *end-of-the-age* hunters, who will be located throughout the world, causing terror (1 Thess. 5:3). However, at the crucial, cataclysmic three-and-a-half-year point (marker), the Antichrist will rage against and invade Jerusalem, defile the sanctuary, take away the daily sacrifices, and set up the abomination of desolation (Dan. 8:11; 11:30–31; 12:11; Matt. 24). Satan's *final hunter* will also war against the children of Israel in Jerusalem, and many shall fall by the sword and flame, while "half the city" is taken *into* captivity (Dan. 8:24; 11:33; Zech. 14). As previously discussed, Messiah warned about this destructive time and commands the children of Israel who are in Judea to "flee *from* Jerusalem to the mountains" (Matt. 24:16), because Jerusalem's appointed time of desolation will have come to fruition. At this troubling and sorrowful time, which is the midpoint of the tribulation period, the prophecy of the fishermen and the hunters will be *completely* fulfilled. Bear in mind: Jeremiah declares the children of Israel are fished and hunted *back* to Jerusalem, which will have occurred up to that destructive and tragic point. Therefore, from the midpoint of the tribulation period unto Messiah's second coming, the *final hunter* and his armies will seize the children of Israel *from* the Promised Land and place them in captivity (Dan. 8:24; 11:33; Zech.14:2–3). Keep in mind, this is when Messiah warns the Jewish people to "flee *from* Jerusalem to the mountains," not make Aliyah to Jerusalem.

Nonetheless, at Messiah's second coming and the beginning of the millennial reign, the children of Israel will make a final Aliyah from the Antichrist's captivity to the Promised Land (Jer. 23). Afterwards, there will not be any more hunters, because *all* of them will be destroyed by Messiah (Rev. 19:11–21). Remember: Jeremiah's prophecy proclaims God's fishermen are sent first, and *afterward*, Satan's hunters, indicating the prophecy will be *completely* fulfilled at the midpoint of the tribulation period. This is to say, when the Jewish people are taken captive by the Antichrist and his armies at the midpoint of the tribulation, they will be saved and redeemed by Messiah, the ultimate fisherman, at His second coming, and there will not be any remaining hunters after Him, which confirms the timetable of Jeremiah's prophecy (Jer. 23).

MESSIAH JUDGES THE NATION OF ISRAEL

At the *time of Jacob's trouble* until Messiah's glorious second coming (seven years), the nation of Israel, and frankly *all* the world, will be severely chastised by the judgments of the Lord God of Israel (Rev. 6–19). Additionally, during the *last* three and one-half years of the age, when Satan's *final hunter* breaks the seven-year "peace covenant," the Almighty will also judge His people by allowing the "cruel master," the Antichrist, and his armies (end-of-the-age hunters), to battle against them with vigorous rage and devastating power. During this terrible and destructive time, the faith and patience of the Lord's remnant will need to be steadfast and unwavering (Rev. 13:10), because the widespread persecution of the saints will be unlike any other time in world history (Isa. 24, Rev. 12).

> Joel 2:1–2: "Blow the trumpet in Zion, and sound an alarm in My holy mountain! Let all the inhabitants of the land tremble; for the day of the LORD is coming, for it is at hand: a day of darkness and gloominess, a day of clouds and thick darkness, like the morning *clouds* spread over the mountains. *A people [Antichrist and his armies] come, great and strong, the like of whom has never been; nor will there ever be any such after them, even for many successive generations.*" (See Ezek. 38–39; Matt. 24:21–22; Rev.12–13.)

> Daniel 8:23–24: "And in the latter time of their kingdom, when the transgressors have reached their fullness, a king shall arise, having fierce features, who understands sinister schemes. His power shall be mighty, but not by his own power; *he shall destroy fearfully, and shall prosper and thrive; he shall destroy the mighty, and also the holy people.*" (See Dan. 7:23–25; 11:29–39.)

> Zechariah 14:1–2: "*Behold, the day of the LORD is coming, and your spoil will be divided in your midst. For I will gather all the*

nations to battle against Jerusalem; the city shall be taken, the houses rifled, and the women ravished. *Half of the city shall go into captivity, but the remnant of the people shall not be cut off from the city.*"

Why does God judge Israel during *the time of Jacob's trouble*? Why does He allow Satan's *final hunter* and his *end-of-the-age* hunters to ravage and terrorize the children of Israel? The predominant reasons are, as a nation, Israel has rejected the chief cornerstone, Yeshua HaMashiach (Jesus the Messiah), or the promised Jewish Messiah and King of Israel, and they have also rejected Moses' law, which prophesies about Yeshua (Deut. 18:15, 18; Ps. 118:22; John 5:31–47; Acts 3:20–23, 26). Additionally, in Jeremiah's prophecy of the fishermen and the hunters, he provides us with another prominent reason for the Lord's judgment upon Israel. After the weeping prophet declares the release of God's fishermen and Satan's hunters (Jer. 16:16), he prophesies the following:

> Jeremiah 16:17–18, 21: "For My eyes are on all their ways; they are not hidden from My face, nor is their iniquity hidden from My eyes. And first I will repay double for their iniquity and their sin, *because they have defiled My land; they have filled My inheritance with their carcasses of their detestable and abominable idols* . . . Therefore, behold, I will this once cause them to know, I will cause them to know My hand and My might; and they shall know that My name is the LORD."

As sovereign and righteous Judge, the Lord God of Israel will allow Satan's *final hunter* and his armies to viciously persecute the children of Israel during the *last* three and one-half years of the *time of Jacob's trouble*. Again, the Almighty allows this because of the Jewish people's rejection of Yeshua, Moses' law, and because of their carcasses and detestable and abominable idols in the Promised Land. Most certainly, if a nation or an individual does not recognize Yeshua as the Lord God, all of that nation's or individual's methods of worship are detestable and abominable before the Lord God's eyes. Therefore, just as Messiah, the sovereign and righteous Judge of all mankind, will pour out His furious vengeance upon the *regions* of Nimrod, Ishmael, Esau, Goliath, the Antichrist, and frankly, the whole world (Isa. 24), God's right Hand (Messiah) will also extend His wrath and indignation upon the nation of Israel.

Jeremiah 25:29–33, 36–38: "*For behold, I begin to bring calamity on the city which is called by My name [Jerusalem], and should you be utterly unpunished? You shall not be unpunished, for I will call for a sword on all the inhabitants of the earth*" [tribulation period] *says the* LORD *of hosts.*' Therefore, prophesy against them all these words, and say to them, "*The* LORD *will roar from on high, and utter His voice from His holy habitation; He will roar mightily against His fold [Israel]. He will give a shout, as those who tread the grapes, against all the inhabitants of the earth [Rev. 14, 19]. A noise will come to the ends of the earth*—for the Lord has a controversy with the nations [Isa. 24]; He will plead His case with all flesh. He will give those who are wicked to the sword," says the Lord' [Rev. 14, 19]. Thus says the LORD of hosts: 'Behold, disaster shall go forth from nation to nation, and a great whirlwind shall be raised up from the farthest parts of the earth. *And at that day the slain of the* LORD *shall be from one end of the earth even to the other end of the earth [Matt. 24:27–28; Rev. 19]. They shall not be lamented, or gathered, or buried; they shall become refuse on the ground* . . . For the LORD has plundered their pasture, and the peaceful dwellings are cut down because of the fierce anger of the LORD. He has left His lair like the lion; *For their land is desolate because of the fierceness of the Oppressor, and because of His fierce anger*'" (Second Coming).

Luke 21:20, 22–24: "*But when you see Jerusalem surrounded by armies, then know that its desolation is near . . . For these are the days of vengeance, that all things which are written may be fulfilled . . . For there will be great distress in the land and wrath upon this people* [Israel]. *And they shall fall by the edge of the sword, and be led away captive into all nations. And Jerusalem will be trampled by Gentiles until the times of the Gentiles are fulfilled* [Second Coming]."

As the time of Jacob's trouble fulfills its apocalyptic seven-year timetable, God will allow Satan's *final hunter* and his end-of-the-age hunters to encircle Jerusalem for the awesome, yet terrible Day of the Lord. The Lord God of Israel will judge His people through the Antichrist, just as He did with Nebuchadnezzar of Babylon (Jer. 25:1–14).

MESSIAH DESTROYS THE REGIONS OF SATAN'S *ORIGINAL HUNTERS*

At Messiah's first coming, God's perfect Servant fulfilled the prophecy of Isaiah 61:1–2, "The Spirit of the LORD is upon Me, because He has anointed Me to preach the gospel to the poor, to heal the brokenhearted, to proclaim liberty to the captives and the recovery of sight to the blind, to set at liberty those who are oppressed, and to proclaim the acceptable year of the Lord" (see Luke 4:16–21). Messiah came as the humbled, suffering Servant and sacrificial Lamb of God to "fish" *all* of mankind through His ultimate sacrifice on the cross (Isa. 53; John 3:16; Phil. 2:5–11). On the contrary, at Messiah's second coming, He will faithfully and truthfully return as the roaring, conquering Lion of Judah (Rev. 5:5; 19:11–16)! Messiah's return to earth will occur on the last day of the *time of Jacob's trouble*, and the *final blood moon of the age* will occur before His glorious appearance!

> Joel 2:31: "The sun shall be turned into darkness, *and the moon into blood before the coming of the great and awesome day of the* LORD." (See Acts 2:20.)

When Messiah returns, He will fulfill the very next part of Isaiah 61:2, which is "to proclaim *the day of vengeance of our God*, to comfort those who mourn" (see Luke 21:22; Rev. 19:11–16). Who will mourn on the Day of the Lord at His glorious appearing?

> Matthew 24:30: "Then the sign of the Son of Man will appear in heaven, *and then all the tribes of the earth will mourn, and they will see the Son of Man coming on the clouds of heaven with power and great glory.*"

For as lightning comes from the east and flashes to the west, *all* of the tribes of the earth will mourn as they realize the moment of truth! There will not be any doubt whatsoever as to who is the King of kings, the Lord of lords, and Faithful and True, when He pours out His vengeance upon the nations (Zech. 9:14; Matt. 24:27; Rev. 19:11–16).

MESSIAH DESTROYS NIMROD'S REGION (SATAN'S ORIGINAL HUNTER)

At Messiah's second coming, He will pour out His vengeance upon the ancient *regions* of Nimrod, Satan's *original hunter*, who *directly* attempted to forbid the Abrahamic covenant from being promised to Abraham. One of the regions of Nimrod is modern-day Iraq, including the cities Babel, Erech, Accad, and Calneh, which were located in the land of Shinar (Gen. 10:10). Let us recall that Satan's *final hunter* is literally named by the prophet Isaiah as "the king of Babylon," which is located in the *region* of Nimrod. Please note that the oracles of Isaiah 11–23 are in the context of the Day of the Lord (Second Coming).

> Isaiah 14:3–6, 9, 11, 16–17, 19: "*It shall come to pass in the day the Lord gives you rest from your sorrow [Second Coming], and from your fear and the hard bondage in which you were made to serve, that you will take up this proverb against the king of Babylon [Antichrist], and say: 'How the oppressor has ceased, the golden city ceased! The Lord has broken the staff of the wicked, the scepter of the rulers; he who struck the people in wrath with a continual stroke, he who ruled the nations in anger, is persecuted and no one hinders. . . .* Hell from beneath is excited about you, to meet you at your coming . . . Your pomp is brought down to Sheol [hell] and the sound of your stringed instruments; the maggot is spread before you, and worms cover you . . . Those who see you will gaze at you, *and* consider you, *saying:* "*Is this the man [Antichrist] who made the earth tremble, who shook kingdoms, who made the world as a wilderness and destroyed its cities, who did not open the house of his prisoners?*"""

Nimrod's kingdom also expanded into ancient Assyria (modern-day northern Iraq), where he built Nineveh (Mosul), Rehoboth Ir, Calah (Nimrud), and Resen (Gen. 10:11). Although these ancient cities are located in modern-day Iraq, it is essential to align the end-of-the-age prophecies to the *regions* the biblical prophets would have been speaking of and writing about *at that specific time*. In the Scriptures we are about to explore, the prophets would have been prophesying about ancient Assyria, which was included in Nimrod's kingdom. At Messiah's second coming, He will pour out His vengeance upon Assyria, the *region* of Nimrod. Keep in mind, Satan's *final hunter* is literally named by the biblical prophets as "the Assyrian," and the "king of Assyria," which is located in the *region* of Nimrod. Again, the context of these Scriptures is the Day of the Lord.

> Micah 5:5–6: "When the Assyrian [Antichrist] comes into our land, and when he treads in our palaces, then we will raise against him seven shepherds and eight princely men. *They shall waste with the sword the land of Assyria, and the land of Nimrod at its entrances; thus He [Messiah] shall deliver us from the Assyrian [Antichrist], when he comes*

into our land [Israel] and when he treads within our borders." (See Isa. 10:24–26; 14:24–26; 30:27–33; 31:8–9.)

Isaiah 10:12, 17–18: "Therefore it shall come to pass, when the LORD has performed all His work on Mount Zion and on Jerusalem [Second Coming], that *He will say, 'I will punish the fruit of the arrogant heart of the king of Assyria [Antichrist], and the glory of his haughty looks.'* . . . So the Light of Israel will be for a fire, and his Holy One for a flame; it will burn and devour his thorns and his briers *in one day [Second Coming]*. And it will consume the glory of his forest and of his fruitful field, both soul and body." (See Isa. 14:12–15; 31:18–19; Dan. 7:11, 26; 8:25.)

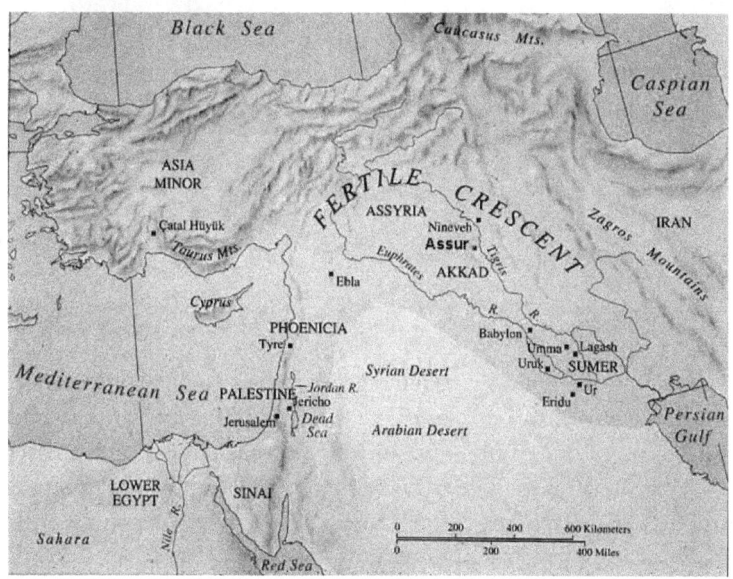

Ancient Assyria

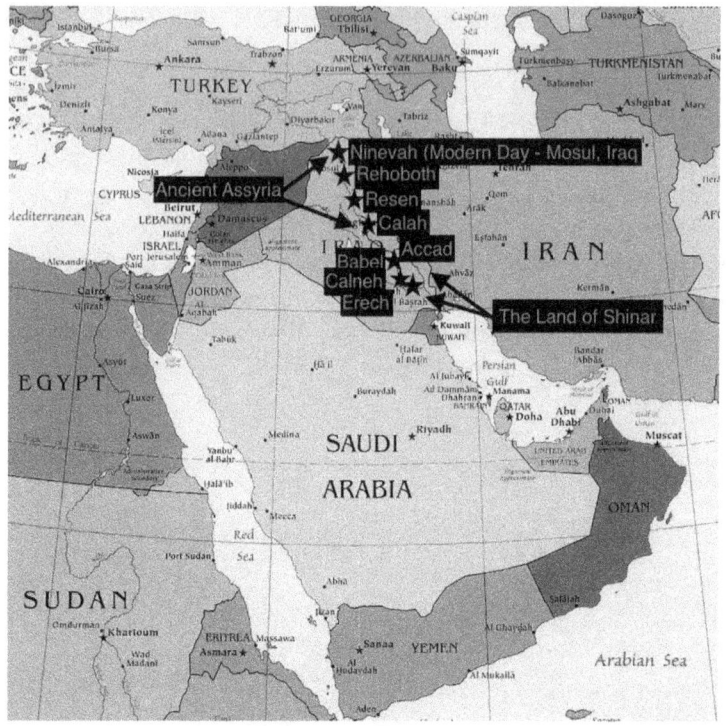

Nimrod

In Isaiah 10, he not only prophesied about the Lion of Judah destroying the *region* of Nimrod and the Assyrian (Antichrist); he also forewarned about the destruction of one of the most ancient cities in the world, Damascus. In Isaiah 17, he validates the Lord's furious anger and unrelenting judgment on the enriched historical city, as he proclaims, "Behold, Damascus will cease from being a city, and it will become a ruinous heap" (Isa. 17:1). According to Greek historian Nicolaus of Damascus, Abram (Abraham) came with his army to Damascus from the land of the Chaldeans. Nicolaus recorded, "Abraham reigned at Damascus, but after a length of time, he took his army and people and journeyed to the land of Canaan, thus Damascus has been in existence for over four thousand millennia." [1] As of this writing, Damascus still exists and is inhabited as a city. Nevertheless, at Messiah's second coming, this sobering, yet candid prophecy will be fulfilled, and this ancient city will be destroyed in *one day* (Isa. 17:14).

MESSIAH DESTROYS ISHMAEL'S REGION (SATAN'S ORIGINAL HUNTER)

On the Day of the Lord, Messiah will pour out His vengeance upon the ancient *region* of Ishmael, Satan's *original hunter,* who *directly* attempted to forbid the Abrahamic covenant from being promised to Isaac. The *region* of Ishmael is located in modern-day Jordan and Saudi Arabia. As we discussed in chapter 4, Flavius Josephus recorded that Ishmael is the "founder of the Arab nation." [2] Of course, there are millions of Arabs who love the Lord God of Israel, Yeshua the Messiah; therefore, this is not a condemnation or judgment upon them, but instead, on the tyrannical Islamic nations and governments (regions) that rule over our beloved Arab brothers and sisters. In fact, during the *time of Jacob's trouble,* Messiah will "fish" the Arab believers from the region of Ishmael before He pours out His vengeance and wrath upon it (Rev. 18:4–5; Isa. 21, 34, 63).

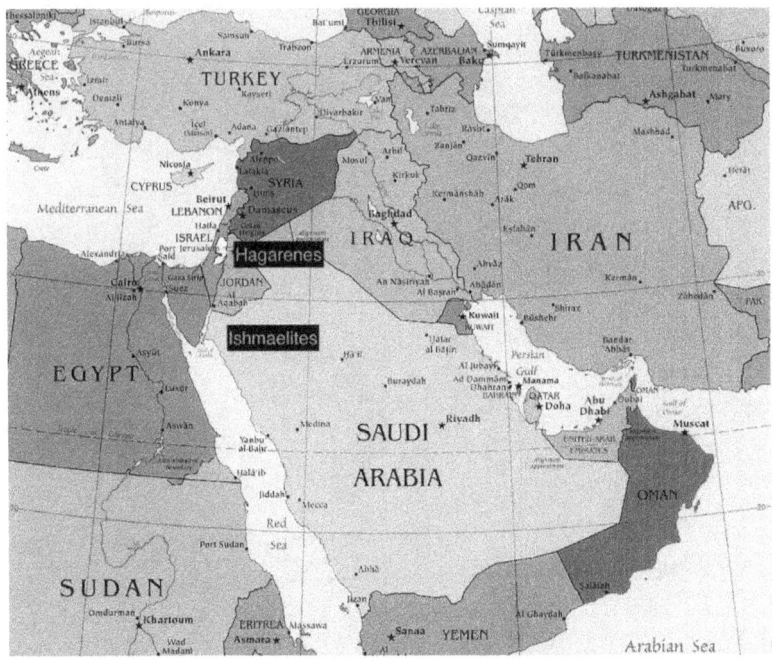

Ishmael

In our book *God's Prophetic Timeline, Messiah's Final Warning,* we build the scriptural case for Mecca, Saudi Arabia, and the kingdom of Saudi Arabia, as the great harlot of "Mystery Babylon the Great" (Rev. 17–18). Saudi Arabia

(Mecca) is the birthplace of Islam, the "mother of all false religions," and it perfectly aligns with *all* of the prerequisites in Revelation 17 and 18. In fact, the prophet Isaiah validates Saudi Arabia as the great harlot, Mystery Babylon (Isa. 21). On the Day of the Lord, Messiah will pour out His vengeance upon the *region* of Ishmael, which is predominantly located in Jordan and Saudi Arabia. Please note: the ancient *regions* of Ishmael and Esau (Edom) geographically overlap the modern boundary lines of Jordan and Saudi Arabia. Therefore, we will discover some biblical prophecies that foretell judgment on both as "one region." For example, in Ezekiel 25, Teman and Dedan are specifically located in *Edom,* which is modern-day Saudi Arabia (Ezek. 25:12–14). In Isaiah 63, Bozrah is specifically located in *Edom,* which is modern-day southern Jordan (Isa. 63:1).

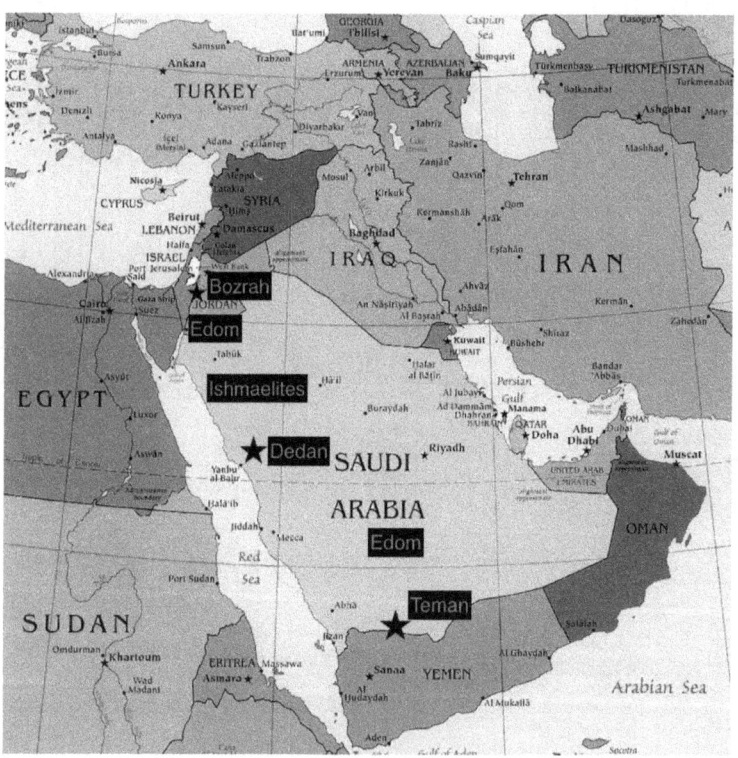

Teman, Dedan, Bozrah

Regardless of the exact modern-day boundaries, the biblical prophets have certainly proclaimed wrath and judgment on both of the *regions* of Ishmael and Esau, who were Satan's *original hunters* against the Abrahamic covenant. Keep in mind, the context of these scriptures are the Day of the Lord.

Ishmael / Esau

Ezekiel 25:13–14: "Therefore thus says the Lord GOD: '*I will also stretch out My hand against Edom, cut off man and beast from it, and make it desolate from Teman; Dedan shall fall by the sword. I will lay My vengeance on Edom by the hand of My people Israel*, that they may do in Edom according to My anger and according to My fury; *and they shall know My vengeance*,' says the Lord GOD." (See Hab. 3:3–7.)

Isaiah 21:1, 9, 13–17: "The burden against the Wilderness [NIV: *Desert*] *of the Sea* [*Saudi Arabia*]. 'As whirlwinds in the South pass through, so it comes from the desert, from a terrible land . . . And look, here comes a chariot of men with a pair of horsemen!' Then he answered and said, **'Babylon is fallen, is fallen!** And all the carved images of her gods He has broken to the ground.' . . . *The burden against* **Arabia**. '*In the forest in* **Arabia** *you will lodge, O you traveling* *companies of Dedanites. O inhabitants of the land of Tema, bring water to him who is thirsty;* With their bread they met him who fled. For they fled from the swords, from the drawn sword, from the bent bow, and from the distress of war.' For thus the LORD has said to me: 'Within a year, according to the year of a hired man, all the glory of Kedar will fail; and the remainder of the number of archers, the mighty men of the people of Kedar, will be diminished; for the LORD God of Israel has spoken *it*.'" (See Isa. 13:6–8, 17–22; 34:5, 8–15; Ezek. 35:1–15.)

Revelation 18:2, 8, 19, 21: "And he cried mightily with a loud voice, saying, '**Babylon the great is fallen, is fallen [Isaiah 21]**, and has become a dwelling place of demons, a prison for every foul spirit, and a cage for every unclean and hated bird!' . . . *Therefore, her plagues will come in one day*—death and mourning and famine. *And she will be utterly burned with fire, for strong is the Lord God who judges her . . . For in one hour she is made desolate.* Then a mighty angel took up a stone like a great millstone and threw it into the sea, saying, 'Thus with violence the great city Babylon shall be thrown down, and shall not be found anymore.'" (See Jer. 49:20–22; 50:41–42, 46; 52:6–7.)

MESSIAH DESTROYS ESAU'S REGION (SATAN'S ORIGINAL HUNTER)

At Messiah's second coming, He will pour out His vengeance upon the ancient *region* of Esau (Edom), Satan's *original hunter*, who *directly* attempted to forbid the Abrahamic covenant from being promised to Jacob. The region of Esau (Edom) is located in southern Jordan and Saudi Arabia. As previously discussed, the ancient regions of Ishmael and Esau overlap the modern-day boundary lines of Jordan and Saudi Arabia, as the region of Edom extends into Saudi Arabia. Accordingly, as we proceed with Messiah's judgment upon Edom (Esau), the region of Ishmael (Saudi Arabia) is encompassed, as well. Again, the context of these Scriptures is the Day of the Lord, and He will avenge Jacob from the generational yoke of his brother Esau (Edom).

Obadiah 1, 8–10, 15, 17–18, 21: "Thus says the Lord God concerning Edom, '*Will I not in that day,*' says the LORD, '*even destroy the wise men from Edom, and understanding from the mountains of Esau? Then your mighty men, O Teman, shall be dismayed, to the end that everyone from the mountains of Esau may be cut off by slaughter. For violence against your brother Jacob, shame shall cover you, and you shall be cut off forever. . . For the day of the* LORD *upon all the nations is near; as you have done, it shall be done to you*; your reprisal shall return upon your own head . . . But on Mount Zion there shall be deliverance, and there shall be holiness; The house of Jacob shall possess their possessions. The house of Jacob shall be a fire, and the house of Joseph a flame; *but the house of Esau shall be stubble; they shall kindle them and devour them, and no survivor shall remain of the house of Esau,*' for the LORD has spoken . . . Then saviors [NIV: deliverers] shall come to Mount Zion to judge the mountains of Esau, and the kingdom shall be the LORD's." (See Joel 3:19–20; Amos 1:11–12.)

Assuredly, just as Esau (Edom) "hunted" Jacob four thousand years ago, and throughout history, Esau's descendants have "hunted" Jacob's descendants (Israel), the *region* of Edom (Jordan, Saudi Arabia) will "hunt" Israel one final time during the *time of Jacob's trouble* (Isa. 46:9–10). However, at Messiah's second coming, He will "hunt" and pour out His vengeance upon the *region* of Esau (Edom), and it "shall be cut off forever" (Gen. 27:40)!

Isaiah 63:1–6: "*Who is this who comes from Edom, with dyed garments from Bozrah, this One [Messiah] who is glorious in His apparel, traveling in the greatness of His strength? 'I [Messiah] who speak in righteousness, mighty to save.* Why is Your apparel red, and Your garments like one who treads in the winepress [Second Coming, Rev. 19:11–16]? 'I [Messiah] have trodden the winepress alone, and from the peoples no one was with Me. For I have trodden them in My anger, and trampled them in My fury; their blood is sprinkled upon My garments, and I have stained all My robes. *For the day of vengeance is in My heart [Isa. 61:2], and the year of My redeemed has come.* I looked, but *there was* no one to help, and I wondered that *there was* no one to uphold; therefore, *My own arm brought salvation for Me; and My own fury, it sustained Me. I have trodden down the peoples in My anger, made them drunk in My fury, and brought down their strength to the earth.*'" (See Ps. 137:7–9; Joel. 3:2; Rev. 14:14–16.)

Please recognize that the Almighty blesses those who bless Israel and curses him who curses Israel (Gen. 12:3). The Lord God of Israel prophesied through the prophet Malachi and proclaimed, "How He loves Jacob [Israel], but hates Esau [Edom] with an *everlasting* indignation." In fact, Messiah will "lay to waste Esau's mountains and his heritage for the jackals of the wilderness, as it will be called the Territory of Wickedness and the people against whom the LORD will have indignation forever" (Mal. 1:2–5). Certainly, Messiah will have a tremendous slaughter of Jacob's ancient enemy in the *region* of Edom on His day of vengeance, His second coming.

> Isaiah 34:5–6, 8, 16: "For My sword shall be bathed in heaven; *indeed, it shall come down on Edom, and on the people of My curse, for judgment. The sword of the LORD is filled with blood . . . For the LORD has a sacrifice in Bozrah, and a great slaughter in the land of Edom . . . For it is the day of the LORD's vengeance, the year of recompense for the cause of Zion . . . For My mouth has commanded it, and His Spirit has gathered them.*"

MESSIAH DESTROYS GOLIATH'S REGION (SATAN'S ORIGINAL HUNTER)

On the Day of the Lord, He will pour out His vengeance upon the *region* of Goliath (Philistines), Satan's *original hunter,* who *directly* attempted to forbid the Davidic covenant from being promised to King David. The *region* of Goliath is Philistia, or better known today as the Gaza Strip, located on the west coast of Israel, where Israel's ancient enemy, the Philistines, inhabited.

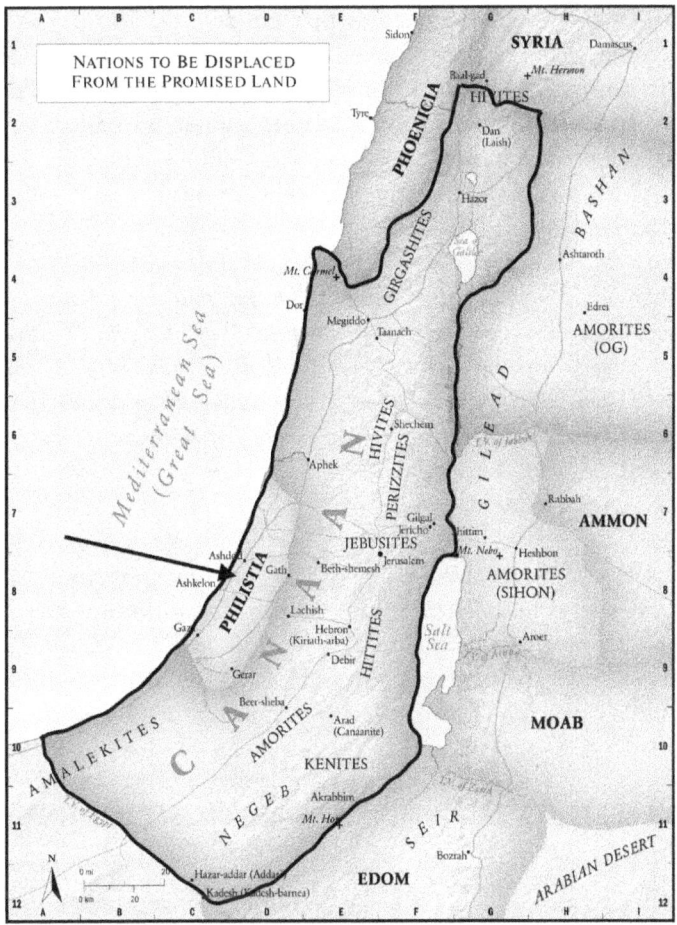

Philistines

Today, the Islamic terror group Hamas (Palestinians/Philistines), which in Hebrew means "violence" (Strong's #2554), predominantly occupies the Gaza Strip. Over the past decades, Hamas has launched attacks, Qassam rockets, suicide bombings, and other provocative measures against God's heritage and people, Israel. As we have discussed, these intentional acts of terror are primarily based on the God-given right to the deed of the Promised Land, which was promised by the Almighty in the Abrahamic covenant. Hamas, and all Islamic groups (Satan's *end-of-the-age* hunters), believe that Ishmael and Esau's lineage has the rights from God to control the land of Israel. On the contrary, God's sovereign and righteous living Word, the Holy

Bible, clearly and specifically records that *His promise, His sworn oath*, the Abrahamic covenant, which is confirmed through the Davidic and new covenants, absolutely deeds this ancient sacred land to the descendants of Abraham, Isaac, Jacob, and David. (Gentiles who are saved in Messiah are heirs according to the promise; see Rom. 11; Gal. 3:26–29; Eph. 2:11–13). Clearly, at Messiah's second coming, He will pour out His unrelenting wrath on the *region* of Goliath (Philistia).

> Zephaniah 2:4–5, 7: "*For Gaza [Philistia] shall be forsaken*, and Ashkelon desolate . . . *The word of the* LORD *is against you, O Canaan, land of the Philistines [Noah's curse]: 'I will destroy you; so there shall be no inhabitant'. . . The coast shall be for the remnant of the house of Judah; They shall feed their flocks there. In the houses of Ashkelon [Gaza Strip] they shall lie down at evening. For the* LORD *their God will intervene for them, and return their captives.*"

> Amos 1:6–8: "Thus says the LORD: '*For three transgressions of Gaza, and for four, I will not turn away its punishment, because they took captive the whole captivity to deliver them up to Edom (Esau). But I will send a fire upon the wall of Gaza, which shall devour its palaces . . . And the remnant of the Philistines shall perish,*' says the Lord GOD." (See Isa. 14:28–32; Ezek. 25:15–17; Zech. 9:5–8; Rev. 14:17–19.)

MESSIAH DESTROYS THE ANTICHRIST'S REGION (SATAN'S FINAL HUNTER)

At Messiah's second coming, He will pour out His vengeance upon the *region* of the Antichrist, Satan's *final hunter*, who will *directly* attempt to forbid God's everlasting covenants from being fulfilled by Messiah.

> Hosea 13:11, "I gave you a king [Antichrist] in My anger, and took him away in My wrath."

In chapter 9, we authenticated the *region* of the Antichrist will be the conglomerate land area of the ancient Babylonian, Medo-Persian, and Grecian empires (10 kings), which also encompasses the *regions* of Satan's *original hunters and his end-of-the-age hunters*. Now, in summary, let us compare Daniel 2 and 7, as they are "brother chapters" that prophesy of the same kingdoms.

A REVIEW OF DANIEL 7'S FOUR KINGDOMS (BEASTS)

1. Babylonian Empire (Iraq)—lion (Dan. 7), which is Daniel 2's gold
2. Medo-Persian Empire (Iran)— bear (Dan. 7), which is Daniel 2's silver
3. Grecian Empire (Turkey)—leopard (Dan. 7), which is Daniel 2's bronze
4. Antichrist's kingdom—iron (Dan. 7) (a conglomerate of the previous three kingdoms, ten kings—Dan. 7 and Rev. 13:2), which is Daniel 2's iron–clay (ten toes/kings)

Babylonian Empire

Medo-Persian Empire

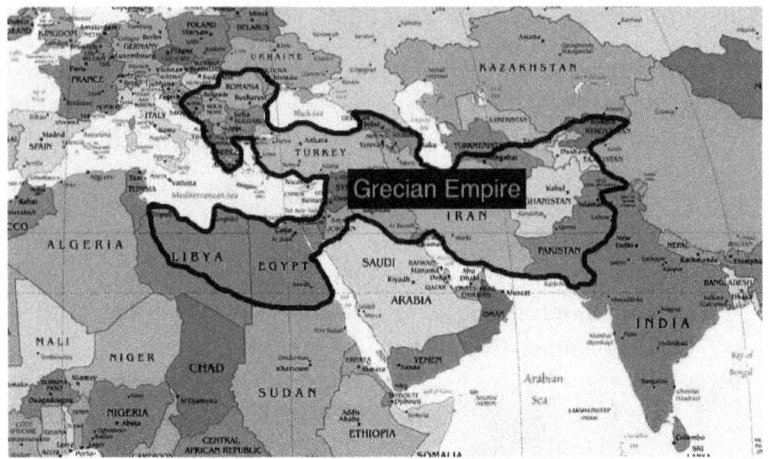

Grecian Empire

Ten Kings

THE TIME OF JACOB'S TROUBLE

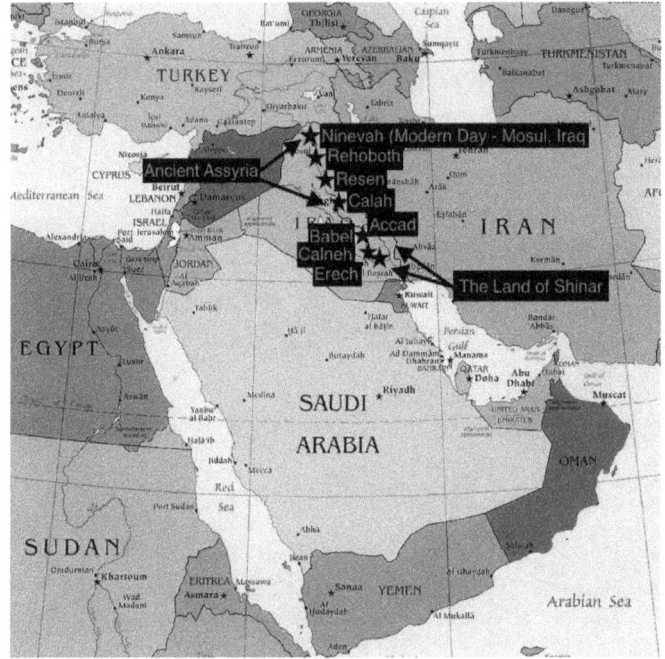

Nimrod

Hagar-Ishmael

Esau-Edom

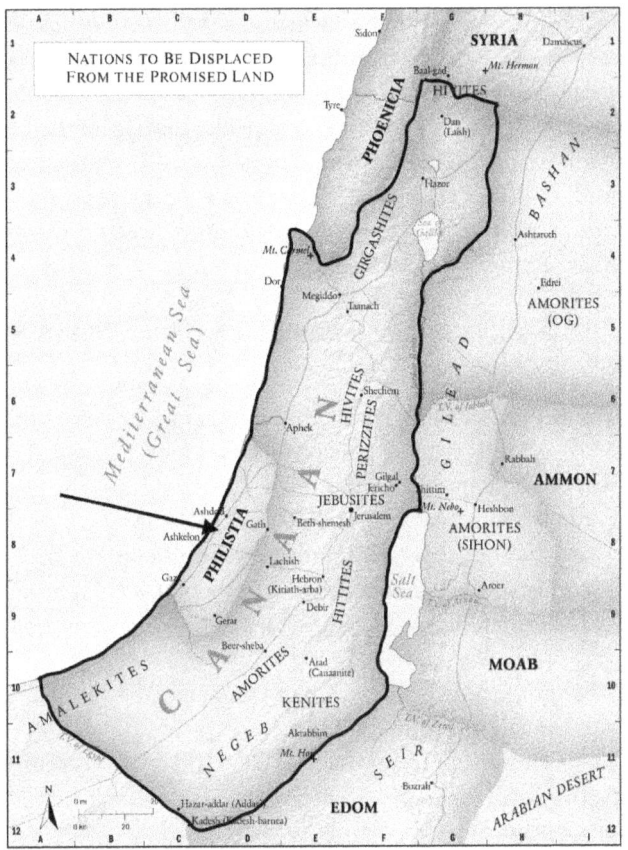

Philistia

In Daniel 2, the account of Nebuchadnezzar's prophetic statue dream, Daniel proves that Yeshua, the Stone the builders rejected, is the Stone who will *crush* the Antichrist's kingdom, which is the fourth kingdom in Daniel 2 and 7. Again, the Antichrist's kingdom will be a *conglomerate of all three previous kingdoms*, which encompass Satan's *original and end-of-the-age hunter's* regions. The prophecy of Daniel 2 is for the "latter days," or the end of the age, when Messiah will "set up His kingdom *in the days of these kings, crushing them together*, as it shall stand forever" (Dan. 2:28, 35, 44). Obviously, Messiah has not fulfilled this prophecy, because the "latter days" were not twenty-five hundred years ago. "Latter days" is an eschatological term for the end of the age. Additionally, *in the days* of Nebuchadnezzar (Babylonian), Cyrus (Persian), and Alexander the Great (Grecian), Messiah did not set up His everlasting kingdom, nor did He *crush* them *all* together.

Daniel 2:34–35: "You watched while a *stone [Messiah] was cut out without hands*, which struck the image on its feet of iron and clay, and broke them in pieces. *Then the iron, the clay, the bronze, the silver, and the gold were crushed together*, and became like chaff from the summer threshing floors; the wind carried them away so that no trace of them was found. *And the stone [Messiah] that struck the image became a great mountain [kingdom] and filled the whole earth"* [second coming and millennial kingdom on earth].

MESSIAH, THE STONE, CRUSHES DANIEL 2'S FOUR KINGDOMS TOGETHER

Following are the kingdoms that will arise in exact order before the awesome and terrible Day of the Lord. "In the days of these kings" (Dan. 2:44), Messiah, the Stone, will *crush* them *all* together (Dan. 2:35), which is the conglomerate fourth kingdom of both Daniel 2 and 7 (Rev. 13). Subsequently, He will set up His eternal kingdom that will stand forever and ever (Dan. 2:44)! For a thorough discovery of these kingdoms, see our book *God's Prophetic Timeline, Messiah's Final Warning* (www.faithfulperformance.com; www.amazon.com).

1. Babylonian Empire (Iraq)—gold (Daniel 2)—fulfilled 2003 with the fall of Saddam Hussein
2. Medo-Persian Empire (Iran)—silver (Daniel 2)—currently existent as of 2017
3. Grecian Empire (Turkey)—bronze (Daniel 2)
4. Antichrist's kingdom—iron, clay (conglomerate of the previous three kingdoms, ten kings—Daniel 7 and Rev. 13:2)
5. Messiah's kingdom (the Stone)

At Messiah's second coming, the Day of the Lord, He will destroy these regions that are literally mentioned by the biblical prophets (Isa. 13–23, Jer. 25:15–37, Jer. 46–51, Ezek. 25–32). Of course, Messiah pours out His vengeance upon the whole world and chastises all nations, including Israel (Isa. 24; Rev. 14:6–20; 19:11–16), but we cannot overlook and neglect the literal references of judgment on these specific kingdoms, which include the *regions* of Nimrod, Ishmael, Esau, Goliath, the Herodian family, the *end-of-the-age* hunters, and the Antichrist's kingdom.

Zechariah 3:8-10: "'Hear, O Joshua, the high priest, you and your companions who sit before you, for they are a wondrous sign; *For behold, I am bringing forth My Servant the BRANCH. For behold, the stone that I have laid before Joshua: Upon the stone are seven eyes.* Behold, I will engrave its inscription,' says the LORD of hosts, 'and I will remove the iniquity of that land in *one day*. In that day,' says the LORD of hosts, 'Everyone will invite his neighbor under his vine and under his fig tree.'"

YESHUA, THE ULTIMATE FISHERMAN, WHO WILL REDEEM THE NATION OF ISRAEL AND SAVE HIS REMNANT AT HIS SECOND COMING

Although the *time of Jacob's trouble* will encompass the most cataclysmic persecution period in world history, an abundant revival will also transpire among the children of Israel. The blessed Holy Spirit will divinely manifest through His two witnesses, the 144,000 sealed saints, whom we discussed earlier, and in other righteous, sovereign ways. This will culminate in a vast remnant that will be saved out of the Great Tribulation (Zech. 13:9; Rev. 11:13). At Messiah's majestic second coming, the remnant of Israel will praise, rejoice, and shout the famous words Messiah Himself prophesied they would proclaim at His return, which will annul the covenant of death (Isa. 28:18).

> Matthew 23:38–39: "For I say to you [Jews], *you shall see Me no more till you say, "Blessed is He who comes in the name of the Lord!"* [Baruch haba b'shem Adonai!]

On God's divine appointment, which will occur on the last day of the *time of Jacob's trouble*, Yeshua will return for His glorious second coming to intervene, deliver, and save His people, His land, and His heritage, Israel. The ultimate and supreme reason for His divine return is to *completely* fulfill the unilateral, unconditional, and irrevocable covenants of the Father to His *original fishermen*, which are the everlasting promises of the Abrahamic, Davidic, and new covenants! Please note, the fulfillment of the everlasting covenants will also eternalize the fulfillment of Noah's prophetic curse on the land of Canaan, which became the Promised Land (Gen. 9:24–27).

> Revelation 19:11–16: "Now I saw heaven opened, and behold, a white horse. *And He who sat on him was called Faithful and True,* and in righteousness He judges and makes war. His eyes *were* like a flame of fire, and on His head were many crowns. He had a name written that no one knew except Himself. He was clothed with a robe

dipped in blood, and His name is called *The Word of God*. And the armies in heaven, *clothed in fine linen, white and clean [Yom Kippur, Leviticus 16),* followed Him on *white horses*. Now out of His mouth goes a sharp sword, that with it He should strike the nations. And He Himself will rule them with a rod of iron. *He Himself treads the winepress of the fierceness and wrath of Almighty God. And He has on His robe and on His thigh a name written: KING OF KINGS AND LORD OF LORDS."*

Luke 1:32–33: "He will be great, and will be called the Son of the Highest; *and the Lord God will give Him the throne of His father David [Davidic covenant]. And He will reign over the house of Jacob forever, and of His kingdom there will be no end"* [Abrahamic and new covenants].

The book of Genesis foreshadows this extraordinary event! In the fascinating story of the well-known messianic figure Joseph, once his brother Judah repented of his sins, Joseph *forgave* and *revealed* himself to Judah and his brothers, thereby saving them from the famine (Genesis 45–46). Equivalently, during *the time of Jacob's trouble*, once Judah (Jews) repents, Messiah will also *forgive* and *reveal* Himself to Judah (Jews) and his brethren, and therefore, they will be saved from Satan's final hunter (Jer. 30:7)!

THE FINAL ALIYAH

After Messiah destroys the *regions* of Satan's *original hunters*, his *end-of-the-age* hunters, and the *final hunter*, the final Aliyah will commence! He will make His triumphal approach into the holy city of Jerusalem from Bozrah (Edom), or the modern-day area of Petra, where Judah will be saved first (Isa. 63; Zech.12:7). Afterward, He will put His almighty feet down on the Mount of Olives in Jerusalem, the exact place where He ascended at His first coming (Zech. 14:4; Acts 1:9–12).

Zechariah 13:7–9: "'Awake, O sword, against My Shepherd, against the Man who is My Companion,' says the LORD of hosts. *'Strike the Shepherd [Messiah], and the sheep [Israel] will be scattered [first coming]; then I will turn My hand against the little ones.* And it shall come to pass in all the land,' says the LORD, *'that two-thirds in it shall be cut off and die, but one-third shall be left in it. I will bring the one-third through the fire [time of Jacob's trouble], will refine them as silver is refined, and test them as gold is tested. They will call on My name, and I will answer them. I will say, "This is My people"; and each one will say, "The LORD is my God [second coming and millennial reign]."'"*

In Jeremiah 23, the weeping prophet provides the children of Israel ultimate encouragement and hope for the *final Aliyah* that will occur at Messiah's second coming and during His millennial reign. Please note the similar but different language in Jeremiah 23 compared to Jeremiah 16.

Jeremiah 23:3–6: "'*But I will gather the remnant of My flock out of all countries where I have driven them, and bring them back to their folds; and they shall be fruitful and increase.* I will set up shepherds over them who will feed them; and they shall fear no more, nor be dismayed, nor shall they be lacking,' says the LORD. 'Behold, *the* days are coming,' says the LORD, that I will raise to David a Branch of righteousness; a King shall reign and prosper, and execute judgment and righteousness in the earth. *In His days Judah will be saved, and Israel will dwell safely; now this is His name by which He will be called: THE LORD OUR RIGHTEOUSNESS.*" (See Mic. 2:12–13, Isa. 4:2–6, Zech. 6:12–13.)

Jeremiah 23:7-8: "Therefore, behold, the days are coming," says the LORD, "that they shall no longer say, 'As the LORD lives who brought up the children of Israel from the land of Egypt,' but, 'As the LORD lives who brought up and **led** the descendants of the house of Israel from the north country and from all the countries where I had driven them.' And they shall dwell in their own land."

Jeremiah 16:14-16: "Therefore behold, the days are coming," says the LORD, "that it shall no more be said, 'The LORD lives who brought up the children of Israel from the land of Egypt,' but, 'The LORD lives who brought up the children of Israel from the land of the north and from all the lands where He had driven them.' For I will bring them back into their land which I gave to their fathers. "Behold, I will send for many fishermen," says the LORD, "and they shall fish them; and afterward I will send for many hunters, and they shall hunt them from every mountain and every hill, and out of the holes of the rocks."

At first glance, Jeremiah 16 and 23 seem to be prophesying about the same event that will be fulfilled at the exact same time. However, these two prophecies will occur at separate times, albeit three and one-half years apart. In chapter 16, Jeremiah prophesied about a specific time when the children of Israel will be brought to the Promised Land from the land of the north and from *all* of the lands, and the prophet warned of exactly how this Aliyah will be accomplished, which is by God's fishermen and Satan's hunters (vv. 14–16). As we have authenticated, Jeremiah 16 will be *completely* fulfilled at the midpoint of the time of Jacob's trouble, or *before* the last three and one-half years of the age initiates.

On the contrary, Jeremiah 23 will be fulfilled at Messiah's second coming and at the beginning of His millennial reign, because during the *last* three and one-half years of the time of Jacob's trouble, half of the people in Jerusalem will be taken into captivity and exiled by the Antichrist (Dan. 11:33, Zech. 14:1–2). Most certainly, there will not be an Aliyah *to* the Promised Land at that devastating time. Remember, Messiah commanded the Jewish people to "flee" Jerusalem, not make Aliyah once the final hunter fulfills the abomination of desolation (Matt. 24:15–16), which will occur at the midpoint of the time of Jacob's trouble (three and a half years). Nevertheless, at Messiah's second coming, He will "bring them out of captivity and *lead* the descendants of the house of Israel from the north country and from all the countries where He had driven them. And they shall dwell in their own land" (Jer. 23:8). Although Jeremiah 16 and 23 parallel in prophetic language of a Jewish Aliyah, these two awesome chapters are prophesying of two separate Aliyah events that are three and one-half years apart.

In Ezekiel 38 and 39, the Battle of Gog-Magog, the prophet substantiates the timeline of the Aliyahs in Jeremiah 16 and 23. Before we confirm, let us realize this battle is the same battle as Armageddon because Ezekiel clearly substantiates the time when this cataclysmic war will occur. The following points in Ezekiel 38 and 39 will verify how the Battle of Gog-Magog absolutely correlates to John's account of Armageddon in Revelation.

In Ezekiel 38, God proclaims, "*All* things who are on the face of the earth shall shake at *My presence*" (vv. 18-20), clearly placing the Lord *on* earth during the Battle of Gog and Magog (Armageddon). Additionally, Ezekiel's description of a great earthquake in Israel (v. 20), and also God's judgments of flooding rain, great hailstones, and fire and brimstone (v. 22), thoroughly corroborates with God's wrath in Revelation 14–19, which preludes the time of Messiah's second coming. Furthermore, Ezekiel proclaims, "*Messiah will magnify and sanctify Himself, and He will be known in the eyes of many nations*" (v. 23), which will only occur at His second coming and during His millennial reign, when *all* nations will know that "He is the Lord" (Rev. 19:11–16, see also Psalm 2). Ezekiel's description of the Battle of Gog and Magog correctly aligns with John's description of the Battle of Armageddon in the book of Revelation, validating it as the same battle.

In Ezekiel 39, the prophet declares several events that will only occur at Messiah's second coming and during His millennial reign.

- The Lord will set His glory among the nations, and *all* the nations will see His judgment that He executes with His hand. (v. 21)
- The children of Israel, as a nation, will understand that Yeshua is the Jewish Messiah and the King of Israel (Matt. 23:39). (v. 22)
- The Gentiles will understand the children of Israel's unfaithfulness to the Lord God and will comprehend their trials and tribulations throughout history. (v. 24)
- All of the children of Israel will return from the final captivity (Aliyah) and they will dwell safely in the Promised Land. (God's everlasting covenants) (v. 25)
- Messiah will be hallowed in the sight of *all* nations, and He will set His glory among all the nations. (v. 27)
- Messiah will pour out His Spirit upon the house of Israel. (v. 29)

In Ezekiel 38 and 39, the prophet clearly emphasizes when this apocalyptic battle will culminate, which is Messiah's second coming (Battle of Armageddon). Now, let us corroborate Ezekiel 38 and 39 with Jeremiah 16 and 23 to authenticate the three and one-half year difference between the chapters.

In Ezekiel 38, the writer prophesies to the Antichrist, "In the latter years you will come into the land *of those brought back from the sword and gathered from many people on the mountains of Israel, which had long been desolate; they were brought out of the nations, and now all of them dwell safely. You will ascend, coming like a storm, covering the land like a cloud,* you and all your troops and many peoples with you" (vv. 8–9). Ezekiel's prophecy validates the timing of the fulfillment of Jeremiah 16, because it confirms the children of Israel will have made Aliyah to the Promised Land due to the *sword* of Satan's *end-of-the-age* hunters (1948, midpoint of time of Jacob's trouble) *before* the Antichrist invades Israel. In other words, in Jeremiah 16, the Lord God will bring the children of Israel to the Promised Land from all nations by the fishermen and the hunters, and then the Antichrist will invade Israel and exile them just as Ezekiel prophesied (Ezek. 38:8–9). As we have discovered, once Jeremiah 16 is fulfilled (God's fishermen, Satan's hunters), which will occur at the midpoint of the time of Jacob's trouble (three and a half years), the final hunter will "come like a storm, covering the land like a cloud with many troops," which connects Jeremiah 16 and Ezekiel 38. Remember: The Antichrist will come in the name of "peace" during the first three and one-half years, which will allow the children of Israel to "dwell safely" before the seven-year "peace treaty" transitions into the covenant of death.

> Ezekiel 38:15-16: "Then you [Antichrist] will come from your place out of the far north, you and many peoples with you, all of them riding on horses, a great company and a mighty army. You will come up against My people Israel like a cloud, to cover the land. It will be in the latter days that I will bring you against My land, so that the nations may know Me, when I am hallowed in you, O Gog, before their eyes."

Ezekiel 38 affirms Jeremiah 16 will be *completely* fulfilled at the midpoint of the time of Jacob's trouble. What about Jeremiah 23 and Ezekiel 39? Does Ezekiel validate the timetable of Jeremiah's prophecy?

In Ezekiel 39, the prophet substantiates the timing of Jeremiah 23, which will be fulfilled at Messiah's second coming and during His millennial reign. Ezekiel prophesies, "Therefore thus says the Lord GOD: *'Now I will bring back the captives of Jacob, and have mercy on the whole house of Israel; and I will be jealous for My holy name—after they have borne their shame, and all their unfaithfulness in which they were unfaithful to Me, when they dwelt safely in their own land and no one made them afraid. When I have brought them back from the peoples and gathered them out of their enemies' lands, and I am hallowed in them in the sight of many nations, then they shall know that I am the LORD their God, who sent them into captivity among the nations, but also brought them back to their land, and left none of them captive any longer. And I will not hide My face from them anymore; for I shall have poured out My Spirit on the house of Israel,' says the Lord GOD"* (Ezek. 39:25–29).

Ezekiel 39 confirms Jeremiah 23 because the Lord God will bring back the captives of Jacob (Israel) to the Promised Land "*after* they have borne their shame [Antichrist's captivity], and all their unfaithfulness in which they were unfaithful to Me, *when they dwelt safely in their own land and no one made them afraid"* (Ezek. 39:26 is speaking of the first three and a half years of the time of Jacob's trouble). At Messiah's second coming, He will be jealous for His holy name and He will be hallowed in the Jewish people in the sight of many nations only *at that glorious time*, which is when He will bring them back to the Promised Land and none of them will be left captive any longer (Jeremiah 23—the Second Coming and millennial reign). At that spectacular time, Messiah will not hide His face from the children of Israel anymore, as He will pour out His Spirit upon the house of Israel (Ezek. 39:29).

Ezekiel 38 perfectly correlates with Jeremiah 16, and Ezekiel 39 exactly aligns with Jeremiah 23, as each respective prophecy corroborates the timing of each Aliyah. Ezekiel 38 validates that Jeremiah 16 will be *completely* fulfilled at the midpoint of the time of Jacob's trouble (three and a half years), and Ezekiel 39 authenticates that Jeremiah 23 will be fulfilled at Messiah's second coming and at the beginning of His millennial reign. "By the mouth of two or three witnesses the matter shall be established" (Deut. 19:15).

It is interesting to note that the children of Israel have been exiled from the Promised Land twice in its history. The Diasporas occurred in 586 BC and AD 70. In biblical numerology, the number three signifies *divine completion*. Therefore, once the children of Israel are exiled for the *third* time by the Antichrist, Messiah will divinely and sovereignly bring them back to the Promised Land for the *third* time, stamping His *divine completion* on the matter forever!

THE FULFILLMENT OF GOD'S EVERLASTING COVENANTS

God's everlasting covenants will be *completely* fulfilled at Messiah's second coming and during His millennial reign! As discussed in chapter 1, through the Abrahamic covenant, God promised a specific piece of land to Abraham, Isaac, Jacob, and their descendants, as an everlasting possession. This was known as the land of Canaan, which is modern-day Israel. The eternal covenant also promised a "Seed," who would eternalize from the patriarch Abraham's lineage, the *pure royal lineage*. God swore through the Davidic covenant that the Abrahamic covenant's "Seed" would become Messiah and King over the Promised Land, including Jerusalem. The Seed, Messiah, and King of Israel is Yeshua Hamashiach (Jesus the Messiah). At Messiah's first coming, Yeshua became the new covenant when He was the ultimate sacrifice for mankind (Matt. 26:27–29; John 3:16; 2 Cor. 5:21). Upon the King's arrival on earth at His second coming, He will fulfill *all* three everlasting promises, as He rules from David's everlasting throne from Zion with the saints (you and me) for a thousand years (Rev. 20)! *At that time*, the new covenant will commence with the house of Israel and the house of Judah (Gentiles are grafted into all three everlasting covenants).

> Psalm 105:8–12: "*He remembers His covenant forever*, the word which He commanded, for a thousand generations, *the covenant which He made with Abraham, and His oath to Isaac, and confirmed it to Jacob for a statute, to Israel as an everlasting covenant*, saying, 'To you I will give the land of Canaan as the allotment of your inheritance,' when they were few in number, indeed very few, and strangers in it."

> Jeremiah 31:31, 33–34: "*Behold, the days are coming, says the* LORD, *when I will make a new covenant with the house of Israel and with the house of Judah* . . . But this *is* the covenant that I will make with the house of Israel after those days, says the LORD: *I will put My law in their minds, and write it on their hearts; and I will be their God, and they shall be My people.* No more shall every man teach his neighbor, and every man his brother, saying, 'Know the Lord,' *for they all shall know Me, from the least of them to the greatest of them, says the* LORD. *For I will forgive their iniquity, and their sin I will remember no more.*"

As previously discussed, the new covenant has not been *completely* fulfilled because the house of Israel and the house of Judah have not accepted Yeshua as their Jewish Messiah and God; therefore, they are not "His people." The good news is He will put His Torah in their minds and write it on their hearts, and both houses will be His people and He will be their God! This extraordinary event will begin the fulfillment of the unilateral, unconditional, irrevocable, and everlasting new covenant, which fulfills the Abrahamic and Davidic covenants. During this awesome and majestic time, the remnant of Israel will *completely* understand that Yeshua is the promised Jewish Seed, Messiah, and King of Israel, who will restore the Jewish kingdom during His millennial reign (Acts 1:6–7)!

> Luke 1:32–33: "He will be great, and will be called the Son of the Highest; and the Lord God will give Him the throne of His father David [Davidic covenant]. And He will reign over the house of Jacob forever [Abrahamic covenant], and of His kingdom there will be no end" [new covenant].

Isaiah 9:6–7: "For unto us a Child is born, unto us a Son is given; And the government will be upon His shoulder. And His name will be called Wonderful Counselor, Mighty God, Everlasting Father, Prince of Peace. *Of the increase of His government and peace there will be no end, upon the throne of David and over His kingdom, to order it and establish it with judgment and justice from that time forward, even forever.* The zeal of the Lord of hosts will perform this."

At this glorious and magnificent time in the future, which is Messiah's second coming and throughout His millennial reign, the house of Israel and the house of Judah will have the Torah placed on their hearts and minds, and they shall be Messiah's people, and He shall be their God! Hallelujah!

Jeremiah 32:37–42: "Behold, I will gather them out of all countries where I have driven them in My anger, in My fury, and in great wrath; I will bring them back to this place, and I will cause them to dwell safely. They shall be My people, and I will be their God; then I will give them one heart and one way, that they may fear Me forever, for the good of them and their children after them. And I will make an everlasting covenant with them, that I will not turn away from doing them good; but I will put My fear in their hearts so that they will not depart from Me. Yes, I will rejoice over them to do them good, and I will assuredly plant them in this land, with all My heart and with all My soul. For thus says the Lord: 'Just as I have brought all this great calamity on this people, so I will bring on them all the good that I have promised them.'"

Jeremiah 33:6–11: "'Behold, I will bring it health and healing; I will heal them and reveal to them the abundance of peace and truth. And I will cause the captives of Judah and the captives of Israel to return, and will rebuild those places as at the first. I will cleanse them from all their iniquity by which they have sinned against Me, and I will pardon all their iniquities by which they have sinned and by which they have transgressed against Me. Then it shall be to Me a name of joy, a praise, and an honor before all nations of the earth, who shall hear all the good that I do to them; they shall fear and tremble for all the goodness and all the prosperity that I provide for it. Thus says the Lord: 'Again there shall be heard in this place—of which you say, "It *is* desolate, without man and without beast"—in the cities of Judah, in the streets of Jerusalem that are desolate, without man and without inhabitant and without beast, the voice of joy and the voice of gladness, the voice of the bridegroom and the voice of the bride, the voice of those who will say: "Praise the Lord of hosts, for the Lord *is* good, for His mercy *endures* forever."'"

Why does the Lord God of Israel, who is Yeshua the Messiah, redeem the nation and remnant of Israel, His Promised Land and heritage? The absolute and resounding answer is, because on account of God Almighty's great and holy name, Messiah will fulfill the everlasting promises He swore to Abraham, Isaac, Jacob, and David, and their descendants, which also includes the believing Gentiles (wild olives), who are grafted into the olive tree and heirs according to God's promises (Rom. 11; Gal. 3:26–29). Both will be included into the commonwealth of the Israel of God (Eph. 2:11–13)!

> Ezekiel 36:22–38: "Therefore say to the house of Israel, *'Thus says the Lord GOD: 'I do not do this for your sake, O house of Israel, but for My holy name's sake, which you have profaned among the nations wherever you went. And I will sanctify My great name, which has been profaned among the nations, which you have profaned in their midst; and the nations shall know that I am the LORD,' says the Lord GOD, 'when I am hallowed in you before their eyes.* For I will take you from among the nations, gather you out of all countries, and bring you into your own land. Then I will sprinkle clean water on you, and you shall be clean; I will cleanse you from all your filthiness and from all your idols. *I will give you a new heart and put a new spirit within you; I will take the heart of stone out of your flesh and give you a heart of flesh. I will put My Spirit within you and cause you to walk in My statutes, and you will keep My judgments and do them. Then you shall dwell in the land that I gave to your fathers; you shall be My people, and I will be your God. I will deliver you from all your uncleannesses.* I will call for the grain and multiply it, and bring no famine upon you. And I will multiply the fruit of your trees and the increase of your fields, so that you need never again bear the reproach of famine among the nations. Then you will remember your evil ways and your deeds that were not good; and you will loathe yourselves in your own sight, for your iniquities and your abominations. *Not for your sake do I do this,'* says the Lord GOD, *"let it be known to you.* Be ashamed and confounded for your own ways, O house of Israel!' *Thus says the Lord GOD: 'On the day that*

I cleanse you from all your iniquities, I will also enable you to dwell in the cities, and the ruins shall be rebuilt. The desolate land shall be tilled instead of lying desolate in the sight of all who pass by. So they will say, "This land that was desolate has become like the garden of Eden; and the wasted, desolate, and ruined cities are now fortified and inhabited." Then the nations which are left all around you shall know that I, the LORD, have rebuilt the ruined places and planted what was desolate. I, the LORD, have spoken it, and I will do it.' Thus says the Lord GOD: 'I will also let the house of Israel inquire of Me to do this for them: I will increase their men like a flock. Like a flock offered as holy sacrifices, like the flock at Jerusalem on its feast days, so shall the ruined cities be filled with flocks of men. *Then they shall know that I am the LORD.*'"

CONCLUSION

THE ROLE OF MESSIAH'S FISHERMEN

What is the role of Messiah's believers at this incredible and exciting yet perilous time? For Jew and Gentile believers, our prophetic commission is to be *Messiah's fishermen* by *"fishing"* all of mankind into His kingdom! Make no mistake: as we rapidly progress along God's prophetic timeline, our generation continues to witness the yearly perpetual escalation and intensification of the *"beginning of sorrows,"* which will imminently culminate with the Bridegroom (Messiah) coming from His chamber to earth, with great power, glory, and authority, for His bride (Joel 2:15–17; Matt. 24–25; John 3:29). Therefore, it is paramount for Messiah's believers to be exceedingly steadfast so we can accomplish our commanded role as *God's fishermen* to the unbelieving world, which will fulfill the Great Commission. Unequivocally, once we are saved in Yeshua, He commands us to be "fishers of men."

> Matthew 4:19: "Then He said to them, 'Follow Me, and I will make you fishers of men.'"

> Matthew 28:18–20: "And Jesus came and spoke to them, saying, 'All authority has been given to Me in heaven and on earth. *Go therefore and make disciples of all the nations, baptizing them in the name of the Father and of the Son and of the Holy Spirit, teaching them to observe all things that I have commanded you*; and lo, I am with you always, even to the end of the age.' Amen."

Once we accept Yeshua as our Messiah, which secures *our* eternal salvation (John 3:16), He *directly* commands us to spread the Good News to others so they have an opportunity to receive *their* salvation! Of course, not everyone is called to be a missionary or travel across the world for this divine purpose. The vital point is for God's fishermen (you and me) to present the gospel of Messiah, including the Hebrew Scriptures (Torah, Prophets, Psalms), throughout our realm of influence (Matt. 5:17–20). Unfortunately, too many believers neglect this command from the Lord God, because they choose to journey through life striving to achieve their own goals, ambitions, and self-seeking pleasures. Messiah sternly warned mankind about this self-centered, vanity-driven behavior.

> Mark 8:34–36: "*Whoever desires to come after Me, let Him deny himself, and take up his cross, and follow Me.* For whoever desires to save his life will lose it, but whoever loses his life for My sake and the Gospel's will save it. *For what will it profit a man if he gains the whole world, and loses his own soul?*"

> Matthew 6:19–21: "Do not lay up for yourselves treasures on earth, where moth and rust destroy and where thieves break in and steal; *but lay up for yourselves treasures in heaven, where neither moth nor rust destroys and where thieves do not break in and steal. For where your treasure is, there your heart will be also.*"

Messiah clearly yearns for His fishermen to build our treasure in heaven by being living sacrifices for Him and His Word, and not for ourselves, just as He was the ultimate sacrifice for mankind (Rom. 12:1). In fact, there is no greater love than to lay down one's life for one's friends, and assuredly Messiah Himself set this standard, because He is the *ultimate Fisherman* (John 15:13). Most certainly, we should follow the King of Israel's example of living according to the Word of God instead of the world (Matt. 5:48). Always remember that *God's heart and desire is for His everlasting kingdom to be full,* and *our* hearts and desires should align with the Almighty's ultimate plan (1 Tim. 2:4; Matt. 22:1–14). Accordingly, His fishermen must *also* be laborers in His field, planting seeds for the blessed Holy Spirit to water and reap the harvest.

> Matthew 9:37–38: "Then He said to His disciples, '*The harvest truly is plentiful, but the laborers are few.* Therefore, pray the Lord of the harvest to send out laborers into His harvest.'"

Brethren, Jews and Gentiles, this is *our* divine moment in time for *our* sovereign calling by the Almighty, in which we are to fulfill *our* prophetic period in time as *God's fishermen* in the Great Commission at the end of the age. According to the Scriptures, our generation aligns with the time of fulfillment of the prophecies associated with the last generation living before Messiah's second coming and millennial reign (Isa. 66:8–24; Ps. 102,16,18). Amazingly, we are living in the most extraordinary prophetic period since Messiah's first coming, which many believers in past generations would have loved to live in! It is absolutely incredible and such a tremendous blessing that you and I have the exceptional privilege of witnessing these magnificent divine appointments of our Lord God! Of course, Jeremiah's prophecy of Satan's *end-of-the-age* hunters, the final hunter, and the time of Jacob's trouble is sobering and frightening. Nonetheless, make no mistake: this is *our* hour, for both Jew and Gentile believers to shine brighter than ever before as *God's fishermen,* regardless of the world's persecution that is occurring around us. Just as the prophet Jeremiah was God's fisherman during a cataclysmic period for the children of Israel (627–586 BC), we have also been commissioned as fishermen in *this* apocalyptic season. Therefore, *all* believers should imitate the weeping prophet's faith, boldness, and love for the God of Israel, His heritage, and His people during this perilous time. Surely, as the dark gets darker, the light *must* shine brighter than ever before! Always hold near and dear: God did not give us a spirit of fear and worry, but one of faith, strength, and courage. Beyond question, He who is within us is greater than he who is in the world (1 John 4:4)! Are you ready to fulfill your prophetic calling as God's fisherman for the kingdom of heaven?

> Matthew 5:14–16: "*You are the light of the world.* A city that is set on a hill cannot be hidden. Nor do they light a lamp and put it under a basket, but on a lampstand, *and it gives light to all who are in the house.* Let your light so shine before men, that they may see your good works and glorify your Father in heaven."

> Joshua 1:9: "Have I not commanded you? Be strong and of good courage; do not be afraid, nor be dismayed, *for the* L<small>ORD</small> *your God is with you wherever you go.*"

EPILOGUE

THE BLUE-BLOOD MOONS OF 2018-2019

Psalm 89:37, "It shall be established forever like the moon, *even like the faithful witness in the sky.*"

In 2018 and 2019, three *blue-blood moons* will occur that *could* be signaling and warning that judgment is imminently coming to the nations. A *blue moon* occurs when there are two full moons in one month, with the second being the *blue moon*. What is so fascinating is that these three *blue moons* will also be *blood moons (total lunar eclipse)*, which is why they are called, *blue-blood moons*. NASA records that it has been 150 years since the last total eclipse of a blue moon (*blue-blood moon*).

Incredibly, when we place the dates of these three *blue-blood moons* on God's calendar, which is the Hebrew/Jewish calendar, it correlates with the biblical prophet's warnings and the signs of the end of the age. The first *blue-blood moon*, which was also a super moon, occurred on January 31, 2018. On the Hebrew calendar, it is Tu B' Shevat, the fifteenth day of Shevat. The second *blue-blood* moon will occur on July 27, 2018, or the biblical calendar date of Tu B' Av, the fifteenth of Av. The *blue-blood* moon trifecta will culminate on January 21, 2019, which again, is Tu B' Shevat!

Therefore, what is the importance of Tu B' Shevat? How does this corroborate to God's fishermen and Satan's hunters? To understand this mysterious phenomenon, let us explore the Holy Bible for answers. Before we proceed, I would like to give credit and thanks to Pastor Mark Biltz of El Shaddai Ministries, who is the author of *Blood Moons: Decoding the Imminent Heavenly Signs.*

TU B' SHEVAT (SHEVAT 15) – THE FIRST DAY ON THE HEBREW CALENDAR THAT BEGINS THE "YEAR OF TREES"

The Hebrew calendar date that begins the year for trees is Shevat 15 or Tu B' Shevat (Jan. 31). Please note: Just as we have different calendars during the year such as fiscal and public school calendars, the Jewish people have four calendars: civil, religious, animal, and tree calendars. In the book of Leviticus, it provides us with great wisdom into why it is necessary to understand the prophetic meaning of the biblical calendar for trees.

> Leviticus 19:23-25, "When you come into the land, and have planted all kinds of trees for food, *then you shall count their fruit as uncircumcised. Three years it shall be as uncircumcised to you. It shall not be eaten. But in the fourth year all its fruit shall be holy, a praise to the* LORD. *And in the fifth year you may eat its fruit, that it may yield to you its increase*: I am the LORD your God."

The Lord God commanded specific instructions to the children of Israel concerning the eating of the fruit of the trees, which explains the importance of keeping an annual calendar for them. In the Word of God, trees are also symbolic for people and nations.

> Psalms 1:3, "*He shall be like a tree planted by the rivers of water, that brings forth its fruit in its season*, whose leaf shall not wither; and whatever he does shall prosper."

The psalmist metaphorically declares that people should resemble trees that brings forth fruit for the kingdom of God. Messiah confirms and boldly proclaims that He chose and appointed us to bear fruit (John 15:16). He also warned believers of the dire consequences of not bearing fruit for the kingdom by giving us a parable of a *barren fig tree*.

> Luke 23:6-9: He also spoke this parable: "A certain man had a *fig tree planted in his vineyard, and he came seeking fruit on it and found none.* Then he said to the keeper of his vineyard, 'Look, for three years I have come seeking fruit on this fig tree and find none. *Cut it down; why does it use up the ground?*' But he answered and said to him, 'Sir, let it alone this year also, until I dig around it and fertilize it. And if it bears fruit, well. *But if not, after that you can cut it down.*" (See Matt. 24:32-34)

Tu B' Shevat is the beginning of the year of *trees,* and it also signals the upcoming change of the season from winter to spring. It is the annual time to inspect the trees for fruit. Now, let us examine the words of the prophet Jeremiah to gain additional insight into the symbolism of trees, as the *almond tree* has special significance for Tu B' Shevat.

> Jeremiah 1:9-11: "Then the LORD put forth His hand and touched my mouth, and the LORD said to me: "Behold, I have put My words in your mouth. *See, I have this day set you over the nations and over the kingdoms, to root out and to pull down, to destroy and to throw down, to build and to plant."* Moreover, the word of the LORD came to me, saying, "Jeremiah, what do you see?" *And I said, "I see a branch of an almond tree."*

The almond tree is among the first trees to blossom in the spring, and the Lord God correlates the season with "the rooting up and pulling down, the destroying and throwing down, and the building and planting of the nations." Interestingly enough, the Hebrew word for "almond" and "to watch" is identical. Remember, Messiah commanded us "to watch" the events of the end of the age (Matt. 24, Mark 13:36, Rev. 3).

Additionally, it is the widely held belief that Aaron's rod/staff was made from a branch of an almond tree. In Numbers 17, Aaron's rod budded, flowered, and produced almonds overnight. The staff also could be used as a blessing or for judgment, depending on the people and the nation's behavior.

Therefore, how does this associate to Tu B' Shevat and the *blue-blood* moons? The prophet Zechariah provides us with this knowledge and understanding.

> Zechariah 1:7, "On the *twenty-fourth day of the eleventh month (Shevat 24),* which is the month Shebat, *in the second year of Darius,* the word of the LORD came to Zechariah the son of Berechiah, the son of Iddo the prophet."

The prophet's vision occurred on Shevat 24, nine days after Tu B' Shevat (Shevat 15), which begins the inspection of the *trees* for fruit. It is worthy to note that in 2018, the *blue-blood* moon on January 31 occurred in the *same month* that Zechariah had this vision. Amazingly, the vision also took place in the *second year* of a Gentile administration (Medo-Persia-Iran), which perfectly aligns with President Trump's second year of his administration

(Gentile). Similar to Darius the Mede, Trump can be substituted for Darius in contemporary prophetic terms, because both were leaders of the world's most powerful nation. Furthermore, as we discussed in chapter 7, Medo-Persia (Iran) is the superpower of the Middle East, just as the United States is today, which makes this even more incredible. As we proceed, Zechariah provides a prophecy that corroborates the blue-blood moons and Satan's *end of the age* hunters of Jeremiah's prophecy.

> Zechariah 1:8-10, "I saw by night, and behold, *a man riding on a red horse*, and *it stood among the myrtle trees in the hollow*; and behind him were horses: *red*, sorrel, and white. Then I said, "My lord, what *are* these?" So the angel who talked with me said to me, "I will show you what they *are*." *And the man who stood among the myrtle trees answered and said, "These are the ones whom the LORD has sent to walk to and fro throughout the earth."* So they answered the Angel of the LORD, who stood among the myrtle trees, and said, *"We have walked to and fro throughout the earth, and behold, all the earth is resting quietly."*

The prophet's vision describes a man riding on a *red horse* as it stood among the *trees*. The man that stood among the trees proclaimed that the Lord God sent them to walk to and fro upon the earth. At that moment, the Angel of the Lord (Messiah) stood among the trees (inspecting fruit), and they responded by stating the earth *is resting quietly*. In Revelation 6, the apostle John explains that a *red horse* symbolizes judgment, terror, violence, war, *with peace being taken away from the earth by the sword* (v.v. 3-4).

Another amazing correlation is that Zechariah's vision occurred at the *end* of the *seventy-year* Babylonian captivity (Zech. 1:11). In 2018, Israel will celebrate its *seventieth* year of its rebirth, which occurred in 1948 (Isa. 66:8). Excitingly, as the vision proceeds, the angel commands Zechariah to prophesy this according to the words of the Lord God of Israel: "I am zealous for Jerusalem and for Zion with great zeal. I am exceedingly angry with the nations at ease; For I was a little angry, and they helped, but with evil intent" (Zech. 1:14-15). Could all of these signs and prophecies tell us that the Lord God is about to fulfill His everlasting covenants to the children of Israel? Is the Lord God about to fulfill the remaining end-of-the-age prophecies to Jerusalem and Zion, which is His heritage and His land?

Zechariah's prophecy continues to proclaim the words of the Most High: "I am returning to Jerusalem with mercy; *My house (temple) shall be built in it* ... My cities shall again spread out through prosperity; The Lord will again comfort Zion, and will again choose Jerusalem. (Zech. 1:16-17). *Could the proclamation of the rebuilding of the temple occur this year?*

In review of the *blue-blood* moons and Zechariah's prophecy:

- Tu B' Shevat is the beginning of the calendar of *trees* (Shevat 15), which symbolizes people and nations.
- Tu B' Shevat encored with a *blue-blood* moon (Shevat 24-Jan. 31), which is a trifecta series that ends on Tu B' Shevat.
- Blood moons signify judgment and persecution, culminating with a Jewish Aliyah to the Promised Land.
- The blood moons occur in the second year of a Gentile administration, perfectly correlating to Zechariah's prophecy.
- The red horse in Zechariah's prophecy was located in the *trees*.
- The red horse symbolizes taking peace away from the earth (trees) by terror, violence, and war.

In conclusion, blood moons are signals for judgment, persecution, and ultimately an Aliyah, and with them occurring on significant dates on God's calendar, their *potential* warning is paramount. Remember, God declares the moon as His "faithful witness in the sky" (Ps. 89:37). Will the red horse, which symbolizes taking the peace away from the earth, be released during this trifecta of *blue-blood* moons? In addition to the blood moon tetrads of 2014-2015 that occurred on the Lord's feast days and escalated widespread anarchy, terror, war, chaos, and civilian unrest, along with the solar eclipse of 2017, which intensified natural disasters and violence in America, could the coinciding of the *blue-blood* moons phenomenon with Zechariah's prophecy of the red horse potentially signify and warn of the same consequential results? Will God's fishermen and Satan's hunters continue their fulfillment as we journey toward Messiah's second coming and millennial reign?

Beloved, I believe the blue-blood moons, along with the other celestial occurrences and prophecies, will escalate and intensify Satan's end-of-the-age hunters on the earth, especially in America. The reason is because the Lord God made an everlasting covenant to Abraham, Isaac, Jacob, and David, and their descendants (Abrahamic, Davidic, New covenant – Gentiles are grafted in – Rom. 11, Eph. 2:11-13, Gal. 3:26-29), and He will fulfill these eternal promises via Satan's hunters, which includes removing peace from the earth by the sword, along with other cataclysmic events (Matt. 24).

Ecclesiastes 3:1, "To everything there is a season, and a time for every purpose under heaven."

Revelation 3:3, "Therefore, if you will *not watch*, I will come upon you as a thief, and you will not know what hour I will come upon you" (See Matt. 24, 1 Thess. 5:1-5).

MY PRAYER

My prayer to the Lord God of Israel is for Jew and Gentile believers to come together as one cohesive body during this cataclysmic time to responsibly proclaim Jeremiah's prophecy to the children of Israel. I pray for Gentile believers to imitate the great example of Ruth, steadfastly standing with the Lord God of Israel and His people during this prophetic time.

> Ruth 1:16: "But Ruth said... 'Your people shall be my people, and your God, my God.'"

Ruth's genuine loyalty and love for Naomi exemplifies how Gentiles should treat the Jewish people. As believers in Yeshua, the *Jewish Messiah*, we are commanded to love God's chosen people and His heritage, because both Jew and Gentile believers will be one *Ecclesia* with the King of Israel, the God of Abraham, Isaac, Jacob, and David (Eph. 2:11–13)! Gentiles should harbor the convictions of Ruth, whose name in Hebrew means "friend" (Strong's #7327). If the Gentiles bless the Jewish people by praying, interceding, supporting, and presenting the gospel of Messiah to them, among other things, the Almighty will surely bless the Gentiles (Gen. 12:3). I pray my fellow Gentile believers will answer the call to this great prophetic calling as Messiah's fishermen.

> Ephesians 2:14-17, "For He Himself is our peace, who has made both one, and has broken down the middle wall of separation, having abolished in His flesh the enmity, *that is,* the law of commandments *contained* in ordinances, so as to create in Himself one new man *from* the two, *thus* making peace, and that He might reconcile them both to God in one body through the cross, thereby putting to death the enmity. And He came and preached peace to you who were afar off

and to those who were near. For through Him we both have access by one Spirit to the Father."

I also pray for the children of Israel to open their spiritual hearts, eyes, and ears to accept Yeshua, their Jewish Messiah (Isa. 6:9–10). And I pray that the current generation of the children of Israel will heed Jeremiah's prophetic warning, unlike the majority of their forefathers from 627 to 586 BC, who did not heed God's prophets' proclamations during that cataclysmic time. In the name that is higher than every other name, Yeshua HaMashiach, Jesus the Messiah, who is the eternal and everlasting God of Abraham, Isaac, Jacob, and David, the Branch of Righteousness, the Holy One of Israel, the King of kings, and Lord of lords, the Almighty, Amen, Amen, and Amen!

> Zechariah 8:2–9, 12–13, 15: "*Thus says the LORD of hosts: 'I am zealous for Zion with great zeal; with great fervor I am zealous for her.' Thus says the LORD: 'I will return to Zion, and dwell in the midst of Jerusalem. Jerusalem shall be called the City of Truth, the Mountain of the LORD of hosts, the Holy Mountain.'* Thus says the LORD of hosts: 'Old men and old women shall again sit in the streets of Jerusalem, each one with his staff in his hand because of great age. The streets of the city shall be full of boys and girls playing in its streets.' Thus says the LORD of hosts: 'If it is marvelous in the eyes of the remnant of this people in these days, will it also be marvelous in My eyes?' says the LORD of hosts. *Thus says the LORD of hosts: 'Behold, I will save My people from the land of the east and from the land of the west; I will bring them back, and they shall dwell in the midst of Jerusalem. They shall be My people and I will be their God, in truth and righteousness.'* Thus says the LORD of hosts: 'Let your hands be strong, you who have been hearing in these days these words by the mouth of the prophets, who spoke in the day the foundation was laid for the house of the LORD of hosts, that the temple might be built . . . For the seed shall be prosperous, the vine shall give its fruit, the ground shall give her increase, and the heavens shall give their dew—I will cause the remnant of this people to possess all these. And it shall come to pass that just as you were a curse among the nations, O house of Judah and house of Israel, so I will save you, and you shall be a blessing. Do not fear, let your hands be strong . . . So again in these days I am determined to do good to Jerusalem and to the house of Judah. Do not fear.'"

Zephaniah 3:14–20: *"Sing, O daughter of Zion! Shout, O Israel! Be glad and rejoice with all your heart, O daughter of Jerusalem! The LORD has taken away your judgments, He has cast out your enemy. The King of Israel, the LORD, is in your midst; You shall see disaster no more.* In that day it shall be said to Jerusalem: 'Do not fear; Zion, let not your hands be weak. *The LORD your God in your midst, the Mighty One, will save; He will rejoice over you with gladness, He will quiet you with His love, He will rejoice over you with singing.'* I will gather those who sorrow over the appointed assembly, who are among you, to whom its reproach is a burden. Behold, at that time I will deal with all who afflict you; I will save the lame, and gather those who were driven out; I will appoint them for praise and fame in every land where they were put to shame. *At that time I will bring you back, even at the time I gather you; For I will give you fame and praise among all the peoples of the earth, when I return your captives before your eyes,' says the LORD."* (Also see Micah 7:14-20)

Jeremiah 31:31–37: "'Behold, the days are coming, says the LORD, when I will make a new covenant with the house of Israel and with the house of Judah—not according to the covenant that I made with their fathers in the day that I took them by the hand to lead them out of the land of Egypt, My covenant which they broke, though I was a husband to them, says the LORD. But this is the covenant that I will make with the house of Israel after those days, says the LORD: I will put My law in their minds, and write it on their hearts; and I will be their God, and they shall be My people. No more shall every man teach his neighbor, and every man his brother, saying, 'Know the LORD,' for they all shall know Me, from the least of them to the greatest of them, says the LORD. For I will forgive their iniquity, and their sin I will remember no more.'

Thus says the LORD, who gives the sun for a light by day, the ordinances of the moon and the stars for a light by night, Who disturbs the sea, and its waves roar (The LORD of hosts is His name): "If those ordinances depart from before Me, says the LORD, then the seed of Israel shall also cease from being a nation before Me forever."

Thus says the LORD: 'If heaven above can be measured, and the foundations of the earth searched out beneath, I will also cast off all the seed of Israel for all that they have done, says the LORD.'"

ENDNOTES

INTRODUCTION

1. Winston Churchill, "Zionism versus Bolshevism: A Struggle for the Soul of the Jewish People," *Illustrated Sunday Herald*, February 8, 1920, 5, http://www.fpp.co.uk/bookchapters/WSC/WSCwrote1920.html.

CHAPTER 1

1. All references to Strong's are from James Strong, *Strong's Concordance with Hebrew and Greek Lexicon*, available online at Eliyah.com, http://www.eliyah.com/lexicon.html.
2. E. W Bullinger, *Number in Scripture*, p. 113, 136 Kregel Publications, 1967.
3. E.W. Bullinger, Number in Scripture, p. 136, Kregal Publications, 1967.
4. Joel Richardson, *When a Jew Rules the World* (Washington, DC: WND Books, 2015), 24–25.
5. Sam Clarke, The Holy One of Israel and His Chosen People, Inspired Authors Press LLC, 36.
6. John J. Collins and Peter W. Flint, eds., *The Book of Daniel: Composition and Reception* (Leiden: Brill, 2002), 64.

CHAPTER 2

1. Taylor, Myron Charles (1942). "Distribution of the Jews in the World". Vatican Diplomatic Files. Franklin D. Roosevelt Presidential Library and Museum.
2. Ira Sheskin, Arnold Dashefsky. Berman Jewish DataBank: Jewish Population in the United States, 2015. Page 15.

CHAPTER 4

1. Kugle, 1998, page 223.

ENDNOTES

2. Flavius Josephus, *The Complete Works*, page 40, translated by William Whiston, A.M., Thomas Nelson, 1998.
3. The Talmud, translated by H. Polano, page 27, The Book Tree, 2003.
4. Ibid.
5. Ibid.
6. The Talmud, Translated by H. Polano, page 31, The Book Tree, 2003.
7. Ibid.
8. The Talmud, Translated by H. Polano, page 32, The Book Tree, 2003.
9. Ibid.
10. Ibid.
11. The Talmud, Translated by H. Polano, page 33, The Book Tree, 2003.
12. Ibid.
13. The Talmud, Translated by H. Polano, page 34, The Book Tree, 2003.
14. The Talmud, Translated by H. Polano, page 34, The Book Tree, 2003.
15. The Talmud, Translated by H. Polano, page 37, The Book Tree, 2003.
16. Ibid.
17. The Talmud, Translated by, H. Polano, pages 37-38, The Book Tree, 2003.
18. The Talmud, Translated by, H. Polano, page 38, The Book Tree, 2003.
19. Ibid.
20. The Talmud, Translated by, H. Polano, page 39, The Book Tree, 2003.
21. The Talmud, Translated by, H. Polano, page 41, The Book Tree, 2003.
22. The Talmud, Translated by, H. Polano, pages 41–42, The Book Tree, 2003.
23. The Talmud, Translated by, H. Polano, page 42, The Book Tree, 2003.
24. The Talmud, Translated by, H. Polano, The Book Tree, 2003, page 43
25. Ibid.
26. Ibid.
27. Bullinger, Number in Scripture, 98.
28. The Talmud, Translated by, H. Polano, page 52, The Book Tree, 2003.
29. Ibid.
30. Flavius Josephus, *The Complete Works*, page 48, translated by William Whiston, A.M., Thomas Nelson, 1998.
31. The Talmud, Translated by, H. Polano, page 60, The Book Tree, 2003.
32. The Talmud, Translated by, H. Polano, pages 42–43, The Book Tree, 2003.
33. The Talmud, Translated by H. Polano, page 86, The Book Tree, 2003.
34. The Talmud, Translated by, H. Polano, page 62, The Book Tree, 2003.

35. Ibid.
36. Ibid.
37. Ibid.
38. The Talmud, Translated by, H. Polano, page 62, The Book Tree, 2003.
39. Flavius Josephus, *The Complete Works*, p.196, translated by William Whiston, Thomas Nelson,1998.
40. E.W. Bullinger, *Number in Scripture*, p. 285, Kregal Publications, 1967.
41. E.W. Bullinger, *Number in Scripture*, p. 50,61,138, Kregal Publications, 1967.
42. Cohen, Shaye. "Roman Domination: The Jewish Revolt and the Destruction of the Second Temple," in *Ancient Israel*, ed. Hershel Shanks. (Biblical Archaeology Society, 1999), p.270.
43. Ibid.
44. Ibid.
45. Levine, Amy-Jill. "Visions of Kingdoms: From Pompey to the First Jewish Revolt," in *The Oxford History of the Biblical World*, ed. Michael D. Coogan. (New York: Oxford University Press, 1998), 357.
46. Richard R. Losch, All the People in the Bible (Grand Rapids: Wm. B. Eerdmans Publishing (2008), p. 155.
47. Aryeh Kasher and Eliezer Witztum, *King Herod: A Persecuted Persecutor: A Case Study in Psychohistory*, pp 19-23; Jan Retsö, *The Arabs in Antiquity: Their History from the Assyrians to the Umayyads*, Routledge (2013), 374; Richard R. Losch, *All the People in the Bible*, Eerdmans (2008), 155.
48. Flavius Josephus, *The Complete Works*, 18.36, translated by William Whiston, A.M., Thomas Nelson, 1998.

CHAPTER 5

1. Elie Wiesel, A Beggar in Jerusalem
2. Sukkah 29a in the Babylonian Talmud.
3. NASA website.
4. Professor B. Netanyahu, *The Origins of the Inquisition*, page 3, Random House, 1995.
5. Henry Kamen, *The Spanish Inquisition*, Yale University Press, 1997.
6. The Edict of Expulsion of the Jews - 1492 Spain" "Edict of Expulsion of the Jews (1492 Spain." www.sephardicstudies.org.
7. Professor B. Netanyahu, *The Origins of the Inquisition*, page 159, Random House, 1995.

8. Joseph Perez, *History of a Tragedy*. P. 17. 2012, 2009, University of Illinois Press, 2007.
9. E. Christopher Reyes, *In His Name*, Volume 3, page 281, Trafford Publishing, 2014.
10. Robert Rusconi, *The Book of Prophecies* Edited by Christopher Columbus, translated by Blair Sullivan, Volume 3, Wipf & Stock Publishers, 1997.
11. Ibid.
12. Jewish Virtual Library.org, Jason Levine, Immigration to Israel.
13. E. W. Bullinger, *Number in Scripture* (Grand Rapids: Kregel, 1967,1980), 235.

CHAPTER 6

1. BBC ON THIS DAY 1973: Israel's Founding Father Dies, BBC
2. The Jewish Agency for Israel, David Ben Gurion (1886-1973), www.jewishagency.org.
3. "Aliyah," The Jewish Agency for Israel, www.jewishagency.org.
4. Zaki, Shalom, Ben-Gurion's Political Struggles, *1963–1967*, Routledge, 2006.
5. Ibid
6. Jewish Agency for Israel, Aliyah Statistics, www.jewishagency.org.
7. Jewish Agency for Israel, About us, www.jewishagency.org.
8. Ibid.
9. Ibid.
10. www.jewishgency.org.
11. Ibid
12. Doyle McManus, *The Courier* (*LA Times*), "US Completes Operation Moses," March 24, 1985.
13. Dr. Vladimir Khanin, "Aliyah from the Former Soviet Union: Contribution to the National Security Balance," 2010.
14. Ibid
15. www.jewishagency.org.
16. Ibid
17. Joel Brinkley, *New York Times*, "Ethiopian Jews and Israelis Exult as Airlift Is Completed," May 26, 1991.
18. The Jewish Agency for Israel, The Urgent and the Important: 2015 Performance Report, www.jewishagency.org.

19. The Jewish Agency for Israel, "Chapter Two, The Seven Years of Herzl," www.Jewishagency.org;
20. "Jerusalem Program 2004," Wzo.org.il.
21. E.W. Bullinger, *Number in Scripture*, p. 235, Grand Rapids: Kregel, 1967,1980.

CHAPTER 7

1. Chadwick Harvey, *God's Prophetic Timeline*, World Ahead Press, 2016.
2. James Pfiffner, *Intelligence and National Security*, vol. 25, no. 1, 76–85, February 2010, "US Blunders in Iraq: De-Baathification and Disbanding the Army."
3. Ibid.
4. The *Economist*, "Can the Joy Last?", September 3, 2011.
5. James Pfiffner, *Intelligence and National Security*, vol. 25, no. 1, 76-85, February 2010, "US Blunders in Iraq: De-Baathification and Disbanding the Army."
6. BBC News, "Iraq study estimates war-related deaths at 461,000," October 16, 2013.
7. Christian Science Monitor/Al-Quds Al-Arabi, March 20, 2006.
8. Liz Sly, The *Washington Post*, "Egyptian Revolution Sparks Protest Movement in Democratic Iraq," February 12, 2011.
9. BBC News, "Protests Engulf West Iraq as Anbar Rises against Maliki," January 2, 2013.
10. Christian Science Monitor, "New Iraqi Leader Seeks Unity at the Wayback Machine," November 2011.
11. *Andrew Hough, The Daily Telegraph, London,* "Wikileaks: King Abdullah of Saudi Arabia 'Wanted Guantánamo Bay detainees microchipped,'"*November 29, 2010.*
12. *Scott Shane; Andrew W. Lehren, New York Times,* "WikiLeaks Archive – Cables Uncloak U.S. Diplomacy", *November 28, 2010.*
13. Michael Weiss, "Trust Iran Only as Far as You Can Throw It," June 23, 2014, www.foreignpolicy.com.
14. BBC News, "Iraq Crisis: Battle Grips Vital Baiji Oil Refinery," June 18, 2014.
15. Mushreq Abbas, Al-Monitor, "IS makes plans to fend off attacks on Mosul," September 23, 2014.
16. Nick Gutteridge, Express News, "ISIS Barbarity: How 100,000 Christians Fled Mosul in ONE NIGHT," October 20, 2015.

17. Fazel Hawramy, *Guardian*, "'They Are Savages,' Say Christians Forced to Flee Mosul by ISIS,'" July 24, 2014.
18. BBC News, "Mosul: Iraq and Kurdish troops make gains in battle," October 17, 2016.
19. https://www.csmonitor.com/World/Middle-East/2017/0811/In-liberated-Mosul-ISIS-still-imperils-the-path-to-city-s-revival.
20. Mosul: Iraq PM to celebrate victory over IS in the city BBC, 9 July 2017.
21. *"Battle for Mosul: Iraq PM Abadi formally declares victory". BBC. 10 July 2017.*
22. The Jerusalem Post, "PM: Iran Risks 'Mortal Peril' By Threatening Israel, Fix or Nix Nuclear Deal, September 9,19, 2017.
23. Adnan Abu Amer, Al Monitor, Palestine Pulse, "Iran, Hezbollah Break with Assad to Support Hamas," July 25, 2014.
24. Patrick Goodenough, CNSnews.com, "Terrorist Chief: 'As Long as Iran Has Money, We Will Have Money,'" June 27,2016.
25. Madeleine Morgenstern, The Blaze, "'Wipe Them Off the Face of the Earth', Iran Issues New Threat to Israel," July 1, 2012.
26. BBC News, "Yemen crisis: Who is fighting whom?", March 28, 2017.
27. Martin Chulov, *Guardian*, "Iran repopulates Syria with Shia Muslims to Help Tighten Regime's Control," January 13, 2017.
28. Ibid
29. Assyrian International News Agency, "Report: 'Seized USB Drives Reveal Turkey's Links to ISIL,'" July 27, 2015.
30. Shoebat.com, "I'll be right there big brother," classified military transcripts leaked to media prove link between ISIS and Turkey," by Andrew Bleszad, February 25, 2016.
31. Shoebat.com, "Wikileaks releases 57,000 emails from Turkish President Erdogan's son-in-law and minister of oil to ISIS terrorists showing his support and how Turkey was involved in finding their smuggling operations," by Andrew Bleszad, December 8, 2016.
32. Walid Shoebat, "Today Major Prophecy Was Fulfilled. The Date August 24th Is Prophetically Significant for Muslims Worldwide Sparking Islam's Caliphate Empire and Is Why Turkey Today Sent a Massive Land Invasion to Syria," August 24, 2016. www.shoebat.com.
33. Steve Contorno, Politifact, "What Obama Said about Islamic State as a 'JV' Team," September, 7, 2014.
34. CNN, "ISIS defeated in Raqqa as 'major military operations' declared over," by Hilary Clarke, Nick Paton Walsh, Eliza Mackintosh, and Ghazi Balkiz, October 17, 2017.

35. http://daily-retirement.com/raqqa-isis-capital-liberated-by-us-backed-fighting-force/
36. Kawczynski 2011, p. 231; Bruce St. John 2012, pp. 279–281.
37. Bruce St. John 2012, p. 286; Human Rights Watch 2012, p. 16.
38. David Smith, *Guardian*, "Murder and Torture 'Carried Out by Both Sides' of Uprising against Libyan Regime", September 12, 2011.
39. Vlasic, Mark (2012). "Assassination & Targeted Killing—a Historical and Post-Bin Laden Legal Analysis." *Georgetown Journal of International Law*: 261.
40. Sputniknews, "Gaddafi's Grim Prophecy Fulfills as Terrorism Spreads Across Europe, July 1, 2016."
41. Nick Meo, The *Telegraph*, "Libya: Revolutionaries Turn on Each Other as Fears Grow for Law and Order," October 31, 2011.
42. Lauren McCauley, "Common Dreams: Libya: Obama Admits Clinton's 'Greatest Moment' Was His 'Worst Mistake,'" April 12, 2016.
43. Chris Stephen, *Guardian*, "War in Libya—*Guardian* briefing", August 29, 2014.
44. Carnegie Endowment for International Peace, "Libya's Legitimacy Crisis", August 20, 2014.
45. *Foreign Policy*, "Why Picking Sides in Libya Won't Work", March 6, 2015."
46. "Egypt Protests a ticking Time Bomb: Analysts". The New Age. South Africa. Agence France-Presse. 27 January 2011.
47. "Egypt: Overview of human rights issues in Egypt". Human Rights Watch.
48. "Egypt torture Centre, Report Says". BBC News, April 11, 2007.
49. Siddique, Haroon; Owen, Paul; Gabbatt, Adam (25 January 2011). "Protests in Egypt and Unrest in Middle East—as it Happened." *Guardian*.
50. "Mubarak Resigns as Egypt's President, Armed Forces to Take Control. *Huffington Post*. February 11, 2011.
51. "Egyptian Parliament Dissolved, Constitution Suspended". BBC. February 13, 2011.
52. "The Simplest Explanation of Egypt's Revolution You'll Ever Read."
53. "Egypt Sees Largest Clash Since Revolution." *Wall Street Journal*. December 6, 2012
54. Kirkpatrick, David D. "Army Ousts Egypt's President; Morsi Denounces 'Military Coup.'" *New York Times*. July 3, 2013.
55. "Egypt Constitution 'Approved by 98.1 Percent.'" Al Jazeera English. January 18, 2014.

56. "Egypt's El-Sisi Bids Military Farewell, Says He Will Run for Presidency." Ahram Online. March 26, 2014.
57. "Former army Chief Scores Landslide Victory in Egypt Presidential Polls." Patrick Kingsley, *Guardian*, May 29, 2014.
58. Al Jazaeera, "The Egyptian Revolution: What Went Wrong?" Omar Ashour. January 25, 2016.
59. CNN, "Egypt: At Least 28 Dead as Gunmen Fire on Bus Carrying Coptic Christians, by Nagwa el-Hamzawi, Housam Ahmed, and Angela Dewan, May 26, 2017.
60. Ibid.
61. Koos, Carlo; Gutschke, Thea (2014). "South Sudan's Newest War: When Two Old Men Divide a Nation".
62. "South Sudan Opposition Head Riek Machar denies Coup Bid", December 18, 2013, BBCNews.com.
63. Niels Kastfelt, *Religion and African Civil Wars*, page 28.
64. "South Sudan Country Profile". BBC News. July 12, 2017.
65. "South Sudan Is Dying, and Nobody Is Counting." News24. 11 March 2016.
66. "50,000 and Not Counting: South Sudan's War Dead." ReliefWeb. 15 November 2014.
67. "UN: Refugees from South Sudan Cross 1.5m Mark". Al Jazeera. 10 February 2017.
68. "Starvation Threat Numbers Soar in South Sudan". aljazzera. 25 November 2016.
69. "South Sudan Declares Famine in Unity State". BBC News. 20 February 2017.
70. Tucker, Spencer C.; Roberts, Priscilla (2008). *The Encyclopedia of the Arab-Israeli Conflict. A Political, Social, and Military*. ABC-CLIO. p. 623. ISBN 9781851098415.
71. Kahalani, *A Warriors Way*, Shapolsky Publishers (1994) pp. 299–301.
72. Friedman, Thomas (2006). *From Beirut to Jerusalem*. New York: Anchor Books. ISBN 0-385-41372-6.
73. "Who Are Hezbollah". BBC News. May 21, 2008.
74. Norton, Augustus (2009). *Hezbollah: A Short History*. Princeton University Press. p. 33.
75. Pape, Robert (2005). *Dying to Win: The Strategic Logic of Suicide Terrorism*. New York: Random House.
76. "2000: Hezbollah Celebrates Israeli Retreat". BBC News. May 26, 2000.

77. "Israel Buries Soldiers Recovered in Prisoner Swap". ABC News.
78. Cody, Edward (August 24, 2006). "Lebanese Premier Seeks U.S. Help in Lifting Blockade". *Washington Post*.
79. "Israeli Warplanes Hit Beirut Suburb". CNN. July 14, 2006.
80. Urquhart, Conal (August 11, 2006). "Computerized Weaponry and High Morale". *Guardian*. UK.
81. SPIEGEL Interview with Lebanese President Emile Lahoud: 'Hezbollah Freed Our Country'. Der Spiegel. July 25, 2006.
82. Deeb, Lara (July 31, 2006). "Hizballah: A Primer". *Middle East Report*.
83. Barak, Oren. "Hizballah." *The Continuum Political Encyclopedia of the Middle East*. Ed. Avraham Sela. New York: Continuum, 2002. p. 350.
84. Filkins, Dexter (September 30, 2013). "The Shadow Commander".
85. *Madani, Blanca (January 2002)*. "Hezbollah's Global Finance Network: The Triple Frontier". *Middle East Intelligence Bulletin*.
86. The Jerusalem Post, "Ya'alon: Israel will destroy Lebanon's Infrastructure in Next War," July 16, 2017.
87. Itamar Rabinovich. Israel in the Middle East. UPNE.
88. The Shifts in Hizbullah's Ideology: Religious Ideology, Political Ideology, and Political Program" by Joseph Elie Alagha. Published by Amsterdam University Press, 2006.
89. Algemeiner.com, "Growing Iranian-Hezbollah Confidence to Take on Israel After ISIS," by Yaakov Lappin, October 11, 2017.
90. Human Rights Watch World Report 2005 Events of 2004, Human Rights Watch 2005.
91. Black, Ian (16 July 2010). "Syrian Human Rights Record Unchanged Under Assad, Report Says". *Guardian*. London.
92. "Un Human Rights Probe Panel Reports Continuing 'Gross' Violations in Syria". United Nations Centre. 24 May 2012.
93. "UN Launches Biggest Humanitarian Appeal, Fearing Deepening of Syrian crisis". ReliefWeb. 16 December 2013.
94. *New York Times*, "Death Toll from War in Syria Now 470,000, Group Finds," by Anne Barnard, February 11, 2016.
95. Syria crisis: Number of refugees rises to 200,000". BBC News. 24 August 2012.
96. Syrian Refugees in Lebanon," *New York Times*, 5 September 2013.
97. "Birth of a Dictator," *European Business Daily*. By Mathias Brüggmann et al. August 12, 2016.

ENDNOTES

98. "Turkey Quickly Sliding into Authoritarian Rule After Move to Increase Erdogan's powers". *The Independent. 30 December 2016.*
99. Braun, Stefan. *"Europarat Sieht Türkei auf dem Weg in die Autokratie" (in German). Süddeutsche Zeitung.*
100. "Turkish Constitutional Referendum: TRexit from Parliamentary Democracy?" *euronews.com.*
101. "'Turkey's president is not acting like the Queen—he is acting like a sultan'." *Telegraph.co.uk. 2 February 2015.*
102. "Rights violations, terror ops threaten Turkey's democratic institutions: PACE." *Hurriyet Daily News. 23 June 2016.*
103. The *Telegraph*, "'Turkey' president says all he wants is same powers as Hitler," by Richard Spencer, January 1, 2016.
104. Lepeska, David (17 May 2015). "Turkey Casts the Diyanet." *Foreign Affairs.*
105. de Bellaigue, Christopher (19 December 2013). "Turkey: 'Surreal, Menacing… Pompous'." *New York Review of Books.*
106. Tim Phillips, "New Report on Human Rights Violations During Turkey's Response to Gezi Park Protests", Activist Defense, 4 October 2013.
107. Arsu, Sebnem (4 June 2013). "Turkish Official Apologizes for Force Used at Start of Riots". *New York Times.*
108. The *Guardian*, "'Isis suicide bomber' strikes Turkish border town as Syrian war spills over," by Kareem Shaheen and Constanze Letsch, July 20, 2015.
109. CNN, "At least 95 killed in twin bombings near train station in Turkey's capital," by Don Melvin, October 10, 2015.
110. Yeginsu, Ceylan, "Suicide Bomber Kills at least 10 in Istanbul District of Sultanahmet," The *New York Times*, January 12, 2016.
111. The Straits Times, World (2 July 2016). "Toll rises to 45 as child dies".
112. The Telegraph, "Eight foreigners among 18 dead after 'terrorist' gunmen attack Turkish restaurant in Burkina Faso," by Agence France-Presse, August 14, 2017.
113. Levin, Ned; Candemir, Yeliz (16 July 2016). "Turkey's Erdogan Reasserts Control After Attempted Coup". *Istanbul: The Wall Street Journal. Archived from* the original *on 16 July 2016.*
114. Kinney, Drew Holland (2016). "Civilian Actors in the Turkish Military Drama of July 2016" (PDF). *Eastern Mediterranean Policy Note. 10: p. 1–12.*
115. Ankara parliament building 'bombed from air' – state agency". RT. *15 July 2016.*
116. "Critics Raise False Flag After Failed Military Coup In Turkey". *Vocativ.* Retrieved 16 July 2016.

117. *USA Today*, "Closer look at empire of cleric accused in Turkey coup attempt". July 21, 2016.
118. *Macdonald, Alastair (18 July 2016)*. "'No excuse' for Turkey to abandon rule of law: EU's Mogherini". *Reuters*.
119. WND, "Rebirth of the Turkish Caliphate—and Why It Matters," by Joel Richardson, August 11, 2017.
120. The Counter-Coup in Turkey". *New York Times*. 2016-07-16. Archived from the original on 2016-07-16.
121. 1,863 Turkish journalists fired during AKP rule, opposition report says". *Hürriyet Daily News*. 27 October 2014.
122. "Erdogan Adversary Begins 250-Mile Protest March in Turkey, by Patrick Kingsley, June 15, 2017. *New York Times*.
123. "Turkish opposition party begins 265-Mile 'march for justice,'" by Zeynep Bilginsoy, June 15, 2017. Fox News.
124. UNHCR Syria Regional Refugee Response—Turkey". *UNHCR Syria Regional Refugee Response*.
125. "Turkey's Erdogan threatened to flood Europe with migrants: Greek website". *Reuters*. 8 February 2016.
126. Germany voices support for accelerating Turkey-EU talks (www.trtworld.com, 12 March 2016).
127. Gatestone Institute, "Germany: The Rise of Islam," by Giulio Meotti, September 14, 2017.
128. WND, Joseph Farah's G2 Bulletin, "Middle East Expert: Turkey Could Be More Dangerous Version of Iran," September 21, 2017.
129. Andrew Bieszad, "ISIS Declares It Is Sending Secret Brigades of Fighters to Terrorize Europe," Shoebat.com, , August 7, 2017, http://shoebat.com/2017/08/07/isis-declares-it-is-sending-secret-brigades-of-fighters-to-terrorize-europe/. The following listed facts are adapted from this article.
130. Ibid.
131. *New York Times*, Alison Smale, "Terrorism Suspects Are Posing as Refugees," Germany Says, Feb. 5, 2016.
132. Express, Aaron Brown, November 18th, 2015 "'Just wait . . .' Islamic State reveals it has smuggled THOUSANDS of Extremists into Europe'."
133. Jerusalem Post, "German study: over 50% of muslim refugees hold anti-Semitic views," June 4, 2017.
134. *Guardian*, "Anti-Semitism on Rise Across Europe 'in worst time since Nazis,'" by John Henley, August 7, 2014.
135. *New York Times*, "Europe's Anti-Semitism Comes Out of the Shadows," by Jim Yardley, September 23, 2014.

136. *USA Today*, "Anti-Semitic violence surged 40% worldwide last year," by Kim Hjelmgaard, April 15, 2015.
137. A Crooked Path, "Hatred of Jews at 'highest level of our lifetimes,' Israeli diplomat tells U.N. Anti-semitism forum," by Ken Pullen, September 8, 2016.
138. BBC NEWS, Charlie Hebco attack; "Three days of Terror," January 15, 2015.
139. Ibid.
140. Ibid.
141. *New York Times*, by Adam Nossiter, Aurelien Breeden, Katrin Bennhold, "Three Teams of Coordinated Attackers Carried Out Assault on Paris, Officials Say; Hollande Blames ISIS," Nov 14, 2015.
142. Ibid.
143. Bloomberg, "French Killer Not on Terror List, Used Islamic State Tactics," by Gregory Viscusi, Alexandre Boksenbaum-Granier, Gaspard Sebag, July 15, 2016.
144. "Louvre attack: Suspect 'confirms' he is Egyptian Abdullah Hamamy". *BBC. 7 February 2017.*
145. NBC NEWS, "French Police Kill Suspected Knife Attacker in Marseille Train Station," by Nancy ING, Alastair Jamieson, October 1, 2017.
146. www.jewishagency.org.
147. Ibid.
148. *Washington Post*, "Germany said it took in more than 1 million refugees last year. But it didn't." Rick Noack, September 30, 2016.
149. WND, "Achtung! Germans the new minority in major German city, "by Paul Bremmer, July 2, 2017.
150. Leo Hohmann, Stealth Invasion: Muslim Conquest Through Immigration and the Resettlement Jihad, (Washington, DC: WND Books, 2017).
151. Gatestone Institute, "Germany: The Rise of Islam," by Giulio Meotti, September 14, 2017.
152. The Local, "Palestinians admit attack on Wuppertal synagogue," January 14, 2015.
153. The *Economist*, "Anti-Semitism in Europe, Fear of a New Darkness," February 21, 2015.
154. The *Telegraph*, "Hate attacks on Jews soared 94% last year, police figures show," by David Barrett, January 21, 2015.
155. Le Parisien, "The driver of the Christmas market in Nantes committed suicide in prison," April 13, 2016.

156. The *Telegraph*, "Anti-Semitism on the March; Europe Braces for Violence," by Justin Huggler, Berlin, and Josie Ensor, July 26, 2014.
157. ABC News, "German-Born Gunman in Munich Attack That Killed 9 Had No Isis Ties, Say Police," by Paul Blake, Emily Shapiro, and David Caplan, July 23, 2016.
158. *New York Times*, by Eddy, Melissa, "At Least 12 Dead in Berlin After Truck Crashes into Christmas Market," December 19, 2016.
159. WND, "Man kills 1, injures 6 in supermarket knife attack shouting, "Allahu Akbar".
160. CNN, "Shooting in German nightclub leaves one dead, by Nadine Schmidt and Hillary Clarke, July 30, 2017.
161. *Washington Post*, "Germany said it took in more than 1 million refugees last year. But it didn't," by Rick Noack, September 30, 2016.
162. Rick Noack, "Leaked document says 2,000 men allegedly assaulted 1,200 German women on New Years Eve," *Washington Post*, July 11, 2016.
163. Martin Lutz, January 10, 2016, "Sexuelle Belastigung: Das Phanomen "taharrush gamea" ist in Deutschland angekommen."
164. *Daily Express*, "Prosecutor: Most Cologne New Year's Eve suspects are refugees," February 15, 2016.
165. *New York Times*, "Europe's Anti-Semitism Comes Out of the Shadows," by Jim Yardley, September 23, 2014.
166. Jerusalem Post, "Berlin Mayor allows Hexbollah to march in 'Zionists out of Israel' rally, June 23, 2017.
167. WND, "Author Warns America Must Reclaim Culture," September 12, 2017.
168. Casert, Raf, "Belgium Ramps up Security for lone suspect in Jewish Museum attack," The *Globe* and the *Mail*. May 25, 2014.
169. Robert Spencer, "Belgium: Muslim rally-goers call for 'Slaughter of Jews,'" July 16, 2014, Jihad Watch.
170. *Guardian*, "Brussels attacks: new footage of airport bombing suspect released," April 7, 2016.
171. *Newsweek*, Jack Moore, "Dramatic Rise in Anti-Semitic Incidents in Austria," April 7, 2016.
172. The Jewish Press, "Austrian Anti-Semitic Incidents Rising", JNI Media, April 21, 2017.
173. The *Telegraph*, "Hate attacks on Jews soared 94% last year, police figures show," by David Barrett, January 21, 2015.
174. *Jerusalem Post*, "Half of Muslim youth in Austria hold anti-Semitic views," by Benjamin Weinthal, June 19, 2017.

175. The *Guardian*, "Barcelona attack: four suspects to face court after van driver is shot dead," August 22, 2017.
176. The *Guardian*, "Cambrils: five terror suspects killed as second attack follows Las Ramblas," August 18, 2017.
177. The *Economist*, "Islamist terrorism in Catalonia leaves the Spanish wondering why," August 18, 2017.
178. Breitbart News, "This place is lost": Barcelona chief rabbi tells Spain's Jews to head for Israel, "by Simon Kent, August 20, 2017.
179. The Gatestone Institute, "The Quiet Islamic Conquest of Spain," by Giulio Meotti, October 2, 2017.
180. "National Antisemitic Crime Audit". *2016-05-01*, www.antisemitism.uk/crime/.
181. . *2016-05-01)*. www.antisemitism.uk/crime/.
182. <u>Report Says Number of Anti-Semitic Incidents in UK Doubles in 2014"</u>. *Sputnik. Community Security Trust. 5 February 2015.*
183. *Jerusalem Online*, "Report: Anti-Semitism in Britain reaches record highs," by Daniel Gilenson, July 28, 2017.
184. Jewishbreakingnews.com, "1 in 3 British Jews have considered leaving UK over anti-Semitism, poll says, August 20, 2017.
185. *Daily News*, "American woman killed, 5 injured in London knife attack," by Keri Blakinger, Meg Wagner, August 4, 2016.
186. "<u>London attack: Four dead in Westminster terror attack</u>". *BBC News. 22 March 2017.*
187. Jerusalem Online: UK: "Increased concern" for terrorist attacks against Jewish community, by Gal Cohen, Jan 17, 2015.
188. *Metro.co.uk, Nicole Morley (23 May 2017).* "<u>Twelve children under 16 are among Manchester terror attack injured</u>". *Metro.*
189. "Manchester attack: Police make tenth arrest". *BBC News. 26 May 2017.*
190. *New York Times*, "London Bridge Attack: The Implements of Terror," by Yonette Joseph, June 11, 2017.
191. *Jerusalem Post*, "ISIS claims responsibility for London metro attack, September 15, 2017.
192. *Hooper, Ryan; Hughes, David (7 May 2016).* "<u>Warm Welcome as Sadiq Khan is Sworn in as Mayor of London</u>". *Press Association.*
193. *Hill, Dave (10 July 2016).* "<u>Sadiq Khan speaks for peaceful Islam at Trafalgar Square Eid festival</u>". *Guardian.*
194. Disobedient Media, "London Mayor's Ties to Extremism Call Commitment to Fighting Terror into Question Muslim Mayor's Ties to Muslim Terrorists," Kenneth Whittle. June 4, 2017.

195. JNS.org, "London Mayor Sadiq Khan faces criticism for refusing Hezbollah terror designation," June 26, 2017.
196. World Israel News, "London Mayor wavers, but supports UK Hezbollah ban," July 9, 2017.
197. Patdollard.com, "Muslim London Mayor sets up task force to jail those who "annoy" Muslims online," August 16, 2016.
198. Ibid.
199. Ibid.
200. Ibid
201. WND, "No-Go Zones Brewing in U.S., Author Warns," by Leo Hohmann, August 27, 2017.
202. The *Economist*, "Anti-Semitism in Europe, Fear of a new darkness," Feb 21, 2015.
203. I Behold Israel, "Netanyahu: To our Jewish brothers and sisters, Israel is your home."
204. The *Times of Israel*, "Netanyahu to French Jews: 'Israel is your home,'" by Justin Jalil and Raphael Ahren, January 10, 2015.
205. The *Jerusalem Post*, by Herb Keinon, February 15, 2015.
206. *USA Today*, Robin Herr, "People in Copenhagen in shock over terror shootings," February 15, 2015.
207. RT.com, "Netanyahu urges European Jews to move to Israel after Denmark attack," February 15, 2015.
208. Ynetnews.com, "Jewish World: Kosher market attack deepens fears among European Jews," January 13, 2015.
209. The Jewish Press, "Thousands Participate in French Aliyah Fair," by Jewish Press Staff, March 30, 2014.
210. Jewishagency.org
211. Ibid.
212. *Guardian*, "Is there really a Jewish exodus from western Europe?" by George Arnett, February 5, 2015.

CHAPTER 8

1. Paul Johnson, *A History of the Jews*, 366
2. The Jews in America 1621–1977, A Chronology & Fact Book. Complied and edited by Irving J. Sloan. Published in 1978 by Oceana Publications, Inc. Dobbs Ferry, New York.

3. Sowell, Thomas, Ethnic America: A History, New York: Basic Books, 1983, p 98-99.
4. Ibid.
5. Ibid.
6. The *Times of Israel*, "New York Jews won't stop winning Nobel Prizes," Mark Schulte, December 9, 2012.
7. David S. Wyman, The Abandonment of the Jews: America and the Holocaust, 1941–1945 (New York, 1984), p. 5.
8. www.jewishagency.org
9. US News, "The 10 most religious countries in the world," by Lauren Boyer, April 17, 2017.
10. "Why Muslims are the world's fastest-growing religious group". *Pew Research Center. 2017-04-06.*
11. US news, "The 10 most religious countries in the world," by Lauren Boyer, April 17th, 2017.
12. The Economist, Cairo, "A Saudi tower: Mecca versus Las Vegas: Taller, holier and even more popular than (almost) anywhere else," June 24, 2010.
13. Venezuela: Oil reserves surpasses Saudi Arabia's at english.ahram.org.eg
14. "Stop the press! Apple is NOT the world's most valuable company". London Loves Business, Charles Orton-Jones, August 21, 2012.
15. "Timeline". *Saudi Embassy.*net.
16. Ramadan in Saudi Arabia". *The Economist. 11 June 2016.*
17. "Saudi Arabia. Wahhabi Theology". *December 1992. Library of Congress Country Studies.*
18. *World Affairs*, "The Saudi Connection: Wahhabism and Global Jihad", May/June 2015, Jamsheed K. Choksy, Carol E.B. Choksy.
19. Mahdi, Wael (March 18, 2010). "There is no such thing as Wahhabism, Saudi prince says". The National. Abu Dhabi Media.
20. Saudi Arabia, Wahhabism and the Spread of Sunni Theo-fascism. By Ambassador Curtin Winsor, PhD.
21. House, Karen Elliott (2012). On Saudi Arabia: Its People, Past, Religion, Fault Lines and Future. Knopf. p. 234. A former US Treasury Department official is quoted.
22. Dawood al-Shirian, 'What Is Saudi Arabia Going to Do?' Al-Hayat, May 19, 2003.
23. *Kepel, Gilles (2003). Jihad: The Trail of Political Islam. I.B. Tauris. pp. 61–62.*

24. *Edward Clifford.* "Financing Terrorism: Saudi Arabia and Its Foreign Affairs". *December 6,2014. brownpoliticalreview.org.*
25. http://www.huffingtonpost.com/dr-yousaf-butt-/saudi-wahhabism-islam-terrorism_b_6501916.html. The *Huffington Post*, by Yousaf Butt.
26. "Fueling Terror". *Institute for the Analysis of Global Terror.*iags.org.
27. "German Vice Chancellor warns Saudi Arabia over Islamist funding", Reuters, Deutsche Welle, 6 December 2015.
28. Daily News, "To see Jimmy Carter's true allegiances, just follow the money
29. Craig Unger, "House of Bush House of Saud," Scribner, 2004, p. 200, 295.
30. Independent, "Julian Assange: Isis and Clinton Foundation are both funded by Saudi Arabia and Qatar," by Gabriel Samuels, November 4, 2016.
31. John MacArthur, "The Vast Power of the Saudi Lobby", April 2007, *Harper's Magazine*.
32. Ibid
33. The *Economist*, "Prince Bandar bin Sultan: Larger-than-life diplomacy", November 6, 2008.
34. The *Atlantic*, Jeffrey Goldberg, Fact-Checking Stephen Walt, December 8, 2010.
35. Hafez, Mohammed M. *Suicide Bomber in Iraq.* United States Institute of Peace Press. ISBN 1601270046.
36. Lee Fang, "As Trump Travels to Saudi Arabia, the Kingdom's D.C. Lobbying Surge Is Paying Off." The Intercept. May 19, 2017.
37. *World Affairs*, "The Saudi Connection: Wahhabism and Global Jihad", May/June 2015, Jamsheed K. Choksy, Carol E.B. Choksy.
38. US NEWS, Lauren Boyer, April 17th, 2017, "The 10 most religious countries in the world."
39. Fox News, by Lucia I. Suarez Sang, "California Imam under fire after asking Allah to 'annihilate' Jews in sermon," July 26, 2017.
40. World Affairs, "The Saudi Connection: Wahhabism and Global Jihad", May/June 2015, Jamsheed K. Choksy, Carol E.B. Choksy.
41. https://freedomhouse.org/report/special-reports/saudi-publications-hate-ideology-invade-american-mosques.
42. Ibid/
43. *World Affairs*, "The Saudi Connection: Wahhabism and Global Jihad", May/June 2015, Jamsheed K. Choksy, Carol E.B. Choksy.
44. US embassy cables: Hillary Clinton says Saudi Arabia 'a critical source of terrorist funding'". *Guardian*. London. December 5, 2010.

45. Ibid
46. Mura, Andrea (2012). "A genealogical inquiry into early Islamism: the discourse of Hasan al-Banna." Journel *of Political Ideologies.*
47. "The Covenant of the HAMAS— Main Points". Intelligence Resource Project. Federation of American Scientists.
48. Husaini, Ishak Musa (1956). *The Moslem Brethren.* Beirut: Khayat's College Book Cooperative. Pp. 62–3.
49. Kull, Steven (2011). *Feeling Betrayed: The Roots of Muslim Anger at America.* Brookings Institution Press. P. 167.
50. Abdelrahman, Abdelrahman Ahmed (Winter 1996). "Administrative Responsibility: An Islamic Perspective." The *American Journal of Islamic Social Sciences.* 13:4:498.
51. Roy, Oliver (1994). The Failure of Political Islam. Translator Volk, Carol. Harvard University Press. P. 110.
52. Oliver. The Failure of Political Islam. P. 110.
53. Ibid.
54. Husain, Irfan; Cohen, Stephen P. (2012). *Fatal Faultlines: Pakistan, Islam and the West.* Arc Manor LLC. P. 60.
55. Lia, Brynjar. The Society of the Muslim Brothers in Egypt: The Rise of an Islamic Mass Movement 1928-1942. Ithica Press, 2006. P. 53.
56. Commins, David. The Wahabbi Mission and Saudi Arabia. I. B. Tauris, 2006, p. 152.
57. Dreyfus, Bob (13 July 2012). "Saudi Arabia and the Brotherhood: What the '*New York Times*' Missed." The Nation.
58. Kepel, Giles, Jihad: The Trail of Political Islam, p. 83.
59. "Social programs bolster appeal of Muslim Brotherhood" IRIN, irinnews.ord/news/2004/10/27/targeted-emergency-food-aid-nampula.
60. Traub, James (29 April 2007) "Islamic Democrats?" *New York Times.*
61. Fawzi, Sameh (8 December 2005). "Brothers and Others," Al-Ahram Weekly.
62. Bradley, John R., *Inside Egypt,* Palgrave MacMilan, (p.65).
63. Eli Lake, "Muslim Brotherhood seeks end to Israel treaty." The Washington Times, February 3, 2011.
64. 'Shariah in Egypt is enough for us,' Muslim Brotherhood leader says." Hurriyet Daily news. 23 May 2011.
65. Interactive: Full Egypt election result, Aljazeera.com, 1 February 2012.
66. Ibid.

67. Dina Bishara (28 November 2012). "Egyptian Labor between Morsi and Mubarak." *Foreign Policy.*
68. "Death toll from Egypt violence rises to 638: Health ministry". *Al-Ahram.* 15 August 2013. Archived from the original on 19 August 2013.
69. "Egyptian military police arrest Brotherhood supreme guide." *Egypt Independent.* 4 July 2013.
70. "Egypt PM labels Brotherhood 'terrorist' group after the bomb kills 14." Dawn AFP. 24 December 2013.
71. "Egyptian Court ordered Death sentence to 529 Members." Dawn 24 March 2014.
72. "Egypt sentences to death 529 supporters of Mohamed Morsi." *Guardian.* 24 March 2014.
73. "Egypt court sentences 183 Muslim Brotherhood supporters to death." Reuters. 2 February 2015.
74. Hendawi, Hamza (16 May 2015). "Ousted Egyptian President Mohammed Morsi Sentenced to Death."
75. Rasoulpour, Khabat (2013) [1392]. Sociologic explanation of establishment of Iranian Call and Reform Organization (Iranian Muslim Brotherhood) and evolution of its discourse. Tarbiay Moallem University.
76. Turkey's relationship with the Muslim Brotherhood." Al Arabiya.
77. Alan Godlas (17 July 1968). "The Muslim Brotherhood in Iraq."
78. The Muslim brotherhood, Nazis, and Al-Queda." *FrontPage.*
79. Higgins, Andrew (24 January 2009). "How Israel Helped to Spawn Hamas." The *Wall Street Journal.*
80. Bar, Shmuel (1998). "The Muslim Brotherhood in Jordan."
81. Islam Hassan (31 March 2015). "GCC's 2014 Crisis: Causes, Issues, and Solutions." Al Jazeera Research Center.
82. Dickinson, Elizabeth (10 December 2014). "Saudi action puts Muslim Brotherhood in Kuwait on spot." Al Monitor.
83. Syria's Muslim Brotherhood is gaining influence over anti-Assad revolt," by Liz Sly, The *Washington Post.* 12 May 2012.
84. Kasolowsky, Raissa (20 September 2012). "UAE Islamists had military wing, planned Islamic State—papers." Reuters.
85. "Yemen's President Saleh Speaks: The Interview Transcript." *Time.* 29 September 2011.
86. "Muslim Brotherhood to Contest Libyan Elections as Independent Party." The *Tripoli Post.* 24 December 2011.

87. Mauritania's Islamists, Carnegie Middle East Center. Carnegie-mec.org.
88. Justice and Development Party, Ikhwanweb, the Muslim Brotherhood's official English language website.
89. "International Religious Freedom Report 2004. Somalia." State.gov. 1 January 2004.
90. Natsios, Andrew S. (2012). Sudan, South Sudan, and Darfur: What Everyone Needs to Know. Oxford University Press. Pp. 84-5.
91. Qaradhawi, Dr. Yusuf (2001). Umat Islam Menyongsong Abad ke-21, Era Intermedia, Solo, pp. 92.
92. Lacroix, Stephane. "Saudi Arabia's Muslim Brotherhood predicament." *Washington Post*.
93. Egypt's Muslim Brotherhood declared 'terrorist group'" BBC.co.uk, December 2013.
94. Resolution of the State Duma, 2 December 2003 N 3624-III GD "on the application of the State Duma of the Russian Federation" on the suppression of the activities of terrorist organizations on the territory of the Russian Federation." Consultant Plus.
95. Alaa Shahine & Glen Carey, Bloomberg News (9 March 2014). "U.A.E. Supports Saudi Arabia against Qatar-Backed Brotherhood." Bloomberg News.
96. Saudi Arabia declares Muslim Brotherhood 'terrorist group.'" BBC March 7, 2014.
97. Lacroix, Stephane. "Saudi Arabia's Muslim Brotherhood predicament." *Washington Post*.
98. Brian Katulis. "Qatar Saudi Arabia Diverge in Battle to Shape Changing Middle East." The Paths of the Arab Spring. *World Politics Review*.
99. "No Satisfaction." The *Economist*. 1 February 2014.
100. Lacroix, Stephane. "Saudi Arabia's Muslim Brotherhood predicament." *Washington Post*.
101. House. On Saudi Arabia. P. 156.
102. Mintz, John; Farah, Douglas (10 Septemeber 2004). "In Search of Friends Among the Foes: U.S. Hopes to Work with Diverse Group." The *Washington Post*.
103. Tamer Elnoury with Kevin Maurer, American Radical: Inside the World of an Undercover Muslim FBI Agent (New York: Penguin, 2017).
104. FrontPage Mag, "Islamophobia: Thought Crime of the Totalitarian Future," by David Horowitz and Robert Spencer, May 8, 2015.
105. "The Muslim Brotherhood Project" investigativeproject.org.

106. "Civilization Jihad: Debunking the Conspiracy Theory." Bridge Initiative Team. 26 February 2016.
107. "The Muslim Brotherhood '"Project".'" investigativeproject.org.
108. "Civilization Jihad: Debunking the Conspiracy Theory." Bridge Initiative Team. 26 February 2016.
109. Elliott, Andrea (30 July 2011). "The Man Behind the Anti-Shariah Movement." *New York Times.*
110. "S.2230—Muslim Brotherhood Terrorist Designation Act of 2015". *Congress.gov. U.S. Library of Congress.*
111. WND, "General: Muslim Brotherhood Inside Obama Administration," by Bob Unruh, January 9, 2014.
112. WND, "Obamas brother linked to Muslim Brotherhood," Jerome R. Corsi, August 20, 2013.
113. WND, "DHS Whistleblower: Why Obama is 'so adamant to protect Islam,'" by Paul Bremmer, June 30, 2016.
114. WND, "DHS Whistleblower: Shariah threatens U.S. like 'dragon' that kills," by Paul Bremmer, July 18, 2017.
115. WND, "Obama 'letting Muslim Brotherhood Run Anti-Terror Ops,'" September 9, 2013.
116. WND, "Ex-Obama advisor roots for more ISIS slaughtering Christians," by Leo Hohmann, May 8, 2017.
117. The *Hill*, "Huma Abedin's ties to the Muslim Brotherhood," by Kenneth R. Timmerman, August 23, 2016.
118. Judicialwatch.org, "New Huma Abedin Emails Reveal Additional Instances of Clinton Sending Classified Information through Unsecured Emails, Special Favors for Clinton Donors," March 29, 2017.
119. WND, "General: Muslim Brotherhood Inside Obama Administration," by Bob Unruh, January 9, 2014.
120. Ibid
121. The *Hill*, "Huma Abedin's ties to the Muslim Brotherhood," by Kenneth R. Timmerman, August 23, 2016.
122. Ibid.
123. Ibid.
124. Ibid.
125. WND, "General: Muslim Brotherhood Inside Obama Administration," by Bob Unruh, January 9, 2014.
126. Shariah, The Threat to America, Report of Team B II, "Who's Who in the American Muslim Brotherhood, www.shariahthethreat.org.

127. The Clarion Project, "Muslim Brotherhood Inside American Colleges," by Meira Svirsky, May 16, 2013.
128. Ibid.
129. Ibid.
130. *Western Journalism*, "Muslim Infiltration in Public Education," by Bradlee Dean, February 15, 2003.
131. Ibid.
132. Israelvideonetwork.com, "LA Public School Teaching Kids 'Allah is the One True God'", August 10, 2017.
133. Ibid.
134. Ibid.
135. Ibid.
136. *Newsweek*, "Anti-Semitic Incidents at College Campuses Nearly Doubled in 2015: ADL," by Stav Ziv, June 24, 2016.
137. *USA Today*. College, "Jewish students battle rising anti-Semitism on campus," by Brianne Garrett, Boston University, November 3, 2016.
138. Ibid.
139. Ibid.
140. ADL, "Audit: In 2014 Anti-Semitic Incidents Rose 21 Percent Across the U.S. in a 'Particular Violent Year for Jews.'"
141. Ibid.
142. Ibid.
143. Ibid.
144. ADL, "ADL Audit: Anti-Semitic Assaults Rise Dramatically Across the Country in 2015."
145. Ibid.
146. Ibid.
147. Ibid.
148. Ibid.
149. Ibid.
150. ADL, "U.S. Anti-Semitic Incidents Spike 86 Percent So Far in 2017 After Surging Last Year," ADL Finds.
151. Ibid.
152. *Jerusalem Post*, "New wave of bomb threats hit 29 Jewish centers in U.S.," February 28, 2017.
153. Ibid.

154. Ibid.
155. Politifact–Florida, "Terrorists from groups besides ISIS crossing U.S.-Mexico border, U.S. Rep. Ron DeSantis says," by Joshua Gillin, April 4, 2016.
156. Ibid.
157. The *Washington Post*, "Texas officials warn of immigrants with terrorist ties crossing southern border," by Reid Wilson, February 26, 2015.
158. Ibid.
159. Politifact–Florida, "Terrorists from groups besides ISIS crossing U.S.-Mexico border, U.S. Rep. Ron DeSantis says," by Joshua Gillin, April 4, 2016.
160. Ibid.
161. The *National Review*, "The Troubling Math of Muslim Migration," by Ian Tuttle, January 13, 2015.
162. WND, "GOP Congress kills legislation banning taxpayer funding of Hamas, "Leo Hohmann, September 12, 2017.
163. *Western Journalism*, "Muslim Immigration to U.S. Staggering—More Evidence Obama Is Attempting to Change America," by L. Todd Wood, February 24, 2015.
164. Limits to Growth, "Islamic Immigration to Increase in America." http://www.limitstogrowth.org/articles/2011/01/28/islamic-immigration-to-increase-in-america/.
165. Ibid.
166. Ibid.
167. The *National Review*, "The Troubling Math of Muslim Migration," by Ian Tuttle, January 13, 2015.
168. *ThinkProgress*, "Islamic Extremists Have Seized Control of U.S. Cities, says NRA Seminar," by Kira Lerner, April 14, 2015.
169. Ibid.
170. Ibid.
171. Ibid.
172. The *Washington Post*, "In the first majority Muslim U.S. city, residents tense about its future," by Sarah Pulliam Bailey, November 21, 2015.
173. Ibid.
174. Ibid.
175. Ibid.
176. Ibid.
177. WND, "Bachmann: Islam Has Transformed My State," by Liam Clancy, July 27, 2017.

178. Ibid.
179. Ibid.
180. USdailynewss.com, "The New America: Muslims take over a small southern town and force absolute hell on their terrified Christian neighbors, "August 12, 2017.
181. Ibid.
182. The *Tennessee Star*, "Nashville preparing to become the most liberal sanctuary city in the U.S.," by Chris Alto, June 20, 2017.
183. WND, "City of Utica 'Gone' because of refugee flood," by Liam Clancy, June 15, 2017.
184. WND, "U.S. refugee program stained by dozens of terror attacks," by Leo Hohmann, July 5, 2017.
185. WND, "City of Utica 'Gone' because of refugee flood," by Liam Clancy, June 15, 2017.
186. WND, "Big List of Muslim Terror Attacks in U.S. Since 9/11," July 16, 2015.
187. BBC NEWS, "San Bernandino shootings investigated as terrorism—FBI," December 4, 2015.
188. *New York Times*, "Orlando Gunman Attacks Gay Nightclub, Leaving 50 Dead," by Lizette Alvaraz and Richard Perez-Pena, June 12, 2016.
189. Yournewswire.com, "Mandalay Bay CEO Gave Money To Islamic Terror Groups, Sold Millions In Shares – Weeks Before Attack," by Baxter Dmitry.
190. DelReal, Jose A. and Kilgannon, Corey (October 31, 2017). "A Mangled School Bus, Bodies Everywhere; "It was surreal"". *The New York Times*.
191. Sukkah 29a in the Babylonian Talmud.
192. Weatherchannel.com
193. www.earthquaketrack.com
194. Las Vegas Sun, "Coroner releases names of all 58 Las Vegas shooting victims," October 5, 2017.

CHAPTER 9

1. The Talmud, H. Polano, page 28-29, The Book Tree, 2003.
2. The River War, by Winston Churchill, Renaissance Classics, 2012.
3. WND Books, "The Islamic Antichrist," by Joel Richardson, pages 52–61, 2015.
4. Ibid., 175–79.

5. Top Executive Media, "God's War on Terror," by Walid Shoebat and Joel Richardson, pages 5–7, 2008.
6. Encouragingly, it is reported that thousands of Muslims have had visions or dreams about Jesus, resulting in their conversions!

CHAPTER 10

1. Flavius Josephus, *The Complete Works*, Book 1, Chapter 12, Sect. 2.
2. Flavius Josephus, *The Antiquities of the Jews*, Book 1, Ch. 7, Sect. 2.

WORLD AHEAD *press*

Authors welcome! Publishing your book with us means that you have the freedom to blaze your own trail. But that doesn't mean you should go it alone. By choosing to publish with WORLD AHEAD PRESS, you partner with WND—one of the most powerful and influential brands on the Internet.

If you liked this book and want to publish your own, WORLD AHEAD PRESS, co-publishing division of WND Books, is right for you. WORLD AHEAD PRESS will turn your manuscript into a high-quality book and then promote it through its broad reach into conservative and Christian markets worldwide.

IMAGINE YOUR BOOK ALONGSIDE THESE AUTHORS!

   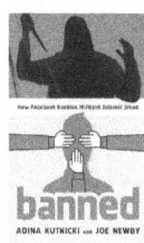 

We transform your manuscript into a marketable book. Here's what you get:

BEAUTIFUL CUSTOM BOOK COVER
PROFESSIONAL COPYEDIT
INTERIOR FORMATTING
EBOOK CONVERSION
KINDLE EBOOK EDITION
WORLDWIDE BOOKSTORE DISTRIBUTION
MARKETING ON AMAZON.COM

It's time to publish your book with WORLD AHEAD PRESS.

Go to www.worldaheadpress.com for a Free Consultation

www.ingramcontent.com/pod-product-compliance
Lightning Source LLC
Chambersburg PA
CBHW020744160426
43192CB00006B/237